Inspirational Quotations

FROM LATTER-DAY SAINT

Women

EAGLE
GATE

Library of Congress Cataloging-in-Publication Data

Inspirational quotations from Latter-day Saint women.
   p. cm.
  Includes bibliographical references.
  ISBN 1-57345-812-0
  1. Mormon women—Religious life—Quotations, maxims, etc. 2. Mormon women—Quotations. I. Deseret Book Company.

BX8641.I67 2001
289.3'32'082—dc21   00-069166

Printed in the United States of America   18961-6698

10 9 8 7 6 5 4 3 2 1

Contents

Thanks to the following, whose efforts helped make this book possible:

VICE-PRESIDENT OF PUBLISHING, DESERET BOOK COMPANY
Sheri L. Dew

MANAGER OF EAGLE GATE IMPRINT, DESERET BOOK
Jana S. Erickson

COMPILER AND EDITOR
Jay A. Parry

EDITORIAL CONSULTANTS
Dee Ann Earl Barrowes
Vicki L. Parry
Kathleen Lubeck Peterson

EDITORIAL ASSISTANTS
Amy Felix
Lisa Mangum
Lindsay McAllister

RESEARCHERS
Necia Brady
Douglas E. DeVore II
Bonnie L. McIntyre
Susan Capson Southworth

ART DIRECTOR
Thomas E. Hewitson

DESIGNER
Jennifer Peterson

ASSISTANT DESIGNER
Sheryl Dickert

DATABASE CONSULTANT
Larry A. Scoffield

TYPOGRAPHER
Laurie C. Cook

PROOFREADERS
Ruth Howard
Doreen McKnight
Judith M. Paller

And special thanks to the hundreds of faithful Latter-day Saint
women from many generations whose words of wisdom
and insight are such a blessing to us all.

Adversity

Adversity Is an Integral Part of Life

BONNIE BALLIF-SPANVILL

Do not be surprised that you have problems. Pain is inevitable in this lone and dreary world. Do not feel that you are being picked on; problems are the fare of this existence. You cannot escape them. When you get through one, others will be waiting to come your way. (In *Every Good Thing*, 131.)

FRANCINE R. BENNION

We wanted life, however high the cost. We suffer because we were willing to pay the cost of being and of being here with others in their ignorance and inexperience as well as our own. (In *Heritage of Faith*, 66.)

We suffer because we are willing to pay the costs of living with laws of nature, which operate quite consistently whether or not we understand them or can manage them. (In *Heritage of Faith*, 66.)

ELAINE CANNON

Surely we understand that just because someone is apple-pie good, strictly obedient, and conscientiously toeing God's marked path every minute, there is no assurance that they will be spared trouble or that there won't be chances to be proven, to suffer, to grow and learn! By design man is faced with choices and adventures that point up the bitter and the sweet. (*Sunshine*, 89.)

One certainty of life is that each of us will meet some mighty test. This is part of the plan. (In *Ensign*, May 1982, 95.)

SHERI L. DEW

Lucifer whispers that life's not fair and that if the gospel were true, we would never have problems or disappointments. . . .

The gospel isn't a guarantee against tribulation. That would be like a test with no questions. Rather, the gospel is a guide for maneuvering through the challenges of life with a sense of purpose and direction. (In *Best of Women's Conference*, 134–35.)

JOY F. EVANS

Death and adversity come to us all, but so does life everlasting! (In *Ensign*, Nov. 1987, 95.)

MARY HALES

Pain in this life is not a sign that the Lord is angry or that we have done wrong. It's just mortality. (In *Hearts Knit Together*, 20.)

ADRIENNE AIKELE HARMER

A life worth living will always have a challenge or a decision in its path. . . . These obstacles can drive away peace and rob us of strength if we are not traveling with the word of the Lord as a lamp unto our feet and a light unto our path. (In *Thy Word Is a Lamp*, 53.)

JANET G. LEE

As hard as it sometimes is to understand, stumbling blocks are essential to our progression. (In *BYU Speeches*, 14 Jan. 1992, 48.)

CHIEKO N. OKAZAKI

Burdens are a part of life, and we all struggle with burdens that are grievous to be borne. There is nothing reproachful about having burdens, and there is nothing wicked in the struggle. (In *Best of Women's Conference*, 410–11.)

KATHRYN S. SMITH

If you think . . . that choosing to follow the pattern set out so lovingly and clearly by our Father in Heaven will remove persecution and temptation and doubt, then you are very young in your gospel experience. (In *Finding the Light*, 155.)

The Source of Our Trials

ARDETH GREENE KAPP

One kind of spiritual growth and refinement comes when we deal with [adversity] . . . for which we are not responsible. . . . It is quite another kind of spiritual growing to deal with feelings and circumstances we *are* responsible for, [including the many] private battles of our own making as we strive to overcome the weaknesses of the flesh. (*Rejoice!* 15–16.)

KATHRYN S. SMITH

The moment we choose God, Satan declares war, and the real artillery begins. It is at this moment that the "qualifying trials" commence their refining process. (In *Finding the Light*, 155.)

BELLE S. SPAFFORD

All must face trials, some of which are more or less personal in nature, and others the trials incident to the day in which we live. These trials are not given us by an unkind providence to crush us. Many of them are manmade, the result of man's weaknesses and imperfections. But, regardless of their source, by a mastery of them we may rise to our fullest stature. (In *Relief Society Magazine*, Nov. 1950, 726–27.)

The Purpose of Trials

BONNIE BALLIF-SPANVILL

Problems hurt, but they also teach wisdom, patience, and an understanding of the good and evil. (In *Every Good Thing*, 131.)

DIANE BILLS

God knows what trials each person needs in order to grow. I believe we are often given the very challenge that is the most difficult for us to face. (*Trust in the Lord*, 22.)

ELAINE CANNON

We are here on earth to be proven, here on earth to endure. Through adversity we gain valuable experience and understanding about life, principles, and the nature of God and his children. (*Gatherings*, 203.)

Adversity can mellow us and prepare us to draw closer to God. Adversity proves whom God can trust. Adversity gives us experience. Adversity brings us closer to the Lord. (*Gatherings*, 203.)

God's plan for us is peppered with a variety of trials to push us to our limit, either by the nature of the problem, the cost of it, or the unrelenting assault of all kinds of struggles. When the ultimate grief strikes—and when it strikes again and then again—it is a wake-up call to look for the lesson and learn! (In *My Soul Delighteth*, 133.)

Neither here nor hereafter are we suddenly going to emerge with qualities we haven't developed or a pattern of living for which we have not prepared ourselves. (In *Ensign*, May 1982, 95.)

Good can come from trouble. Trauma can enliven the heart and enrich the soul. Clouds do have silver linings, and the leaf will burst again on the dry branch. (In *Ensign*, May 1982, 95.)

Part of our precious legacy—to be remembered and renewed—is that though deepening trials throng our way, we know that our afflictions can be consecrated to our good. (In *Ensign*, May 1982, 95.)

MARY ELLEN EDMUNDS

One of the most important lessons we learn from our own adversity . . . is a deeper appreciation and love for our Savior. . . . Through afflictions, we learn to trust the Lord completely, knowing that whatever happens . . . everything will be sorted out, everything will be fair, wrongs will be made right, tears will be wiped away, no one will be hungry or thirsty or naked or sick or imprisoned or frightened or lonely or hurting. (In *Arms of His Love*, 228–29.)

JAROLDEEN ASPLUND EDWARDS

Adversity brings strength, sorrow brings joy, and pain brings us the most priceless gifts. The value of something is often the equal of its price, so it is logical that the gifts of pain are infinitely precious—they are so dearly bought. (*Things I Wish I'd Known*, 58.)

Through suffering, we gain an increased awareness of love for all mankind. It illuminates our hearts and minds and gives us a burning desire to help, lift, and protect. Once harmed or hurt, we gain a great desire to care for others who are in need or pain. (*Things I Wish I'd Known*, 63.)

MARY F. FOULGER

We need to strip ourselves of consuming earthly cares in order to remember who we are and to realize that these very adversities are the reason why we are here. (In *As a Woman Thinketh*, 71.)

RUTH MAY FOX

Life brings some hard lessons. The sturdiest plants are not grown under glass, and strength of character is not derived from the avoidance of problems. (In *Keepers*, 41.)

Our Heavenly Father loves us best of all, yet he permits us to suffer pain and sorrow, to come in contact with the winds and the flood, the desert and mountain, that we may develop character and gain strength to overcome obstacles, that we may not only have dominion over the fish of the sea, the fowls of the air and the beasts of the field, but dominion over ourselves, which is the greatest conquest of all. (In *Young Woman's Journal*, Aug. 1905, 359.)

SUSA YOUNG GATES

Patience, hope, resignation, charity for others' pain or weakness, mercy, love, long-suffering, trust in God, all these are taught in suffering's school. (In *Young Woman's Journal*, Dec. 1894, 135.)

MARJORIE P. HINCKLEY

Even a failure can be counted as a success because it will give you experience. (In *Glimpses*, 227.)

PATRICIA T. HOLLAND

The Lord does allow darkness and struggle and pain. He often uses it to call us to him. (In *BYU Speeches*, 11 Sept. 1984, 2.)

ELAINE L. JACK

Know that trials and adversity teach and train us. Recognize them for what they are and how they make us strong and effective. (In *BYU Speeches*, 5 Jan. 1997, 131.)

LUCILE JOHNSON

Our personal growth and development, our increased spirituality, or our improvement in relationships all have different kinds of price tags. They do not come free. (*Sunny Side Up*, 132.)

Tribulation is often the paintbrush God uses to create a masterpiece on the canvas of our lives. (*Enjoy the Journey*, 77.)

ARDETH GREENE KAPP

Times of difficulty try the faith of all who profess to be Latter-day Saints and follow the prophets. (*Joy of the Journey*, 13.)

How do we handle unfulfilled expectations? . . . We must accept the reality that this life is not intended to be free of struggle. In fact, it is through struggle that we are given opportunities to fulfill the very purpose of this mortal life. It is the fiery trials of mortality that will either consume us or refine us. (In *Ensign*, Feb. 1989, 22.)

The blessings of adversity usually come in such disguise that we would likely decline them if we could. But when we better understand the place of adversity, and even learn to be grateful for this important part of our mortal experience, we will see that the experiences that drive us to extremity also bring us to Him who can and will succor us in all our infirmities (see Alma 7:12). (*Rejoice!* 37–38.)

SUZANNE EVERTSEN LUNDQUIST

Just prior to my divorce, I was driving to work on a brittle winter day. My [six] children were suffering; my soul could not be comforted. I cried unto the Lord. I don't want to be tried; I don't want to be a God. All I want is a complete, righteous family. The Lord quickly responded, . . . That is all I want. (In *As Women of Faith*, 101.)

DIANE L. MANGUM

Life is not about stillness. To grow is to change. Righteousness cannot even exist in a vacuum. To be righteous is to face choices and conflict. To have joy is to know sorrow. Peace is not about the storm that is absent. Peace is about the storm that is weathered. (In *Balm of Gilead*, 104.)

LAURA OWEN

All of the lessons about enduring through trials and building faith, even when we get a raw deal, are partly for us, but I am convinced they must be partly for those people we run into later who may also need to hear what we have learned so far. (In *Thy Word Is a Lamp*, 140.)

BROOKIE PETERSON

As we suffer we learn, and as time heals we can reach for a brighter day. (*Woman's Hope*, 10.)

LYNN F. PRICE

We are here to be tried. We all have, have had, or will have problems that will try our faith. If we do not know sorrow, we will never really know joy. If we stripped everything from our character and personality that we have gained through trials, we would end up with a bare shell of what we are. (In *Balm of Gilead*, 97.)

DOLORES RITCHIE

One cannot have things both ways; one cannot remain comfortable and secure in a predictable and constant world (if there is such a thing), and also experience growth, independence and adventure. (In *Mormon Women Speak*, 184.)

WENDY EVANS RUPPEL

We cannot choose eternal life unless we've had the painful as well as joyful experiences upon which to base our choices. (In *Clothed with Charity*, 170.)

KATHRYN S. SMITH

We are here to prove our loyalty, to prove our ability to commit ourselves, to prove our love. (In *Finding the Light*, 155.)

ELIZA R. SNOW

We cannot comprehend all the glory that pertains to this great work. Before Zion is redeemed every heart will be tried to the core; the Lord will have a tried people. (In *Woman's Exponent*, 1 Oct. 1887, 70.)

BELLE S. SPAFFORD

While trial may bring pain and suffering, the ability to rise above it or master it brings compensatory inner satisfactions and joy as well as eternal rewards. (*Today's World*, 211.)

EMMA LOU THAYNE

The unpredictable in life is often the best teacher. (*As for Me*, 59.)

M. CATHERINE THOMAS

Life's path is strewn with seemingly unsolvable dilemmas so that people will be driven to God for help. (*Selected Writings*, 72.)

EMMELINE B. WELLS

Does not passing through deep sorrow and walking in thorny paths prepare one to enjoy a fuller and more complete happiness when the dark hour is over, when the path which was rough has been trodden down by patience, perseverance and constant toil, and become smooth and easy to walk in? (In *Woman's Exponent*, 15 Dec. 1877, 105.)

Adversity Purifies

ANITA R. CANFIELD

Many people rise to greatness not in spite of their trials but because of their trials. (*Young Woman*, 68.)

ELAINE CANNON

The agony in one's life, like a sand speck in an oyster, can become a rare jewel, unblemished and singularly satisfying to behold—a treasured blessing of inner strength and grace. (*Count Your Blessings*, 90.)

DIXIE R. CLIFFORD

We want to reach our spiritual potential and cannot do so without being stretched and made malleable in the fiery trials of life. Gold is obtained from raw ore only when it is smelted and fired and thus refined to yield something precious. So it might be with our human souls. (In *Thy Word Is a Lamp*, 109.)

MARTI AND MARCIE HOLLOMAN

The Lord . . . molds you and leaves his mark upon you after you have gone through the refiner's fire—while you are hot and glowing and humble. (In *Clothed with Charity*, 231.)

CAMILLA EYRING KIMBALL

We are inclined to long for ease in our lives, but it is a common observation that those who struggle and overcome are the ones who have the greatest satisfaction. (*Writings*, 18.)

MARY FIELDING SMITH

It is through suffering that we are to be made perfect, and I have already found it to have the effect of driving me nearer to the Lord and so suffering has become a great blessing to me. (*Mary Fielding Smith*, 37.)

PEGGY ST. CYR

We are not required to go through the trials that Christ did. . . . But we are required to go through *our own* trials and remain faithful; our doing so proves that we are willing to go through whatever the Lord asks of us. We, too, need to strive for perfection. . . . We have to be purified by remaining faithful through our own Gethsemane. (*Conversion to Commitment*, 71.)

EMMELINE B. WELLS

The women of the past . . . who have endured the severe trials and persecutions . . . developed the most admirable traits of character while passing through such terrible ordeals, driven from their homes, wanderers in the wilderness without food or shelter, for the sake of their religious faith. (In *Woman's Exponent*, Jan. 1908, 48.)

HELEN MAR WHITNEY

Trials are necessary to separate the dross from the pure metal. (*Woman's View*, xiv.)

Attitude or Response toward Trials

MARILYN ARNOLD

Trials of any kind are a test of our mettle, and we can choose to grow from them . . . or we can choose to be destroyed by them. (In *My Soul Delighteth*, 63.)

SHERLENE HALL BARTHOLOMEW

We can accept life's challenges with faith in the Lord's power to change human hearts—especially our own—when we exercise agency to invite him into our life. (In *To Rejoice As Women*, 87.)

We can, at least ultimately, be grateful for life's pain, for only through opposition are we able finally to comprehend joy in all its rich measure. (In *To Rejoice As Women*, 87.)

MARILYN S. BATEMAN

So often the things that teach us the most and give us the greatest insights into God's ways happen while we are struggling. If we turn to God for strength, feelings and sure knowledge pour into our thinking through the light that quickens our understanding. (In *Best of Women's Conference*, 32.)

ELAINE CANNON

Attitude in adversity turns hopeless to hopeful. (In *Keepers*, 133.)

At the beginning of any tribulation, it hardly seems possible to imagine that there will be a time to praise God in gratitude for the burdens. (*Count Your Blessings*, 39.)

In difficult times, the struggling person who . . . deliberately skims off the shallow aspects of life reaches in the depths of God's real purpose where true joy is. (*Count Your Blessings*, 90.)

It is for us to find at last that in the midst of winter we have within us an invincible summer. In a world filled with adversity we can reach for joy. (In *Ensign*, May 1982, 95.)

KAREN LYNN DAVIDSON

As we strive to see life steadily and see it whole, we need not allow any dark moment of the past to dim the present or the future. (In *Women and the Power*, 15.)

The father of a friend of mine underwent what was thought to be a simple operation, but he was found to have inoperable cancer. The doctors told the family the terrible news. One of the man's daughters, in the immense distress of the moment, kept saying, "I can't go on! I can't go on!" Finally her sister said, "Well, what exactly do you plan to do instead?" (In *Women and the Power*, 15.)

JOY F. EVANS

It is true for all of us that the winds will blow and beat upon our houses. It is true, also, that our houses will stand if they are built upon the rock of Jesus Christ. Whatever adversity or difficulty we experience can be met with courage and faith, and even joy. (In *Behold Your Little Ones*, 90.)

ADRIENNE AIKELE HARMER

Times of trouble are times for us to search diligently for the Lord's light so that we may not be consumed by the darkness, no matter what the reward of the world. The glory of the world exists only until it fades into a lack of satisfaction. (In *Thy Word Is a Lamp*, 58.)

BEPPIE HARRISON

It's not having problems that distinguishes us from each other; it's the way we choose to deal with them. (*Plain and Precious*, 32.)

MARJORIE P. HINCKLEY

It is the trials of life that make us humble and make us strong. . . . I am indeed grateful that there have been . . . times in my life that I have had to depend entirely on the Lord for my well-being and comfort. (In *Glimpses*, 92–93.)

The only way to get through life is to laugh your way through it. You either have to laugh or cry. I prefer to laugh. Crying gives me a headache. (In *Glimpses*, 107.)

PATRICIA T. HOLLAND

When the winds blow and the sea is storm tossed, we must not give in to self-pity. God is with us; Christ is our sure foundation; there is a safe haven ahead. . . . In this mortal journey, all learning, all personal growth, all spiritual refinement carry with them the possibility of a little motion sickness. (In *Arms of His Love*, 366.)

When we can feel sure that God has not forgotten us—nor will he ever—and that he is blessing us in his own way, then the world seems a better, safer place. (In *Clothed with Charity*, 4.)

ELAINE L. JACK

Difficulty is an essential element in the bedrock underlying mortality and does not preclude rejoicing. Everything doesn't have to be marvelous for us to rejoice. (In *BYU Speeches*, 3 Jan. 1993, 49.)

The wonderful thing about life is that despite the injustices of this world, each of us still has the choice to believe. (In *Women of Wisdom*, 37.)

LUCILE JOHNSON

When we know that the Lord's work and his justice and mercy will ultimately prevail, we can gain peace of mind and consolation, even when things do not go as well as we had hoped or planned; and especially when they do not comply with our personal timetable. (*Enjoy the Journey*, 80.)

Storms have their place, but they always pass. The buffeting of storms in our lives can bring about

personal integrity if we weather the storm with courage and optimism. . . . But the secret of happy living in the midst of the storm is to hold fast to our belief that the sunshine will return. That makes the dark skies bearable. (*Sunny Side Up*, xv.)

ARDETH GREENE KAPP

Difficulties are just God's errands. If we are sent upon them, it is an evidence of his confidence. Therefore, let us be glad, be happy, for it is a way of being wise. (In *Ensign*, Nov. 1986, 89.)

CAMILLA EYRING KIMBALL

Forget self-pity and look for mountains to climb. Everyone has problems. The challenge is to cope with those problems and get our full measure of joy from life. (*Writings*, 143.)

MARILYNNE TODD LINFORD

When we stop expecting life to be easy, we take a giant step forward. We may not be able to control the events around us as we would like, but we can control what we think about those events and about ourselves. (*Woman Fulfilled*, 10.)

Expecting life to be difficult, but being grateful for every minute it isn't, is a healthy thought. If we expect highs and lows, seasons and cycles, blue days, maybe even a few black days along the way, we will be better able to cope. (*Woman Fulfilled*, 11.)

Amy Brown Lyman

In these days of anxiety let us regard one another with tenderness, love, and sympathy; let us put our trust in the Lord and unite in fervent appeals to Him for strength and courage to meet life each day as it comes with faith and composure, and to turn men's hearts to ways of peace. (In *Relief Society Magazine*, Mar. 1942, 196.)

Ann N. Madsen

It isn't a test unless it stretches us, unless it's really hard. There must be an honest choice. We must find ourselves on a path that forks and choose to go towards Christ or to move away from him. Our individual tests will vary, but the pattern of giving our all will not. (In *Redeemer*, 49.)

Diane L. Mangum

It doesn't matter if all the angels in heaven are bending down to give you a hand if you won't reach up to take hold. . . . Storing up your grief brings no awards, only weariness. . . . I don't need to carry anguish. I can set the whole list down. I can reach my hand up. I can turn my face to the light. (In *Balm of Gilead*, 105.)

Kathleen "Casey" Null

Life has always been full of disappointments, and it always will be. . . . We may have good reason to be miserable, but is that enough reason to comply? Pain is inevitable . . . but misery is optional. (*People My Age*, 13.)

Chieko N. Okazaki

Not all adversity is evil. . . . Some of it is just the normal accidents, the ill health, the bad luck that accompanies being alive. But adversity always hurts. And it always requires strength to deal with it. So seek in yourself for that rocklike strength to endure adversity. (*Disciples*, 159.)

Anne Osborn Poelman

Sometimes we suffer adversity as a consequence of someone else's exercise of agency. That which we can't control, we must often endure. However, what we *can* control is our response to that adversity. . . . That's the part that is up to us. (*Amulek Alternative*, 122.)

The Lord . . . knows us intimately and individually. He's in charge. He can work miracles, both small and large, in our lives. . . . Our knowledge that the Lord understands, cares, and will guide us— *sometimes in ways we may recognize only in retrospect*—can give us hope, reassurance, and the confidence to cope with adversity. (*Simeon Solution*, 7.)

Lynn F. Price

The scriptures don't tell us to hang on by our fingertips. They tell us to be grateful for all things. I believe that also means we should be grateful for the trials that can prove us worthy to return to live with our Father some day. (In *Balm of Gilead*, 97.)

HEPZIBAH RICHARDS

I had learned . . . to anticipate affliction and sorrow, knowing that it would surely come, and I am confident that nothing will be laid upon me which I shall not be enabled to endure. (In *Women's Voices*, 77.)

IONE J. SIMPSON

Every one of us will have challenges. We can let those challenges control us, or we can take charge. (In *Hearts Knit Together*, 118.)

Develop a good attitude. It is so easy to feel sorry for yourself. Don't. (In *Best of Women's Conference*, 492.)

BARBARA B. SMITH

It is less the traumas of childhood that shape our ability to adjust to . . . change. It is more often the quality of sustained relationships . . . that makes the difference. Positive, supportive, ongoing relationships are a valuable resource in times of major change in one's life. (In *Ensign*, Nov. 1981, 100.)

At one time or another, we all will have occasion to choose between a life of bitterness and a life of beauty. We have the power within us to make such a choice. (In *Ensign*, Feb. 1983, 60.)

Blessings come only after the struggle. It is not as if we had our choice to pay a certain price for a desired measure of personal growth. Growth comes only if our spirits remain teachable during profound

hardship. This truth may not be discernible before the fact of suffering. (*Grandmothering*, 26.)

MARY FIELDING SMITH

I have, to be sure, been called to drink deep of the bitter cup; but you know . . . this makes the sweet sweeter. (In *Their Own Words*, 98.)

ELIZA R. SNOW

I will go forward. I will smile at the rage of the tempest, and ride fearlessly and triumphantly across the boisterous ocean of circumstance. (In *Elect Ladies*, 40.)

I have learned to acknowledge the hand of the Lord in all things; in sickness, in trials, in pain, and in everything. God rules and over-rules in all things for the welfare of His people. Do we keep in view that God sent us here to hold high and responsible positions? We? Yes, we! the daughters of the Most High God. (In *Woman's Exponent*, 1 Oct. 1887, 70.)

Our hardships and privations were sufficient to have disheartened any but the saints of the living God—those who were prompted by higher than earthly motives, and trusting in the arm of Jehovah. (In *Women of Mormondom*, 145.)

BELLE S. SPAFFORD

It was not intended that our lives should be a succession of confused, wearisome, frustrated days. Rather, it was intended that they should be orderly, fruitful days of true joy as we triumph over evil and rise above tribulation. This comes about as we approach our problems positively in the light of gospel teaching. (*Woman's Reach*, 121.)

[As] children of the Father we have within us resources of power and strength great enough to enable us to meet valiantly whatever adversities this earth life may bring. (In *Relief Society Magazine*, Nov. 1950, 727.)

It is not what comes to us by way of experience but how we meet the difficulty that counts. (*Today's World*, 96.)

GWEN SQUIRES

Whatever our circumstances, we have the option to choose our attitude toward them. We can choose to let them overwhelm and defeat us, or we can choose to find the beauty, humor, and good in each day. (In *Hearts Knit Together*, 108.)

MARY STOVALL

Each of us will experience over our lifetime physical pain, emotional anguish, heartache, grief, even betrayal in one form or another. If we attempt to deny the problem or to cover it with a facade of forced sweetness and light, we . . . deny the healing that can result from the love, strength, and insights of true friends. (In *As Women of Faith*, viii.)

TERI H. TAYLOR

None of us will escape tragedy in our lives. We will feel despair, sadness, and grief. It's important to allow ourselves to feel those emotions. Then we each need to find a way to move on, to pass through the pain, and to find happiness again. (In *Clothed with Charity*, 245.)

EMMA LOU THAYNE

To ask why? or why them? or why me? can be the least productive of concentrations. (*As for Me*, 59.)

MERCY FIELDING THOMPSON

As long as memory lasts will remain in my recollection the squeaking hinges [as the door of Liberty Jail] closed upon the noblest men on earth. Who can imagine our feelings as we traveled homeward, but would I sell the honor bestowed upon me by being locked up in jail with such characters for gold? No! No! (*Mary Fielding Smith*, 86.)

ELOUISE TROTTER

Center our lives in Christ. I don't care what else goes on around us. We will never fail if we center our lives in Christ. (In *Clothed with Charity*, 178.)

Remember that no matter what you're going through, it will not last. The Book of Mormon has a phrase that you read over and over again: "And it came to pass." Remember that whatever comes into your life, it came to pass—it didn't come to stay. (In *Clothed with Charity*, 178.)

EMILY BENNETT WATTS

Some mountains would be better if they were considered molehills. (In *Arise*, 191.)

EMMELINE B. WELLS

God has given us [the] faculty of calling to remembrance the "light of other days" to help us to endure our lives with better grace. (In *Woman's Exponent*, 1 May 1877, 177.)

God Helps in Adversity

LINDA R. ARCHIBALD

Sometimes [our] trial is within us. . . . Other times it is the burden of a wayward or suffering loved one. . . . We need to be willing to cast our burden at His feet, ask Him to take it from us, allow Him to intervene. (*Sunshine in My Soul*, 85.)

DIXIE DRAWHORN BAKER

There are some things I will not understand in this life. That's just part of Heavenly Father's plan. I discovered that the peace he sends in place of complete understanding makes the trial something you can tolerate. With time the trial becomes a blessing. (In *Balm of Gilead*, 68.)

SHERLENE HALL BARTHOLOMEW

No personal challenge is beyond hope in Christ, when we are willing to do our part. (In *To Rejoice As Women*, 87.)

MARILYN S. BATEMAN

When we are exhausted from the trials of the day, the Lord through his spirit refreshes our spirit and prepares us for a new day. Our purpose is not to escape problems but to overcome them with the Lord's help. (In *Wisdom's Paths*, 108.)

SUSAN EASTON BLACK

The Book of Mormon Saints taught us how the Lord shows his love in times of trials. Sorrow eventually becomes glory. Persecution proves a crown of righteousness. (*Finding Christ*, 77.)

The Lord will not leave his devoted followers comfortless. In affliction, persecution, and suffering, the Lord sends heavenly aid. (*Finding Christ*, 77.)

ELAINE CANNON

In the worst of times only God can ease the pain. He's good at this in part because he has been through it. (*Count Your Blessings*, 39.)

MARY ELLEN EDMUNDS

Trials and adversity can be sanctifying and purifying, whether we are left on this earth or taken Home. God is with us, and we will come through all right if we can endure patiently. (*Happiness*, 86.)

MARIE K. HAFEN

The Lord does give us strength to deal with a world that can sometimes be dreary, but often that help comes only as we do all we can do. (In *LDS Women's Treasury*, 316.)

BEPPIE HARRISON

When we are tossed about by the storms and tempests of our lives on this earth . . . we have . . . certainties to hang on to. Our Father in Heaven will always be there. The gospel will always be there. The eternal laws will always be there. (*Plain and Precious*, 10.)

JANE F. HINCKLEY

[When our lives are out of balance,] there is only one source of help—the Savior. We cannot do it alone. We need to lay our burdens at the Lord's feet and move on. When we have done all we can and know it is not enough to meet the day's requirements, we must trust the Lord. We must rely on him for strength. He will not fail us. (In *Arms of His Love*, 261.)

PATRICIA T. HOLLAND

The light that comes into our lives in times of great personal need, the light that dispels the clouds of darkness and rends the veil of unbelief . . . is the marvelous light of God's goodness. (In *To Rejoice As Women*, 98.)

MARTI AND MARCIE HOLLOMAN

If in the storms of crisis, . . . you feel you can never be whole again, . . . look at your experience from an enlarged perspective. Out of one shattering experience, you have the opportunity to take each piece of your broken heart, bind it with the pure love of Christ, and come out of your trial of fire. (In *Clothed with Charity*, 231.)

ELAINE L. JACK

Despite trials, worldly confusion, and caustic voices, we can trust in the Lord and go forward with happy hearts, knowing that with every challenge or problem, there's the strength to go on. Why? Because we know His promises are real, that He does know us by name and has a plan for each of us. He will help us learn what it is and give us joy in doing it. (In *Ensign*, May 1992, 91.)

VIRGINIA U. JENSEN

When we tremble, when we bleed, when we suffer, either in body or in spirit, [Christ] understands. None is better qualified to see us through our mortal trials than he who "descended below all things" (D&C 88:6). (In *May Christ Lift Thee Up*, 32.)

We have once seen. Every now and then the spirit whispers to us of remembered light. We are not lost in a black cave. We know the source of all light! (In *May Christ Lift Thee Up*, 38.)

ARDETH GREENE KAPP

Can we tell [Jesus] anything about struggle or suffering that he does not know and understand—anything about loneliness, about rejection, about abuse? Do you think he understands about sorrow? And though he was without sin himself, do you think he knows of the consequence of sin, when he voluntarily took upon himself the weight of all our sins and transgressions? If we choose to follow him, he will be with us even in the fiery furnace. (*Rejoice!* 47.)

Yes, the struggle is real. It must be, if we are to break from the spiritual shell and become all God intends us to be. But we are not left alone to find the way. We know the path, and others before us have succeeded. Because of God's great love for us, he has provided the way for our victory, if we will just do our part. (*Rejoice!* 96.)

To become saints, we must endure trials. Through our covenant relationship with Jesus Christ we do all that we can do, and by the grace of God he does the rest. (*Joy of the Journey*, 14.)

Camilla Eyring Kimball

Christ . . . has not promised us that the road will be easy. . . . But the problems will help us to grow in strength. He has assured us that he stands ready to help us and to guide us all the way if we but seek him in earnest prayer continually. (*Writings*, 85–86.)

Janet G. Lee

Our Heavenly Father wants us to grow through our own experiences. . . . But he will help us and

give us direction. As *we* do the work, our Father in Heaven will help lift our burdens. You might think of it as a joint effort. (In *BYU Speeches*, 10 Sept. 1991, 10.)

Amy Brown Lyman

Our greatest source of help and comfort at any and all times lies in the Gospel of Jesus Christ and in the spiritual security which comes from a testimony of its truthfulness. (In *Relief Society Magazine*, Mar. 1942, 196.)

Deborah Eldredge Milne

I don't remember one earth-shattering experience that instantly helped me overcome the trauma of my youth. I remember slow progress, year after year, as I read and prayed daily. . . . The scriptures taught me then, and still teach me today, that it's possible to transcend *any* problem through faith. (*Reflections*, 90.)

Chieko N. Okazaki

If we allow . . . pain to make us focus all our attention on ourselves, then we can't find peace and comfort under Christ's wings. (*Disciples*, 5.)

Kathy D. Pullins

The Savior knows our times, and he knows our hearts. He also understands the effect that . . . unrest can have upon our souls, and he offers perspective that allows us to find joy even amidst the tribulation. (In *May Christ Lift Thee Up*, 18.)

CAROLYN J. RASMUS

Challenges, temptations, hardships, and difficulties will not always be removed from us; but by the power of faith in the Savior we can feel peace, experience comfort, and realize a strength and power which comes only through belief in him. (*In the Strength of the Lord*, 48.)

When we are discouraged, uncertain, overwhelmed, anxious, confused, or feeling inadequate, we can turn to the true sources of strength and power. Increasingly, we can "lay aside the things of this world, and seek for the things of a better." (In *Wisdom's Paths*, 230.)

ELLIS R. SHIPP

My faith in my Heavenly Father wavered not. I relied upon Him. I believed He would let nothing come upon me but what would be for my good even though it should be want and suffering and I resolved to bear patiently whatever might come. (*While Others Slept*, 246–47.)

CHERRY B. SILVER

Life presents difficult choices. We don't always pick our route. But we can choose our guide. Our basic choice of eternal values helps us maneuver through the obstacles on our road. (In *Knit Together in Love*, 29.)

BATHSHEBA W. SMITH

[As pioneers] we traveled through storms of snow, wind and rain— . . . roads had to be made, bridges built, and rafts constructed— . . . our poor animals had to drag on, day after day, with scanty feed— . . . our camps suffered from poverty, sickness and death. We were consoled in the midst of these hardships by seeing the power of God manifested through the laying on of the hands of the elders, causing the sick to be healed and the lame to walk. The Lord was with us, and his power was made manifest daily. (In *Women of Mormondom*, 321–22.)

EMMA SMITH

Was it not for conscious innocence, and the direct interposition of divine mercy, I am very sure I never should have been able to have endured the scenes of suffering that I have passed through. (In *Personal Writings of Joseph Smith*, 388.)

MARY ELLEN SMOOT

In cooking and in life, if we gave up after every time our gravy was lumpy or our bread sagged in the middle, we'd all go hungry. Lumpy gravy is part of what mortality is all about. We all have challenges, trials, and upsets. The Lord's plan of happiness does not eradicate difficulty; it teaches us how to endure it. (*Sweet Is the Work*, 10.)

ELIZA R. SNOW

Our exposures and privations [as pioneers] caused much sickness, and sickness increased destitution; but in the midst of all this, we enjoyed a great portion of the spirit of God, . . . with rich manifestations of the gifts and power of the gospel. (In *Women of Mormondom*, 317–18.)

The mind must be fixed on God that the cheering influence of his spirit may elevate our hopes above the power of changing circumstance; then will the aged rejoice and the young be encouraged, even amid scenes of difficulty and peril. (*Personal Writings*, 56.)

HEIDI S. SWINTON

The Lord doesn't often reach down and move the mountains to clear our way. Usually he helps reorient our thinking and gives us added strength. (In *Arms of His Love*, 239.)

EMMA LOU THAYNE

Pray not so much for "Please, with your omnipotence change all this," as for "Please, with your strength help me to manage."

It is not easy to learn, like Job, that kind of asking, but it can be a gift given—if I take time and am willing to wait for the teachings that accompany everything that happens in a day—or night. (*As for Me*, 59.)

WENDY L. WATSON

When we feel that no one understands us, that there is no one we can trust, that we need someone who will always be there, we can turn to the Lord, even in our despair, in our disappointment, and also later in our gratitude. (In *May Christ Lift Thee Up*, 50.)

ZINA D. H. YOUNG

Never can it be told in words what the Saints suffered in our days of trials, but the sweet spirit of the Comforter did not forsake us. (In *Elect Ladies*, 49.)

I pray thee, O Heavenly Father, . . . let the angel of thy peace attend me and never forsake me, but may I ever have grace to listen to the Spirit of truth forever more. (In *Their Own Words*, 74.)

Agency

Agency Is Essential to Growth and Salvation

JUTTA BAUM BUSCHE

Achieving our full potential in our journey here depends on our free choices. That message needs to penetrate every act of our daily lives. (In *Best of Women's Conference*, 69.)

ELAINE CANNON

Our job is to search for the full truth and apply it in our lives. (In *Ensign*, Nov. 1980, 99.)

BEPPIE HARRISON

Free agency offers us much more than a decision between good and evil: it opens before us a splendid panorama of choices between an infinite number of alternatives, many just as good as others. (In *Woman's Choices*, 54.)

SHARON G. LARSEN

The world's two opposing forces seek our commitment. On the one hand, there is the reality of Satan, and on the other, the more powerful love of the Savior. (In *Ensign*, Nov. 1999, 11.)

Agency Must Be Preserved

SUSAN NOYES ANDERSON

Just as we are free to act for ourselves, our children are free to act for themselves. We are not commissioned as parents to deny children this freedom, nor can we exercise it in their behalf. The Lord will not allow it. What He does allow are consequences: some natural, some God-given, some parental. . . . Rules and limits should be in keeping with higher laws as well, all with an eye toward helping our children achieve self-mastery. (*End of Your Rope*, 32–33.)

SUSA YOUNG GATES

God may have marked out a certain path for a soul to follow while in this life, but there is as surely an opposite direction which that soul can only too easily take if the agency is exercised in doing wrong instead of right. (In *Young Woman's Journal*, Aug. 1891, 524.)

ANNE OSBORN POELMAN

Unlike agency, our freedom—the opportunity together with the ability to exercise our agency—*can* be compromised. It may be restricted by others, . . . limited by circumstance, . . . [or] curtailed or willingly surrendered by our own choices. . . .

But agency itself cannot be surrendered or taken away. Agency is preserved under the most severe conditions, the most extreme circumstances. (*Amulek Alternative*, 29–30.)

MOLLIE H. SORENSEN

Trying to force another to accept the gospel is not pleasing to our Father. He cares not only that they return again to him, but also that they do so of their own free will and choice. He wants them to discover for themselves that the truths he has given are right and good and will bring the greatest joy. (In *Building a Love*, 172–73.)

Agency and Accountability

RUTH E. BRASHER

We, as spirit children of our Father in Heaven, had the opportunity to choose in the premortal existence because we possessed agency. . . . We chose the plan with agency—a plan which required that *we* must direct our own lives. . . . We knew what we were choosing, and, thereby, we accepted responsibility for the decisions we make and the actions we undertake. (In *BYU Speeches*, 30 May 1995, 195–96.)

ELAINE CANNON

Spiritual maturity is understanding that we cannot blame anybody else for our actions. . . . Being accountable for how we use our agency means being answerable for our own behavior. (In *Ensign*, Nov. 1983, 88.)

We are like children walking a path in the rain. We can walk in or around the mud of life as we desire, but with our choices come the consequences. And we are rapidly becoming what we are choosing to be for all eternity. (In *Ensign*, Nov. 1983, 88.)

Accountability is the natural product of agency and is the basis of the plan of life. We are responsible for our own actions and accountable to God for what we choose to do with our lives. Life is God's gift to us, and what we do with it is our gift to him. (In *Ensign*, Nov. 1980, 99.)

SUZANNE L. HANSEN

We need to stop looking for someone to blame for our unhappiness or loneliness or depression. If *you* are unhappy or sad or feel unliked or uncared about, it may be because of your choices. (In *High Fives*, 66.)

CAMILLA EYRING KIMBALL

Our parents may have had wonderful testimonies and may have lived well, but it is our individual responsibility to make our own way to eternal life. (*Writings*, 81.)

Choice in life is not just an occasional thing. We are afloat on a sea of choices. And we ought not to think that we can avoid accountability by refusing to make a choice, because refusing to decide is itself a choice—a choice to be borne wherever external forces will take us. (*Writings*, 20.)

Our free agency, the right to choose, is a God-given privilege, but we must remember that the actual results of these choices may be far from what we had desired. . . . Too often we choose foolishly, and the price we must ultimately pay is completely outside our expectations. What we do today vitally affects our tomorrows. (*Writings*, 97.)

You are your own constant companion through every day of life and throughout all eternity. You cannot escape yourself. (*Writings*, 99.)

SHARON G. LARSEN

Deciding for oneself dictates consequences, which are not always what we want. We want the freedom without consequences. (In *Ensign*, Nov. 1999, 12.)

ELAINE SORENSEN MARSHALL

None of us travels the road of mortality by chance. Every decision, every act, every thought, moves the direction of our lives to one path or another. (In *Ensign*, Mar. 1983, 31.)

ANNE OSBORN POELMAN

Moral agency is inextricably linked with personal responsibility and accountability. Our choices often beget consequences that reverberate far beyond the borders of our own lives. (*Amulek Alternative*, 100.)

BARBARA B. SMITH

Ultimately *we* are responsible for our own happiness. It is our attitude, our acceptance, our intelligent understanding that make the difference. (In *Ensign*, Apr. 1976, 68.)

There is a light given us by the Lord. It is the same light that he gave yesterday and that he will give forever. . . . It will give direction to make every dream of eternity come true. But one has to choose to keep it or . . . trade it away. The ultimate responsibility for living lives in accord with that heavenly light rests with each of us. (In *Ensign*, Apr. 1976, 68.)

BELLE S. SPAFFORD

We may feel and know that there is no spot so dark and no place so far removed that the all-seeing eye of God is not upon us, and that we will be held accountable for our deeds. (*Today's World*, 35.)

EMMELINE B. WELLS

Do we order our lives with reference to the hereafter, keeping the conviction continually in view, not in fear, not in dread, but guiding, directing, inspiring us to achieve a work of which we need not be ashamed when we go home again into the presence of our Father? (In *Woman's Exponent*, 1 Jan. 1876, 114.)

We must [ultimately] render an account . . . without help from others; without the influence of friends; not resting upon another's faith; not trusting to another's knowledge; our own acts, our own merits must speak for themselves. (In *Woman's Exponent*, 1 Jan. 1876, 114.)

The Power to Choose

NORMA B. ASHTON

Others may be responsible in the beginning for some of our problems, but they are not responsible for the way we act or the way we solve our problems. (In *Best of Women's Conference*, 19.)

JANETTE HALES BECKHAM

God has given each of us power—the power to act, to choose, to serve, to love, and to accomplish *much good*. Perhaps it is time to take control of ourselves. (In *Ensign*, Nov. 1995, 11.)

AFTON J. DAY

We have all been given the freedom and responsibility to control only one person—ourselves. (In *Building a Love*, 122.)

SHERI L. DEW

We are free to choose how we live, where we spend our temporal, emotional, and spiritual resources, and to what and whom we devote ourselves. (In *Arms of His Love*, 389.)

MICHAELENE P. GRASSLI

The Lord has given you control of your life. . . . You will not always be able to control what others may say or do, but you can control how you will react to them. (In *Ensign*, Nov. 1988, 91.)

When you follow God's plan, you can know what to do, and that's when you are in control. You can decide whether or not you are going to be happy by making choices that will lead you close to your Heavenly Father and away from Satan. You can decide what *you* will say and do. (In *Ensign*, Nov. 1988, 91.)

ARDETH GREENE KAPP

We are free to choose to follow or not to follow, to abide by the law or to disregard it, to have freedom or to forfeit our freedom, to claim our inheritance or to leave it unclaimed. (In *BYU Speeches*, 1 Feb. 1987, 99.)

SHARON G. LARSEN

To become a committed follower of Christ, we must have the option to reject Him. So Satan is permitted to exercise his power, and yielding our will to God can sometimes become difficult. Yet it is in this exercise of acting for ourselves that we grow. (In *Ensign*, Nov. 1999, 11.)

Agency is the power to think, choose, and act for ourselves. . . . It is a blessing and a burden. Using this gift of agency wisely is critical today because never in the world's history have God's children been so blessed or so blatantly confronted with so many choices. (In *Ensign*, Nov. 1999, 11.)

DEBORAH ELDREDGE MILNE

I am not a victim of fate or of other people's mistakes because I am free to choose my own responses and free to learn something positive from my pain. I believe God wants me to write my own story of life as I go. (*Reflections*, 112.)

I . . . acknowledge all that I can't control in my life, including the choices made by my friends and family. I acknowledge that at any given moment, accident, death, or disease could strike me or the people I love. But I also know that no matter what the external event, God has given me the freedom to choose how I will react. (*Reflections*, 125.)

CHIEKO N. OKAZAKI

We are free to choose because we were made free from the beginning, and [Christ] honors our agency and our right and ability to choose. The choice He offers is life, and life offers hope. Any other choice is a choice of spiritual death that will bring us into the power of the devil. (In *Ensign*, Nov. 1996, 90.)

VIRGINIA H. PEARCE

We've all seen ourselves as victims of someone else's behavior. Changing our thinking to focus on . . . our responsibility for current choices can be liberating. (In *To Rejoice As Women*, 37.)

BARBARA B. SMITH

We may not realize it at the moment of choice, but our response is an infallible index of what we have become. (In *BYU Speeches*, 16 Feb. 1982, 92.)

PAULA THOMAS

Along with Christ's coming to atone for our sins, he would show us by his example that our freedom of choice, or agency, is not just the right to choose between good and evil but also the right to choose every minute of every day how we will respond to life's experiences and to the people who share those experiences with us. The life of Jesus was a constant example of choosing the higher ground. (In *Finding the Light*, 68.)

Choosing to Choose

ELAINE CANNON

Though we are free to act, we are not free to decide what is right or wrong. That was determined eons ago. . . . We cannot alter God's laws, his truth. We can choose to use truth wisely and reach our goal, or we can refuse to learn truth, to live it, and then pay the inevitable penalty. (In *Ensign*, Nov. 1980, 99.)

ARDETH GREENE KAPP

It is while a person stands undecided, uncommitted, and uncovenanted, with choices waiting to be made, that the vulnerability to every wind that blows becomes life-threatening. (In *Best of Women's Conference*, 237.)

SHARON G. LARSEN

Too often, we try to stand neutral, undecided, and uncommitted. It is in this atmosphere that we become vulnerable to the influence of Satan. (In *Ensign*, Nov. 1999, 12.)

ANNE OSBORN POELMAN

Each of us makes choices between good and evil, between right and wrong, several times a day. . . . We must select our path firmly and courageously. We must be steadfast and unwavering in our determination to choose the right and resist the wrong. (*Amulek Alternative*, 56.)

BARBARA B. SMITH

You will have occasion to choose between a life of bitterness and a life of beauty. You have the power within you to make such a choice, and the Lord has promised that you can count on him for sufficient help to have an abundant life if you choose to live by the principles that lead you to personal growth and development. (*Love,* 53.)

MARY ELLEN SMOOT

No matter what our status in life, no matter what choices were made in the past, we can choose to be on the Lord's side now. (In *May Christ Lift Thee Up,* 82.)

We may need to redesign some of our dreams, we may need to renew some of our covenants, but we can choose the Lord's plan for happiness today. (In *May Christ Lift Thee Up,* 82.)

Making Good Choices

ELAINE CANNON

To use our agency wisely we need information to act upon. We need a knowledge of the laws of life, with their accompanying blessings and protective punishments. When we know the gospel, the elements of the "thou shalts" and the "thou shalt nots," we'll make better choices. (In *Ensign,* Nov. 1980, 99.)

BEPPIE HARRISON

Only seldom do we encounter pure black or pure white. Most of the time most of us make our way through an ever-changing world of grays, trying to do the best we can. The choices are all there. (In *Woman's Choices,* 54.)

ARDETH GREENE KAPP

A good measurement to ask concerning every important decision is whether or not this decision will move you toward or away from making and keeping sacred covenants and preparing for the ordinances of the temple. (In *Ensign,* Nov. 1990, 95.)

When we do something different than we know we should, it is like going into a final examination and putting down the wrong answer, even though we know the right one. (In *Best of Women's Conference,* 241.)

JO ANN LARSEN

Through goodness we experience the wondrous rapture of being alive and ultimately discover the path to happiness and inspired meaning in our lives. (*Heart of Goodness,* ix.)

Originating and flowing from God's own perfect essence, goodness is its own reward, endowing us all with comfort, peace, love, and security while simultaneously bettering our world. (*Heart of Goodness,* ix.)

MARGARET D. NADAULD

The Lord will help you after you have done all you can to make good decisions. He will bless you as you serve him and his children. (In *BYU Speeches,* 2 Nov. 1997, 12.)

ANNE OSBORN POELMAN

The small and seemingly insignificant choices we continually make can become either stumbling blocks or stepping-stones on the pathway to a joyful, balanced day-to-day life and—ultimately—eternal life and exaltation. (In *Joy*, 50.)

SALLY TAYLOR

If you listen humbly to the whisperings of the Spirit, [your] future can be directed toward the joy and happiness your Father in Heaven wants you to have. . . . Pray for guidance and then humbly and quietly listen. . . . Decision making is hard. Let the Holy Ghost be your partner in the process. (In *BYU Speeches*, 5 Nov. 1996, 77–78.)

EMMELINE B. WELLS

We are not as much to blame for ignorantly committing an error as we are for neglecting that which we know to be a duty because of lack of thought, or consideration for others. (In *Woman's Exponent*, 15 Sept. 1879, 59.)

BARBARA W. WINDER

The right and wrong of our decisions and actions should be consistently determined in light of the plan of salvation. There [is] a standard of righteousness—this standard will enlighten and aid our decision process. (In *BYU Speeches*, 12 Nov. 1985, 44.)

The crucial test of life is not between fame and obscurity or between wealth and poverty. The greatest decisions of life are between good and evil. (In *BYU Speeches*, 12 Nov. 1985, 46.)

Aging

CAMILLA EYRING KIMBALL

There is no place nor time when one can justify idly sitting by to vegetate. Keeping mentally, physically, and spiritually growing constantly is the way to continue the happy, useful life. (*Writings*, 61.)

The later years of a woman's life should be viewed as a time that can be socially and professionally productive. When a mother's children are reared, or if she is childless, the years after forty or fifty may begin to look bleak. Her real life's work may seem done, when in reality it has only changed. (In *Ensign*, Mar. 1997, 58–59.)

I can take a little teasing, but people need to remember that the problems of growing old are not really very funny to those who have them. (*Writings*, 147.)

Old age does allow one time for reflecting with some satisfaction on the joys and accomplishments of a lifetime. (In *Best of Women's Conference*, 273.)

EILEEN GIBBONS KUMP

I have a line or two from a letter of a great-aunt. . . . Note how she felt about old age: . . . "It never occurred to me that a period of time would be given me when there was nothing else to do but think, and learn. See how foolish of me to think there was nothing for me to do! There is so much to think about, to reason out, so much knowledge which I might gain that these quiet, all-alone hours are only blessings." (In *Woman's Choices*, 109.)

CAROLINE EYRING MINER

Our golden years truly can be golden if we interact with family and friends and continue to serve God, maker of all great and wonderful creations. (In *Ensign*, July 1997, 66.)

CAROLYN J. RASMUS

Lessons of life that come with increasing years come in quiet, often solitary ways. . . . Perhaps the physical body slows and tires a bit more quickly so that we might have increased time to ponder and reflect and meditate. (In *Wisdom's Paths*, 231.)

MARILYN RICHARDSON

Despite all the problems involved with caring for our elderly parents, we must not lose sight of their humanity. Don't let them simply devolve into a burden to be borne. They are still the people who loved and reared us. We owe them consideration, dignity, and love. (In *Arms of His Love*, 329.)

BARBARA B. SMITH

With careful planning, a family can have loving, rewarding experiences in caring for its elderly members. There is no better way to teach children respect for the elderly and the need for everyone to prepare for that time in life than by helping to care for their older relatives. (In *Ensign*, May 1978, 85.)

We can make service to others a lifetime habit; the older years may bring even more time for service as the hours once devoted to earning a livelihood or rearing a family can be used to enrich the lives of others through church and community service. (In *Ensign*, May 1978, 85.)

We can . . . enrich our own lives by learning new skills after our fulltime occupation has relaxed its demands. Learning should be a lifetime pursuit. (In *Ensign*, May 1978, 85.)

There may be times when the medical and physical needs of the aged can only be met by institutional care. . . . After a family member enters a health care institution, the family and the Church need to continue their supportive interest with regular visits and expressions of love. (In *Ensign*, May 1978, 85.)

Priesthood and Relief Society leaders must be aware of the great potential of those . . . who are in their later years and can give useful service. . . . A wonderful world of service may emerge for those with time and skills to offer! (In *Ensign*, May 1978, 85.)

We can begin now to develop good attitudes toward the later years. We can learn to respect the wisdom, experience, and value of older people. We can strengthen our family ties and appreciate the assets of many generations in a family. (In *Ensign*, May 1978, 85.)

[The] loneliness [of the elderly] can be as debilitating as disease, and their isolation a prison from which there seems to be no escape. For many, their constant companion is a feeling of worthlessness or inconvenience. We have the responsibility to include them, and the greater opportunity to learn from them. (In *Ensign*, Nov. 1981, 99.)

Relief Society's response to aging sisters . . . must take into account the physical impairment that often accompanies old age, and must determine how to be helpful. We should be happy and willing to assist our older sisters. Their loneliness can be as debilitating as disease, and their isolation a prison from which there seems to be no escape. For many, their constant companion is a feeling of worthlessness or inconvenience. We have the responsibility to include them, and the greater opportunity to learn from them. (In *Ensign*, Nov. 1981, 101.)

Eliza R. Snow

Court the society of the aged who have trod the path of life before you—those who have accumulated wisdom by length of years and practical experience. Listen respectfully to their instructions, and profit by their counsels. (*Personal Writings*, 70.)

We thought the days of our youth was the time of happiness and enjoyment. I can bear my testimony to my young sisters that the older I grow the happier I am. (In *Heroic Mormon Women*, 131.)

Belle S. Spafford

Loneliness is . . . one of the tragedies of old age. The physical presence of someone else in the home doesn't always dispel loneliness. Loneliness is the absence of a positive feeling of closeness, of companionship, of being important in the minds of others—being cut off from the currents of life about one. (*Today's World*, 180.)

The gift of age should be viewed in its true light as the fortunate destiny of an ever-increasing number of Americans who, rich in experience, mature in wisdom, resourceful in meeting the demands of life, can continue to contribute to national well-being and live happy, well-adjusted personal lives. It is the responsibility of both the individual and society to make it so. (*Today's World*, 174.)

Atonement of Jesus Christ

The Significance of the Atonement

LINDA R. ARCHIBALD

In [premortality], we shouted joyfully because we were excited to have the opportunity for eternal progression and because we had faith that Jesus could and would do all He promised to do. By making us perfect through the power of the Atonement, He would make it possible for us to return to our heavenly home. We will give that same joyful shout in mortality when we understand the all-encompassing nature of His mission. (*Sunshine in My Soul*, 48.)

SHERI L. DEW

In this, the twilight of the dispensation of the fulness of times, when Lucifer is working overtime to jeopardize our journey home and to separate us from the Savior's atoning power, the only answer for *any* of us is Jesus Christ. (In *Ensign*, May 1999, 67.)

MARIE K. HAFEN

Because we lack the power to compensate fully for the effects of our sins, we are utterly dependent on Jesus Christ. Without his holy atonement, no amount of agonizing repentance could return us to God's presence. We dare not trifle with so sacred a reality. (In *BYU Speeches*, 9 May 1995, 172.)

NEILL MARRIOTT

We are at present in a fallen state, but a healing power is always available to empower us. The atonement of Jesus Christ is that power. Only his atonement can heal the wounds in our heart, the sins in our past, the fears for our future so that we may return home, rejoicing in one another's achievements to live God's life, eternally. (In *Hearts Knit Together*, 128.)

LOUISE PLUMMER

Without the atonement of Jesus Christ, our virtues, whatever they are, are meaningless. (In *Best of Women's Conference*, 460.)

M. CATHERINE THOMAS

The Lord Jesus Christ himself is [the] consolation, [the] compensation, designed from the foundation of the world to comfort the human pain of fallenness, to compensate men and women for their earthly reductions and sacrifices. Only the Atonement, or more expressly, the At-one-ment, can heal the pain of the Fall. (In *BYU Speeches*, 7 Dec. 1993, 46.)

The Atonement Is Personal

CAMILLE FRONK

The profound interaction Jesus Christ had with countless individuals shows that he lived and died for each one of us. I am convinced that if there was only one of our Father's children who needed the Savior's sacrifice for salvation, Jesus would have gone through all the pain and suffering for that one. (In *Redeemer*, 172.)

JAMIE GLENN

He took upon himself our insecurities and personal failings and pains and sicknesses. He took upon himself our weaknesses of mind, will, and character. When we feel that no one understands, he may say, "I do understand." (*Walk Tall*, 38.)

PATRICIA T. HOLLAND

Christ's compassionate atonement is more powerful than even a mother's love. (In *BYU Speeches*, 15 Sept. 1987, 15.)

BETTE S. MOLGARD

Our Savior felt the pain of our everyday battles in the Garden of Gethsemane. He felt every fear, discouragement, every single hurt the adversary can throw at us. . . . He somehow individually felt and fought every single one of my battles, and every single one of your battles. He did it so that he would know exactly how to comfort and succor us. (*Everyday Battles*, 12.)

CHIEKO N. OKAZAKI

Do you know that if you were the only person in the world who needed his atonement, he would still have died for you—just for you? (*Sanctuary*, 95–96.)

We know that Jesus experienced the totality of mortal existence in Gethsemane. It's our faith that he experienced everything—absolutely everything. . . . We talk in great generalities about the sins of all humankind, about the suffering of the entire human family. But we don't experience pain in generalities. We experience it individually. (In *Women and Christ*, 6.)

Even during the hardest moments of your life, when your powerlessness seems absolute and your isolation total, you are not alone. The Savior is with you. . . . Your survival and even your triumph are assured through his atoning sacrifice and his love. (*Sanctuary*, 95.)

It is in the goodness of God, not in the goodness of ourselves, that our hope of the Atonement lies. We must have faith in Christ—not only that he is *the* Savior, but that he is *our* Savior. (*Lighten Up!* 209.)

The Atonement Covers More Than Sin

JOYCE BACA

With repentance and the hope that comes from it, we can realize that there is really no obstacle to becoming who we want to be. Whatever pain in rejection we may feel, whatever grief we suffer, or whatever bitterness we harbor is lost in the marvelous healing power of the atonement. (*Divorce*, 82.)

MARILYN S. BATEMAN

As we go through pains, sicknesses, afflictions, and temptations of every kind, our Savior will be there to succor us. He has paid the price through his atoning sacrifice to know us and to know how to help us. He knows how to deliver us safely back home. He is our Deliverer—our all! (In *Best of Women's Conference*, 32.)

JANIEL REEVE CARVER

The Atonement is not just for sinners. Its effects relieve every burden that we will place before our Lord and Savior. (In *Balm of Gilead*, 141.)

CATHERINE CHRISTENSEN

The Savior suffered for our sins, and he suffered for our lack of understanding, for our loneliness, for our struggle, and for our pain. The healing of our wounds is a gift given to us because of the Atonement, and finding peace is the realization of that gift. (In *Balm of Gilead*, 48.)

SHERI L. DEW

The Lord knows the way because He *is* the way and is our only chance for successfully negotiating mortality. His Atonement makes available all of the power, peace, light, and strength that we need to deal with life's challenges. (In *Ensign*, May 1999, 67.)

M. CATHERINE THOMAS

The ultimate object of all the deliverances is to bring that which is miserable, scattered, alienated, and spiritually dead back into living oneness with Christ: deliverance is a function of the power of at-one-ment in Jesus Christ. (*Selected Writings*, 61.)

MERCEDES WIEDERHOLD

When in the dead of the night, I am unable to sleep because of physical discomfort, my thoughts turn to the Garden of Gethsemane. I know I am not alone. He is there. He understands better than anyone else any physical, emotional, or spiritual pain that I am asked to bear. We are in partnership on this project called mortality. (In *Balm of Gilead*, 29.)

The Blessing of Grace

JAMIE GLENN

[Jesus Christ] bridges the gap between life and death, making eternal life possible for us. More immediately, he bridges gaps in our lives with forgiveness, with healing, with increased patience, with strength when our strength seems to be gone, with knowledge beyond our own learning, with new understanding, and with peace that only he can give. We cannot make it in life alone. We cannot make it without him. (*Walk Tall*, 118.)

There are times when we have gone to our limit and have done all that we can do but more needs to be done. . . . Through the Atonement, Jesus Christ is the one who can bridge the gaps in our lives and do those things we cannot do for ourselves. (*Walk Tall*, 117–18.)

MARIE K. HAFEN

The Lord's forgiveness is ultimately an act of grace. It comes as his gift, not as something we have a right to, even though we must repent as a condition of receiving it. (In *Women in the Covenant*, 21.)

JANE F. HINCKLEY

When we have done all we can and know it is not enough to meet the day's requirements, we must trust the Lord. We must rely on him for strength. He will not fail us. (In *Arms of His Love*, 261.)

LUCILE JOHNSON

Only in Christ is there power to transform the human mind and heart to make true growth possible. Only in Christ can we learn who and what we are. Only in Christ can we effect the changes as needed. (*Enjoy the Journey*, 39.)

ARDETH GREENE KAPP

Sometimes we feel that we need to do it all—and all at once. But that is not the case. When we give what we have according to our time, according to our energy, according to where we are at this moment in our development, then the Lord will take what we have to offer and he will make up the difference. That is the grace of God. (In *Women and the Power*, 46.)

CAROL CORNWALL MADSEN

How often has God told us, My grace is sufficient for you? . . . He wants us to . . . yield ourselves to that unearned blessing more often so that it might lighten our spiritual load and diminish our sense of inadequacy. I think it means to depend more than we do on the enabling power of God's grace to accept and meet our daily commitments. (In *Women in the Covenant*, 7.)

There is a beautiful symmetry in the doctrines of grace and works. . . . God's grace unlocks the door to salvation, and our faith and works lead us through it and take us closer to him. Both grace and works are freewill offerings—doing for others what they cannot do for themselves: God for us through his grace, and we for others through our works. (In *Women in the Covenant*, 6.)

We may not fully understand the theology of the Atonement nor completely comprehend the depth of God's love and mercy for us in giving us the free gift of life by the sacrifice of his Son. But I think we all yearn to feel the touch of grace in our lives, moments that capture the soul and hold it, a willing hostage, away from the assaults and demands of the unjust world in which we live. (In *Best of Women's Conference,* 334.)

ELAINE SORENSEN MARSHALL

Anyone who would be a disciple of Christ kneels sometime at [a] Gethsemane. But . . . we need not stay. When we can find the courage to surrender, to accept the gift of the Savior—who already suffered there—we can stand and move on to another garden. Grace offers the quiet promise of that safe passage. (In *Women in the Covenant,* 267.)

Grace intercedes to change our focus from what we can or cannot do to who we are. (In *Women in the Covenant,* 265.)

If we are earnest and obedient in our strivings, we are promised the help and comfort of our Heavenly Father. We are His children, and we are rearing His children. His will is our growth, refinement, progress, and influence for good. (In *Woman's Choices,* 32.)

CHIEKO N. OKAZAKI

"We know that it is by grace that we are saved, after all we can do." (2 Nephi 25:23.) Sometimes I've heard people quote that scripture in a way that gives me the impression that I am floundering in a river, being swept toward a great waterfall. . . .

My feeling about Nephi's statement is very different. Christ is in the river with us, not standing on the shore. He is the master of wind and wave, the creator of the river and the falls. He can walk on the water and command the storms to obey him. Yet he is in the water with us, feeling the batterings of the same current. He lends us his strength so we can try. He gives us his vision so that we can see the shore. He whispers encouragement in our ears. When we are exhausted, his arm is there for us to lean on. It may be true that we can always do more—but not because we have no limits. It's because he has none. (In *Women in the Covenant,* 249.)

ELIZA R. SNOW

The grace of God is sufficient; therefore, I will not fear. I will put my trust in Him who is mighty to save; rejoicing in his goodness and determined to live by every word that proceedeth out of his mouth. (In *Their Own Words,* 52.)

Partaking of the Blessings of the Atonement

ELAINE CANNON

Keep a strong, close relationship with the Lord. . . . He died so that you might live eternally. He shows you how and helps you do those things that will take you home to heaven again. He is your example and friend. He'll see you through each day, if you will let him. He will comfort you when others can't or don't! But he doesn't force himself on you. Jesus waits so you can *choose* to have him part of your life. (*Bell Ringer*, 110.)

SHERI L. DEW

Our responsibility is to learn to draw upon the power of the Atonement. Otherwise we walk through mortality relying solely on our own strength. And to do that is to invite the frustration of failure and to refuse the most resplendent gift in time or eternity. (In *Ensign*, May 1999, 67.)

I fear that some Latter-day Saint women know just enough about the gospel to feel guilty that they are not measuring up to some undefinable standard but not enough about the Atonement to feel the peace and strength it affords us. (In *Best of Women's Conference*, 128.)

Do you believe that the Savior will really do for *you* what he has said he will do? . . . An unwillingness to believe that the Savior stands ready to deliver us from our difficulties is tantamount to refusing the gift. It is tragic when we refuse to turn to him who paid the ultimate price and let him lift us up. (In *May Christ Lift Thee Up*, 193.)

VIRGINIA U. JENSEN

The Savior trod the rockiest ground of all, the path of Calvary. Having experienced mortality, he is "acquainted with grief" (Isaiah 53:3) and asks only our meek petition for his rescuing arm. (In *Best of Women's Conference*, 228.)

ARDETH GREENE KAPP

It is in our struggles, while striving to qualify, that our spirits reach out in greater humility and gratitude, and we are better prepared to receive the gift because we so desperately need it—in fact, we must have it if we are to receive our eternal rewards. (In *BYU Speeches*, 5 May 1981, 80.)

One of the sure signs that a person has accepted the gift of the Savior's atonement is that person's ability to love. An acknowledgment of his love for us makes us more sensitive, more gracious, more anxious to reach out. (*Joy of the Journey*, 28.)

ANNE OSBORN POELMAN

The Savior himself knows what we know, has experienced what we experience, and indeed feels what we feel. Knowing that fact can comfort us and give us hope, enabling us to put aside old hurts and look to the future with confidence. (*Simeon Solution*, 32.)

WENDY C. TOP

The Savior [said to Peter,] "If I wash thee not, thou hast no part with me" (John 13:4–8). If we do not let him serve us and wash us clean and make us new, no matter how faithful we think we are being, we have no part with him. We cannot save or free ourselves. (*Getting Past the Labels*, 36.)

Body, Physical

CONNIE L. BLAKEMORE

The opportunity to feel the influence of the Holy Ghost is a compelling reason to reverence our body and allow it to be as sensitive to the Spirit as possible. (In *BYU Speeches*, 28 July 1998, 10.)

SARA LEE GIBB

If we understand the significance of the body in the eternal plan of salvation in even a small way, could we permit ourselves to be dressed immodestly, to allow our bodies to be defiled or to defile that of another, . . . to weaken the body with inappropriate substances, to try to strengthen the body with inappropriate substances, to allow our muscles to atrophy and become weakened through lack of movement and disuse, to deny nourishment to the point of anorexia, or allow other destructive behavior? (In *BYU Speeches*, 27 June 1989, 138.)

We are living, springing, dynamic beings whose vital systems all depend upon movement and use. We rarely lose our physical capabilities in normal living, but we give them up through nonuse. . . . We were made to move. Our bodies do adapt to the stresses placed upon them—gradually, carefully, respectfully, little by little. (In *BYU Speeches*, 27 June 1989, 137.)

BONNIE L. GOODLIFFE

When the mind is tired, exercise the body; when the body is tired, exercise the mind. (In *Hearts Knit Together*, 205.)

PATRICIA T. HOLLAND

Anyone who reads a newspaper or magazine is constantly reminded that proper diet, appropriate exercise, and plenty of rest increase our daily capacities as well as our life span. But all too many of us put off even these minimal efforts, thinking our family, our neighbors, and our other many responsibilities come first. Yet in doing so, we put at risk the thing these people need most from us: our healthiest, happiest, heartiest self. When they ask for bread, let us not be so weary and unhealthy that we give them a stone. (In *LDS Women's Treasury*, 95.)

MARGARET D. NADAULD

Women who love God would never abuse or deface a temple with graffiti. Nor would they throw open the doors of that holy, dedicated edifice and invite the world to look on. How even more sacred is the body, for it was not made by man. It was formed by God. We are the stewards, the keepers of the cleanliness and purity with which it came from heaven. (In *Ensign*, Nov. 2000, 15.)

Grateful daughters of God guard their bodies carefully, for they know they are the wellspring of life and they reverence life. They don't uncover their bodies to find favor with the world. They walk in modesty to be in favor with their Father in Heaven. (In *Ensign*, Nov. 2000, 15.)

TESSA MEYER SANTIAGO

If Satan can get us to fixate on our bodies, either in vanity or self loathing, then he has caused us to misunderstand completely the role our bodies play in our salvation. (In *Best of Women's Conference*, 477.)

BARBARA B. SMITH

We do have great physical powers within us to create life, to control our abilities and capacities, and to compensate for disabilities; and these physical powers require us to take good care of our bodies. At the very least we should obey the Word of Wisdom, eat properly, sleep and exercise regularly, and abstain from taking anything into our bodies that will destroy their powers, for we will be held accountable for them. (*Love*, 50.)

The state of our health affects every facet of our life—our feeling of personal well-being, our approach to work, our social interactions—even our service to the Lord. (In *Ensign*, Nov. 1978, 77.)

LEAH D. WIDTSOE

Your body is sacred as the tabernacle of one of God's chosen spirits.

It belongs to you to cherish, to keep healthy and clean that your life on earth may be more joyous thereby. (In *Improvement Era*, Apr. 1938, 220–21.)

Physical Appearance

MILDRED CHANDLER AUSTIN

Much study has been given to the psychological effect of the clothes people wear and how one's costume really does affect one's behavior. . . . People's perceptions of themselves as well as other people's perceptions of them are greatly affected by the clothing worn. (*Divine Destiny*, 41.)

VIVIAN R. CLINE

People make assumptions about us based on the way we look and act. If we wear immodest clothing, chances are that people will assume that we are immodest. They will treat us accordingly, even though they may be mistaken about us. (In *Sharing the Light*, 44.)

Educators have found that people test better and score higher when they are clean and well dressed. (In *Sharing the Light*, 47.)

AFTON J. DAY

The old standby, cleanliness, is still most important. . . . There's nothing mysterious about it, people are just more comfortable around other people who look and smell good. (*Coming Up*, 97.)

At least for this life, our bodies and our spirits are inseparably joined together, and if you like yourself it will show in the way you dress and the way you wear your hair. (*Coming Up*, 97.)

AMY HARDISON

Value is not dependent on appearance. . . . Physical beauty is ephemeral; personal value is eternal. (*How to Feel Great*, 17.)

SHARLENE WELLS HAWKES

Modesty is about more than the style of clothes we choose to wear. It starts with a core belief that we are literal heirs of God, and as such, we must portray dignity, self-assurance, and determination to preserve all that is sacred. (*Living*, 46.)

ARDETH GREENE KAPP

You must be alert to the aggressive advertising of immodest fashions. Often the desire and practice of wearing such fashions begins innocently and early. Some mothers dress their little girls in ways that unknowingly train their appetite for the immodest fashions of the world. And when they are teenagers, the pattern is set and it's so hard to change. (In *Ensign*, Nov. 1990, 94.)

MARGARET D. NADAULD

You can recognize women who are grateful to be a daughter of God by their outward appearance. These women understand their stewardship over their bodies and treat them with dignity. They care for their bodies as they would a holy temple. (In *Ensign*, Nov. 2000, 15.)

BARBARA B. SMITH

A person can be well dressed by paying close attention to the purchase of a dress with a style that will have a long life and by paying only casual attention to the faddish elements of the new season. (In *Best of Women's Conference*, 502.)

The Body and the Spirit

CONNIE L. BLAKEMORE

The spirit controls the body until the body catches up. I believe our challenge is to get the body and spirit functioning together in harmony—eventually both at a celestial level. To do this, we must value each as sacred. (In *BYU Speeches*, 28 July 1998, 8.)

PATRICIA T. HOLLAND

It is no coincidence that we speak of "feeding the spirit" just as we would speak of feeding the body. We need constant nourishment for both. The root word *hale* (as in hale and hearty) is the common root to words like *whole, health, heal, and holy*. Our health and our wholeness are unquestionably linked with our holiness. (In *BYU Speeches*, 13 Jan. 1987, 85.)

We need very much for body, mind, and spirit to come together, to unite in one healthy, stable soul. (In *BYU Speeches*, 13 Jan. 1987, 85.)

SHERRIE JOHNSON

"Onement" begins as we make the body and spirit one. To do this the spirit has to become stronger than the flesh; or in other words, we have to follow the promptings of the spirit instead of the promptings of the flesh. (*Man, Woman, and Deity,* 88.)

One of the great tests of life is whether our body or our spirit will determine our choices in life. (*Man, Woman, and Deity,* 88.)

As with all other pursuits of "onement," making the body and spirit one is a life-long challenge and not something easily arrived at. The discipline gained in the pursuit, however, is necessary to succeeding the other tests of life. (*Man, Woman, and Deity,* 88–89.)

CHIEKO N. OKAZAKI

You're a temple—a living, breathing, walking temple on two legs with a spirit that's in motion, seeing the needs of many, meeting the needs of many, sometimes tuned in fully and beautifully to the indwelling Spirit of the Lord. (*Lighten Up!* 73.)

WENDY C. TOP

Before we came to earth, we were anxious to have a body of any kind. We understood what a transcendent gift it would be to have a body, even if it were not perfect. Now that we are here, many of us hate and berate our bodies when they deserve and need to be loved, respected, and cared for just as our spirits do. . . . Such negative attitudes can't help but take a toll on both body *and* spirit. (*Getting Past the Labels,* 8.)

Character

AFTON J. DAY

Strength and bravery are great qualities, but true strength is developed through an acceptance of natural laws and the fortification of spirit that comes from living in accordance with those laws. (*Perfect Wife,* 99.)

JANET D. GOUGH

Honor is one of the highest qualities of moral character. (In *Living the Young Women Values,* 74.)

BEPPIE HARRISON

Just as our children seem to need repetition to learn both simple ideas . . . and complicated ones . . . so we seem to need to learn the same lessons over and over again. (*On Being a Parent,* 16.)

ARDETH GREENE KAPP

Our values . . . are not to be tucked away for safekeeping. They are to be carried daily, used continuously, tested against our performance regularly, and literally worn out as a constant measuring device that keeps us accountable. (*I Walk by Faith*, 111.)

CAMILLA EYRING KIMBALL

Much unhappiness has been suffered by those people who have never recognized that it is as necessary to make themselves into whole and harmonious personalities as to keep themselves clean, healthy, and financially solvent. (*Writings*, 13.)

Our pressing responsibility is to build up a personality worthy of our heritage as children of God. (*Writings*, 82.)

ELIZA R. SNOW

The impressions made in childhood and youth give indelible stamp to character. (*Personal Writings*, 7.)

The manner in which you improve the present period will have a bearing on your conditions and character hereafter. (*Personal Writings*, 68.)

BELLE S. SPAFFORD

No community can be any stronger morally than the combined moral strength of the individuals who comprise it. (In *Relief Society Magazine*, Jan. 1959, 33.)

The place where good character is most effectively built is the home. This has always been true; it is true today. If attention is not conscientiously and continuously given to this important matter in the home, it is not to be expected that it will be accomplished elsewhere. (In *Relief Society Magazine*, Jan. 1959, 33.)

Good character is developed through love, acceptance, and feelings of security. (In *Relief Society Magazine*, Jan. 1959, 33.)

Evil has always been abroad upon the earth. The greatest fortress against it and the strongest defense weapon one may possess, has ever been and always will be good character—character developed through continually seeking to know and understand the will of God, through daily communion with him, and through obedience to his counsel and commandments. (In *Relief Society Magazine*, Nov. 1959, 720.)

In the building of strong character, one of mankind's most powerful allies has always been prayer. (In *Relief Society Magazine*, Nov. 1959, 720.)

There must be in one's makeup a strong spiritual fiber out of which there grows a certain nobility of character—character that is elevated above anything that is selfish, degrading, or uncharitable; character that squares with the principles of truth and righteousness. (In *BYU Speeches*, 11 Mar. 1969, 9.)

Integrity

VIVIAN R. CLINE

This is a normal pattern: first, we claim to have integrity; second, that integrity is questioned or tested; third, we experience pain or opposition. But when we determine to hold true thereafter, we experience great rewards. (In *Feeling Great*, 117.)

JANET D. GOUGH

Honesty is one of the basic elements of integrity. But honor is probably a better synonym because it encompasses all types of honesty. (In *Living the Young Women Values*, 74.)

MICHAELENE P. GRASSLI

To fail to have and exercise the courage of our convictions would not be in keeping with the charge we have to stand for righteousness in all times and all places. (*What I Have Learned*, 73.)

ARDETH GREENE KAPP

The greatest tests come when there seems to be so much at stake and our integrity will be tested in the fierce fire of temptation. To make our actions consistent with our knowledge of right and wrong is the test. Those times of severe temptation will be customized for our individual growth. (*Joy of the Journey*, 147.)

Holding to principles without compromise, we become trustworthy. (*Lead*, 45.)

The most destructive threats of our day are not nuclear war, not famine, not economic disaster, but rather the despair, the discouragement, the despondency, the defeat caused by the discrepancy between what we believe to be right and how we live our lives. (In *BYU Speeches*, 29 Jan. 1985, 68.)

CAROLYN J. RASMUS

Oh, that we might learn to act with integrity, having the moral courage to make our actions (our doing) consistent with our knowledge of right and wrong, to be able to say with Job, "Till I die I will not remove mine integrity from me" (Job 27:5). (In *Best of Women's Conference*, 467.)

There is often a discrepancy between what we say we know and what we do. . . . It is this discrepancy that creates inner strife and turmoil—a literal wrenching of our souls. (In *Best of Women's Conference*, 467.)

ELIZA R. SNOW

It is better to suffer than do wrong. (*Personal Writings*, 80.)

The very few who have strength of mind, reason, and stability to act from principle is truly astonishing, and yet only such are persons worthy of trust. (*Personal Writings*, 81.)

Honesty

ARDETH GREENE KAPP

Honesty is like the foundation of character. The foundation must be sound if the building is to stand erect. Our strength of character, our reputation, our trustworthiness, and ultimately our peace of mind rest heavily on the foundation of honesty. (*Joy of the Journey*, 146.)

CHIEKO N. OKAZAKI

Make the truth your own shield. Lies will not protect you. Don't use them. And don't allow anyone else to persuade you to shade the truth. (*Disciples*, 240.)

One of the most important ways we can be pure before the Lord is to be scrupulously honest in our words and deeds. (*Sanctuary*, 18.)

BELLE S. SPAFFORD

To be honest in word and deed requires constant appraisal of one's self, one's attributes and character traits. It requires a penetrating evaluation of the motives that prompt what one says and does. It demands of one a determined effort to adhere to truth. (*Woman's Reach*, 140.)

I believe that honesty grows easier with practice just as dishonesty grows easier with practice. (*Woman's Reach*, 140–41.)

Dishonesty takes many forms. . . . It asserts itself in thinking and in motives. . . . It may be directed against man and God, and there are many who are dishonest with self. No matter what its form or against whom it is directed, dishonesty is destructive and demoralizing. It injures the one who practices it and wrongs the one against whom it is directed. It in no way builds nor strengthens nor benefits. (In *Relief Society Magazine*, Feb. 1945, 88–89.)

The entanglements of lying, of dishonesty, bring sorrow and bondage. The Lord . . . regards dishonesty as sin. (In *BYU Speeches*, 11 Apr. 1972, 6.)

BARBARA B. SMITH

Trust is to human relationships what faith is to gospel living. (In *Ensign*, Nov. 1981, 83.)

Envy

MARIE CORNWALL

Do not covet your neighbor's life. You may want what appears to be her special blessings and opportunities; but life is a package deal, and it is not likely that you would be so covetous of her difficulties if you really understood them. (In *Women of Wisdom*, 5–6.)

KARLA C. ERICKSON

It seems easier to help people when they are suffering than to extend love and congratulations when they are successful. (*Make Time Count*, 12.)

Why is it so difficult to be sincerely happy about another's good fortune? Blessed is the person whose friends are sensitive to needs when ill fortune has crossed his path. Twice blessed is the person who has a friend who can sincerely exult with his good fortune. (*Make Time Count*, 12.)

JILL C. MAJOR, LAUREN C.
LEIFSON, AND HOLLIE C. BEVAN

Jealousy and its near-kinsman envy have numerous faces—all of them hideous. They are bitter, invidious feelings that can slither past our best spiritual guards to send messages of misery to our minds. (*Encircled by Love*, 44.)

Our Heavenly Father loves each one of us in a way that is far beyond our comprehension. With his divine help, we can conquer jealousy, envy, or any of our other weaknesses—and win! (*Encircled by Love*, 47.)

By stripping away jealousy, envy, and the other foes of love, we can create a happier life for ourselves and all those around us. We can tap that great power to build, lift, and nurture that is part of our divine inheritance. (*Encircled by Love*, 50.)

Chastity

MILDRED CHANDLER AUSTIN

The challenge comes in looking for a way to teach premarital sexual abstinence without hampering a couple's ability to become one after they are properly married.

One friend of mine . . . teaches her seminary students to consider themselves to be sexually fasting before marriage. Fasting is a concept that they can easily identify with, and though they recognize it as a difficult discipline, they can endure it because they look forward to the eventual feasting. Applying this concept to sexual behavior helps young people remain chaste without growing up with the damaging feeling that sexual feasting is inherently wrong. (*Divine Destiny*, 51–52.)

KATHLEEN RAWLINGS BUNTIN

The Lord's rules for physical intimacy are given to us not to deny us pleasures of the flesh but to protect us. We have the assurance that if we follow his guidelines, we will experience physical intimacy only where there is an equally strong emotional intimacy and under the protection of a long-term commitment. (*All Alone*, 76.)

ELAINE CANNON

Sex is for a wife and her husband. It is the way a couple can develop oneness. It is saved for marriage for the sake of the couple and the children that may come to that couple. It is the ultimate act of intimacy that God has provided to unite a certain special woman with her certain special man so that they come to know each other as they are not known to anybody else. Also, so that they may have the incredible blessing of being earthly parents to others of Heavenly Father's spirit children. (*Love You*, 29.)

VIVIAN R. CLINE

There is a special glow that men possess when they are morally pure and clean—an inner strength of confidence and self-assuredness that women can feel. (In *Feeling Great*, 116.)

AFTON J. DAY

Sex holds an attraction for the youth with low self-esteem, especially if he feels isolated or alienated. Often it is not sex itself which is so attractive, but the attempt to fill the emotional void inside. (*Coming Up*, 55.)

ERIN ELDRIDGE

It might seem as though "the Church" doesn't understand what it's like to struggle with same-sex attraction. Christ does understand, and He is at the head of The Church of Jesus Christ of Latter-day Saints. (*Born That Way?* 55.)

To find and keep a homosexual life is to lose eternal life with Christ. To give up that homosexual life for Christ's sake is to find eternal life. We choose which course we will take. (*Born That Way?* 51.)

Some people struggling with same-sex attraction fear they will have to spend the rest of their lives alone, without a close relationship with someone. But what "alone" feels like in the midst of the struggle is not what it feels like later. . . .

I am not alone. I now have a close, personal relationship with the Lord Jesus Christ. And I prefer a close relationship with the Savior over a homosexual relationship. It is impossible to maintain both. (*Born That Way?* 84–85.)

JOY F. EVANS

There are lesbian women, as well as homosexual men, in the Church. The Lord God has decreed, "Thou shalt not." And however hard the task, these people must likewise keep the commandments. Marriage and intimate relationships are to be reserved for husbands and wives, and any sexual relationship outside of marriage, whether between men and women or between those of the same sex, is forbidden. (In *Ensign*, Nov. 1987, 94.)

SUSA YOUNG GATES

The girl who is chaste and pure in her thought can never lose her most valuable possession, her virtue. (In *Young Woman's Journal*, Dec. 1895, 139.)

CAMILLA EYRING KIMBALL

God's law of chastity will be in force as long as time lasts, no matter what others may say. (*Writings*, 100.)

One of the most distressing lies being circulated among youth is that they can violate the law of chastity with impunity. No one can transgress this law and find peace without fully repenting. (*Writings*, 98.)

Pornography is the opening wedge to serious sin. (*Writings*, 99.)

Perhaps the greatest sin of our day is unchastity, and pornography propagates the pernicious lie that premarital sex is acceptable in society and before the Lord. (*Writings*, 99.)

Children

Children Are a Blessing

JOANNE B. DOXEY

A group of Relief Society sisters [were] making candy called "divinity" at the home of one of the sisters. Two little boys in the family were allowed to eat all of the divinity they could scrape from the spoons, pans, and bowls. It was the weekend of general conference and . . . one of the speakers said, "There is a spark of divinity in each of us." One of the little boys jumped up and said, "A spark of divinity? Wow, I'm full of it!" Yes, children are full of divinity. Surely the angels attend them. (In *Ensign*, Nov. 1987, 90.)

Children, being pure and holy, teach us something of our heavenly home. (In *Ensign*, Nov. 1989, 91.)

JOAN B. MACDONALD

We were commanded to multiply and replenish the earth that we might have joy in our posterity. But joy is not the only thing our posterity brings us. It also brings experience, learning, understanding, patience, and selflessness. In short, raising children propels us in our quest for greater spiritual maturity. (*Holiness of Everyday Life*, 57–58.)

MARGARET D. NADAULD

Celebrate the fact that girls are different from boys. Be thankful for the position they have in God's grand plan. (In *Ensign*, Nov. 2000, 16.)

KATHLEEN "CASEY" NULL

Children teach us that sometimes it's much, much wiser to keep our meaning simple. . . . Children teach us to slow down, to appreciate dandelion seeds that can be blown all over a lawn in one puff, sow bugs, simplicity, and play—all the things that can be appreciated only in the present, which is the only place we can live anyway. (In *As a Woman Thinketh*, 115.)

NAOMI M. SHUMWAY

Tomorrow comes marching forward on the feet of little children. The strength or weakness of tomorrow lies in the hands of our children. (In *Ensign*, Nov. 1979, 104.)

BARBARA B. SMITH

Babies come into families in many ways. The blessings of God come to sanctify each new addition to a family if there is faith and testimony and a humble heart. (*Grandmothering*, 118.)

SHIRLEY W. THOMAS

One of the most difficult challenges in our responsibilities with children lies in enjoying them fully—delighting in their imagination and talk, their wonder, their fancies, and even their silliness and fun, all that makes them children—while at the same time taking them seriously, learning from them and helping them to learn. . . . Paramount to the process is recognizing the sanctity of every child's spirit. (In *Behold Your Little Ones*, 141–42.)

Our Sacred Obligations to Children

JANENE WOLSEY BAADSGAARD

Remember the Savior's love for little children and His statement that we must become as a little child to inherit the kingdom of heaven. He saw children's energy, curiosity, and enthusiasm as attributes to be nurtured, not merely tolerated. (*Life after Birth*, 71.)

Each child who comes into the world comes with a message that our Father in heaven has not given up on mankind. He has entrusted to our care His most treasured possessions. (*Life after Birth*, 96.)

Fifty years from now it won't matter at all what kind of car I drove, or what kind of house I lived in. . . . Fifty years from now, my life will have meaning only if I've taken the time to be a positive influence in the life of a child. (*Family Finances*, 18.)

MARIAN R. BOYER

As Latter-day Saint homebuilders, our greatest challenge is to bring up our children in light and truth—to develop the spiritual nature of each family member. (In *Ensign*, Nov. 1980, 108.)

SUSA YOUNG GATES

To every child who crosses your path be . . . a second mother. (In *Young Woman's Journal*, Nov. 1893, 93.)

MICHAELENE P. GRASSLI

Each of us, whatever our circumstances, can help a child in a particular, important way that no one else can. We can give them life-giving water, food, love, comfort, and more importantly we can offer the "living water" of the gospel. (In *Ensign*, Nov. 1992, 94.)

The children need our help. They need us to prepare them. They need us to help them obtain the peace of the Lord. Today is neither too early nor too late to prepare the children, and anyone can do it. . . . All of us can teach children of the Lord. (In *Ensign*, Nov. 1988, 78.)

Kindness to a child can be expressed in so many ways by anyone.

You don't have to be a child's parent or teacher. You don't have to add kindness to a list of things to do later. You can be kind to a child today. (In *Ensign*, Apr. 1994, 64.)

Our children . . . are among the most valiant spirits to come into the world. We have a sacred responsibility to bestow on them a legacy of peace. (*What I Have Learned*, 104–5.)

Our families, our society, our church are only as solid or virtuous as today's generation of children. (*What I Have Learned*, 98–99.)

Imagine what tomorrow's Church could be like if we fulfill the needs of our children today. Imagine what it will be like if we don't. (In *Ensign*, Nov. 1992, 94.)

We can *behold* our children in their eternal perspective and see that they *all* know of the Savior and learn the significant truths of his gospel. We can help them witness marvelous spiritual events. They can hear our earnest prayers in their behalf. And we can be their ministering angels on earth if we follow the Lord's example. (In *Ensign*, Nov. 1992, 94.)

We care what happens to our children. They are precious to our Heavenly Father, and they are our hope for bringing about good in the world. (In *Ensign*, Nov. 1994, 12.)

MARGARET D. NADAULD

In your mind's eye, do you see yourself as nurturers of precious sons and daughters of Heavenly Father? You can practice now by being loving and gentle to little children and by saying the kindest things in the kindest way in your home. (In *Ensign*, May 1998, 90.)

EMMA SMITH

I particularly desire wisdom to bring up all the children that are, or may be committed to my charge, in such a manner that they will be useful ornaments in the Kingdom of God. (In *Elect Ladies*, 17.)

EMMELINE B. WELLS

Children can never be too happy, the happier you make them, the richer and purer will be the fountains of their thoughts, and the growth of high and holy feelings depend in a great measure upon the influences and surroundings of one's childhood. (In *Woman's Exponent*, 15 Mar. 1877, 155.)

HELEN MAR WHITNEY

We can never be young but once in this life and I like children to enjoy themselves while they can for they will grow old soon enough. (*Woman's View*, 116.)

Teaching Children

JANENE WOLSEY BAADSGAARD

Our efforts with our young children are not going unnoticed by our Father in heaven. . . . The time will come when we can meditate during the sacrament and can concentrate on the speaker's words instead of trying to keep our two-year-old from pulling the hair of the woman in front of us. But for now we are introducing our children to their spiritual roots. We are teaching them about reverence. (*Life after Birth*, 71.)

BARBARA TIMOTHY BOWEN

I have come to learn that . . . my children are not mine. They belong to their Heavenly Father. . . . They are only loaned to me for a brief period on earth. . . . As much as I want to be a central figure in their lives, I want the Savior to be more central in their lives. I need to teach them all I can in our brief but precious time together and then let them go to find their own path. (In *Emotional First Aid*, 34.)

ELAINE CANNON

Children have agency to act and think on their own, but we must help them learn correct principles before they try to govern themselves. A believing mother is more likely to rear up a believing child. A believing child is apt to cope with all the shifting prisms of life. (*Mothering*, 52.)

LINDA J. EYRE

Children come with their own personalities. Some are freer spirits than others and some think in different patterns than I do. We should never give up teaching them correct principles, but we have to allow them to be themselves in applying

those principles to their own lives. (*I Didn't Plan to Be a Witch*, 55.)

Our children are not lumps of clay that we can mold into whatever shape we like. They're seedlings. . . . We can't blame ourselves for every branch that shoots off in the wrong direction, because there is sap inside every tree that contains something called agency. (In *Emotional First Aid*, 173.)

SUSA YOUNG GATES

Nothing, ever so great or ever so small, [should] be passed on to our children that is not informed and inspired by the Spirit of all truth. (In *Relief Society Magazine*, Sept. 1921, 501.)

MICHAELENE P. GRASSLI

When you teach the principles of the gospel, you have given the child one of the greatest gifts you could give. (In *Ensign*, Apr. 1994, 64.)

We want to enable our children to recognize error and take action. . . . This is much more than simply telling them what to think and what to do. It is helping them seek for and love truth and choose independently to act according to it. (In *Ensign*, Nov. 1994, 13.)

Our children need to know that if we read the scriptures and the words of the prophets and heed the whisperings of the Spirit, we are learning from the source of all truth. (In *Ensign*, Nov. 1994, 13.)

Immerse the children in the stories of Jesus so that they can know him. . . . Tell them about the Savior so they'll trust him, so they'll develop a desire to be like him, and want to be with him again. (In *Ensign*, Nov. 1988, 79.)

Peace in the Lord can give [children] freedom from self-doubt, freedom from fear, freedom from the confinement of their environment, freedom from enslaving habits. His peace can free them to unfold from the tender buds they are to the mature and fruitful adults they can be. (In *Ensign*, Nov. 1988, 78.)

We begin by teaching what we are. The children need us; they need to see in us what they can become. They need to see us keeping the commandments. *We* must come unto the Lord and seek for the peace of the gospel in *our own* lives. (In *Ensign*, Nov. 1988, 78.)

Trust the feelings and impressions that come to you and act on them, and you will bless the life of a child, and the child will bless yours. (In *Ensign*, Nov. 1989, 92.)

It really isn't very hard to develop a relationship with a child. Anyone can do it! Just, one, understand them; two, listen to them; three, be kind to them; and four, share the gospel with them. (In *Ensign*, Nov. 1989, 92.)

MAY GREEN HINCKLEY

We touch and mold the lives of the children in more ways than by the spoken word. It is what we are that registers in their lives rather than what we say. (In *Children's Friends*, 55.)

ARDETH GREENE KAPP

It is in teaching diligently that we are instructed more perfectly. Those who are privileged to have a calling to teach the children for a short time can enhance and hasten their spiritual understanding as they are teaching, not just as they are being taught. (*My Neighbor*, 52.)

When someone, especially a parent, has confidence in a child, and that confidence is expressed consistently, the child's ability seems almost magically commensurate with the expressed confidence. (*Gentle Touch*, 50.)

CAROLINE EYRING MINER

Let your grandchildren know that you expect good behavior and respect from them. They will rise to your expectations. And set a good example yourself. Be what you expect *them* to be. (In *Ensign*, Aug. 1986, 61.)

PATRICIA P. PINEGAR

Children do have spiritual insights when they are very young, but they need parents and family members and loved ones to give them language to express the feelings and love that they have for the Savior. (In *Arms of His Love*, 284.)

As we bear testimony in Primary, the Spirit will confirm to the children the truths we teach. It is important that we teach them how to identify the feelings that accompany the Spirit. Children are more likely to progress in the gospel when they feel the Spirit and understand how the Spirit will help them in their lives. (In *Ensign*, Feb. 1999, 9.)

ELLIS R. SHIPP

What greater reward could a parent desire for all [the] years of loving care than to have her children good and *noble*, wise and intellectual, with a love of truth, virtue, and God in the hearts. (*While Others Slept*, 257.)

NAOMI M. SHUMWAY

Children need to be taught the gospel, so that when temptations come to them they . . . have a foundation of true principles. (In *Ensign*, Apr. 1978, 20.)

Children need to have a spiritual experience every time they go to Primary—and they need to have fun, too. Children should look forward to Primary, and teachers and leaders can give them that feeling. (In *Ensign*, Apr. 1978, 23.)

BATHSHEBA W. SMITH

Teach your children to love the Gospel . . . so that they can have a testimony for themselves; every soul that is honest in heart may receive a testimony that they cannot deny. (In *Woman's Exponent*, June 1905, 7.)

MARIAN P. SORENSEN

Prayer can be one of the most effective ways of teaching children many of the concepts that parents desire to have their children learn. (In *Ensign*, May 1973, 33.)

ANNE G. WIRTHLIN

When our children feel our love for the Lord and our unconditional love for them, then our example becomes a meaningful guide to them as they develop their own spiritual strength. (In *Ensign*, Nov. 1995, 81.)

RUTH B. WRIGHT

Our children respond best when taught with respect and love. (In *Ensign*, May 1994, 85.)

DWAN J. YOUNG

We are all teachers of children—parents, aunts, uncles, grandparents, priesthood leaders, ward members, neighbors. Children are always watching and learning. We teach them through our behavior as well as by what we say. (In *Ensign*, May 1988, 78.)

We must take time to teach the children about the important things of life—about Heavenly Father, the Savior, and the Holy Ghost. We must teach them about repentance, baptism, honesty, and doing good to others. . . . They listen to the voices of their parents and to the voices at church. . . . We must teach them at an early age to listen to the right voices. (In *Ensign*, May 1988, 78.)

Mothers and fathers need to read the words of the Lord with their children and discuss the scriptures constantly. It is only through hearing the word and watching it manifest itself in our lives that children come to be familiar with the voice of the Good Shepherd. (In *Ensign*, Nov. 1983, 86.)

In the soft and gentle arms of a mother's love, children can come to know the voice of the Lord. Then, in later years, when the stress of living comes, the soul has at its command the teachings and the tools by which to overcome. (In *Ensign*, Nov. 1983, 86.)

A young child's self-esteem is based largely on how he thinks others perceive him. He needs to know he will always be loved, will always have a friend. What better way, then, to provide self-esteem than to help a child understand he is a child of God—that Heavenly Father and Jesus love him no matter what. (In *Ensign*, Mar. 1986, 42.)

ZINA D. H. YOUNG

Teach your children the principles of the Gospel, the Gospel is the bread of life. Let the children learn of the peace of the Gospel at home. (In *Woman's Exponent*, 15 Nov. and 1 Dec. 1899, 74.)

Childlessness

LISA JOHNSON BOSWELL

Fortunately, as the months and years pass, most couples recognize that their adversity is not a God-given punishment but simply a natural consequence of physical limitations. (In *Women Steadfast in Christ*, 198.)

One infertile woman said that her crisis of faith had been healed by the example of the Savior. She had wanted her faithful prayers to heal her infertility. . . . Finally she realized that . . . Christ's perfect faith had not altered Gethsemane but rather helped him to endure it. This woman came to see her faith . . . not as an imperfect faith that had been insufficient to remove her trials but as a vibrant faith that could help her endure them. Not faith to remove mountains but faith to climb them. (In *Women Steadfast in Christ*, 199.)

[For one] woman . . . infertility had been the loss of a dream. Losing her dream helped her empathize with all women who had experienced loss—whether visible losses, such as the loss of a loved one or of health, or less obvious losses, such as the loss of self-esteem or the loss of hope. . . . Her life would not be filled with many children, but it would be a life filled with love. (In *Women Steadfast in Christ*, 200–201.)

JANET NELSON CHRISTENSEN

The most difficult aspect of infertility to overcome was the effect that it had on my feelings of self-worth. During those pain-filled years, I mistakenly felt that because I could not have children, I must be of no worth. . . . Through prayer and scripture study, I learned that the source of my depression was Satan and that his influence can be overcome by going to the Lord for help and then acting upon the impressions received. (In *LDS Women's Treasury*, 154.)

LOUIE B. FELT

Perhaps, like me, there are some who have been denied the great privilege of being a mother. . . . But God has given me many, many lovely children through other mothers, that I may pray for, think of, and love. (In *Children's Friends*, 9.)

TAMARA A. ILICH

I believed my long unanswered prayers for a baby meant that I was not loved. This realization brought me once again to my knees. I prayed for myself, but now my prayer did not concern my childlessness. What I asked was simply, "Do you love me?" As soon as I uttered that question, I was overwhelmed with a feeling of love, joy, and peace. (In *Ensign*, Aug. 2000, 60.)

ARDETH GREENE KAPP

For those of us without children, the choices may seem incredibly difficult to make. What would the Lord have us do? To what extent do we seek medical attention? What about adoption and foster children? What about no children? If that is the choice, then what do we do with our lives? The choices are never simple. . . . From my own experience, I've learned that the only lasting peace is the peace that comes when we learn the Lord's will concerning our opportunities in life. (In *Ensign*, Feb. 1989, 22.)

The characteristics of motherhood, which include concern for others, sacrifice, service, compassion, teaching, encouraging, and inspiring can be the noble labor for each one of us now, with or without children. The fate of each spirit in the eternities to come depends so much on the training it receives from those here and now who are willing to help another gain eternal life. (In *Ensign*, Feb. 1989, 23.)

If I have any comforting message for others, it is this: Peace of mind comes from keeping an eternal perspective. Motherhood, I believe, is a foreordained mission. For some, this glorious blessing may be delayed, but it will not be denied. Motherhood is an eternal reality for all women who live righteously and accept the teachings of the gospel. (*My Neighbor*, 128.)

I have come to know that we can all rejoice in the sacred calling of motherhood. To give birth is only one part of this sacred mission, the miracle of life. But to help another gain eternal life is a privilege that is neither denied to nor delayed for any worthy woman. And to be a mother in Israel may be within reach of every righteous woman even now. (*My Neighbor*, 136.)

We who do not have children can wallow in self-pity—or we can experience "birth pains" as we struggle to open the passageway to eternal life for ourselves and others. (In *Ensign*, Feb. 1989, 23.)

Church of Jesus Christ

The Mission of the Church

ELAINE CANNON

Our Creator has given us the principles and procedures to get through life and to guide us back into his presence. . . . His church is named after him—The Church of Jesus Christ of Latter-day Saints. We meet in the name of the Lord. We pray in his name. We covenant in his name. We take his name upon us in sacred ordinances. (In *Best of Women's Conference*, 97.)

AMY BROWN LYMAN

The Church as an institution has a passion for righteousness, a feeling for the kinship of mankind, a recognition of human brotherhood; and it can instill in the individual a passion for righteousness that will not only be the contributing factor in his own life, but the contributing factor in inspiring him to human helpfulness. (In *Relief Society Magazine*, Nov. 1936, 701.)

VIRGINIA H. PEARCE

A ward is [one] place where there is enough commitment and energy to form a sort of "safety net" family for each of us when our families cannot or do not provide all of the teaching and growing experiences we need to return to Heavenly Father. (In *Ensign*, Nov. 1993, 79.)

BARBARA B. SMITH

The purpose of the Church is not to condemn or discourage. Instead, the Church gives us identity and direction, stars to steer by. (In *Ensign*, Mar. 1979, 22.)

MARY ELLEN SMOOT

What matters is not our house, clothes, cars, or many of the things with which we busy our lives. It's not even our Church callings. The Relief Society and all Church organizations and programs are designed to strengthen the family—not the other way around. (*Sweet Is the Work*, 93.)

M. CATHERINE THOMAS

The purpose of the Church in any dispensation is to prepare the Saints by the power released through priesthood ordinances to acquire the divine nature and stand in God's presence. (*Selected Writings*, 110.)

Church Government

JOYCE BACA

The Church has designed programs to meet the needs of its members. But . . . Church programs can be only as effective as the members allow them to be. (*Divorce*, 5–6.)

SUSA YOUNG GATES

This Church is divinely organized, and is illumined, day by day, by the spirit of life and the voice of inspiration. Were it not for the revelations by which this Church was organized and the light which guides it daily, it would fall to pieces. (In *Relief Society Magazine*, Jan. 1922, 3.)

Contemplating the Church as a whole, with its general and local authorities, its temples, its auxiliary societies, its missionary and educational systems, one is lost in wonder and admiration at the simplicity, and yet the exactitude, the completeness, of the whole plan; and yet the individual liberty which is encompassed by this divine plan makes it perfect in detail and in execution. (In *Relief Society Magazine*, Jan. 1922, 3–4.)

Not all great men are called to high positions in this Church and Kingdom, but certain it is, that no man, however great may be his capacities, will ever be put in charge of responsibilities until he has shown fully and completely his willingness to be led and guided by those over him. (In *Improvement Era*, Aug. 1905, 738.)

MICHAELENE P. GRASSLI

The Lord's house is a house of order. He gives the Church direction about accomplishing its mission in an orderly way—through the priesthood line of authority. (*Leader-Talk*, 30.)

ARDETH GREENE KAPP

When members of a presidency pray with each other and for each other and for those they serve, they will be blessed beyond their natural abilities. They will feel a greater unity that will make them better able to serve. (*Lead*, 97.)

The role of a counselor is to counsel. Counselors are an essential part of a presidency, bringing insights, experience, skills, and perceptions that magnify the capacity of the president. (*Lead*, 96.)

PATRICIA P. PINEGAR

Councils are where we listen to one another and share concerns. Councils are where we solve problems and formulate and implement plans to help one another. (In *Ensign*, June 1996, 73.)

Church Meetings and Conferences

MARY HALES

When we think we didn't get anything out of a meeting, we need to reflect on why we go to church. The reality is we don't go to church to *get*. The Lord commanded us to go to sacrament meeting so that we could *give* our worship, *renew* our covenant to keep his commandments, and *support* and love each other. (In *Hearts Knit Together*, 17.)

BETTY JO JEPSEN

As members of His true Church, perhaps we do not need to be taught new things as much as we need to be reminded of what we already know. (In *Ensign*, Nov. 1992, 76.)

JOAN B. MACDONALD

As a church, we would be wise and . . . greatly blessed if we . . . came together for an hour as a community to wholly and completely worship God together [in sacrament meeting]. Done well and with meaning, this kind of worship-in-community reaches deep into our souls, nourishing our love for God and for each other. (*Holiness of Everyday Life*, 128.)

BELLE S. SPAFFORD

The Church, through the sacrament meeting, offers its members opportunity for worship on the seventh day of rest. Too often the sacrament meeting as a meeting designed for worship is lost sight of by Latter-day Saints, and its value is measured in terms of the fluency and ability of the speaker. (In *Relief Society Magazine*, June 1942, 402.)

Church gatherings should be the most friendly gatherings in the world because the Church is built upon the divine principle of brotherhood. (*Today's World*, 57.)

ZINA D. H. YOUNG

It is a blessing to meet together. The Spirit of God is here, and when we speak to one another, it is like oil going from vessel to vessel. (In *Women in the Covenant*, 14.)

Welfare Program of the Church

MARILYN ARNOLD

We have . . . little personal responsibility for the honesty and motives of those who seek help, but we have considerable responsibility for what is in our own hearts. If others lack integrity, that is their problem; but if we lack charity, that is our problem. (*Sweet Is the Word*, 95.)

MARIAN R. BOYER

When you, the individual member, put into daily practice the principles of welfare, you are *personally* reducing the woe of the world. (In *Ensign*, Nov. 1981, 103.)

AMY BROWN LYMAN

The spirit back of the [welfare] program is unselfishness, the Golden Rule, fraternal friendship for those less well-off, brotherly love based on the Christian ideals of the brotherhood of man, reverence for human personality, and recognition of the value of the soul. (In *Relief Society Magazine*, May 1940, 346.)

LOUISE Y. ROBISON

We want to administer to the strength, and not the weakness, of our people, and it is administering to their weakness to do anything for them that they can do for themselves. (In *Relief Society Magazine,* May 1937, 306.)

BARBARA B. SMITH

The history of our people has magnificent moments when we have taken of our "plenty" and given sustenance to those who were suffering. From those moments we know the joy which comes when need is relieved. (In *Ensign,* Nov. 1979, 85.)

The basic welfare principles fortify and secure. Through them, the home becomes a stronghold, a protection against society's offenses, a haven in time of storm. (In *Ensign,* Nov. 1981, 84–85.)

If we who believe will give all that we have, a way will be opened so that we can alleviate suffering as it comes to our attention. None of us is exempt from dedicating our lives to this principle. (In *Ensign,* Nov. 1979, 85.)

Relief is only temporary, but welfare is eternal. (In *Ensign,* Nov. 1981, 85.)

SHIRLEY W. THOMAS

The welfare services of the Church include multiple systems and long-range plans, but the *constant* through all its development is the application of gospel principles in loving concern for another's need. (In *Ensign,* May 1980, 86.)

Unity among the Saints

JULENE BUTLER

One of Satan's strongest tools is to isolate us from each other, to turn our thoughts away from those around us and, in so doing, prevent us from reaching out to others and finding strength through unity. (In *Best of Women's Conference,* 76.)

Satan does not want Zion to flourish, and he knows he can stop it most easily by attacking its roots, by dividing righteous people from one another. (In *Best of Women's Conference,* 76.)

MICHAELENE P. GRASSLI

When we can accept one another, even if we do not always approve of others' behavior, we will make considerable progress toward achieving unity with one another. (*LeaderTalk,* 49.)

Unity in the Church is not necessarily being alike or agreeing on everything all the time, but it is agreeing on purpose, goals, or outcomes. (*LeaderTalk,* 45.)

When we serve together in the Church, the mission of the Church and the purposes of our organizations should form unifying foundations for what we do. (*LeaderTalk,* 45–46.)

ELAINE L. JACK

"Them and us" are not the words the Lord uses to talk about us. He has called us his children, his friends, his sheep, his lambs. He has admonished us to be one with each other, to follow the pattern he and his Father have set for us. (In *BYU Speeches*, 2 June 1991, 132.)

KATE L. KIRKHAM

We, being many, will be varied in our experience and yet can be one in our willingness to create Zion among us. (In *BYU Speeches*, 12 Apr. 1994, 143.)

If we only examine our differences, we may lose the opportunity to apply the love, patience, and service that gathers difference into the whole. (In *BYU Speeches*, 12 Apr. 1994, 143.)

AMY BROWN LYMAN

There is nothing truer, I think, than that the Gospel breaks down barriers and transforms strangers into friends, into brothers and sisters. (In *Relief Society Magazine*, Nov. 1938, 758.)

CHIEKO N. OKAZAKI

Our unity grows from what we have in common all around the world. They are the doctrines and ordinances of the gospel, our faith in the Savior, our testimonies of the scriptures, our gratitude for guidance from living prophets, and our sense of ourselves as a people striving to be Saints. (In *Ensign*, May 1996, 13.)

EMILY MADSEN REYNOLDS

The Holy Ghost draws us together with his revelations, erasing with mercy the boundaries we sometimes draw, teaching us how to be members one of another, bringing to our remembrance the atonement of Jesus Christ, healing the wounds that divide us. (In *To Rejoice As Women*, 44.)

MARY ELLEN SMOOT

We become one as we turn our backs on sin, selfishness, materialism, and self-indulgence. We become one as we look to God and give our lives to him. (In *Best of Women's Conference*, 517.)

Unity in our Relief Society, unity in our homes, unity in our hearts, is born of banishing ill feelings and taking renewed courage to be more earnest in our endeavors. As sisters in Zion, we can be nothing less than unified. (In *Best of Women's Conference*, 517.)

Satan would have us be divided, for our unity could spell the demise of his oppression. (*Sweet Is the Work*, 160.)

SUSAN CHAMPION SOMMERFELDT

While we must make our own footsteps, we journey with other voyagers. . . . Although the use of our agency and the private nature of our own inspiration promotes individuality, we travel through life together. The gospel of Jesus Christ gives us common ground in exploring our paths. (In *Thy Word Is a Lamp*, 170.)

DONLU DEWITT THAYER

We are different. But we need not contend. If we are to be exalted, we must, even with our differences, become one. We must, by the grace of God, find communion, find moments when love brings Zion, when love discloses the kingdom of God among us. (In *Women and Christ*, 143.)

M. CATHERINE THOMAS

We have to practice at-one-ment here so that we will know how to act when we get to heaven. (*Spiritual Lightening*, 91.)

CLARISSA S. WILLIAMS

Let us not harbor in our communities, in our organizations, any ill feelings that would tend to diminish the beauty and the blessings of the Spirit of the Lord. (In *Relief Society Magazine*, Dec. 1921, 696.)

Communication

Positive Communication

KATHLEEN H. BARNES

A simple expression of feelings can often diffuse an attack. So when all else fails, just speak from your heart. (In *Arise*, 276.)

ANYA BATEMAN

I suspect one word of encouragement is equivalent to about fourteen thousand words of criticism when it comes to the motivation to improve that they instill. (*Talent Race*, 96.)

ELAINE CANNON

Good communication is a sign and principle of love. It depends upon our forgetting self-interest, personal ego, and the need to be right; it depends upon developing Christlike love. (*Gatherings*, 150.)

Christlike love will give us an honest desire to understand another person's perceptions, emotions, and real underlying message. . . . Understanding may not bring agreement, but it will improve relationships. . . . Seek first to understand, then to be understood. (*Gatherings*, 150–51.)

AFTON J. DAY

The key to all human relationships, whether parent-child, teacher-student, or husband-wife, is honest respect for the other individual. *Honest* respect . . . implies respect for a person's right to be himself, whatever that may be. (In *Building a Love*, 122–23.)

SUZANNE L. HANSEN

Remember, we are known to others, perhaps more than anything else, *by the words we speak*. Having a positive, loving attitude, when speaking to anyone, can brighten some of the darkest days. (In *Sharing the Light*, 70.)

JO ANN LARSEN

A smile . . . communicates approachability and establishes or enhances emotional connections with others. (*Heart of Goodness*, 371.)

We never know when our observations may uplift others, fortifying their self-confidence and gracing their lives with comfort and sweetness. (*Heart of Goodness*, 353.)

People have a way of living up or down to the opinions of others. . . . They respond willingly to and even thrive on positive responses. . . . In a world organized to highlight the negatives, most of us could better serve ourselves and the world by increasing our flow of positives to friends and strangers alike. (*Heart of Goodness*, 346.)

MARILYNNE TODD LINFORD

Praise is a form of service that raises another. Bits and pieces of well-placed praise can mold and build and create positive attributes and self-esteem as nothing else. (*Standing Ovation*, 42.)

Praise is catching a person being good. Praise provides hope for the future because praise raises. (*Standing Ovation*, 44.)

JILL C. MAJOR, LAUREN C. LEIFSON, AND HOLLIE C. BEVAN

Make it a point to observe good things about people, and when you do observe the good, tell the person so immediately. Don't ever let an opportunity pass to build up someone. (*Encircled by Love*, 43.)

M. CATHERINE THOMAS

The very words we speak . . . carry a spirit which stirs that same spirit in the person who hears them. . . . How easy it is to create a Spirit-filled atmosphere of peace so as to produce continually a higher spiritual influence for ourselves and those around us. (*Selected Writings*, 231.)

WENDY L. WATSON

A soft voice penetrates positively. . . . Harsh, loud voices grieve life, grieve the Spirit, and shrink your spirit. (In *May Christ Lift Thee Up*, 46.)

One of the marvelous things about commendations, as opposed to condemnations, is that they increase the likelihood that our other words will be received with increased influence. (In *Every Good Thing*, 49.)

Listening

ELAINE CANNON

Collisions in conversations can be avoided if you follow your primary school rules for pushing through traffic. Stop. Look. Listen. (*Bell Ringer*, 60.)

The most frequently ignored social trait is listening. . . . Listening is unselfish. It also can be educational, delightful, and rewarding. . . . Listen with your facial expression, your eyes, and your mind. Listen with your heart as well as your ears. (*Bell Ringer*, 60–61.)

AFTON J. DAY

Real communication results more from a high quality of listening than from a large quantity of talking. (*Perfect Wife*, 39.)

SUSA YOUNG GATES

A good talker is sometimes welcomed in society; I say sometimes, but a tactful, gracious listener is always the most delightful of companions. (In *Improvement Era*, Apr. 1905, 443.)

MICHAELENE P. GRASSLI

Listen with your heart, and listen for the unspoken message. (In *Ensign*, Apr. 1994, 62.)

BEPPIE HARRISON

Unrequested advice is [a] treasure that would be best kept to myself. Possibly the world *would* be better if it were left to me to organize, but I won't be harmed by keeping still about it. (*Plain and Precious*, 13.)

LINDA BENTLEY JOHNSON

Our need to be listened to, to be taken seriously, to be understood, and to have a sense of belonging is as powerful as our need for air. When we listen, we help others breathe. (In *Every Good Thing*, 87.)

Listening without judgment doesn't mean that we condone what is being said. After we have done the work of listening, we can clarify values, solve problems, share similar experiences, and give challenges and suggestions. But people have to be heard before they can hear. (In *Every Good Thing*, 87.)

JO ANN LARSEN

To listen with one's own soul and thereby possibly engage another's soul, one must become fully present. To listen is thus to pay absolute attention, to enter others' worlds, to try seeing things from the inside out. (*Heart of Goodness*, 343.)

To listen is to refrain from adding to, or changing, others' perspectives. In listening, one does not judge, twist, or embellish information. One simply receives the thoughts and feelings flowing from others' minds and hearts. (*Heart of Goodness*, 343.)

To listen is . . . to verbally walk with people, to emotionally hold hands, and to experience what they experience. (*Heart of Goodness*, 343.)

MARILYNNE TODD LINFORD

Listening is hard. Listening takes time. Listening takes concentration.

Listening takes control. As I work on being fully present in conversation, I find that active listening is a changing experience for both listener and speaker. The listener is focused, respectful, empathetic, encouraging, interested, but not nosey. The speaker is heard, respected, encouraged, and given the chance to express feelings. Both listener and speaker keep confidences; both use reinforcing phrases and words—never turnoffs or put-downs. Both are involved in and gain from the experience of listening, because the speaker is listening to herself too. (*Woman Fulfilled*, 36–37.)

JILL C. MAJOR, LAUREN C. LEIFSON, AND HOLLIE C. BEVAN

Once you start hearing, then you can listen. The two have some of the same elements, but they are not the same action. Listening is deeper than hearing. (*Encircled by Love*, 68.)

Listening—not just passively tuning in, but actively listening—is the most important part of a conversation. It communicates love. (*Encircled by Love*, 68.)

When you listen, you are using your ears not only to process words, but also to interpret the tone of voice. You are using your eyes to see facial expressions, body movement, and responses. You separate yourself from your own life and from your own emotions at that time so that you can feel what the other person is going through. (*Encircled by Love*, 68.)

To hear, you must have a one-track mind, and it must be on the same track as your friend's. (*Encircled by Love*, 68.)

CAROLINE EYRING MINER

When we are speaking we are only giving forth what we already know, but when we listen we may learn something new. (In *Relief Society Magazine*, Apr. 1964, 270.)

ANN WHITING ORTON

I've learned to listen to the identity-seeking children. Listening to their words must be coupled with listening to their actions. Teenagers speak with gestures, body language, attitude, and sometimes meaningful words. With careful observations, you find you can actually communicate with an independence-seeking child. It's not easy, nor does it work consistently, but occasionally you detect a message that's meaningful. (In *Emotional First Aid*, 146.)

VIRGINIA H. PEARCE

The surest way to increase our love for someone is to listen with patience and respect. I believe that our baptismal covenant demands this. How can we "mourn with those that mourn" and "bear one another's burdens" (Mosiah 18:8–9) if we don't listen to know what those burdens are? (In *Ensign*, Nov. 1993, 80.)

JANICE MADSEN WEINHEIMER

Listening isn't a passive thing where only our ears are involved. Listening entails much more. It requires concentrating on what is being said, then repeating back to the teenager, in our own words, what has been said to make sure we understand. (*Families Are Forever*, 91.)

Negative Communication

EARLENE BLASER

Living under constant criticism is demeaning to the spirit. Husbands, wives, and siblings who constantly berate each other are harming the whole divine system of families. (In *Emotional First Aid*, 76.)

ELAINE CANNON

Always remember and never forget that the human soul is tender and that God considers every one of us worthwhile and precious. (*Gatherings*, 45.)

SUSA YOUNG GATES

The moment you begin to argue, reason leaves you, and feeling or prejudice steps in and breeds dissension and strife. (In *Improvement Era*, May 1905, 503.)

ELAINE L. JACK

To avoid offense we must be serious about neither giving nor taking it. We will always have to deal with thoughtless people. . . . Unquestionably, opportunities to give and take offense are plentiful. I suggest, however, that we never intentionally litter the lives of our associates with offenses. And we can also refuse to pick up an offense when others drop it. (*Eye to Eye*, 89.)

LUCILE JOHNSON

Faultfinding is putting personal prejudice and personality in place of principle. It is so easy to drift from principle—determining *what* is right, to personality—worrying about *who* is right. (*Sunny Side Up*, 53.)

Perhaps there is no sin more common than the sin of faultfinding. . . . True, not all criticism is bad. There is constructive criticism, but there is a difference between being critical and hypercritical. (*Sunny Side Up*, 52.)

JO ANN LARSEN

Just as, over time, love flourishes and deepens with an abundance of loving behaviors, so love slowly fades in exposure to the same abundance of abrasive behaviors. (*Heart of Goodness*, 19.)

MARILYNNE TODD LINFORD

When we receive criticism the message may hurt and the time, word, and place choices of the messenger may be completely inappropriate. But no matter how the message is sent or by whom, criticism can be a commodity of high value. (*Woman Fulfilled*, 82.)

BETTE S. MOLGARD

Elevating ourselves while saying derogatory remarks about someone else is gossip. The setting and motive are irrelevant. (*Everyday Battles*, 84.)

VIRGINIA H. PEARCE

When fellow ward members complain, blame others, and repeat negative tales, it takes self-discipline to stop ourselves from adding more fuel to their fire of disgruntlement. Mutual murmuring is a smoldering fire that can burst into flame and destroy a ward. (In *Ensign*, Nov. 1993, 79.)

BARBARA B. SMITH AND SHIRLEY W. THOMAS

Cutting words inflict damage both to the victim and to the one by whom they were spoken. It is true that one individual has the power to break another's heart through unkindness, but not without hurting herself. (*Words for Women*, 78.)

Criticism and finding fault have a contagion that allows them to grow in kind and amount, until they can cause harm and even heartbreak, sometimes involving many people. (*Words for Women*, 78.)

PEGGY ST. CYR

Although we share common values with other members of the Church, we should not expect them to be just like us or to do things exactly as we would do them. Because we share common values, we have many similarities, but we are not clones of each other. We are of different ages, come from different backgrounds, and are at different levels of growth. When we criticize others we sometimes hurt them and we always hurt ourselves. (*Conversion to Commitment*, 59.)

WENDY L. WATSON

Words do matter. They lodge in our cells and in our souls. (In *Every Good Thing*, 42.)

Consecration

JULENE BUTLER

We are expected to live the law of consecration. We are to consecrate our time, our means, and our talents to building up Zion. We are each given different types and amounts of talent and time and material goods. And we covenant to consecrate what we have. (In *Best of Women's Conference*, 79.)

RUTH MAY FOX

[Tithing] was revealed for the benefit and blessing of the Church individually and collectively. Individually it is a stepping stone to a higher law. . . . It is a test of loyalty to the Church we love; a test of faith and trust in our Heavenly Father. (In *Relief Society Magazine*, July 1938, 470.)

SHERRIE JOHNSON

The law of consecration is a law of great power and spiritual strength. It is also a principle that, when correctly lived, brings joy to the soul and peace to the mind. (*Spiritually Centered*, 96.)

As with all of God's laws, the blessings and rewards of living the law of consecration far surpass any of the earthly sacrifices we might make to live it. (*Spiritually Centered*, 96.)

Consecration means to set our hearts upon righteousness and to put the things of God first in our lives. (*Spiritually Centered*, 96.)

ARDETH GREENE KAPP

Our Father in Heaven knows us. He asks each of us to commit not a particle more than we can give, but not a particle less. He doesn't want just our money or our time or our work; he wants us—all of us, heart and soul, all that we are and all that we might yet become. He wants our total commitment, and in return we are invited to come and partake of the blessings, to become joint heirs with Jesus Christ. (*Rejoice!* 120.)

PAM KAZMAIER

Seeking the kingdom of God first is *hard*. Usually I find I have to sacrifice something of the world to do it. (In *Best of Women's Conference*, 272.)

JOAN B. MACDONALD

To consecrate our lives to God means to bring every thought to the obedience of Christ. (*Holiness of Everyday Life*, 136.)

Consecration surrenders all to God and sees God in everything and everywhere. Consecration makes each moment of our lives moments of worship. Consecration sanctifies our life and makes it holy. (*Holiness of Everyday Life*, 136.)

Covenants

CHERYL BROWN

We are invited to lift up our hearts and rejoice and to cleave unto the covenants we have made. They are sure sources of guidance and strength. (In *To Rejoice As Women*, 148.)

The covenants we make on this earth are designed to lead us through our complexities and help us decide what to do when we do not understand, or when demands press upon us, or when we feel as if we cannot hold on one second longer. (In *To Rejoice As Women*, 148.)

JOANNE B. DOXEY

Ordinances and covenants are an anchor to safety for the family, both here and hereafter. (In *Ensign*, Nov. 1987, 91.)

PATRICIA T. HOLLAND

The reason the keeping of covenants is so important to us is at least partly because it makes the contract so binding to God. Covenants forge a link between our telestial, mortal struggles and God's celestial, immortal powers. (In *Arms of His Love*, 372.)

Though we may see our part in the matter of faithfulness going by fits and starts, by bumps and bursts, our progress erratic at best, God's part is sure and steady and supreme. We may stumble, but he never does. We may falter, but he never will. We may feel out of control, but he never is. (In *Arms of His Love*, 372.)

ELAINE L. JACK

A mother I know of . . . had given up on religion. One night she dreamed that she stood before Jesus on the Day of Judgment. . . . "I begged, I pleaded, I promised to change," she said. . . . "I knew in my heart [Jesus] was right. I was bound by my baptism the same as he was bound by covenants. I awoke with the most physical, heartbreaking pain. . . . I was at church the next week and have never missed since." (In *To Rejoice As Women*, 10–11.)

Covenants are not invisible. They reach out from what we say, do, and create to touch others. Keeping our covenants . . . brings blessings from the Lord. These bless-

ings may come as a gentleness of spirit, a light in our eyes, and a peace in our souls that speaks dramatically of the goodness of God. (In *Best of Women's Conference*, 212.)

Kept, honored, renewed, and held sacred, covenants bind us to God. (In *Best of Women's Conference*, 204.)

Covenants are active, two-way commitments that bring the Savior into our very lives and change us. (In *Best of Women's Conference*, 204–5.)

Our willingness to take seriously our covenants brings comfort amid sorrows, joy amid pain, blessings amid suffering. (In *Ensign*, Nov. 1993, 99.)

ARDETH GREENE KAPP

When we understand that our covenants with God are essential to our eternal life, these sacred promises become the driving force that helps us lighten our load, prioritize our activities, eliminate the excesses, accelerate our progress, and reduce the distractions that could, if not guarded, get us mired down in mud while other wagons move on. (In *BYU Speeches*, 13 Nov. 1990, 50.)

CAMILLA EYRING KIMBALL

Gospel ordinances are designed to remind us again and again of our commitments. (*Writings*, 21.)

CHIEKO N. OKAZAKI

There will be many times when you will be tried, when your covenants will seem hard to you—even confusing, perhaps. At these difficult moments, cleave to your covenants. Behave with honor and dignity in keeping the promises you have made. Trust the promises of the Lord in return, for there is great rejoicing in store if you do. (*Disciples*, 250.)

BONNIE D. PARKIN

If you have slipped in your covenants, take heart! The Savior so wants us to fulfill our promises that He has provided an everlasting atonement. (In *Ensign*, May 1995, 79.)

Covenant keeping will help you recall the One with whom you're yoked, and your burden will be lighter. (In *Ensign*, May 1995, 79.)

Covenants anchor us to solid ground, which, amidst the storms, makes our promises *not only meaningful for eternity but vital for today*. (In *Ensign*, May 1995, 79.)

Father in Heaven knows us as individuals. The covenants that we make with Him are performed one-on-one. (In *Ensign*, May 1995, 78.)

Sacrament

ARDETH GREENE KAPP

When our performance falls short in spite of our striving for perfection, we will find ourselves eagerly and anxiously and more gratefully than ever before, drawn to the Sabbath day and the sacramental altar where we can feel the glorious transformation of the healing of our wounded spirits as we commit to strive again and again to follow him. (In *BYU Speeches*, 5 May 1981, 83.)

We must come to the sacramental altar hungry—a spiritual hunger and thirst for righteousness. It is a time for self-evaluation, a time to rectify our courses, if necessary, and to make right our lives. It is a time and place for us to judge ourselves and come to better understand the magnitude of that sacred divine gift and the reality of being allowed to have his Spirit with us always to direct every act of our lives. (In *BYU Speeches*, 5 May 1981, 81.)

ANN N. MADSEN

The tiny cup of water offered us in the sacrament is enough to gradually cleanse the inner vessel—that part of us that only the Lord sees. (In *Best of Women's Conference*, 347.)

By partaking of the symbols of Christ's body and blood, when attended by the Spirit, we are washed clean, rinsed from the grime and filth of the world in completion of the changing process we call repentance. (In *Best of Women's Conference*, 347.)

BELLE S. SPAFFORD

There is never a time in the life of the Latter-day Saint when he can afford to forgo partaking of the sacrament. (In *Relief Society Magazine*, June 1942, 401.)

Discipleship

Turning Our Hearts to Christ

NANCY BAIRD

What an amazing offer Christ makes—to permanently satisfy and heal a soul. This is the path of comfort, the balm of Gilead—to truly live by his word. (In *Clothed with Charity*, 213.)

FRANCINE R. BENNION

Peace grows from direct experience with God . . . and His Son Jesus. . . . Some peace may be found in what we choose to believe of Them, and in ritual attention to Them, but great peace, joy, and uncommon love are to be found in our experience with Them, not just in knowing what has been said of Them and what we have thought of Them. (In *Behold Your Little Ones*, 45.)

ELAINE CANNON

Never forget, whether you turn to Jesus or not, he goes on loving you, waiting for you to love him back. (*Bell Ringer*, 110.)

AILEEN H. CLYDE

It is a response of the soul when we sense and accept the loving promises that Christ extends to us. (In *Ensign*, May 1995, 27.)

PATRICIA T. HOLLAND

The eternal kingdom of God is all important. If I want to be chosen as well as called . . . then my devotion must be to a ruler who is King of Kings and Lord of Lords, who knows me and knows my needs and to whom I must be loyal. (In *Ensign*, July 1980, 24.)

Each of us—each of you—must *want* the right things, must *pursue* the right things, and must give all that we have to the kingdom with an eye single to God and the covenants we've made. (In *Ensign*, July 1980, 25.)

ARDETH GREENE KAPP

Every act of our lives *can* become a sacramental experience when we take upon us his name. (In *BYU Speeches*, 5 May 1981, 83.)

JAYNE B. MALAN

When we are baptized and take on the name of Christ, we assume a great responsibility. We become his representatives here on earth, and wherever we go, whatever we do reflects on his name. Our prime responsibility is to make of ourselves what Heavenly Father has designed that we should become. (In *Living the Young Women Values*, 20.)

CHIEKO N. OKAZAKI

We all need to have a primary relationship with the Savior—a first-hand relationship . . . a personal, intimate relationship, one that is based on our own experiences with the Savior, our own answered prayers, our own knowledge of what the Spirit feels like, our own obedience to its guidance, our own knowledge that Christ atoned for us. (*Aloha!* 105.)

Sometimes, when I am feeling lonely and tired, I take the name of the Savior upon me like a warm blanket. I wrap myself in it . . . and I feel warmed and comforted. If I am feeling vulnerable, sometimes I take the name of Christ upon me like armor, feeling it solid and bright and impregnable, so that no opposition can puncture it and so that no wound can devastate me. Sometimes I take the name of Christ upon me like Joseph's coat of many colors, a beautiful garment in which to dance and rejoice and praise the Lord. (*Aloha!* 49–50.)

Making [Christ] the center of our hearts enlarges our hearts in wonderful ways. You'll be amazed at how much room there is for other people, for kind words, for swift acts of service, for happy thoughts and gestures when your heart is filled with the love of Jesus. (*Cat's Cradle,* 165.)

MARY ELLEN SMOOT

The most important conversion for any of us is our own. If we are to bring the light of the gospel into others' lives, it must shine brightly in our own. . . . Only when we are converted to the Lord Jesus Christ are we in a position to strengthen others. (In *Ensign,* Nov. 2000, 90.)

Becoming Disciples of Christ

MARILYN S. BATEMAN

It is through meeting the challenges of our mortal journey that we become disciples of Christ. As we put our trust in him, he will bless us according to our faith. (In *Best of Women's Conference,* 32.)

SHERI L. DEW

Not long ago I visited a ward [and] at the conclusion of sacrament meeting I was a little surprised when a woman approached me and asked, "Are you the woman I think you are?" Her question referred to my identity, but it is one that has haunted me. *Am* I the woman I think I am, the woman I want to be? More importantly, am I the woman the Savior needs me to be? (In *Ensign,* Nov. 1997, 92.)

As our testimony of [Jesus] expands and matures, we begin to care more about life forever than life today, and we have no desire but to do what He needs us to do and to live as He has asked us to live. (In *Ensign,* Nov. 1997, 92.)

CAMILLE FRONK

The goal of a disciple is not to be different from everyone else but to be more like the Master. (In *Arms of His Love*, 57.)

Being a disciple is not a single event but a spiraling process that begins at baptism and continues throughout our lives. (In *Arms of His Love*, 57.)

A disciple is not only one who follows Christ after accepting his gospel but one who also spreads his good news to others. (In *Arms of His Love*, 57.)

BEPPIE HARRISON

The only key that will unlock our great potential is our trust in Jesus Christ and our obedience to his principles. (*Day at a Time*, 78.)

MARJORIE P. HINCKLEY

All kinds of things—you could call them miracles—happen to all kinds of people when they lose themselves in the work of the Lord. (In *Glimpses*, 210.)

JENI HOLZAPFEL

A woman's qualification for discipleship was and is the same as a man's: all must accept him as their Lord and Master. Any person who truly accepts him consequently becomes a witness of him as the source of Living Water. (In *Every Good Thing*, 365.)

ELAINE L. JACK

The time is past when we can merely believe in this gospel; we must be passionate in our belief and in our commitment to Jesus Christ and His plan. We must know, unequivocally, that He is with us, that He will guide and direct us. (In *Ensign*, May 1997, 74–75.)

ARDETH GREENE KAPP

It won't matter if we play center stage or in the wings if our Lord and Savior is at the very center of our life. (In *BYU Speeches*, 4 June 1989, 126.)

SHARON G. LARSEN

Some may say [the Savior's] yoke is restricting, that we are not free to go wherever we want to go. That is true—unless where we want to go is where he is. Then we will always want to be in step with him. (In *Arms of His Love*, 34.)

CHIEKO N. OKAZAKI

We're not trying to balance the Savior or our spiritual life against any other aspect of our life. The Savior is the fulcrum of the balance, the pivot point of the balance, the trunk and roots of the tree that keep the branches in balance. We're trying to keep this feeling about the Savior sweet and strong, because then, questions of priorities and how to spend our time will be easy and clear. (*Aloha!* 74.)

Let's make Jesus the center of our lives. Let the consciousness of

Jesus Christ permeate our thinking until we live in a Christ-centered world. (*Cat's Cradle*, 165.)

To love the Savior with all of our heart, might, mind, and strength doesn't mean that we never think about anything else, never love anyone else, never work at anything else. It means that we think about other things in the presence of the Spirit of Christ. It means that we love others with the same kind of love that he gives us. (*Cat's Cradle*, 165.)

When we make room in our hearts for Christ and his abundant love for us, we are fulfilling the cause of Christ. When we think, speak, and act with love, we are carrying forward the cause of Christ. This is a great cause. It is the greatest cause we will ever know. (*Cat's Cradle*, 163.)

Our choice to become Christians is not a matter of saying a few words or signing a piece of paper or going to a certain set of meetings on Sundays. It involves a change of heart. We must choose to become Christ's. We must choose it freely. We must choose obedience to his way. (*Sanctuary*, 55–56.)

Virginia H. Pearce

As we concentrate on pleasing the Lord rather than others and continue to work hard, doing the things we don't know how to do yet, we will experience personal growth. We will increase our confidence in Heavenly Father and his Son, Jesus Christ. This faith assures us that in the end, we will not only survive but we will know great joy and happiness. (In *Ensign*, Nov. 1992, 91–92.)

M. Catherine Thomas

Spiritual refinement, as well as coming to the greater light and knowledge, are accomplished through an all-encompassing sacrifice, usually made over time. (*Selected Writings*, 152.)

Barbara Sorenson Wilde

When we are living within the light of Christ, his light is reflected in our countenances. We are not the light, however; the Lord is the light. We can only carry the lamp of Christ and reflect the light of Christ. (In *Thy Word Is a Lamp*, 82.)

Dwan J. Young

When we are converted, we can stand alone against the storms around us, secure in the knowledge of the revealed truth. (In *BYU Speeches*, 15 Feb. 1983, 83.)

Becoming Like Christ

Francine R. Bennion

According to my understanding of scripture, we are not preparing now to begin in the next life to become more like God. We are not simply waiting to get started with the process. We are in it here and now. (In *Heritage of Faith*, 66–67.)

JUTTA BAUM BUSCHE

Our efforts should not be to *perform* nor to *conform* but to be *transformed* by the Spirit. (In *Best of Women's Conference*, 72.)

CAMILLE FRONK

Only after we begin to know, love, and have faith in Christ can we commence to live like him. We cannot embody his attributes until we embody him. When we are truly converted in our hearts, our behavior begins to mirror our inner conviction. (In *Redeemer*, 125.)

MARIE K. HAFEN

We must push ourselves to develop a dependence upon the Lord so that he can mold us spiritually into the kind of people we must become. (In *Clothed with Charity*, 44–45.)

ARDETH GREENE KAPP

Ask yourself, are the comparisons you may make of yourself and others based on the model of the Savior's life, or do they come from trying to fit your life into the pattern of others' lives? (In *Ensign*, Nov. 1990, 89.)

We follow our Savior, not by filling the same mission that he filled, but by seeking to do the will of the Father who has sent us and to do it in such a way that, at the close of our ministry and our mortal life, we might be able to say, as did Jesus, "I have finished the work thou gavest me to do." (*Joy of the Journey*, 167.)

When Christ becomes our constant companion, it will make our whole day different, and with his Spirit . . . slowly, day by day, our conduct will become more unselfish, our relationships more tender, our desire to serve more constant, and we will find ourselves going about doing good. Always. We will have taken upon us not only his name, but his image in our countenances also (see Alma 5:14). (In *BYU Speeches*, 5 May 1981, 81.)

MARY B. KIRK

[God] will pour out his holiness upon us at the rate that we open our eyes and perceive, open our ears and understand, and open our hearts and invite him in. And then we'll become like him. (In *Best of Women's Conference*, 283.)

JANET G. LEE

If we let [Christ's] light shine in us, we will receive "his image in [our] countenances" (Alma 5:14). . . . He will know us because our total beings will reflect his image. And we will know him because we recognize his light in us. (In *BYU Speeches*, 11 Jan. 1994, 68.)

AMY BROWN LYMAN

In this day of world confusion, we are challenged as are all other Christian groups to preserve and maintain the ethical, moral and religious standards and ideals set up by the Master. Let us dedicate ourselves to these ideals. (In *Relief Society Magazine*, Nov. 1939, 777–78.)

MARGARET D. NADAULD

Our outward appearance is a reflection of what we are on the inside. Our lives reflect that for which we seek. And if with all our hearts we truly seek to know the Savior and to be more like Him, we shall be, for He is our divine, eternal Brother. But He is more than that. He is our precious Savior, our dear Redeemer. (In *Ensign*, Nov. 2000, 14–15.)

CHIEKO N. OKAZAKI

If we see every place, every job, every responsibility as an opportunity to be with another precious child of God who needs our ministry . . . as a disciple of Christ, then even a very busy schedule doesn't feel like juggling any more. Something has taken the fragmentation out of it and given us a unified purpose. (*Aloha!* 54.)

I don't have to rely on my own goodness to be good. I can rely on the Savior's goodness filling my heart when I am worthy and willing to receive it. I don't have to rely on my own capacity for love to be loving. I can rely on the Savior's love to fill my heart. . . . I don't have to rely on my own patience, my own generosity, my own forgiveness, or my own steadfastness. . . . If I am willing to make room in my heart for the Savior, . . . and if I fix my thoughts and desires and hopes on him, then in some miraculous way, I can think the thoughts of Jesus, I can feel the feelings of Jesus, and I can do the works of Jesus. (*Aloha!* 131.)

SANDRA ROGERS

The Beatitudes are truly the simple yet eternal guide to becoming closer to God and more like him— and to becoming Christlike friends. (In *Arms of His Love*, 196.)

WENDY L. WATSON

Because the Savior never changes, the changes that occur through our interactions with the Savior will all be in us. And as we change, our capacity to show love, to express love, to enter into life-changing and life-giving relationships will be our absolute reward. (In *May Christ Lift Thee Up*, 51.)

The Savior changed eyes. And he can give you the eyes to see what you need to see in order to change your life. He will open the eyes of your understanding. Just ask him.

The Savior changed ears. And he can help you hear his voice. . . . Ask him.

He changed limbs that were weak. And he can change your mobility and direction to help you move to the next level of your life and help you in your efforts to shore up the feeble knees that are around you. Ask him.

He changed a few fishes and a couple of loaves of bread into enough to feed 5,000 people. And he will take your widow's mite of time, energy, and ability and magnify them, multiply them, so that there is enough and to spare. You just need to ask him. (In *BYU Speeches*, 7 Apr. 1998, 220.)

The ultimate and only true and living change agent is the Savior. He is the source of all change. . . . As you turn to him, he will bring the very best out of you. He will indeed rescue all that is finest down deep inside of you. And what a celebration that will be! (In *BYU Speeches*, 7 Apr. 1998, 220.)

Divorce

DEANNE ERNST ALLEN

It was in the early days after our separation that I began to understand [that] I had a choice between bitterness and blessings. Many people have chosen bitterness and existed in misery. . . . When I let go of bitterness, . . . I feel peace and contentment as I eagerly look forward to my future. (In *Ensign*, Oct. 1992, 30–31.)

MARILYN ARNOLD

We in the Church have rightly been taught that divorce and broken homes are destructive to society and to individual happiness, but certainly we have not been taught that we, therefore, have the right to judge divorced people as evil. They are usually, in fact, people who have suffered much anguish, who are burdened with a terrible sense of their own failure, and who have made a decision to separate only when it seemed to them that no other avenues were open. . . . Such a decision is perhaps the most difficult of their lives. Only the Lord . . . is in a position to make a judgment against them. (In *Ensign*, June 1975, 48.)

JOYCE BACA

One of the prime requisites in being able to help anyone experiencing divorce is to withhold judgment. We cannot know what is in the heart of another person. . . . We cannot know fully the experiences the individuals in a marriage have been through. (*Divorce*, 34.)

Hostility and anger, bitterness, backbiting, an unforgiving spirit—these are all common reactions after divorce, yet they all separate a person from the Spirit. (*Divorce*, 32.)

After divorce we create our own environment. Choosing to make it a nurturing environment supports growth and brings us closer to God. (*Divorce*, 26.)

For many, severing the marriage tie brings a sense of uncomfortable disassociation—a sense of identity loss. . . . This is an opportunity to find out who you really are, what you stand for and believe in, and what your goals are. (*Divorce*, 22.)

LORI BERG

It's easy for single parents to berate themselves for failing at the very thing the Church emphasizes most—keeping families together. Divorce is hard on one's self-esteem. But I do know the Lord loves me. At times I have gone to him, complaining about how unfair life seems, and he puts his arms around me and enfolds me in his love. I know I am not alone. (In *Ensign*, Feb. 1993, 49.)

SANDRA BOULEY

The worth of a soul is great in the sight of the Lord. Sometimes that soul is a person victimized by divorce, or one responsible for divorce. All who are coping with various degrees of broken hearts and contrite spirits have a great need for understanding, encouragement, and visible support that communicates love and acceptance. (In *Ensign*, June 1983, 58.)

SUZANNE LITTLE DASTRUP

Peace may seem so distant that you feel you will never reach it. . . . Having peace within doesn't mean you will never hurt again. It means that you are understanding yourself and liking yourself. . . . Without a doubt, however, our personal relationship with the Savior will be an unfailing source of peace. (In *Women in the Covenant*, 57.)

KAREN LYNN DAVIDSON

As Latter-day Saints, we cherish our picture of the traditional family pattern. But we should not let our ideal keep us from acknowledging and appreciating the many thriving, praiseworthy families that have another pattern. . . . Throughout the Church are families establishing their own identity even though no husband and father is present. (*Thriving on Our Differences*, 68.)

NEDRA HARDY

A marriage is a commitment between two people that is designed to last for eternity. One person cannot carry that commitment to fruition alone. When it is not being upheld by both parties, it ceases to be eternal. . . . A hopeless marriage need not be forever; an abusive situation need not be tolerated. . . . My marriage ceased being eternal years before we entered the divorce courts. (In *Women in the Covenant*, 55.)

KIMBERLEY BURTON HEUSTON

Feelings of suspicion and mistrust sown by divorce can persist for decades and often compromise [a] child's ability to form lasting relationships as an adult. (*Single Parenting*, 58.)

Although divorce ends a marriage, it doesn't end a relationship, especially when there are children involved. Patterns of anger, guilt, blame, and shame forged in the heat of a turbulent marriage may persist and even intensify between family members. (*Single Parenting*, 57.)

MARY JANE KNIGHTS

Divorce often creates feelings of bitterness. These feelings are not unusual, but peace will come to you only when you learn to forgive both your former mate and yourself. (In *Ensign*, Aug. 1985, 50.)

MARILYNNE TODD LINFORD

If divorce is an end, it is also a beginning. . . . A woman who is divorced has opportunities to forgive. She has opportunities to forget. She has opportunities for Christlike love. (In *LDS Women's Treasury*, 163–64.)

ELAINE SORENSEN MARSHALL

Peace after divorce comes in the process of living. It happens after learning hard lessons. It occurs over time alongside family, friends, and professionals who care. It happens privately but also with many others who share the experience and understand. Peace emerges from pain and accompanies healing. (In *LDS Women's Treasury*, 179.)

Understanding and using resources appropriately can be critical, . . . in divorce. The confidence and support of a bishop or stake president are important for spiritual counsel, of a lawyer for legal counsel, of a therapist for emotional help, of an accountant for financial guidance, of friends and family for love. But it is equally important not to confuse the roles of such valuable relationships. The bishop is not the accountant; the lawyer is not the therapist. (In *Women in the Covenant*, 48–49.)

Emotional Health

Anger

SALLY H. BARLOW

Anger is hard to hang onto forever. The Lord only asks us to do those things that will benefit us in the long run. Surely there is something wise about finding a way to rid ourselves of the canker of hatred, even if it is justified. (In *Wisdom's Paths*, 92.)

LUCILE JOHNSON

If we are not dealing with the conflict, whatever the cause, in a healthy, loving manner, we are allowing cracks to remain in the seams of the relationships, which may destroy them. (*Enjoy the Journey*, 228.)

JO ANN LARSEN

Only when anger is absent can a heart experience caring or the deep abiding love it has for another person. (*Heart of Goodness*, 401.)

Depression

KARLA C. ERICKSON

Learn to recognize your energy cycles. . . . When your energy level is "down," select people projects which are less demanding. . . . Instead of saying "depressed days," I prefer to call them "low-energy days." Dwelling on the bleak word "depression" usually worsens the situation. Thinking in terms of energy brightens the picture. (*Make Time Count*, 15.)

PATRICIA T. HOLLAND

Depression, conflict, or negativism is often a message to us that we are not growing toward the full measure for which God has created us. Our pain—emotional pain—is a demand that we stop and take time for change in our life because we may be getting off course. (In *LDS Women's Treasury*, 97.)

JO ANN LARSEN

Like a weather front, clinical or chemical depression often comes subtly and the symptoms are often mild enough to permit a sufferer to go through the motions of life at home and at work. As months go by, the sadness, the mood swings, the low tolerance for stress, the withdrawal from people, numbed feelings, and other symptoms that gradually develop seem normal to the depressed person, who often forgets what she felt like before the depression descended. (*I'm a Day Late*, 165.)

JUDY NORMAN

Everyone involved with a depressed individual . . . must remember to be patient. When energy, appetite, sleep, and mental functioning are still significantly impaired, suggestions for more physical activity or social contact can lead the person to feel more helpless, more guilty—yes, even more depressed. Reminding her how blessed she is may well have the same effect. We can listen, and we can encourage her to do what she is able to do. (In *Clothed with Charity*, 252.)

Emotional Healing

SALLY H. BARLOW

Many people bear unseen burdens, or perhaps unhealed wounds within their souls. . . . Before coming to the peace necessary for a secure foundation in Christ, we may need to reexamine these wounds. (In *Wisdom's Paths*, 84.)

Unreconciled wounds may actually damage both our spirit and our body because wounds carry the power to interfere with our mental and physical growth, and therefore our mortal and immortal identity. (In *Wisdom's Paths*, 84.)

KATHLEEN RAWLINGS BUNTIN

Somewhere along the line, we assume—erroneously so—that what happens to us *causes* our happiness or unhappiness. This is not true. It is how we *perceive* what has happened to us and how we act upon that perception that results in the emotional reaction we feel. We cannot always control what happens to us, but we can most certainly control the way we react to what has happened. (*All Alone*, 42.)

Emotions are intrinsically neither good nor bad; they just *are*. . . . It's what we do with those emotions that determines whether they will have negative or positive effects. (*All Alone*, 42.)

ELAINE L. JACK

As you take stock of yourself and your situation, base your evaluation of where you are on your own criteria, not that of another person. . . . Can you imagine how different our world would be if we concentrated . . . on what all of us do right, on the positive acts of ourselves and others? That's maturity. (In *Clothed with Charity*, 50.)

Maturity allows us to accept ourselves even when we're not all we want to be. Maturity allows us to accept who we are and where we are. We should never abandon the quest for a better self, but neither should we allow ourselves to become immobilized, thinking we are nothing. Accepting ourselves, knowing we are progressing, frees us to reach out to others in charitable ways. (In *Clothed with Charity*, 50.)

CARROLL HOFELING MORRIS

During our earthly life, we are separated to one extent or another from our eternal nature by the veil. We are also separated from our brothers and sisters, not being of one mind and one heart, and we are separated from our Father in Heaven. Overcoming these separations is our prime task; helping others overcome them is our mission. (*"Why Do I Hurt?"* 132.)

We are never able to connect with others meaningfully until we begin to connect with our true selves. (*"Why Do I Hurt?"* 132.)

Dealing with Abuse

TAMMY B. HEATON

Abuse is a denial of the victims' rights. . . . Your listening to them confirms their right to be themselves . . . ; your validation of their right to have their own feelings will help restore and feed their self-esteem. . . . [This] will require great patience on your part; I implore you to hang in there for their sakes, to encourage the healing process. (In *Women and the Power*, 250–51.)

CARROLL HOFELING MORRIS

Victims of every age and either sex are in great need of having their self-worth reaffirmed. They need to know that regardless of what has happened to them, their Father in Heaven has not ceased to love them. Victims of sexual abuse in particular need the reassurance that they are "still clean in the eyes of God and others." (*"Why Do I Hurt?"* 130.)

Members of the Church often feel that because we have the blessing of the restored gospel, we also have—or ought to have—some immunity from the relationship problems faced by the population as a whole, including abuse. However, this does not seem to be the case. (*"Why Do I Hurt?"* 13.)

MARYBETH RAYNES

No matter what happens to us in life, whether . . . through abuse or violence, or . . . by being abusive or violent ourselves, we are not beings who are irreparably harmed. . . . Even serious misdeeds do not have to reverberate forever. . . That is the message of the Atonement. (In *Women and the Power*, 179.)

MICHELE R. SORENSEN

What can you [say] about healing a broken heart—a heart that's been . . . 'soul-murdered' [because of abuse]? . . .

[There are] many things: . . . the healing power in love, . . . the importance of the wounded person wanting to let go of the pain and to be willing to be healed, and of how doing that requires humility and faith. . . . Nothing short of the atonement of Jesus Christ can heal such a wound. . . . Only the healing power of the Master Physician can actually resurrect tissues that have died. (*Chainbreakers*, 171.)

WENDY C. TOP

No woman is expected to put up with physical or sexual abuse in any degree, no matter how much she loves her husband or how high his position in the Church. She is not doing herself,

him, or their children any favors by covering up for him. . . . His salvation is in jeopardy, and . . . she has a responsibility to do every righteous thing in her power to get help for him to end such unrighteous behavior. (*Getting Past the Labels*, 95.)

Dealing with Substance Abuse

ANNE OSBORN POELMAN

God can give us strength and power beyond our own to overcome all things. Addiction is no exception. (*Amulek Alternative*, 43.)

MICHELE R. SORENSEN

Certain behaviors such as drinking, doing drugs, or promiscuity are not the actual problem. They're symptoms of a deeper need for healing. They show us that something else is out of balance. (*Chainbreakers*, 147–48.)

M. CATHERINE THOMAS

Recovering alcoholics recognize what they call "stinking" thinking. If they want to get well and understand what the Lord's rest is, they have to repent of bad mental habits: fear, self-pity, self-condemnation, bad memories, unforgiveness, certain kinds of fantasizing. [As a child of a recovering alcoholic,] I found I did not have this power fully in myself to reshape and heal my mind, but Christ did. (In *Women and the Power*, 189.)

Faith

Acquiring Faith

NANCY BAIRD

We cling to our sins and our comforts, like a child with her blanket, instead of putting aside our fear and choosing faith. (*Every Good Thing*, 17.)

JANETTE HALES BECKHAM

As we gain experience in this demanding "real world," we sometimes fail to see the sacred nature of our seemingly routine daily tasks. Fundamentals of daily living—scripture reading, prayer, family home evening, the conversation at dinner—these provide the experiences that make faith a reality. (In *Ensign*, Nov. 1997, 76.)

CHERYL BROWN

Sooner or later everyone has to choose to believe or not. We have to choose to recognize the sweetness of the Spirit that comes when we think about the Church being true. We have to acknowledge, when we pray and ask the Lord if the Church and the Book of Mormon are true, that the thought that we already know that they are comes from the Being who knows our thoughts. We have to admit that, indeed, we do know

they are true. (In *BYU Speeches*, 11 May 1993, 105.)

MICHAELENE P. GRASSLI

In . . . instances, when we desire to believe but find faith faltering, if we will continue in our desire and in patiently praying, walking through each day doing the necessary and good, we will find belief growing stronger. If we are watching for it, we can see a phrase, a word, a lesson, a paragraph, a comment, or an experience shared by someone that will increase our faith and belief. But the *desire* to believe is a critical component, because it demonstrates our willingness to put ourselves in the hands of our Father; to turn ourselves over to him and to trust in him. (*What I Have Learned*, 27–28.)

SUZANNE L. HANSEN

Belief is what moves us forward while fear is what holds us back. (In *Serving with Strength*, 128.)

ARDETH GREENE KAPP

It is relatively easy to be faithful, but faith is born out of study, fasting, prayer, meditation, sacrifice, service, and, finally, personal revelation. (*My Neighbor*, 73.)

The first principle of the gospel is faith in the Lord, Jesus Christ. To have faith in Him is to know Him, to know His doctrine, and to know that the course of our life is in harmony with and acceptable to Him. (*My Neighbor*, 73.)

CAMILLA EYRING KIMBALL

Faith must be won with the help and power of God, each within himself. Even with help each must discover within himself those deep wellsprings of faith upon which life's eternal goals and achievements depend. Parents and grandparents may have perfect faith, but they cannot transmit it to their descendants. (*Writings*, 88.)

JEANIE MCALLISTER

Concentrating on what is certain, giving thanks for blessings, and living righteously all increase our faith. (In *LDS Women's Treasury*, 335.)

CHIEKO N. OKAZAKI

We can't rely on someone else's faith in the Savior. We can't depend on someone else to get answers to prayers for us. We can't ask someone else to listen to the whisperings of the Holy Ghost for us. We have to do it ourselves. (*Sanctuary*, 15.)

All of us face different family circumstances and home situations. All of us need strength in dealing with them. This strength comes from faith in the Savior's love and in the power of his atonement. If we trustingly put our hand in the Savior's, we can claim the promise

of the sacramental prayer to always have his Spirit with us. All problems are manageable with that strength, and all other problems are secondary in urgency to maintaining a strong spiritual life. (In *Ensign*, Nov. 1993, 94.)

We have to develop our own faith in Christ—not in substitutes for Christ. Even if we have wonderful marriage partners upon whom to rely, even if we have the most devoted and kindly bishops in the world, and even if we have developed much strength in ourselves, our ultimate faith must be in the Savior, not in any human being. (*Sanctuary*, 145.)

LOUISE Y. ROBISON

Faith is peculiar—it can grow stronger even in the face of hardship and sorrow, or it can and does leave if one neglects to nourish it. The more prayer becomes a regular habit, the easier faith grows. (In *Relief Society Magazine*, May 1939, 349.)

Exercising Faith

LINDA R. ARCHIBALD

It was faith that allowed us to shout for joy in our premortal life, and it is faith that will again give us the power to proclaim our joy over and over again in mortality. We believe the first principle of the gospel is faith in the Lord Jesus Christ. (*Sunshine in My Soul*, 48.)

JANETTE HALES BECKHAM

The greatest goal is that you would constantly choose experiences that would exercise or strengthen your faith in our Savior, Jesus Christ. (In *New Era*, Nov. 1994, 41.)

BEPPIE HARRISON

You can't separate honest faith and works. You show that faith exists by the works that you do. (*Plain and Precious*, 236.)

PATRICIA T. HOLLAND

Even through the darkest of shadows, we can walk in comfort and consolation if we lovingly trust God. (In *Arms of His Love*, 369.)

ARDETH GREENE KAPP

Even tiny drops of water steadily dropping on a solid rock can cause a crack and eventually split the rock. Continual doubts about our ability are actually an indication of lack of faith, and can be destructive of the very gifts waiting to be magnified. As we move forward in faith, not fear, we magnify our gifts and our callings. (*Lead*, 153.)

We are on a stormy sea. These are threatening times and we may be ignoring or even cutting ourselves loose from the very signals that would save us. (In *BYU Speeches*, 29 Jan. 1985, 68.)

MARILYNNE TODD LINFORD

Confidence in God is called faith. Faith is often misunderstood. Faith is not hope. Hope precedes faith. Hope is the wishing, the planning, the thinking. Faith is the action, the work, the try and try again that makes something a reality. . . . Show your faith in him by working to make the things you pray about come to be. Listen for his still, small voice and act on his promptings. (*Mother's Self-Esteem*, 21.)

AMY BROWN LYMAN

Sublime faith is one of the greatest of all gifts. Let us pledge our allegiance to our faith. Let us as individuals say, "No man may destroy my faith and hope and belief and leave me a stone." (In *Relief Society Magazine*, July 1926, 382.)

The Lord helps those who help themselves. . . . Faith without works is dead. And so we are committed to the idea of work and service as well as faith. (In *Relief Society Magazine*, May 1934, 286.)

BETTE S. MOLGARD

Trusting our Heavenly Father and his Son also means trusting their timetable for our desired blessings. (*Everyday Battles*, 39.)

CHIEKO N. OKAZAKI

When we have faith, nothing is impossible, because faith connects us to a source of power beyond all our ability to imagine. (*Sanctuary*, 146–47.)

ANNE OSBORN POELMAN

Trusting implicitly in the light of Christ, using it as a spiritual "navigational aid" to move unafraid and with confidence through life's many foggy moments, is an inestimably precious spiritual gift. (*Simeon Solution*, 13.)

ESTHER RASBAND

The Lord reminds us that faith the size of a mustard seed can move mountains. The reason this is true is that it is not the power of our faith that moves mountains of the spirit, but the fact of our faith in the power of God. Even a mustard-seed's worth of desire can lead us to faith in the power and perfection of God. (*Confronting the Myth*, 87.)

LOUISE Y. ROBISON

Each one of us . . . could bear a beautiful testimony of the healing of some members of our family, but do we have that faith sufficient in our lives to keep us from complaining. It is that faith that makes us equal to things that are almost impossible to bear, it is faith that brings . . . Peace. (In *Relief Society Magazine*, Dec. 1925, 650.)

KATHRYN S. SMITH

You and I want our faith to be the force behind us, but we live in a world where things we can see and touch and feel seem the most real. Our job is to learn to exchange "sight" for faith in God. (In *Living the Legacy*, 202.)

MARY FIELDING SMITH

The Lord knows what our intentions are and He will support us and give us grace and strength for the day as we continue to put our trust in Him and devote ourselves unreservedly to His service. (In *Mothers of the Prophets*, 96.)

ELIZA R. SNOW

Our trust is in God. . . . His kingdom will move steadily forward, until wickedness shall be swept from the earth, and truth, love and righteousness reign triumphantly. (In *Women of Mormondom*, 393–94.)

M. CATHERINE THOMAS

Grasping the Lord's outstretched hand for help requires reaching into the unknown for the unseen. (*Selected Writings*, 61.)

SHIRLEY W. THOMAS

The ultimate in counting blessings is to learn to count on the Lord. (In *Ensign*, Feb. 1982, 62.)

SALLY M. TODD

Trust in the Lord, even in the face of opposition and trial. We never know the role of opposition in our development and growth. (In *BYU Speeches*, 8 July 1997, 310.)

MARGARET J. WHEATLEY

Are we not of little faith when we believe that we can only cry out to God from the depths of our despair? Life is so much nicer, so much easier, so much more fun when we call upon the Lord in our moments of pleasure, when we call upon the Lord for companionship, for enjoyment, when we call upon the Lord for every little need, not just the big ones. (In *Women and Christ*, 43.)

BARBARA W. WINDER

Facing some of life's challenges may require a "leap of faith," where we walk forward with only our faith and trust in the Lord to lead us. It will require all the heart and soul we have to act, to move, to reach out and grasp handholds the Lord will extend to us in times of extremity. (In *BYU Speeches*, 13 Mar. 1990, 103.)

Faith and Fear

DIANE BILLS

When we face trials or challenges, getting on our knees and *staying there* until we feel the Spirit can be the key to having our fears replaced with faith. As we pray humbly, the fear will dissipate and our faith will grow. (*Trust in the Lord*, 79.)

When we have fears in our hearts, we deny ourselves the blessings of heaven. But when we replace our fears with faith, the powers of heaven can be brought down in our behalf. (*Trust in the Lord*, 77.)

JEANIE MCALLISTER

Even when we are trying to do our best, fearing that blessings may not come will weaken what faith we have been able to develop. Fearfulness is not of the spirit of the Lord. . . . Fear works against us. (In *LDS Women's Treasury*, 335.)

VIRGINIA H. PEARCE

The uncertainties of earth life can help to remind each of us that we are dependent on [our Father in Heaven]. But that reminder is not automatic. It involves our agency. We must *choose* to take our fears to him, *choose* to trust him, and *choose* to allow him to direct us. We must make these choices when what we feel most inclined to do is to rely more and more on our own frantic and often distorted thinking. (In *Ensign*, Nov. 1992, 90.)

As we try to live his commandments and pray to [our Heavenly Father], there are things he will direct us to do that will help calm our fears. These actions often require great courage and direction from the Holy Ghost. . . . He will support us as we face our fears and try to do things that we have never done before. (In *Ensign*, Nov. 1992, 90.)

ELIZA R. SNOW

I will not fear. I will put my trust in Him who is mighty to save; rejoicing in his goodness and determined to live by every word that proceedeth out of his mouth. (*Personal Writings*, 52.)

Let us have no fear; fear and faith do not dwell in the same bosom; let us lay aside fear and have faith in God our Father. (In *Woman's Exponent*, 1 Oct. 1887, 70.)

DEBRA WOODS

Learning to trust is an active process for me. When I find myself overwhelmed by worry or fear, I pause to pray for peace and clarity. With the help of the Spirit, I determine if there is some action I should take to address the source of the fear. I earnestly search the scriptures for answers and comfort. (In *Thy Word Is a Lamp*, 132.)

The Fruits of Faith

LINDA R. ARCHIBALD

It is by faith that we conquer any fears, for faith vanquishes doubt and propels action. (*Sunshine in My Soul*, 48.)

JANETTE HALES BECKHAM

After Primary a few weeks ago our four-year-old grandson, Michael, reported to his parents, "When I pray, my heart feels like a roasted marshmallow." Already Michael is recognizing the feelings associated with faith. How fortunate that he is willing and able to identify and talk about his feelings with his parents. (In *Ensign*, Nov. 1997, 75.)

DEANNA EDWARDS

Those who have a deep, intrinsic faith seem able to call upon that faith for strength and comfort when faced with tragedy. (*Grieving*, 193.)

SUSA YOUNG GATES

Faith teaches us to control fears, doubt, hatred, and strife. (In *Young Woman's Journal*, May 1900, 232.)

ARDETH GREENE KAPP

Faith in the eternal plan helps fill the cavity of emptiness when we feel alone or homesick. (*Rejoice!* 87.)

AMY BROWN LYMAN

Religious faith helps us to put our trust in the Lord, to rest our case with Him and to trust in Him for the final outcome. (In *Relief Society Magazine*, May 1933, 293.)

The greatest help and comfort that can come to anyone in any kind of distress is faith in Divine Providence—faith in God, who, we believe, will surely protect and help those who love and serve Him and put their trust in Him. (In *Relief Society Magazine*, May 1934, 286.)

Faith in our Heavenly Father and in his Son Jesus Christ is an asset to any individual. It helps him to be a brave and courageous individual. It helps to make him a positive and forceful character as opposed to a negative and vascillating one. It helps him to have confidence in himself and confidence in others; to believe in himself and to believe in others; to be generous to those in need and charitable to those less fortunate; to be cheerful, hopeful and optimistic. (In *Relief Society Magazine*, July 1926, 381.)

CHIEKO N. OKAZAKI

The miracle of faith in the Savior is that it runs through our whole lives, like a drop of food coloring in the icing for a cake, transforming every bit. Our goal isn't to whittle away our material lives so that all we have left is the spiritual. Our aim isn't to expunge and erase our physical lives so that there is this pure cube of spirit left. No, it's to infuse our whole physical lives *with* the Spirit. We want there to be no activity, no thought, no word, no gesture of service, no impulse that is not steeped in the Spirit. (*Disciples*, 95.)

Through faith in the Savior, we can magnify our opportunities, cope with our problems, and keep both of them in perspective. (In *Ensign*, Nov. 1993, 94.)

The goal of faith is not a problem-free life. The goal of faith is salvation. (*Sanctuary*, 17.)

VIRGINIA H. PEARCE

We all know that more faith won't make our problems disappear. But I believe as our faith increases, we become more able to not only survive the hard times but become better because of them. I believe faith is the answer. (In *Ensign*, May 1994, 92.)

SYDNEY SMITH REYNOLDS

When we are confident of our own core beliefs, no human theory will upset us. (In *Ensign*, Mar. 1984, 20.)

LOUISE Y. ROBISON

There is a great strength which comes to us when we mingle with those of strong faith, because faith is a strong dynamic power, and its influence is felt by those who come in contact with those who possess it. (In *Relief Society Magazine*, Dec. 1923, 618–19.)

SANDRA ROGERS

Deep, abiding faith in the Savior brings a peace that surpasses understanding, but it also creates the environment and the need for the deepest and least-fettered curiosity and inquiry. (In *BYU Speeches*, 28 June 1994, 180.)

We must have an immaculate faith in and a profound reverence for the one stable thing in our lives—the Savior Jesus Christ and his atonement. This steadying faith can, I testify, carry us through all manner of challenge, disagreement, difficulty, and hurt. (In *BYU Speeches*, 28 June 1994, 183.)

ELLIS R. SHIPP

Our merciful Creator [will] overrule even our deepest afflictions for our eternal joy. This seems to me the only source of peace and consolation in the life of mortal trial and divine test. (*While Others Slept*, 56.)

My blessed faith, the rock upon which I leaned and found a holy strength and peace, enabled me to endure [my trials in the gospel]. . . . Therefore I felt that I could, at any self-sacrifice, join heart and all the powers of my being, in all that was in my *mortal* power assisted by the divine, to be courageous—never doubting, never failing in a cause I fully believed divine! (*While Others Slept*, 52–53.)

How very wonderfully are all things overruled for the good of those who have faith, and trust in the wisdom of God. (*While Others Slept*, 258.)

MARY ELLEN SMOOT

We simply cannot afford to lose sight of the purpose of life, fail to find meaning in our daily struggles, or wander aimlessly from one cause to another. Faith is power: power to

remain true to our divine inheritance as daughters of God. (*Sweet Is the Work*, 17.)

ELIZA R. SNOW

My life, as well as the lives of many others, was preserved by the power of God, through faith; and not on natural principles, as comprehended by man. (In *Women of Mormondom*, 318.)

HELEN MAR WHITNEY

Our faith and enthusiasm have been equal to every emergency. (*Woman's View*, 151.)

Faithfulness

CAROL K. ANDERSON

When people stop respecting themselves and others, confidence and hope die. We all stand near an avalanche; life is unpredictable, and terrible things happen, taking everything with them. But we can stand firm in doing right. (In *Balm of Gilead*, 73.)

JANENE WOLSEY BAADSGAARD

Pioneers were simple people who dusted themselves off, even when the way was rough, and just kept putting one foot in front of the other. (*Families Who Laugh*, 45.)

JANETTE HALES BECKHAM

When we establish a pattern of righteousness in our lives, we com-

mit to our Heavenly Father to do all in our power to help others reproduce this pattern in their lives. (In *Ensign*, May 1991, 84.)

The powers of heaven are available to everyone through righteousness. (In *Ensign*, Nov. 1995, 11.)

GENEVIEVE DeHOYOS

Our inspired leaders . . . remind us again and again that eternal principles are unchangeable, that the ways of the Lord are ultimately and invariably more successful than the ways of men, that there can be no greater challenge than to obey the Lord, and that exaltation cannot be gained without sacrifice. (*Stewardship*, 103.)

Mary Ellen Edmunds

Opposition is evidence of the truth at work. (In *LDS Speaker's Sourcebook*, 302.)

Kim Novas Gunnell

Although it's true that any journey begins with the first step, most journeys don't end there. As important as first steps are, they must be followed by lots and lots of other steps. (In *Living the Legacy*, 75.)

Beppie Harrison

Achieving virtue—indeed, achieving anything but the most superficial forms of competence—is impossible without the Lord. The harder we try to make it on our own, the more certainly we fail. (*Day at a Time*, 78.)

Elaine L. Jack

Patience is an expression of spiritual maturity. (In *BYU Speeches*, 5 Jan. 1997, 132.)

We should not make the mistake of viewing patience as being idle, indifferent, apathetic, or nonchalant. Patience does not abdicate responsibility, nor does it simply give us a seat on the sideline of events. Patience brings balance and perspective. (In *BYU Speeches*, 5 Jan. 1997, 128.)

Patience displays confidence that "not my will, but thine, be done" (Luke 22:42), that all things will be accomplished in the Lord's way. (In *BYU Speeches*, 5 Jan. 1997, 128.)

Virginia U. Jensen

Christ's light and the gospel message of light and salvation can be darkened in our own lives only by our disobedience and lack of faith. In like manner the Savior's light *increases* in our lives as we keep the commandments and strive continually to be like Him. (In *Ensign*, Nov. 2000, 63.)

If we could truly recall for a few moments some dim memory of our premortal existence, we would do anything to assure our return to the Father who sent us here. (In *May Christ Lift Thee Up*, 38.)

Ardeth Greene Kapp

When we live with the Light of Christ in our lives, through our preparation and works of righteousness, we will contribute in a very real way to the dawning of a brighter day in a dark and troubled world. (*Joy of the Journey*, 61.)

Sooner or later, either privately or publicly, we will all be tested. We must be prepared to defend our values, our standards, our commitments, and our covenants to stand as a witness of God at all times, in all things, and in all places. (In *Ensign*, Nov. 1990, 93.)

We are pioneers on a new frontier. . . . When we are determined with every fiber of our being that nothing will stop us from our commitment to follow Christ at all costs, the angels will push our cart and we will make it home. (*Rejoice!* 118–19.)

Commitment requires a level of self-mastery, self-discipline, the ability to make ourselves do what we ought to do until it becomes what we want to do. (*Lead*, 37.)

VIRGINIA H. PEARCE

The people of the city of Enoch are remembered by us as so good—so incredibly good—that the whole city was taken up into heaven. But if we read carefully we see that the city of Zion was taken up into heaven "in process of time" (Moses 7:21). Just like the pioneers, just like you and me, it must have been a *process* of walking forward, step by step, over a long period of time. (In *Ensign*, May 1997, 87.)

BROOKIE PETERSON

Sometimes we think that righteousness will bring relief from trial, but righteousness brings peace, not an easy life. (*Woman's Hope*, 130.)

MARY ANN PRATT

If there are only three who hold firm to the faith, I will be one of that number. (In *Women of Mormondom*, 406.)

LOUISE Y. ROBISON

Our parents and grandparents gave evidence of . . . loyalty. Hundreds of them who had established homes were asked to leave them and take their families into even more unsettled places. As descendants of these brave people we are proud of their devotion, and we cannot do less when the Prophet of God speaks in our day. (In *Relief Society Magazine*, Nov. 1938, 768.)

SANDRA ROGERS

What marvelous principles those early pioneers teach us: To plant the best of seeds without concern for praise or glory; to plant for the use of someone else and not just for ourselves; to contribute something to the lives of people we may never see again; to plant seeds where we are now because it is the right thing to do, even if no one applauds. (In *BYU Speeches*, 28 June 1994, 182.)

MARTHA H. TINGEY

It requires more real courage, force of character and faith in God, to battle with adversity, to meet and overcome the trials and temptations that are the heritage of man, and keep oneself pure and uncontaminated, than is required to face a raging torrent or a roaring cannon. (In *Young Woman's Journal*, Nov. 1907, 545.)

RUTH B. WRIGHT

[Be] true when you are tempted, [be] true when you don't want to be, [be] true when it means standing alone from the rest of the world. (In *Ensign*, Nov. 1990, 79.)

The Heart Is the Key

JUTTA BAUM BUSCHE

One great stumbling block to our progress in faith is rule-keeping that does not spring from an honest heart. (In *Best of Women's Conference*, 69.)

Jesus Christ never condemned the honest in heart. (In *Best of Women's Conference*, 69.)

ELAINE L. JACK

The heart is the key to our influence, for it counts and measures each kindness, each effort, each time we lift, praise, teach, or cheer one another. (In *Ensign*, Nov. 1996, 91.)

We are told to attend Church meetings, work hard in callings, go to the temple, be generous in offerings to the Lord, hold family home evening, and visit one another. But simply being there does not sanctify us; statistics do not drive eternal progression. (In *Ensign*, May 1994, 15.)

ARDETH GREENE KAPP

What lies behind us and what lies before us are not as important today as what lies within us. (In *Arms of His Love*, 2.)

ANN N. MADSEN

We can pray any place, any time—beside a mountain trail . . . kneeling in a closet, anywhere. We are the ones who choose the when and the where. No time is wrong. The only prerequisite is a broken heart and a contrite spirit. And I think *broken* can mean more than the painful process we think of in repentance. *Broken* can also mean open, not hardened and inaccessible but open and ready to receive, to

make place for the Lord's direction. (In *Clothed with Charity*, 94.)

CAROL CORNWALL MADSEN

In the end, whatever our store of good works and pile of accomplishments, or whatever our weaknesses, mistakes, and unfulfilled intentions, God looks on the heart and knows us by what he sees there. (In *Best of Women's Conference*, 332.)

CHIEKO N. OKAZAKI

The Savior does not call us to abandon the world; he calls us to come unto him so that he can heal us and make us whole. But to do that, we have to bring him our hearts—all of the pieces we have given elsewhere. . . . He asks us to take care of our daily activities with a heart centered on him. With whole hearts we can worship him through all those quite ordinary activities of our mortality. (*Lighten Up!* 172–73.)

VIRGINIA H. PEARCE

A pure heart is both the antecedent and consequence of sacrifice. We make sacrifices out of the purity of our hearts. We purify our hearts through sacrifice. (In *Arise*, 269.)

KATHRYN S. SMITH

The Savior taught us that when he comes again in all his glory, all the nations will be gathered, and he will separate them as a shepherd divides his sheep from the goats. . . . I don't think he will look at our clothes, or our muscles, or our skills.

I don't think he will ask to see our bank accounts or the cars in our garages. I think he *will* evaluate the quality of our hearts. (In *Sharing the Light*, 153.)

PEGGY ST. CYR

Commitment will keep our feet on the path that leads us to eternal life in our Heavenly Father's kingdom. (*Conversion to Commitment*, 5.)

Blessings of the Faithful

KAREN J. ASHTON

It's hard to remain downcast or overwhelmed when you realize how blessed you are. . . . Our Heavenly Father has given us "every good thing." . . . He wants us to be successful. We have living prophets to guide us, the Holy Ghost to inspire us, scriptures to enlighten us, priesthood to bless us, and covenants to reassure us. (In *Behold Your Little Ones*, 61–62.)

If we remain faithful we have the Lord's assurance that "ye shall have eternal life" (2 Nephi 31:20). This knowledge should make us the most optimistic, hopeful, cheerful people on the face of the earth. We can go forward with faith, enjoying all that is good in the process. (In *Behold Your Little Ones*, 62.)

MARILYN S. BATEMAN

If we remain true and faithful to the gospel of Jesus Christ and endure to the end, the Lord tells us that the promised land will be ours. The blessings and the riches of eternity will be our inheritance. (In *Best of Women's Conference*, 32.)

ANITA R. CANFIELD

Eternal life is to have the kind of life God has. It is to inherit all that the Father has. But it is much, much more even than that. It is to become like Jesus Christ—to possess every attribute, every sympathy, every quality, every bit of divinity possessed by the Savior himself. It is to be all that we struggle and stretch to be in this life—and more. It is to be free from the pains and chains of weakness and to be full of the love of God. It is the greatest hope there is. (*Perfect Brightness*, 12.)

MICHAELENE P. GRASSLI

There is no question in my mind that my earthly and eternal blessings are dependent upon whether I love God and obey his commandments, keep my covenants, and endure faithfully to the end. . . . I know that if we submit humbly to the will of our Father in Heaven and obey him and follow his prophets, we will be blessed with all the Father has for us. . . . The opportunities open to us now and eternally are limitless! (*LeaderTalk*, 32–33.)

SUZANNE L. HANSEN

Are you afraid that the Lord won't bless you because of past problems you've had? Then you are cheating yourself of blessings he is waiting to bestow on you, right now! (In *Serving with Strength*, 128.)

KIMBERLEY BURTON HEUSTON

The promise of comfort, protection, and power that comes as a result of a life carefully lived according to gospel principles is real. (*Single Parenting*, 64.)

ARDETH GREENE KAPP

When we want what Jesus wants, we will get all that we want and much, much more. We will become joint-heirs with him and receive all of the blessings the Father has promised. (*Joy of the Journey*, 81.)

As children of God we are his heirs, but first we must be tested before we can be trusted with our inheritance—the power and blessings of God our Eternal Father. (In *BYU Speeches*, 1 Feb. 1987, 100.)

CHIEKO N. OKAZAKI

Sometimes blessings flow to us like water from a spring, but more often, I think, they come to us from a well, when we are willing to do the hard work of letting down a bucket and then pulling it up, heavy and dripping. Faithfulness brings forth these blessings. (*Disciples*, 34.)

We have taken upon ourselves the name of Jesus and the way of the disciple. Our way will also lead to gardens of anguished prayer, to crosses, to tombs. At those times, we, like the apostles, must endure in faith and love. We must endure despite our pain, with our pain, in the depths of our pain, until the moment of the resurrection in us when we understand the greater purpose in the cross and the tomb. I testify to you that those moments of understanding and acceptance will come. (*Aloha!* 101.)

PATRICIA P. PINEGAR

Our Father has blessings and eternal rewards available for each of His children, whether they are married or single, parents or childless. Our circumstances may be different, our opportunities may be varied, but the end result of our righteousness can be the same— eternal parenthood, eternal lives. (In *Ensign*, May 1997, 13–14.)

NAOMI M. SHUMWAY

We can . . . be as strong as we must be [only] when we are truly committed. (In *Ensign*, Nov. 1979, 104.)

EMMA SMITH

If we humble ourselves, and are as faithful as we can be we shall be delivered from every snare that may be laid for our feet. (Letter to Joseph Smith, 25 Apr. 1837, Joseph Smith Letterbooks, LDS Archives.)

LUCY MACK SMITH

I covenanted with God that if he would let me live, I would endeavor to get that religion that would enable me to serve him right, whether it was in the Bible or wherever it might be found, even if it was to be obtained from heaven by prayer and faith. At last a voice spoke to me and said, "Seek, and ye shall find; knock, and it shall be opened unto you. Let your heart be comforted. Ye believe in God, believe also in me." (*History of Joseph Smith*, 48.)

ELIZA R. SNOW

We were happy in the rich blessings of peace, which, in the spirit of brotherly and sisterly union, we mutually enjoyed in our wild mountain home, and what we had, seemed to be multiplied as we carefully and thankfully used it. (*Personal Writings*, 30.)

The eyes of the great God are [continually] upon you, and let his approbation be esteemed the richest reward. (*Personal Writings*, 69.)

If you are faithful and true to the profession you have made, you are to become the companions of angels. (*Personal Writings*, 70.)

How awkward you would feel to be introduced into the society of beings filled with intelligence and surrounded with glory if entirely unprepared for such society. (*Personal Writings*, 70.)

BELLE S. SPAFFORD

The richest of spiritual blessings . . . will not come to us, as individuals, through inertia or indifference—they will come only as the result of faithfulness and diligence. They come through knowledge and obedience, sacrifice and service. They come through keeping ourselves attuned to the mind and will of the

Father. (In *Relief Society Magazine*, Oct. 1943, 612.)

Always must we remember that great blessings bring great responsibilities. (In *Relief Society Magazine*, Feb. 1943, 113.)

We all know that everything of worth in life has its price tag. A person must pay the price if he would possess it. In all too many cases, people desire the best but they are unwilling to make the full investment required to obtain it. Our rewards are pretty much commensurate with our investments. (*Woman's Reach*, 124.)

To *endure* is to maintain the capability of holding out, of lasting, of continuing in the same state without weakening or perishing. It is the power to continue under pain, hardship, discouragement or suffering without being overcome. History is replete with goals that have been realized and battles that have been won, not by those who made a brilliant beginning or an impressive first stand but by those who had the power to remain firm, patiently to overcome obstacles, to be constant in their efforts. (*Today's World*, 45.)

ELMINA S. TAYLOR,
MARIA Y. DOUGALL, AND
MARTHA H. TINGEY

We are anticipating a heaven where all our loved ones are a hundred fold dearer to us than now; where we will enjoy each other's society as husbands and wives, and parents and children, where every link in the family chain will be more firmly welded; where every tie that makes our associations pleasant and desirable here, will be purified, intensified and perfected there. (In *Young Woman's Journal*, Feb. 1891, 237.)

DONLU DEWITT THAYER

Eternal life is a state of being, a quality of existence, not a quantity of spiritual acquisitions. (In *Women and Christ*, 132.)

M. CATHERINE THOMAS

One day, when we seek, ask, and knock and the heavenly gate is opened, and we ask permission to enter, I think we will have to present something in ourselves recognizably heavenly in order to gain entrance. (*Spiritual Lightening*, 91.)

We will never meet all the challenges of this dispensation unaided. . . . Only those who have learned how to receive the Holy Spirit for their guide will be able to read the signs and abide those days (D&C 45:57); only those who have studied how to draw on grace, on the divine enabling power of the Lord Jesus Christ, will escape through the means the Lord will provide. (*Selected Writings*, 39–40.)

EMMELINE B. WELLS

Things may look very dark and gloomy, men may be in prison and in bonds, and Satan may have power to afflict the Saints, but they will always have the strength and courage to endure if they live faithful and keep the Spirit of God in their hearts, and when their integrity to God and His Kingdom is sufficiently proven He will come out of His hiding place and manifest His power in the deliverance of His chosen people. (In *Woman's Exponent*, 1 May 1885, 180.)

BARBARA W. WINDER

As we keep a time for regular scripture study and quiet time for prayers, we receive knowledge and inspiration. Then, through obedience, we put that information into action. We are sanctifying ourselves one step at a time as we accept personal responsibility for our actions and honor the covenants we make at baptism, in the temple, and as we take the sacrament each Sunday. We progress by living worthy to receive the blessings available to us, responding to those promptings to serve others, by loving one another, and by trying to obey the prophet's voice in all things. (In *Ensign*, Nov. 1985, 96.)

ELIZABETH ANN WHITNEY

That this is God's work and not man's should be apparent to all those who are acquainted with the history of the saints, their persecutions, their trials, their difficulties, and the marvelous means of their deliverance— when dangerous and various untoward circumstances environed them. (In *Their Own Words*, 203.)

Fasting

SUZANNE BALLARD

Fasting does not change the will of God, but it helps us *learn* His will. (In *Serving with Strength*, 16–17.)

MARY ELLEN EDMUNDS

Charity is developed as we try to more fully live the law of the fast. This important law of God . . . seems tied to responding to those who are hungry, thirsty, and experiencing other needs. And, oh, the promises! As we reach out to others, we will always find God is there. (In *Knit Together in Love*, 44.)

BEPPIE HARRISON

One reason fasting is such a source of spiritual strength [is that] we take advantage of all the continual reminders our bodies give us, and use them as reminders to pray. Without prayer, fasting is simply missing a couple of meals. (*Needles*, 76.)

SHERYL CONDIE KEMPTON

Fasting is an integral part of . . . joy. It is a crucial element in our effort to eliminate every weakness, strengthen every talent, [and] become perfect so that we can rejoin our Father in heaven. (In *Ensign*, Jan. 1978, 13.)

It gives me a wonderful feeling of joy to realize, when I fast, that I am joining the rest of the Church

membership . . . and that we can gain power through unity. (In *Ensign*, Jan. 1978, 12.)

JANET G. LEE

We usually fast alone and in private, but as we draw near to our Heavenly Father, feelings of loneliness disappear. The sacred process of fasting prepares us to receive the guidance and comfort we need. (In *Wisdom's Paths*, 45.)

The prophet Isaiah tells us the Lord promises rich blessings to those who fast, that they will be free from heavy burdens and oppression (see Isaiah 58:6). . . . Through my own fasting, burdens have been lifted as the absence of temporal feasting feeds my spirit. (In *Wisdom's Paths*, 44.)

When we need spiritual strength, or when sadness consumes us, we can turn to the Lord with prayer and fasting. Fasting humbles us in preparation for our request for blessings. (In *Wisdom's Paths*, 45.)

BELLE S. SPAFFORD

Fasting engenders a love for the Lord and for one's fellow men. Those who neglect to fast neglect to fully develop within themselves the true spirit of love for God and man. (*Today's World*, 71–72.)

God the Father

Belief in God

AMY BROWN LYMAN

How anyone can believe there is no God I cannot understand; how anybody can believe that this great earth exists, moves, produces life, by chance; that matter and force, with no supervising intelligence and purpose back of them, could create an earth and could create human life. (In *Relief Society Magazine*, June 1928, 339.)

BELLE S. SPAFFORD

There is no finer, no more wholesome, no more powerful restraining influence than an unwavering belief in God, a God who is continually watching over us. Our belief in God becomes strong through prayer. (*Today's World*, 35.)

M. CATHERINE THOMAS

In the Sacred Grove, Joseph could obviously see that there were two separate, glorified, anthropomorphic beings in the Godhead before either of the Gods had spoken. In a split second Joseph apprehended a truth that had the power to end eighteen hundred years of speculation and pointless philosophizing, centuries of making mysteries out of plainness. (*Selected Writings*, 162.)

God Is a Personal God

JILL TODD BANFIELD

Our Father is interested in all our activities that affect our eternal welfare. He pleads with us to come to him often in prayer and wants us to remember him throughout each day. . . . His arms are outstretched to us in hope that we will reach out for him. (*Draw Near unto Me*, 13–14.)

It is essential that we beckon him to be a part of our lives. It is our responsibility to open the door to him by living a life which will invite him to enter. (*Draw Near unto Me*, 14.)

Somewhere, . . . we have to come to know God. (*Draw Near unto Me*, 82.)

JAMIE GLENN

Heavenly Father is aware of us, our every feeling, and our every need even when we feel far away. He could not love us any more, know us any better, or be more aware of us if we were his only child. (*Walk Tall*, 28.)

PATRICIA T. HOLLAND

We owe it to that divine potential in us to look up to God *without fear*. . . . He knows every one of you and loves you dearly and can call *each* of you by *name*. (In *BYU Speeches*, 15 Sept. 1987, 14.)

CAMILLA EYRING KIMBALL

When we think how fervently earthly parents want their children to grow up in faithfulness, we can appreciate in some small measure the great desire our Heavenly Father has that his beloved children may find their way back to him. (*Writings*, 13.)

AMY BROWN LYMAN

There is something directing this great earth; there is a pilot directing it, together with these great physical forces. It is our Heavenly Father, who is accessible to all of us. When we keep his commandments and obey his words, we can draw near unto and receive help from him. (In *Relief Society Magazine*, June 1928, 340.)

ANN N. MADSEN

Dare the encounter with God. It is up to each of us. We must choose. God does indeed stand with His arms outstretched, waiting, and a voice within us demands that we ascend. (In *As Women of Faith*, 165.)

DEBORAH ELDREDGE MILNE

It's comforting to know that I will never live in this world without parents, even when my mom and dad die. Although circumstances may make me feel abandoned or alone, I am less than inches away from a Heavenly Father who loves me more than I can imagine. (*Reflections*, 36.)

ELLIS R. SHIPP

In my own abilities I have no confidence, but there is One whom I can trust, One upon whom I can rely. No other friend is near to guide and aid me. Without Him I would be all alone, *all alone*. (*While Others Slept*, 226.)

BARBARA B. SMITH

A personal relationship to God is essential for a firm foundation. (In *Best of Women's Conference*, 497.)

M. CATHERINE THOMAS

As the unredeemed soul . . . closes the gap between himself and his Maker, he perceives the contrast as so overwhelmingly great that he is sorely tempted to shrink back, to give up the quest. Those who will not be redeemed do shrink, overcome by fear of this encounter (e.g., the Israelites in Exodus 20:18–21); but those who are determined to be redeemed press boldly on, and, exercising mighty faith, penetrate the veil, and receive the transformation they so desire. (In *Temples*, 392.)

MARGARET J. WHEATLEY

It is true that when we suffer, we very often draw closer to the Lord. One path to the Lord is through trials and tribulations. . . . There are other ways God will participate in our lives if we invite him. I believe we spend far too much time appreciating the difficulties by which God tests us and not nearly enough time celebrating how easy life can be in the hands of this loving, creative, and artistic being who is our Father in Heaven. (In *Women and Christ*, 36–37.)

God's Love

LINDA R. ARCHIBALD

As children of our Father in Heaven, we are loved by Him in the only way His perfection allows Him to love us: perfectly, unconditionally. This means that He loves us always, under all circumstances. His love does not increase or decrease as a result of who we are, how we look, what we have, or what we do. (*Sunshine in My Soul*, 60.)

CHERYL BROWN

It is no small thing to turn a regular person into something godly. . . . This is the work in which he who is the greatest of all, who understands the real worth of all things, who could be engaged in any work he desires, this is the very work in which he is engaged. (In *BYU Speeches*, 11 May 1993, 108.)

ELAINE CANNON

One blessing to be grateful for is this knowledge of God's love for his covenant children. Regardless of what we suffer or how we are tried, he will help us and we can then be humble witnesses of him, for we know things that other people don't know yet! (In *Sunshine for the LDS Woman*, 114.)

Heavenly Father yearns for our success in life and our safe return to his presence. (In *Sunshine for the LDS Woman*, 114.)

The love of God assures us of the purpose of life. He knows of our crises and our deepest cares. Not always will he eliminate our trials at the moment. But he will love, support, sustain, and supply us with hope that all things will work to our good. We are not forgotten by him. He takes our burdens on his back. He weeps with us, so to speak, and does not leave us alone in our trials. (*Love You*, 56.)

God loves us because *he* is good, not because we are. (*Love You*, 129.)

RUTH HARDY FUNK

The one whose name this church bears has equal and unconditional love for each of his children—both those who know him and those who do not know him so well. Whatever your current situation, . . . he reaches out to you. (In *New Era*, Jan.–Feb. 1979, 38.)

BARBARA DAY LOCKHART

Knowing that Heavenly Father truly loves us and trusting that it is vital to Heavenly Father that we come home to him are some of the greatest motivators that we can have to give us the genuine desire to be true to him. (In *BYU Speeches*, 12 May 1992, 97.)

Filled with [God's] love, we love God, we lose our desire to do evil, and, more than anything, we want to be like him and be with him. (In *BYU Speeches*, 12 May 1992, 102.)

When we realize that each and every person is loved by Heavenly Father, it prompts us to love each and every person, too. (In *BYU Speeches*, 12 May 1992, 102.)

Once we are filled with [God's] love, we cannot help but stand in awe of his love for us and be grateful for who we are. (In *BYU Speeches*, 12 May 1992, 102.)

KATHLEEN LUBECK

[Heavenly Father] sees the great good inside of us; he knows what we can do and what we can be. He also knows our weaknesses, and he has provided the gospel to help us overcome them. . . . He loves us so much that he sent his Son, Jesus Christ, to pay the price for . . . mistakes we make—to atone for our sins. He let his Son suffer for each of us so we can repent, be washed clean of our sins, and return again . . . , pure and sweet. (In *Living the Young Women Values*, 2.)

Heavenly Father loves each of his children—always, unconditionally, and with such an intensity that it is hard to fully understand. When we're hurting . . . he is concerned and is there to help us. When we need someone to talk to, he is always there. . . . When we rejoice and are happy about something, he is happy for us. He will comfort us, bless us, watch out for us, guide us, help us to be the best we can be—and teach us how to grow stronger when we have problems. (In *Living the Young Women Values*, 2.)

JILL C. MAJOR, LAUREN C. LEIFSON, AND HOLLIE C. BEVAN

You are a child of our Heavenly Father and oh, how he loves you! . . . He loves you! And our Savior pleads with each of us to "remember the worth of souls is great in the sight of God." (D&C 18:10.) This includes your soul! (*Encircled by Love*, 53.)

LOUISE Y. ROBISON

We may doubt the word of man, but we cannot doubt the word of God. He has given us his word, that he is with us always, although we are not where we can see him. (In *Relief Society Magazine*, June 1928, 335.)

BARBARA B. SMITH

God's dealings with us are not capricious. He loves us too much for that. His dealings with us are predicated upon eternal principles of righteousness. (In *BYU Speeches*, 9 Feb. 1978, 15.)

KATHRYN S. SMITH

In what may seem to be the darkest of times, if we will but reach up to our Father . . . he will hold our hand through the ordeal. It may be that he will tenderly lead us out of the "flames." *But if not*, we must still demonstrate which team we are on in each decision each day of our lives. (In *Feeling Great*, 37.)

MARY FIELDING SMITH

I have sometimes of late been so filled with the love of God, and felt such essence of his favor as has made me rejoice abundantly indeed. (*Mary Fielding Smith*, 37.)

A. D. SORENSEN

Divine love has for its ultimate aim that humankind avoid [spiritual] death and realize everlasting fulness of life. The achievement of that aim represents . . . the highest possibility of humankind, their ultimate good, and the final purpose of God. . . . Divine love also makes possible, indeed literally constitutes, fulness of life. (In *As Women of Faith*, 55.)

Gospel of Jesus Christ

Plan of Salvation

ELAINE CANNON

What will never change is God's system and his principles—the laws irrevocably decreed in heaven before this earth was—established for man's fulfillment, success, and happiness. (*Not Just Ordinary*, 22.)

MARY ELLEN EDMUNDS

The plan of our Heavenly Father is a great plan of happiness! . . . It is not just a good idea or an interesting thought. It is great; there is nothing greater. And it does lead to happiness—not just in future time, but today, this very minute, moment, and inch of eternity. (*Happiness*, 9.)

CAMILLE FRONK

There was no mysterious alternative gospel taught by prophets of God in ages past. God *is* the same yesterday, today, and forever. There is security in knowing that the rules don't change; the principles and ordinances necessary for salvation are understood and taught by prophets in all dispensations of time. (In *Voices*, 186.)

ARDETH GREENE KAPP

Our Father in Heaven is with us all the way, and he has set the pattern for us. It is a pattern that does not change. It is a pattern based on love and obedience, sacrifice and service. It is a pattern made possible through the atoning sacrifice of Jesus Christ and realized when we make and keep sacred covenants. (In *Arms of His Love*, 2.)

AMY BROWN LYMAN

The plan of salvation includes the principles of the gospel and practical religion, the latter covering instructions on how to conduct our lives, on our duties, on our relationship to our

Heavenly Father, and on our relationship to one another. (In *Relief Society Magazine*, June 1929, 327.)

Fundamental Truths of the Gospel

PAULA CARLSON

Faith is first—faith in the Lord Jesus Christ and in myself that I can do anything through him. . . . Next, hope in his word—a perfect brightness of it. Hope is, for us, a choice. . . . I choose hope. . . . Finally, there must be charity—the pure love of Christ—for all with whom I come in contact. (In *Thy Word Is a Lamp*, 17–18.)

CAMILLA EYRING KIMBALL

The gospel message today is the same as it has always been: love God, follow Christ, serve one another, develop self-mastery and spiritual power, keep the commandments with the assurance that thereby God will be pleased and you will obtain eternal joy, never give up in well doing, continue faithful to the end. (*Writings*, 81.)

Surely Christ is the head of this church. The name of the church is the Church of Jesus Christ. Every prayer is in his name. His life's example and his gospel are the foundation of our faith. His teachings are our constant guide. (*Writings*, 88.)

We . . . say to all who will listen, "Here is more truth than can be found anywhere else in this world because God has established his church to teach his children. . . . Come and share with us!" (In *LDS Women's Treasury*, 323.)

We reject no truth or good to be found anywhere, but we are anxious to share that added truth which we have. All truth is a part of the gospel. (In *LDS Women's Treasury*, 323.)

AMY BROWN LYMAN

Many people . . . are realizing . . . that prayer, faith in God, spirituality, morality, and all the old virtues as taught in the Bible, such as the Ten Commandments and the teachings of the Savior, are worth more than all the modern philosophies of men. (In *Relief Society Magazine*, Nov. 1940, 734.)

It is our faith and our knowledge, based upon the great example of the Savior, that we shall be resurrected. And in this hope of immortality is the apex of the glory of the earth life. (In *Relief Society Magazine*, May 1936, 295.)

Some say, prove immortality. Our answer would be prove truth, prove love. Immortality is its own proof, as truth is its own vindication. (In *Relief Society Magazine*, May 1936, 295.)

BARBARA B. SMITH

The gospel, correctly understood, embraces all that is virtuous, lovely, of good report and praiseworthy. (In *Ensign*, May 1982, 96.)

Purpose of the Gospel

MARILYN S. BATEMAN

The way we are gathered is through the restored gospel and its priesthood and by fully living its precepts. Its purpose is to make us one with Christ and with each other. (In *BYU Speeches*, 5 Jan. 1999, 100.)

SHERI L. DEW

The gospel of Jesus Christ is all about people. It's about leaving the ninety and nine and going into the wilderness after those who are lost. It's about bearing one another's burdens. (In *Ensign*, Nov. 2000, 95.)

MARIE K. HAFEN

The gospel has been given to heal our pain, not to prevent it. (In *LDS Women's Treasury*, 316.)

BARBARA B. SMITH

The gospel is heaven sent. It is the light by which we find our way through darkness and difficult times. (In *Ensign*, May 1982, 97.)

BARBARA W. WINDER

The gospel helps us to put things in their proper perspective, to see the eternal nature of things, and, through faith, to overcome our problems and recognize that many of them are blessings in disguise. (In *BYU Speeches*, 7 June 1987, 154.)

Living Gospel Principles

COURTNEY CARR DAVIES

The Savior's light is always burning brightly for each of us. Its batteries never die, and its bulbs will not burn out. We hold the switch and can turn it on through study, prayer, and personal application of the gospel. Christ's teachings are a lamp unto our feet and a light unto our path, the path that will lead us back to our Heavenly Father. (In *Thy Word Is a Lamp*, 38.)

SUSA YOUNG GATES

Those among us who are true to the teachings of our faith are a mighty light in the world. (In *Young Woman's Journal*, Feb. 1903, 86.)

MICHAELENE P. GRASSLI

If we only dip a toe in the Church, we can't even begin to know what opportunities there are for our personal and temporal growth as well as our spiritual growth. We need to jump in full force with both feet. (In *Children's Friends*, 153.)

ARDETH GREENE KAPP

Much of the emotional and social illness of our day is caused when people think one way and act another. The turmoil inside is destructive to the Spirit and to the emotional well-being of one who tries to live without clearly defined principles, values, standards, and goals. (*Joy of the Journey*, 5.)

When we get the gospel on the inside and make it part of our very being, we have not just changed our habits; our habits have literally changed us—a mighty change. (In *BYU Speeches*, 1 Feb. 1987, 105.)

CAMILLA EYRING KIMBALL

Living the gospel is not the easiest way of life, but it is the most rewarding way. (*Writings*, 86.)

AMY BROWN LYMAN

The finest standards of living are the gospel standards. (In *Relief Society Magazine*, May 1932, 298.)

It is much easier to believe and to testify of our beliefs, than it is to live them. (In *Relief Society Magazine*, June 1929, 327.)

The gospel of the Master is the greatest source of spiritual strength known to man. It is a philosophy of unselfishness and brotherly love, gentleness and peace, faith and hope. If the Christian peoples of the world who are believers could live it, they would not only experience the greatest happiness, joy and satisfaction they have ever known, but they would be a blessing to their fellowmen. (In *Relief Society Magazine*, May 1941, 345.)

The most powerful and sustaining force in helping us to meet the realities of life is religion. (In *Relief Society Magazine*, May 1933, 293.)

ANN N. MADSEN

Truth demands our allegiance, but to accept and love others, we need neither adopt their ideas nor be condescending. We can be strong in testimony, shining with that light which cannot be hid. When others differ from us in these essential matters, we must learn to see with eyes that separate people from their traditions and/or sins. Mistaken beliefs may be held by good people. (In *BYU Speeches*, 20 July 1982, 185.)

BARBARA B. SMITH

We speak often in our worldwide Church about translation. Computers are being employed to assist, and hundreds of language specialists are engaged in this important work. But the translation for which we each bear personal responsibility is converting the words of the gospel into actions, attitudes, and habits. (In *Ensign*, Nov. 1982, 82.)

The word of the gospel as it is preached and learned is, for each of us, the beginning. "Knowing" alone is not always sufficient to bring the promised light. We have to live by every word. (In *Ensign*, Nov. 1982, 82.)

It is often said to me that the ideal is too much to strive for, because in falling short of perfection there is too much pain, too much sorrow, too much guilt. But it is the responsibility of the Church and its leaders to teach correct principles. Each individual must apply those principles as best he can—trying, failing, repenting, trying again, and finally succeeding. (In *Ensign*, Mar. 1979, 22.)

We who have the gospel need to organize our lives to do what has to be done, . . . and in the doing to come to know strength in the Lord. That strength comes when we prepare for his blessings, recognize them, and use his gifts to make his ways our ways. (In *Ensign*, Nov. 1983, 85.)

Mary Ellen Smoot

The gospel of Jesus Christ allows for and encourages diversity, but not at the expense of sacred components and tenets of righteousness. . . . Don't let Satan lead you to believe that your potato salad has to be just like mine, but also don't think you can make potato salad without potatoes. Essential ingredients of the gospel plan must always be in place. (*Sweet Is the Work*, 9.)

Belle S. Spafford

Big trials and little ones seem to be the lot of man. Evil influences are threatening our homes and our families. . . . What are we to do? . . .
There is but one answer: "As for me and my house, we will serve the Lord." In this commitment lies our hope, our peace, our comfort, our strength, and our promise. In this commitment we fulfill our earthly mission, earning for ourselves exaltation in our Father's kingdom. (*Today's World*, 12.)

Heidi S. Swinton

Righteousness is the accumulation of day-to-day living when we live by the words of the Lord. (In *Arms of His Love*, 241.)

Leah D. Widtsoe

No matter what your life work may be—and all well done work is ennobling—seek to understand and live daily the Gospel of Jesus Christ. (In *Improvement Era*, July 1936, 472.)

Barbara W. Winder

If we rely on the Lord, live his gospel, converse with him daily, and are obedient to his teachings, he will provide the way for us to accomplish his work! (In *BYU Speeches*, 7 June 1987, 154.)

Blessings of the Gospel

Sheri L. Dew

The gospel is the Good News that provides us the tools to cope with the mistakes, the heartaches, the disappointments we can expect to experience here. (In *Ensign*, Nov. 1998, 94.)

Joanne B. Doxey

The gospel of Jesus Christ teaches us a way of life that, if followed, will help us avoid the stumbling blocks and the detours that draw us off course and beckon us to follow the ways of the world. (In *Ensign*, Nov. 1989, 89.)

MARY ELLEN EDMUNDS

Because of the gospel, we are privileged to have confidence in our dreams of a better world and an eventual place of peace, rest, and endless happiness. (*Happiness*, 29.)

This gospel of Jesus Christ is our source for a perfect brightness of hope. (*Happiness*, 29.)

RUTH MAY FOX

When one calls to mind the spiritual darkness under which the world labored for so many centuries and the confusion and perplexity of the nations at the present time, it is indeed a cause for rejoicing that we are living in a day when the Everlasting Gospel has been restored and with it the keys and laws for its administration. (In *Relief Society Magazine*, July 1938, 470.)

RUTH HARDY FUNK

The gospel is the vehicle whereby almost every life you touch is touched and changed in some miraculous sort of way for good if you allow the Holy Ghost to lead you. (In *Keepers*, 117.)

SUSA YOUNG GATES

There is a heavenly peace and communion within the folds of the gospel which the world can neither give nor take away. (In *Improvement Era*, Apr. 1907, 452.)

FLORENCE S. JACOBSEN

What people seek . . . is in their midst. It is so close, they do not see it, and it is so simple, they cannot understand it: the gospel of Jesus Christ. (In *New Era*, Nov. 1971, 36.)

AMY BROWN LYMAN

No better plan of life can be offered anywhere for improving the world than the Gospel Plan of Life and Salvation. (In *Relief Society Magazine*, May 1934, 289.)

BARBARA B. SMITH

When we live the principles [of the gospel], we are promised that they will be a light unto us. As we come to know that light, it will lead us through the mist of darkness, and as we begin to bring that light into our homes, it can become a beacon to our children, and to their children, and to theirs. (In *Ensign*, Nov. 1982, 85.)

MARY FIELDING SMITH

The more I see of the dealing of our Heavenly Father with us as a people, the more I am constrained to rejoice that I was ever made acquainted with the everlasting covenant. (*Mary Fielding Smith*, 100.)

ELIZA R. SNOW

We shall be held accountable to God not only for the privileges we inherit from our fathers, but also for the blessings we enjoy as Latter-day Saints. (In *Keepers*, xii.)

BELLE S. SPAFFORD

The spirit of the gospel . . . causes [women] to reach out for immortal treasures; it leads them into experiences that bring enduring joy; it subdues selfishness and crowds out the spirit of criticism and fault-finding; it dissipates fear and builds confidence; it engenders a recognition of and a respect for an inspired Church leadership . . . ; it lifts them above the mean and petty things in life into the realm of that which is of good report and praiseworthy; it enables them to live useful, happy lives. (*Today's World*, 4.)

MARY KAY STOUT

There is no more inclusive and effective approach to lifting our burdens than understanding and living the gospel of Jesus Christ. (In *To Rejoice As Women*, 292.)

ELIZABETH ANN WHITNEY

The gospel has been to me . . . a fresh revelation of the Spirit day by day, . . . [and] a most implicit faith in a divine power, in infinite truth emanating from God the Father, the fountain from which we must never depart . . . if we mean to conquer as individuals. (In *Woman's Exponent*, 1 Aug. 1878, 33.)

ZINA D. H. YOUNG

It is through obedience and humility that we gain the blessings of the Lord. (In *Woman's Exponent*, 1 Nov. 1887, 85.)

The Lord has been so merciful to us and the Gospel is so grand and so glorious, there is in it such an inspiration, a power, a peace that the world knows nothing of. It is a very foretaste of heaven . . . —it is so soul-satisfying that we have no room for hard feelings. (In *Woman's Exponent*, 15 Mar. 1899, 118.)

Gratitude

GERALDINE P. ANDERSON

There isn't a word in all the English language with more magic in it than the word *gratitude*. Love makes fertile the soil for things to blossom and to grow, and love begins with gratitude. (In *Ensign*, Mar. 1971, 53.)

People who take time to truly pour out their hearts in gratitude, who frequently count their blessings before [the Lord] verbally and praise him for his goodness, are the ones who talk to him in an easy and personal manner. Isn't this the way all great prophets have approached their Maker? (In *Ensign*, Mar. 1971, 53.)

JANENE WOLSEY BAADSGAARD

I believe we uncover the place of rest deep inside us when we allow a space in our hearts for gratitude, when we open ourselves to the realization of life's abundance. We are never truly prosperous until we realize that our lives are full of riches that money can't buy. (*Family Finances*, 132.)

JOYCE BACA

It is important to cultivate the attitudes of appreciation and gratitude. No matter how bad the situation is, some good can always be found. (*Divorce*, 19.)

JILL TODD BANFIELD

No matter what the reason or how awesome the task may appear, we cannot excuse ourselves from the responsibility of returning thanks to God. (*Draw Near unto Me*, 19.)

We must seek to make thanksgiving our initiative to find [God] before our lives are crippled with trials and we are compelled by despair. (*Draw Near unto Me*, 21.)

ANYA BATEMAN

If we are to express our gratitude and give credit where credit is due for our Father's gifts to us, then we have to identify what those gifts are. Acknowledging our gifts is a righteous endeavor, not an unrighteous one. And who can better help us identify our gifts than he who gave them to us? (*Talent Race*, 38.)

ELAINE CANNON

Consciously and deliberately counting my own blessings has long been a healing therapy for me. I strongly recommend the method as superior for a satisfying life. . . . Remembering the blessings we do have crowds out desperation and self-pity. How sweet it is to name our blessings one by one—to literally marvel at what God has done! (*Gatherings*, 186.)

It is good for the soul of both giver and receiver when gratitude is exchanged. (*Count Your Blessings*, 63.)

ELAINE S. DALTON

I am grateful for the dailyness. . . . Nature shows the strength and joy of dailyness. I am grateful for daily sunrises and sunsets, for the stars' and moon's appearance daily. In times of great stress and trial, the routine things sustain us—daily prayer and daily scripture study. (In *Every Good Thing*, 249.)

MARY ELLEN EDMUNDS

I have been making a conscious effort to expect less and appreciate more. This change is making a noticeable difference in my life. (In *LDS Women's Treasury*, 352.)

Remembering is tied to gratitude and contentment. When we forget about our abundance of blessings, we tend to become unhappy. Forgetting can bring feelings of impatience, selfishness, and greed. Remembering, on the other hand, helps us feel happy in our abundance and more responsive to promptings to share it. (*Happiness*, 168–69.)

Sometimes our stress and discouragement, our unhappiness, our feelings of burnout and hopelessness, are a result of forgetting . . . how much Heavenly Father has helped us in the past, and . . . how much He wants to help us now and in the future. We forget to ask for His help. We forget how much He has promised to those who knock, seek, and ask. (*Happiness*, 168.)

SUSA YOUNG GATES

Ask Him to show to you what your real blessings are, and to make your burdens so light and desirable that you will become a shining pillar of glory to every one around you. (In *Young Woman's Journal*, Oct. 1894, 31.)

MARJORIE P. HINCKLEY

"Thank you" is a wonderful phrase. Use it. It will add stature to your soul. (In *Glimpses*, 91.)

Never let a day go by without saying thank you to someone for something—and especially to your Heavenly Father. (In *Glimpses*, 91.)

A grateful heart will give you a touch of refinement that can come in no other way. (In *Glimpses*, 90.)

ELAINE L. JACK

People who are spiritually mature are people who are truly grateful. (In *Ensign*, July 1995, 49.)

When we see most clearly, we see the Lord's hand in everything. (In *Ensign*, July 1995, 50.)

The truly grateful . . . dwell on the goodness of life, even while acknowledging there may be more adversity than there are words to write it. (In *Ensign*, July 1995, 50.)

To thank the Lord for his blessings to us is to understand how good life is, even when it seems unpleasant, unsuccessful, or just plain hard. (In *BYU Speeches*, 3 Jan. 1993, 51.)

There is a definite link between gratitude and spirituality. To begin to feel gratitude, we first have to recognize and be aware of the blessings around us. . . . I believe that personal peace and increased humility often follow our expressions and feelings of gratitude. (*Eye to Eye*, 34.)

LUCILE JOHNSON

It is no secret that ungrateful people are discontented people, and thankful people are happy. Discontent is a by product of ingratitude. (*Enjoy the Journey*, 16.)

BROOKIE PETERSON

Gratitude will help us cultivate so many virtues! It provides a fertile seedbed for a humble heart; it promotes an obedient heart. Best of all, it prepares a heart to develop faith in the Lord Jesus Christ. (*Woman's Hope*, 119.)

Our Father requires our thanks and our worship of him, not for his own gratification but for the good of each one of us, his children. He knows that through appreciation to him for his blessings we can develop faith in him. (*Woman's Hope*, 118.)

Through appreciation and prayers of thanksgiving we grow spiritually. (*Woman's Hope*, 118.)

ESTHER RASBAND

When we are truly and fully grateful, we also see those personal gifts that God has given us. We see the good in ourselves because it would be ungrateful not to see it. It is an awareness that is associated with God, however, and not with ourselves. It is gratitude and worship. It is peace, not pride. (*Confronting the Myth*, 66.)

Happiness requires gratitude, and gratitude creates happiness. (*Confronting the Myth*, 101)

MARY ELLEN SMOOT

One of the best ways to invite the Holy Ghost into our lives is to be grateful. When we kneel in sincere prayer and give thanks, the windows of heaven open for us. At such moments, we cannot help but be filled with charity. (*Sweet Is the Work*, 68.)

ELIZA R. SNOW

To be able to perform the many duties and labors of love required of me is certainly worthy of a higher tribute of gratitude to God, the Giver of all good, than I am capable of expressing. (*Personal Writings*, 42.)

SHIRLEY W. THOMAS

We all, at times, succumb to the tendency to discount what we have or fail to realize the value in what we have because of focusing so much on what we want. (In *Ensign*, Feb. 1982, 61.)

While we count [blessings], we concentrate our attention upon the encouraging, the positive, the happy. It gets our mind away from loneliness or pain. . . . We need to count our blessings because it causes us to look more closely and not miss those quiet blessings beyond price. (In *Ensign*, Feb. 1982, 60, 62.)

LISA RAY TURNER

Gratitude is more a virtue, like hope or faith—something that may not come naturally but can be learned (or relearned) by becoming as little children. (In *Ensign*, July 1992, 52.)

MERCEDES WIEDERHOLD

Gratitude is the much-needed miracle salve that can heal our spiritual wounds. When I generously apply the balm of gratitude on a painful spiritual sore, not only does the wound heal but instead of unhealthy tissue, I have much stronger, pliable skin that can withstand inclement circumstance. (In *Balm of Gilead*, 29.)

Sin is usually so easy to commit but so very hard to deal with in its effects. When I use the balm of gratitude to cleanse the wound left by sin, I find our Savior comes to add his strength to complete the task. Gratitude not only creates in me a desire to forgive, but it also helps me to understand that I am forgiven. (In *Balm of Gilead*, 30.)

Grieving

KATHLEEN RAWLINGS BUNTIN

Grief is not a luxury. It is not a self-indulgence. It is not a sign of weakness. Grief is a psychological necessity. It is making "real" inside of ourselves an event that has already occurred outside of ourselves. It is teaching the heart what the head already knows. It cannot be forced or consciously controlled or scheduled to a timetable. It is a pain that must be felt and processed. Grief is work. (*All Alone*, 8.)

Resolving grief is more than just accepting the death. It involves gradually reinvesting that emotional energy, not in the past, but in the future; not in pain, but in growth. (*All Alone*, 62.)

ELAINE CANNON

Grief must have its day. We have been counseled to weep and mourn for those we have loved well. But let us not forget the value of God's counsel that we seek help as he has provided, that we may get on with life, with our individual mission on earth and not waste time unduly in self-pity or adjustment. (*Gatherings*, 266.)

The partners in a celestial marriage know they'll be reunited some day. So it's more than mere comfort that's needed when the trial of supreme loneliness comes; it is direc-

tion for living without being more lonely than one can bear, a method for arriving at peace and keeping hope in one's heart. (*Ensign*, May 1973, 41.)

LUCY GRANT CANNON

Sorrow and joy [are] two of the great factors that come into life to make it real. (In *Keepers*, 62.)

AFTON J. DAY

It is not weak to allow yourself to grieve at the loss of someone you love, but it is weak to be so engulfed in grief that you refuse eventually to look forward to the time when the grief will have passed. (*Perfect Wife*, 99.)

Because of our religious beliefs as Latter-day Saints, death does not have the aspect of hopelessness and finality that can be overwhelming. It is comforting to know that death is simply the passing of a spirit from one realm to another. The comforting powers of the Holy Ghost, too, can be of tremendous help in times of bereavement. (*Perfect Wife*, 100.)

CHRISTINE DURHAM

Mourning opens us up. Pain softens our hearts. Hurt renders us available to messages and teachings that we would otherwise not heed. (In *Every Good Thing*, 330.)

DEANNA EDWARDS

The process of grief . . . involves reconciliation and forgiveness. We have to forgive the person who died for leaving us with loneliness and unfamiliar responsibilities. We need to forgive ourselves for those acts of omission and commission we suspect hurt the person who died. . . . We need to forgive those who say and do insensitive things. . . . We need to forgive others whose carelessness or neglect contributed to the death of someone we loved. . . .

Without forgiveness we become stuck in the quicksand of the pain and resentment of unresolved grief. But complete forgiveness frees us. . . . It allows us to discover our talents and abilities and complete our own missions on this earth. (*Grieving*, 52–53.)

There is a difference between "good grief" and "bad grief." Good grief will propel us into a process of growth that will give us a deeper spiritual understanding of eternal progression. It will help us to see why there has to be opposition in all things, and we will come to see the benefits of pain. . . .

Bad grief is the act of internalizing pain to such an extent that we begin to focus only on ourselves. . . . Our own needs become so great that we begin to drain the energies and resources of the people around us. Our feelings of low self-esteem can create dependence on the goodness offered us, and foster a subtle resentment on the part of loved ones. (*Grieving*, 98.)

God has a great heart! Only He knows of the conditions and circumstances that cause people to take their own lives. . . . To be nonjudgmental is the most important attribute we can have when we are trying to help a family who has experienced this tragic loss. (*Grieving*, 155.)

It is important to remember . . . that we do not have to leave a loved one who dies behind. . . . If we are going to be together through the eternities we might just as well get used to having them here with us in mortality, if only in spirit. . . . Do something special in memory of your loved one. . . . The veil is very thin. (*Grieving*, 187.)

CARROLL HOFELING MORRIS

Some in the Church have the mistaken notion that if a person grieves a loss—especially the loss of a loved one—it indicates that they are lacking in faith. . . . Because of this attitude, they do not know how to perform one of the important tasks of a baptized member of the Church, to mourn with those who mourn and comfort those who stand in need of comfort. (*"Why Do I Hurt?"* 109.)

CHIEKO N. OKAZAKI

Grieving is a process. It's okay to experience that process. To deny the bitterness of the sorrow is to deny some of the sweetness of the comfort when it comes. (*Disciples*, 171.)

Holy Ghost

Blessings from the Holy Ghost

ANITA R. CANFIELD

The Holy Ghost has the power to come to our level and help us get to God's level. (*Young Woman*, 51.)

ELAINE CANNON

The Holy Ghost . . . witnesses that Jesus is the Christ, the Son of God, and the Creator. The Holy Ghost also warns of danger, instructs in sacred knowledge, and helps the individual discern right from wrong. This is an awesome blessing from God. (*Not Just Ordinary*, 134.)

SUSANNE JOHNSON DAVIS

The Holy Ghost is the revealer and testifier of all truth. Even though he is a spirit, he has the form and likeness of a man. He can only be in one place at one time, but his influence can be felt everywhere at the same time. Because he has no body, he can dwell in us to help guide and direct us in paths of righteousness. He is our Heavenly Father's messenger and is a sacred gift to us. (In *BYU Speeches*, 5 Aug. 1997, 352.)

Having the Holy Ghost as our constant companion brings peace to our hearts and minds and allows us to understand the things of God. (In *BYU Speeches*, 5 Aug. 1997, 352.)

The Holy Ghost can temporarily guide a person without that person receiving the "gift of the Holy Ghost," but the guidance will not continue unless one is baptized and confirmed a member of The Church of Jesus Christ of Latter-day Saints, and then only if one lives worthily. (In *BYU Speeches*, 5 Aug. 1997, 352.)

AFTON J. DAY

The person who is guided from within has several advantages. First, she seldom has trouble establishing priorities; second, by relying on the Spirit for direction she is also in a position to expect, and receive, extra heavenly help; and third, by receiving affirmation that she is doing the Lord's work she is less likely to become angry with other people for attempting to manipulate her or control her life. (*Coming Up*, 20.)

SHERI L. DEW

The Holy Ghost enlarges our minds, our hearts, and our understanding; helps us subdue weaknesses and resist temptation; inspires humility and repentance; guides and protects us in miraculous ways; and gifts us with wisdom, divine encouragement, peace of mind, a desire to change, and the ability to differentiate between the philosophies of men and revealed truth. (In *Ensign*, Nov. 1998, 95.)

The Holy Ghost is the minister and messenger of the Father and the Son, and He testifies of both Their glorious, global reality and Their connection to us personally. Without the presence of the Spirit, it is impossible to comprehend our personal mission or to have the reassurance that our course is right. No mortal comfort can duplicate that of the Comforter. (In *Ensign*, Nov. 1998, 95.)

LAUREN A. DICK

It is not . . . the light that I can see that brings me security or fills my lamp and sheds light upon my path. Rather, it is a light that I can feel, a light that fills my soul and envelops me with a knowledge that I am, indeed, loved by Heavenly Parents, who watch over me. (In *Thy Word Is a Lamp*, 87.)

BARBARA DI CONZA

The light that emanates from the servants of the Lord as they articulate his word seems very nearly visible. The answering light within me responds and fills my entire being with warmth and power until I feel I will burst. (In *Thy Word Is a Lamp*, 6.)

CHRISTINE DURHAM

My experiences of being filled with the Holy Ghost have been like being visited with fire. It's an experience of beauty, of transcendence, of moving up and outside of one's self, and of seeing one's life from a completely different perspective. It's an experience of going from emptiness to fullness. (In *Every Good Thing*, 333.)

ANN N. MADSEN

The Holy Ghost guides us into the will of God and away from temptation. He speaks directly to my spirit. (In *Clothed with Charity*, 96.)

The Holy Ghost translates and delivers our pleadings and praises to our Father even when we can't find the words to express our deepest joy or darkest sorrow. When you can't find words, trust the Spirit. (In *Clothed with Charity*, 96.)

CATHERINE W. OCKEY

Pride and negligence may close the blinds of my soul, causing my step to falter, but a simple plea, a humble prayer, opens them again. Then the word of the Lord comes to me through the still, small voice of the Holy Ghost, seeping through the cracks and illuminating my whole being. (In *Thy Word Is a Lamp*, 102.)

CHIEKO N. OKAZAKI

The Spirit of Christ is not a luxury to be enjoyed only when we have achieved an ideal environment. It is the essential transforming power that can lift and strengthen us amid the trials of real life, even when our situations are far from perfect. (*Aloha!* 5.)

LOUISE Y. ROBISON

It is necessary that we keep in the homes the spirit of the Lord. . . . There is nothing that can comfort, and cheer, and enable us to see the good there is in life [as well as] the spirit of God. (In *Relief Society Magazine*, May 1932, 294.)

I believe the thing we need now most of anything in the world, is the Spirit of God, to enable us to meet life with trust and faith. (In *Relief Society Magazine*, May 1934, 264.)

MARY ELLEN SMOOT

The gift of the Holy Ghost helps you to see through the fog of this world and find your way back to your Father in Heaven. (In *BYU Speeches*, 10 Feb. 1998, 169.)

The Holy Ghost helps you recognize distractions for what they are. He also gives you strength to resist temptations, and peace when you are faced with difficult . . . conditions. All in all, the Holy Ghost clears the window of your soul and gives you the visibility needed. (In *BYU Speeches*, 10 Feb. 1998, 169.)

ELIZA R. SNOW

I realized the baptism of the Spirit as sensibly as I did that of the water in the stream [during my physical baptism]. . . . I felt an indescribable, tangible sensation . . . commencing at my head and enveloping my person and passing off at my feet, producing inexpressible happiness. (*Personal Writings*, 10.)

MICHELE R. SORENSEN

[My] confirmation [at eleven years old] was a supremely beautiful event. For the first time in my life, I had a name for my most trusted companion. This was my only true friend, the only one who had never deserted me. When I needed it most, that little voice had whispered for me to run. In quiet moments, it had wordlessly spoken peace to my heart. It had always spoken love. Now I knew why the voice was wiser than I was. I knew where it came from, and I knew how I could ask for its guidance. (*Chainbreakers*, 87–88.)

M. CATHERINE THOMAS

When I began to taste the Spirit, I could feel the effects it was having on my emotions, how they were clearing up, how life was smoothing out, how sweet some moments in life were starting to be. (*Spiritual Lightening*, 84.)

The Holy Ghost is the tool for dispersing the mists of darkness, for hearing and interpreting spiritual messages. (*Selected Writings*, 235.)

SHIRLEY W. THOMAS

Making the right decisions matters. God wants us to succeed. He wants us to return to him. And the Holy Ghost is our great ally. He sheds the light of truth on decisions we face, until right choices become clear. (In *To Rejoice As Women*, 70.)

The Holy Ghost is . . . a means for the Father to stay close to us. As the Spirit touches our lives, the truth he conveys bears witness of the Father's love. (In *To Rejoice As Women*, 70.)

In the scriptures we learn of the breadth of the role of the Holy Ghost. Besides bringing wisdom, understanding, a sound mind, boldness, power, revelation, testimony, and healing, the Holy Ghost sanctifies. (In *To Rejoice As Women*, 75.)

When we are filled with the Spirit, we have no more disposition to choose anything contrary to the Lord's will; we purify our souls and yield our hearts unto God. That is not always easy. (In *Best of Women's Conference*, 555.)

It is amazing to me that a member of the eternal Godhead can actually be a companion to me and to you. (In *Best of Women's Conference*, 553.)

ANNA TUELLER

The Spirit comforts. . . . How often the Spirit is there healing the broken-hearted, giving rest to the weary, pushing us up one more mountain until we hit a valley, granting us a lull in the storm until we are ready to face it again, . . . dispensing comfort and assurance that all is well, that it is going to be okay. (In *Best of Women's Conference*, 560.)

The Spirit cares, letting us know through a rain-washed spring day, through a speckled sunset, or through the gesture of a grateful student that we matter in this big, silent universe,

that we are not alone, that if the journey seems long, it is not forever. (In *Best of Women's Conference*, 560.)

GAYLA WISE

Any of us who have received the gift of the Holy Ghost are entitled to his companionship. The more purified we become, the more filled we will be by his Spirit. (*Sign of the Son*, 84.)

In a real way, we can grow in the amount of light we have from the Holy Ghost that surrounds us. Eventually we can shine with a glory of our own. (*Sign of the Son*, 84.)

Recognizing the Holy Ghost

ANITA R. CANFIELD

At times we need to "burn" in our hearts, as we do when we ask if the Church is true. At times we feel "warm," as when we listen to an inspired talk. At times we feel calm, as in the face of danger. Probably all these assorted descriptions really do feel very much alike. Depending on our personality and emotions, we find different ways to express the feeling. The most important part is that we are able to recognize the Spirit when we feel it. (*Perfect Brightness*, 114–15.)

The Comforter is described not only as a voice but also as a feeling. Burning, swelling, calmness, warmth, comfort, assurance—these are all words we've heard used to describe the feelings the Spirit brings. (*Perfect Brightness*, 114.)

BARBARA DI CONZA

I have come to recognize the light that accompanies . . . truth as a familiar friend—not so much learning as remembering, not charting new territory but coming home at last. When the Light is turned on, an answering light within us is ignited, which, if we will protect and nurture it, will illuminate our way back to its eternal Source. (In *Thy Word Is a Lamp*, 6.)

CAROLYN J. RASMUS

If we are to be in tune with the Spirit of the Lord we must "turn off" the noise of the world in order to listen, truly listen, to his voice. (*In the Strength of the Lord*, 70.)

SHIRLEY W. THOMAS

What's important is that we identify the Spirit, however it is manifest, and not only recognize it but act upon it. (In *Best of Women's Conference*, 553.)

Most daily decisions we make are guided by peaceful feelings or by promptings—the quiet workings of the Holy Ghost—still and small. (In *Best of Women's Conference*, 554.)

Many decisions must be made quickly, and for me, it is in these, with the continual fine-tuning of my will to the Lord's that these require, that I most often sense the com-panionship of the Holy Ghost. (In *Best of Women's Conference*, 554.)

Spiritual Gifts

MARILYN S. BATEMAN

Gifts of the Spirit, especially charity, are like a gyroscope. They are internal. Like a gyroscope they are steady and sure amidst the changing fads of the world. As part of our education for eternity, we must seek a principle-centered life. This is a life where the gyroscope—our real self—maintains an equilibrium and direction based on eternal truths rather than on the signals generated by others. (In *BYU Speeches*, 9 Sept. 1997, 11.)

JAYNE B. MALAN

Not all are given every gift, but what each person has been given is important to the whole. And to all of us he has given the ability to love, to care for, and to nurture others. He expects us to use these gifts to bless the lives of others. (In *Living the Young Women Values*, 21.)

Conditions of Receiving the Holy Ghost

DONNA LEE BOWEN BARNES

Although through the Spirit of Christ we can be given all the help, strength, and comfort necessary, to gain . . . spiritual help for ourselves certain things are expected: that we are righteous, that we obey the precepts and commands of the gospel, and that we seek help from the Lord on our knees in prayer. . . . [The Spirit] is available to those who truly desire it and are willing to humbly do as they are commanded. (In *As Women of Faith*, 80.)

DIANE BILLS

The Holy Ghost is the light or lamp that guides our lives. It is not possible for us to share our oil, which is the price we have paid to have the companionship of the Holy Ghost. The oil is everything we do in our lives that helps us to have the Holy Ghost as our guide. (*Trust in the Lord*, 36.)

ELAINE CANNON

When you were baptized and confirmed you were given the gift of the Holy Ghost. Cultivate that gift. Invite the Holy Ghost into your life. Live purely since the Holy Ghost cannot function in impurity. It is a most precious gift and will tell you right from wrong, instruct you, guide you, and witness to you that you are a child of God, who loves you. (*Bell Ringer*, 50.)

The Holy Ghost cannot—repeat, *cannot*—dwell in an unclean being. . . . The Holy Ghost cannot function where there is wickedness or disobedience before God. And if you don't have the Holy Ghost, it's a big loss. (*Not Just Ordinary*, 134.)

XANTHE K. FARNWORTH

The light [of the Holy Ghost] has eased my burdens, brought warmth and healing to my physical body and spirit, given me protection, flashes of wisdom, changes to my countenance, and testimony. This light is strongest when I walk steadily down the road. It grows weaker when I'm distracted by the pleasantness of large and spacious fields away from the bumpy road. (In *Thy Word Is a Lamp*, 47.)

SHERRIE JOHNSON

It is next to impossible to change directly from a negative emotion to a positive one. . . . But if instead we just concentrate on moving the negative emotion to "neutral," or in other words stop the negative actions and feelings until we have control enough to think and reason, then we can follow the promptings within us and move to the positive emotion. In neutral we can gain the help of the Spirit that is necessary to move to the positive. (*Spiritually Centered*, 93–94.)

ARDETH GREENE KAPP

To have the companionship of the Holy Ghost, you must be clean; and to be clean, you must keep the commandments of God. (In *Ensign*, Nov. 1990, 94.)

MARILYNNE TODD LINFORD

What drives the Holy Ghost away? . . . Arrogance, cockiness, breaking any commandment, . . . wickedness, envy, pride, malice, retaliation, intolerance. If we don't want to drive his promptings away, we need to keep the lines of communication open and clear. We must listen and obey. (*Standing Ovation,* 79.)

PATRICIA P. PINEGAR

The Holy Ghost will direct your paths if you listen to His promptings. He will help you discover what you can do to build the kingdom as you open your ears to hear the word of God and open your heart to understand and feel the desire to help. (In *BYU Speeches,* 7 Mar. 1999, 171.)

SALLY TAYLOR

Some knowledge comes quickly, some is revealed little by little, and some will need to be revealed later—in God's time. Some blessings and healings will come later or even in the next life. Sometimes suffering must come before the comfort. If we are humble and submit ourselves to God's will, we will be comforted. (In *BYU Speeches,* 5 Nov. 1996, 80.)

Importance of Obeying the Still, Small Voice

SHERI L. DEW

Is it possible that in this twilight season of the dispensation of the fulness of times, when Satan and his minions roam the earth inspiring deceit, discouragement, and despair, that we who have been armed with the most potent antidote on earth—the gift of the Holy Ghost—don't always fully partake of that gift? Are we guilty of spiritually just "getting by" and not accessing the power and protection within our reach? Are we satisfied with far less than the Lord is willing to give us, essentially opting to go it alone here rather than partner with the Divine? (In *Ensign,* Nov. 1998, 95.)

ELAINE L. JACK

We have within us the Spirit of the Lord to guide us on the path of righteousness. Daily, we choose between temptation and sanctification. We seek spiritual moments as we read the scriptures. We pray and carry that prayer in our hearts. We know the peace that comes from hearing . . . that still small voice that whispers ever so softly. We listen less to the world and more to the promptings from on high. (In *Ensign,* Nov. 1993, 99.)

JILL C. MAJOR, LAUREN C. LEIFSON, AND HOLLIE C. BEVAN

It is important always to act upon . . . little promptings and impressions that you receive. . . . Decide now not to miss any opportunities to show love. Don't dismiss that feeling—act on it! (*Encircled by Love,* 30.)

CHIEKO N. OKAZAKI

Learn to hear what the Spirit tells you. The Lord knows you in ways other people couldn't possibly. (*Lighten Up!* 74.)

We need to listen to that still small voice rather than to the thunderous crashes of public opinion, or the fiery words of people who want us to follow their solutions, or the earthshaking fears and disapprovals of our associates. (*Lighten Up!* 74.)

ANNE OSBORN POELMAN

Listen to and heed promptings from the Holy Ghost! If we're open to those spiritual impressions, the Lord will guide our lives. We can trust him. He will open the right doors, at the right time, and in the right sequence. (*Simeon Solution*, 54.)

MARY ELLEN SMOOT

A still, small voice speaks to us and encourages righteous living. We must listen carefully to His beckoning and search our souls. As we do, clouds of darkness will dispel and the glorious light of God will fill our beings. (In *Ensign*, Nov. 1998, 89.)

HEIDI S. SWINTON

The world may . . . cry . . . loudly for attention, but the still, small voice speaking to the hearts of the Saints will have a far greater impact. (In *Best of Women's Conference*, 532.)

The still, small voice can be heard above the noise of the crowd or in the quiet of our silent prayers. It can catch our attention when we're thinking about something else or sound so loud that we will change direction and go another way. It is a miracle, really, one that reminds us who we are because of who is talking and who we will become if we will listen. (In *Best of Women's Conference*, 532.)

Home and Family

The Importance of Home

MARIAN R. BOYER

That is how the world will be saved—by strengthening every child of God in every home. (In *Ensign*, Nov. 1980, 108.)

JAROLDEEN ASPLUND EDWARDS

If we succeed in creating that subtle miracle called a home, what we create will become the rock that gives substance, meaning, and purpose to life. A home is the beginning of the promises of eternity. (*Things I Wish I'd Known*, 39.)

ELAINE HANSEN HATCH

We today must build a strong, worthy foundation for the return of the Savior. This must be done home by home, family by family. (In *Behold Your Little Ones*, 19.)

MARJORIE P. HINCKLEY

Home is where you are loved the most and act the worst. But I have come to the conclusion that it is in the home where we are tested the most. (In *Glimpses*, 60.)

The trouble with the world . . . is that we don't love each other enough. And if we do, we don't bother to show it, or we don't bother to say it. If the world is to know love, it has to begin at home. It has to be in your heart and mine. And the place to begin is home. (In *Glimpses*, 59.)

VIRGINIA U. JENSEN

In that most important of places, our homes, we learn best how it is that "out of small things proceedeth that which is great," for life at home is a series of small things that combine to create an eternal family. (In *Ensign*, Nov. 2000, 93.)

AMY BROWN LYMAN

If high standards are set and maintained in the home and riveted in the minds and lives of children, they are apt to remain as a guide and influence throughout life. They will form the strongest weapon of defense, and will become as mighty armor in the battle of life. (In *Relief Society Magazine*, Mar. 1936, 142.)

We are a family agency. We believe in the family. We have faith in the family. We feel that the most vital concern of society should be the cultivation and conservation of the family and its restoration and rehabilitation where necessary. (In *Relief Society Magazine*, Nov. 1939, 777.)

CAROL C. OTTESEN

Viewed in its totality, family life has the potential of providing peak experiences not available in any other social situation, as well as potential for being the world's most efficient support system. (In *Mormon Women Speak*, 105.)

VIRGINIA H. PEARCE

Learning in groups is so important that Heavenly Father planned for us to be born into a group—the most basic, most hallowed, and most powerful group on earth: the family. (In *Ensign*, Nov. 1993, 79.)

LOUISE Y. ROBISON

It is in the home, in the intimate contacts of life in the family group, where cooperation, self-sacrifice and service are learned and consequently where appreciation of one another is greatest, and love reaches its highest human level. (In *Improvement Era*, Apr. 1936, 215.)

Home—Family! These words represent not only the highest ideals of life, but they are the stabilizing force of any nation. Security, peace and development depend upon the status of the home. (In *Improvement Era*, Apr. 1936, 214.)

BARBARA B. SMITH

The kingdom of God is made up of sovereign individuals who use their agency to choose to live the laws of heaven. This is the way to exaltation. Eternal truths are best taught and immortal lives are best shaped in a good home. What a challenge it is to be the maker of such a home! (In *Ensign*, Mar. 1979, 22.)

A family provides the best laboratory in mortal existence for developing Christlike qualities. (In *Ensign*, Apr. 1976, 68.)

MARY ELLEN SMOOT

The family unit . . . is an essential element of our Father in Heaven's plan of happiness. (In *BYU Speeches*, 10 Feb. 1998, 167.)

Can you see how families are critical to our mortal experience? We laugh with them; we cry with them; we live for them; we die with them. We need strong families. (*Sweet Is the Work*, 79.)

BELLE S. SPAFFORD

The home should be the first to establish the gauge that will enable youth to measure the true values of life. (In *BYU Speeches*, 8 Nov. 1961, 4.)

The gospel gives to Latter-day Saint mothers the loftiest concept of home and family life known to mankind. (In *Relief Society Magazine*, Nov. 1958, 716.)

[The home] must teach [young people] that they owe something to the world, not that the world owes them, and that the world which lies ahead for them will be of their own making. (*Woman's Reach*, 40.)

MARTHA H. TINGEY

Home is the nursery for tender human plants, where they must receive the careful training that will enable them to grow healthy and strong, physically, mentally, morally and spiritually, that they may develop into useful, noble, Godlike characters. (In *Young Woman's Journal*, Sept. 1903, 398.)

LEAH D. WIDTSOE

The home is the keynote and the beginning of joy and happiness, of stability and progress. (In *Relief Society Magazine*, July 1958, 422.)

JERI J. WINGER

The face of any nation mirrors the family life of her people, for the home is the child's first country and the family the first citizenry. (In *Woman's Choices*, 161.)

Where there is love at home, there will be love of country. Where there is trust at home, there will be trustworthiness in business. Where there is freedom to communicate honestly within the family, there will be courage to communicate honestly in politics. (In *Woman's Choices*, 161.)

ANNE G. WIRTHLIN

Home can be an oasis in the world. It's a place where every child has a right to feel safe. (In *Ensign*, Nov. 1995, 82.)

The Ideal Home

MARIAN R. BOYER

Even the humblest house, if clean and neat, has the foundation for a happy home. . . . To cross its threshold is to know a bit of heaven. (In *Ensign*, Mar. 1976, 76.)

A clean, well-ordered, happy home provides the climate where love and peace abide, where family members find refuge from the troubled world about them. (In *Ensign*, Mar. 1976, 76.)

Every home has a body and a spirit. . . . The physical structure— the material components of food, clothing, and shelter—make up the body; while the faith, devotion, attitudes, feelings, purposes, and love which prevail within the home make up the spirit. (In *Ensign*, Mar. 1976, 75.)

A home is more than a house or a room to live in. . . . The home should be a place of learning, a place where prayer can point the way to eternal life. (In *Ensign*, Nov. 1980, 108.)

In well-ordered homes we must keep bright the spark of testimony and build faith within each heart. (In *Ensign*, Nov. 1980, 108.)

FLORENCE S. JACOBSEN

The home is the castle, the husband the king, the mother the queen, the children the princesses and princes. (In *New Era*, Nov. 1971, 36.)

JANET G. LEE

If we are listening to the Spirit, we will surround ourselves with truth and goodness in each of our earthly homes, making the pathway to our ultimate heavenly home more direct and attainable. (In *BYU Speeches*, 12 Sept. 1989, 20.)

ANN N. MADSEN

There is a spirit that accumulates in a home as righteous people come and go there. (In *Best of Women's Conference*, 315.)

CAROLINE EYRING MINER

The gospel should not be a secret, unacknowledged part of our lives, but basic to our relationships with our children and grandchildren. (In *Ensign*, Sept. 1978, 68.)

MARGARET D. NADAULD

We need to have more reverence in our lives, more holiness, more times of quiet and peace and calm. We need a place where our souls can be nourished and tutored and blessed. Temples are such places. Homes can be such places. (In *BYU Speeches*, 2 Nov. 1997, 11.)

Refinement can add a gentle spirit to a home. (*Write Back Soon!* 87.)

CHIEKO N. OKAZAKI

A sanctuary isn't a fortress that bars people from entering it, and it's not a mausoleum where everything is hushed and still. It's a place of holiness, a place of happiness, and a place of love. Your children, your friends, and your neighbors will be able to feel if your home offers a sanctuary. (*Sanctuary*, 5.)

BARBARA N. RICHARDS

Our children, and their children, must be given every opportunity to be raised with every aspect of their lives in tune with the Spirit. (In *Behold Your Little Ones*, 121.)

LOUISE Y. ROBISON

This is one truth that life has taught us—that the supreme joy comes in the home, where there is harmony, peace, unity and love. Surely this source of joy is worthy to endure! (In *Improvement Era*, Apr. 1936, 215.)

ELLIS R. SHIPP

Where religion and learning are combined what a happy household there could be. (*While Others Slept*, 243.)

BARBARA B. SMITH

There may be exceptions but the pattern is clear: an ideal home has both a home-maker and a father-provider. (In *Ensign*, Mar. 1979, 24.)

We need to create a home environment in which the highest qualities of the human spirit—those that bring us individually back to our heavenly parents—can be developed. (In *Ensign*, Mar. 1979, 24.)

A family begins with individuals—with two people who become one, and as children are added, in the spiritual arithmetic of family unity, they will still be one. Parents can provide a protecting shelter, a safe place, and children are made strong by the bonds of their love. (In *Ensign*, Nov. 1981, 83.)

BATHSHEBA W. SMITH

Let love and cleanliness and order rule in every home that our children may not desire to leave the fireside for idle pleasures. (In *Woman's Exponent*, 1 Jan. 1902, 67.)

BELLE S. SPAFFORD

Home as a sanctuary for family members—a place of love, understanding, the sharing of responsibilities, and peace—is far more important than its physical and material character. (*Woman's Reach*, 12.)

If mothers would have the spirit of the home right, they must maintain homes in which the Spirit of the Lord may dwell—homes that daily meet the requirements of righteousness. They must be obedient to the commandment of the Lord to teach their children. (In *Relief Society Magazine*, Nov. 1959, 717.)

Within a good home there must be parental authority, righteously exercised. (*Today's World*, 245.)

The sister with a testimony knows the place and importance of the home and family in the eternal scheme of life. She knows "the earthly home has its pattern in the heavens." (In *Relief Society Magazine*, Nov. 1953, 717.)

Destructive Influences on the Home

SALLY PETERSON BRINTON

Strengthening the family is more vital with each passing day, as new challenges to the strength and solidarity of the home arise. Never before in history have so many insidious influences threatened the family. (In *Woman's Choices*, 84.)

GENEVIEVE DeHOYOS

Today in our age of confusion, everything connected with the proper order of the family is attacked by the forces of Satan and of the world. (*Stewardship*, 103.)

JOANNE B. DOXEY

The adversary, who is the enemy to all righteousness, seeks to thwart the efforts of the Lord's people. His deadly forces are arrayed against our homes. He plans every move with accuracy and precision. There is nothing haphazard or careless about his plan.

Then, can there be anything haphazard about our plan and our efforts to teach this generation in righteousness? (In *Ensign*, Nov. 1989, 89.)

ARDETH GREENE KAPP

In times of war . . . the enemy's first effort is focused on destroying the communication center. In families as well as in nations, when the communication breaks down, the war rages. (*Rejoice!* 67.)

Satan's effective strategy is to do everything possible to stop [a family's] communication and to separate us, if not physically, then emotionally and spiritually. If possible, his plans would have us eating, but not together; praying, but not together; living in the same house, but apart. When parents and youth are isolated and insulated from each other by the lack of communication, there is danger in our homes. (*Rejoice!* 67.)

BARBARA W. WINDER

Do not forget that the Lord desires strong marriages and families. These are not easily achieved in today's world where "siren sounds" of materialism, infidelity, and carnal mindedness pull us toward selfishness and pride. The family is in critical condition! (In *BYU Speeches*, 13 Mar. 1990, 105.)

Strengthening the Family

MARILYN S. BATEMAN

Marriage is the critical relationship in a family. Generally, as the marriage goes, so goes the family. (In *Arms of His Love*, 344.)

JANETTE HALES BECKHAM

It is in an environment of trust that growth takes place. We feel safe to acknowledge mistakes and make corrections. We are more likely to do our best when we feel love and security. It is a place where the Spirit can be felt. (In *BYU Speeches*, 7 Aug. 1994, 190.)

ELAINE CANNON

The most memorable family experiences . . . touch the heart and enrich the spirit. What a family feels together will weld them in an eternal way. (In *Ensign*, Dec. 1973, 5.)

SANDRA MERRILL COVEY

One of the main functions of family life is to build positive memories that tie the children to an eternal family, to teach them the gospel, and to teach them how to love and serve each other and the Lord, so they will have a solid foundation. (In *Wisdom's Paths*, 165.)

It is never too late to begin again. It is never too late to show interest in a child or a grandchild. . . . One sure way to live forever is to build and develop a meaningful relationship with your children and grandchildren. (In *Wisdom's Paths*, 175.)

KARLA C. ERICKSON

Go to your parents for advice. They have traveled the way before and they have learned through experience some of the pitfalls. . . . We need to respect the knowledge and inspiration which our parents previously learned. (*Dandelions*, 72.)

ARDETH GREENE KAPP

It's okay that your parents aren't perfect; no one's are. And it's okay that they didn't have any perfect children either; no one's are. (In *Ensign*, Nov. 1984, 97.)

Our whole purpose is to strive together in righteousness, overcoming our weaknesses day by day. Don't ever give up on each other. (In *Ensign*, Nov. 1984, 97.)

Disappointment and sacrifice can provide the struggles that make you pull together, or become the enemy that will divide and destroy families. You will decide which it will be. (In *Ensign*, Nov. 1984, 97.)

CHIEKO N. OKAZAKI

When you perceive a need in your family, pray for inspiration. Draw on the spiritual strength of . . . your family. . . . Have faith in your inspiration. Have the discipline to be obedient to the whisperings of the Spirit. (*Disciples*, 82–83.)

BARBARA B. SMITH

Accountability is a necessary condition of work. Responsibility brings system to the workings of a family and order to a marriage. Defining responsibilities and planning a method of reporting back fosters freedom from family discord and is also a meaningful stage in developing personal discipline. (In *Ensign*, Nov. 1981, 84.)

BELLE S. SPAFFORD

The knowledge . . . the gospel gives us of the eternal organization of the family is precious to all true Latter-day Saint mothers and serves as a guide in all of their activities in relation to their families. (In *Relief Society Magazine*, Nov. 1958, 716.)

MARTHA H. TINGEY

The strongest and most important foundation stones in home-building are the spiritual and moral influences which pervade the atmosphere, and perfect unity and harmony in the governing powers. (In *Young Woman's Journal*, Sept. 1903, 398.)

WENDY L. WATSON

Commend your loved ones publicly. The best-kept secret in many families is the strengths that mothers see in their children and spouses. (In *May Christ Lift Thee Up*, 47.)

LEAH D. WIDTSOE

Encourage your menfolk to honor and exercise their Priesthood. It is in reality a key that may unlock the door of joy and accomplishment so that all may progress together. (In *Relief Society Magazine*, Nov. 1933, 667.)

Family Life

JANENE WOLSEY BAADSGAARD

Parents spend a lifetime creating a home that the children must leave. It hurts on both ends to learn the difficult art of roots and wings. (*Family Finances*, 20.)

Children and parents grow up together, and it's hard sometimes. We affect each other's lives more than anyone else. We're both struggling to sort out life in each other's presence. (*Family Finances*, 19.)

AFTON J. DAY

This business of educating the eternal family was never supposed to be easy, or painless, or free from opposition. Most growing pains do not occur in the bones or muscles, but rather in the heart. (*Perfect Wife*, 104.)

MARJORIE P. HINCKLEY

Most of us have developed a pretty good set of company manners that we exercise at school and socials and church and other places, but it is what we are at home that tells the true story of what we really are. (In *Glimpses*, 60.)

AMY BROWN LYMAN

In the home the child gets his first lessons in government, religion, and industry. Through the relationships here he learns the meaning of love and service; self-sacrifice and self-restraint; obedience and authority. The members of the family learn to cooperate, to adjust to one another, to adjust to conditions, and to rules and standards of the home. The home environment thus plays a large part in the development or lack of development of its members. (In *Improvement Era*, Mar. 1933, 267.)

BARBARA B. SMITH

Often a woman who is feeling discouraged about her lot lacks nothing more than appreciation from those she serves. It is easy for a family to grow accustomed to the pleasant circumstances of a home and fail to remember the management necessary or the energy and skills required to keep a house running smoothly. (In *Ensign*, Nov. 1981, 84.)

One . . . council in which every member of the Church may participate [is] the family council. It is the one for which all of the others exist. (In *Ensign*, Nov. 1979, 85.)

BELLE S. SPAFFORD

Important as may be the so-called physical aspects of the home . . . we must never lose sight of the fact that the spirit of the home is the lasting element. Its influence goes on long after the physical is forgotten. (In *Relief Society Magazine*, Nov. 1959, 717.)

Memories of the patterns and practices of the parental home, its traditions and ideals, become sweet and treasured possessions which children consciously or unconsciously perpetuate in their own households. (*Today's World*, 230–31.)

In a good home children are genuinely happy and the patterns of life are so favorably impressed upon them

as they contribute to their happiness and well-being that these patterns remain unforgotten and are generally carried over into the homes which the children themselves establish. (*Today's World*, 230.)

Family Prayer

MARIAN R. BOYER

The home should be a . . . place where prayer can point the way to eternal life. (In *Ensign*, Nov. 1980, 108.)

MARJORIE P. HINCKLEY

It is good to kneel as a family and to hear daily expressions of gratitude to our Heavenly Father for the blessings we enjoy. The Lord intended His children to enjoy the good things of life. . . . We must also have grateful hearts. We must teach our children not to take all that they have for granted. (In *Glimpses*, 92.)

BELLE S. SPAFFORD

Prayer unites every heart within the household. It brings composure to the home and peace to the soul. It offers comfort and guidance. It allays fears. It fortifies against evil. (In *Relief Society Magazine*, Nov. 1959, 720.)

There is perhaps no single factor more important in a spiritual home and in building spiritual strength in our children, than the teaching and practice of prayer. (*Today's World*, 28.)

Family Scripture Reading

ELAINE CANNON

In the home, when direction is needed, when a problem or misunderstanding arises, I pray that we may open the scriptures with our youth beside us and find the law irrevocably decreed upon which blessings are predicated. Reading the will of God in the language of God builds reverence and witness and commitment, and we will all live more purely. (In *Ensign*, May 1984, 26.)

ARDETH GREENE KAPP

We must not underestimate our children's ability to respond to the scriptures. We do not always have to feed them a watered-down storybook or animated version of the Bible or Book of Mormon. The language of scriptures has a power and majesty all its own. (*Stripling Warriors*, 54.)

KRISTEN D. RANDLE

We live in a house made of scriptures. They are our walls and ceiling, our foundation and the roof under which we rest. Their words and wisdom are the weave that holds the house together, the windows through which we see all the world. They are the conduit through which so much of our fresh air comes. (In *My Soul Delighteth*, 87.)

A family cannot achieve the kind of depth of love and understanding we Latter-day Saints seek without constant use (do not read *use* as simply *reading*) of the scriptures, that the counsel and wisdom of the prophets and the very words of the Lord can get us through some very tough situations, especially when diligent use of these scriptures is coupled with humility, prayer, and love. (In *My Soul Delighteth*, 79.)

BELLE S. SPAFFORD

The hours spent together with the word of the Lord are bound to develop a close family unity, which, in itself, will bring rich rewards. (In *Relief Society Magazine*, Nov. 1962, 799.)

Family Traditions

SANDRA MERRILL COVEY

When parents, grandparents, and children cultivate traditions that are meaningful to them, and then repeat these traditions, the family is strengthened. (In *Wisdom's Paths*, 153.)

Through traditions, you reinforce the connection of the family. You give a feeling of belonging, of being supported, or being understood. You are committed to each other. You are a part of something that is greater than yourself. (In *Wisdom's Paths*, 153.)

CAMILLA EYRING KIMBALL

Traditions that embody truth and righteous doing reinforce our good intentions. Traditions also provide a link to the past, tying us to those whose traditions we follow. . . . But what the traditions are may be less important than that we establish some pattern. Continuity contributes to a sense of security. (*Writings*, 123.)

BARBARA B. SMITH

Many times . . . it is tradition which preserves life and values when all else seems to conspire to destroy. (*Grandmothering*, 64.)

Love at Home

MARILYN JEPPSON CHOULES

A child will best learn to be kind through having a kind mother and/or father and by being taught the nature and necessity of kindness. (In *Behold Your Little Ones*, 94.)

The child who receives consistent, dependable kindness from a parent is surely among the most fortunate and most blessed of children. (In *Behold Your Little Ones*, 94.)

CAROL L. CLARK

It is from [my friend Blythe that] I learned the great line, "family by affection." . . . Just think of it—we can feel related to the people we love. And this means we can choose to make our family by blood also our family by affection. We can "adopt" and enfold them through the love we feel for them. (In *Knit Together in Love*, 72.)

SHERRIE JOHNSON

I have often wondered what the world would be like if every time a child looked into his mother's face he saw love reflected there. That is possibly one of the best ways to make home a heaven on earth. (*Spiritually Centered*, 12–13.)

ARDETH GREENE KAPP

Our home can be a first-aid station where wounds of all kinds are healed. (*My Neighbor*, 118.)

JENNIE B. KNIGHT

Kindness is an essential qualification in successful parentage. (In *Relief Society Magazine*, Jan. 1940, 56.)

BARBARA B. SMITH

There is perhaps no greater laboratory in the world for the expression of Christlike love than exists in the family. In the close day-to-day contact, we come to know more about giving love than in most situations. (In *BYU Speeches*, 9 Feb. 1978, 18.)

BELLE S. SPAFFORD

Let us make of our homes a sanctuary, a place where the sweet spirit of the Lord may dwell, regardless of the confusion in the world about us. (In *Relief Society Magazine*, Nov. 1950, 727.)

The love and the sanctity of the home should be zealously safeguarded. (In *Relief Society Magazine*, Nov. 1958, 717.)

Children should be cherished with the strongest bonds of affection; there should be the greatest solicitude on the part of the parents for their children. No effort should be too much, no sacrifice too great to protect them from evil and preserve them in righteousness, that none shall be deprived of his eternal blessings. (In *Relief Society Magazine*, Nov. 1958, 717.)

Let each of our homes be a place of such faith, peace, and understanding companionship that wherever family members may go, or whatever experiences they may pass through, the sweet memory of home will bind them to it, buoy them up, and help them to endure without yielding. (In *Relief Society Magazine*, Nov. 1950, 727.)

Love must abide in a well-ordered home, fostered from the very beginning by joyous preparations and a happy welcome for each new life sent by the Father. (*Today's World*, 245.)

The home protects love against destructive influences such as quarreling, bickering, fault-finding, selfishness. Love is nourished by happy, harmonious family relationships, by understanding and an appreciation of one for another, by unselfish consideration of one another, by thoughtful kindness and, at times of special need, by open affectionate tenderness. (*Today's World*, 245–46.)

Zina D. H. Young

Where can we find pure love? In the homes of the Latter-day Saints; there it sits enthroned. If sorrow and death visit such a household there is comfort and relief at hand. (In *Woman's Exponent*, 1 Mar. 1885, 149.)

Hope

We Must Have Hope

Elaine L. Jack

Hope is a personal quality, essential for righteous living. In fact, hope is one of the personality traits of godlike men and women. (In *Ensign*, Mar. 1992, 10.)

[The] three good friends—faith, hope, and charity—become stronger because of their association with each other. Perhaps what is most important about them is that they exist together. (*Eye to Eye*, 6.)

Don't defer hope. Don't put it off, postpone it, or delay it. . . . Physically, emotionally, and spiritually, hope deferred sickens our hearts. To prevent illness, grab onto and hold onto your hope. (In *Ensign*, Mar. 1992, 15.)

Hope holds us steady, firmly bound to our moorings, grounded and settled in our understanding. (In *Ensign*, Mar. 1996, 19.)

Hope is not a fulfillment of what we want but an understanding and peace that comes from living God's laws and valuing his ways. (In *Ensign*, Mar. 1996, 19.)

Hope is a steadying influence. . . . Hope, the anchor, is essential in this world so full of tidal waves. Sometimes those waves slap us from behind. Sometimes we see them coming but cannot stop them or get out of the way. In all cases, hope ties us to safety. (In *Women Steadfast*, 11.)

ARDETH GREENE KAPP

Hope comes from the sure conviction that when we have done our very best, the Savior, by the grace of God, will do the rest. (*Joy of the Journey*, 36.)

COLLEEN H. MAXWELL

How vital it is . . . that we convey hope to our families and a feeling that we are living in extraordinary times with many blessings and opportunities. (In *Arms of His Love*, 384.)

If we choose to do what is right, our eternal hopes are fixed. Disappointments of the day are not to affect our ultimate hopes. We must not mistake today's local cloud cover for general darkness. (In *Arms of His Love*, 378.)

CHIEKO N. OKAZAKI

The sources of hope are the sources of life itself. That's why hope persists, even when experience, reason, and knowledge all say there is no reason to hope. Hope does not calculate odds. . . . It is prepared for either sunny or stormy weather. To choose hope is to choose life. To choose hope is to choose love. (In *Ensign*, Nov. 1996, 89–90.)

Because we are mortal, death is entangled with life. We can choose to feed the darkness and death in our lives, or we can choose to feed the brightness of hope in our lives. (In *Ensign*, Nov. 1996, 90.)

Despair comes when we feel powerless to influence events and when the sources of meaning in our life disappear. Despair is a kind of disorientation so profound that we lose contact with the sources of life itself. (In *Ensign*, Nov. 1996, 89.)

ANNE OSBORN POELMAN

Hope is essential to life. Without it, people can literally shrivel up and die. With hope, they struggle valiantly in the face of long odds. (*Amulek Alternative*, 118.)

MICHELE R. SORENSEN

Hope is the beginning of resurrecting what seems entirely lost. (*Chainbreakers*, 197.)

REBECCA GWYNN STRADLING

Hope grows out of our faith that we are the sons and daughters of

God and that we can be like him. What great expectations that hope will build in us! (In *Ensign*, July 1981, 29.)

Hope gives us the ability to expect that, when we see as we are seen and know as we are known, what we are will be good. Hope of this eventual perfection gives us strength to repent of small and serious weaknesses alike. (In *Ensign*, July 1981, 29.)

DWAN J. YOUNG

Despair is the enemy of our souls. It can paralyze us, halt our progress, and cause us to lose our way. But hope awakens us like a light shining in the darkness. (In *Ensign*, Nov. 1986, 86.)

The Lord wants us to be filled with hope—not just because it points us to a brighter tomorrow, but because it changes the quality of our lives today. (In *Ensign*, Nov. 1986, 86.)

Hopeless may be the saddest word in our language. (In *Ensign*, Nov. 1986, 86.)

Our Hope Rests in Christ

KAREN BAKER

Peace may be obtained in part by developing spiritual maturity. The influence of the Spirit then secures our hope of eternal life. Those who place their hope in the Savior know that his atonement balances all unequal earthly equations, and that the Lord has his own perfect timetable and scales. (In *Balm of Gilead*, 132.)

ELAINE CANNON

The daily work of the Lord involves changing hopeless to hopeful—for all of us. And it is for us to find at last that in the midst of winter we have within us an invincible summer. In a world filled with adversity we can reach for joy. (In *Ensign*, May 1982, 95.)

DEANNA EDWARDS

The concept of faith is inexplicably tied to the necessity for hope. Faith leads to hope in Christ. As we cultivate the hope that life is eternal, we move closer to experiencing what faith really is. (*Grieving*, 193.)

ELAINE L. JACK

My hope and my joy in life are based upon the atonement of our Savior and the restoration of the gospel in these days. I base my life on it; therefore, I have reason for my hope. (In *Ensign*, Mar. 1992, 14.)

COLLEEN H. MAXWELL

We can let the gospel fill us with a brightness of hope in him in whom we can place our absolute trust. That is what it means to have a perfect brightness of hope, an everlasting hope. (In *Arms of His Love*, 384.)

CHIEKO N. OKAZAKI

Hope is one of the three great Christian virtues because Christ Himself is the master of life and therefore the master of hope. (In *Ensign*, Nov. 1996, 90.)

MICHELE R. SORENSEN

Being able to keep your hope alive depends on whom you place it in. (*Chainbreakers*, 79.)

Hope will give birth to trust and faith, and upon them Christ will add His grace, which is sufficient for everyone. (*Chainbreakers*, 197.)

REBECCA GWYNN STRADLING

Hope generated by the promises of the Lord to the righteous has been the motivator for many mighty works by servants of God. And power to do anything with the hope of the Lord quite literally depends upon the degree to which we are willing to hope for, and to expect, that help. (In *Ensign*, July 1981, 28.)

DWAN J. YOUNG

Hope is knowing that whatever comes, the Lord can whisper peace. Our hope in Christ gives us an unchanging reason to rejoice. (In *Ensign*, Nov. 1986, 86.)

We can endure all things when our hope is centered in one who will never fail us—our Savior, Jesus Christ, who is the light of the world. (In *Ensign*, Nov. 1986, 86.)

Humility

ANYA BATEMAN

Teachability is [an] important element of humility. How beautiful is the person who thirsts for learning and progressing and doesn't care what others think or who knows it. (*Talent Race*, 48.)

Throughout his life Christ gave credit not to himself but to his Father in Heaven. Glory to his Father, we sense, was his purpose. Could humility be the willingness to recognize the source of our powers, abilities, and strengths? Could it simply be giving credit where credit is due? (*Talent Race*, 38.)

JOANNE B. DOXEY

Man proposes, but God disposes; we only petition, we cannot control. (In *Ensign*, Apr. 1987, 32.)

RUTH MAY FOX

[The Lord] has always done better for me than I could have done for myself. (In *Keepers*, 49.)

SUSA YOUNG GATES

The only power that a superior mind should really seek is the power to make others, less favored, happily unconscious of any difference between the two. (In *Improvement Era*, Aug. 1905, 739.)

MICHAELENE P. GRASSLI

Humility is knowing that you sin—and feeling sorrow for those sins—but not writing yourself off as being hopeless or unworthy of God's help and love. (*What I Have Learned*, 41.)

Humility enables us to truly rejoice at others' successes and mourn with them through trouble. . . . Humility is recognizing your limitations and even your failures, but not concluding that you are a failure. (*What I Have Learned*, 37, 41.)

Humility and meekness do not preclude the exercise of courage. (*What I Have Learned*, 73.)

BEPPIE HARRISON

Humility means . . . not getting carried away with your own importance. . . . It means being receptive to all the commandments. . . . It means being prepared to see merit in the virtues of others. . . . It means being ready to listen to other people. . . . It means recognizing your need for the Lord's hand in your life even when everything is going splendidly, instead of only acknowledging your dependence when things have gotten into a mess and you need some help to get back on your feet. (*On Being a Parent*, 90.)

PATRICIA T. HOLLAND

Humility comes from an honest and balanced recognition of both our limitations and our strengths. (In *BYU Speeches*, 6 Sept. 1988, 25.)

To recognize areas of vulnerability and needed growth in our life is to recognize a chance for divine influence. (In *BYU Speeches*, 6 Sept. 1988, 25.)

SANDRA ROGERS

Without humility, our unity [as saints] can become self-serving, restrictive, and haughty, directing us straight up the steps of a latter-day rameumptom instead of into the sandaled, dusty footprints of the Master. (In *Hearts Knit Together*, 3.)

HEIDI S. SWINTON

Humility and meekness are manifest in "Thy will be done." (In *Best of Women's Conference*, 531.)

DONLU DeWITT THAYER

True humility is found only in the self-forgetfulness of a self-existent being. We can only find ourselves by losing ourselves—not by exhausting ourselves in resentful service, but by giving ourselves freely to increase the joy in the universe. (In *Women and Christ*, 142.)

We cannot acquire humility by paying attention to (quantifying, and being proud of) our efforts at humility. We cannot find humility by subjecting ourselves to humiliation and certainly not by attempting to conquer and humiliate others. (In *Women and Christ*, 142.)

SHIRLEY W. THOMAS

Of all Christlike attributes, humility is one of the easiest to grasp, probably because it is taught over and over through experience. It also may be one of the most difficult qualities to make a consistent part of our lives. It is easy to put it on, but then it slips off. It is the quality that seems to run most directly counter to the world in which we live. (In *Wisdom's Paths*, 10.)

Meekness

ELAINE CANNON

Meekness indicates a full-scale awareness of how much a troubled person cannot walk the way of trial without heavenly help. (*Count Your Blessings*, 39.)

CHRISTINE DURHAM

Meekness refers to the ability to turn our hopes, desires, and ambitions over to God, to accept God's time, to accept God's hand as it operates in our lives, and to let his words, his doctrine, his teachings, and his love affect our hearts and transform our spirits. (In *Every Good Thing*, 332.)

Submissiveness

LILLIAN S. ALLDREDGE

When you place yourself in the Lord's hands for his use, marvelous things happen. With every challenge comes a blessing. With every struggle comes the lifting of one's spirit. (In *Wisdom's Paths*, 193.)

DIANE BILLS

Faith can replace fear and peace can come even as we are experiencing our trials. Peace comes from aligning our lives with what God desires us to do. We must find out God's will for us, then let go of the things that are not important and focus on the things he would have us do. (*Trust in the Lord*, 81.)

AFTON J. DAY

When you submit yourself to the will of your Heavenly Father you find yourself becoming the kind of wife you know you should be. You're more generous, flexible, and loving, partly because in becoming aligned with the forces of good you become a stockholder in the eternal reservoir of love, and partly because you are more likely to feel good about yourself and are therefore able to become less defensive and give more of yourself. (*Perfect Wife*, 27.)

DEANNA EDWARDS

We can place faith in others when we know they care about us, and that is precisely why we can turn all that we are over to God, because He loves us. At that moment of turning our lives over to Him we remember, above all, that He loves us. (*Grieving*, 196.)

In The Lord's Prayer the phrase, "Thy will be done," is still one of the most vital aspects of prayer, not in the sense that all bad things that happen are God's will, but in the sense that we can turn our lives, possessions, and all that we are over to a higher power and have faith in the source of our trust. (*Grieving*, 196.)

Mary Sturlaugson Eyer

To know the will of God is the greatest knowledge; to suffer the will of God is the greatest heroism; to do the will of God is the greatest achievement; and to have the Lord's approval on your work is the greatest happiness. (*He Restoreth My Soul*, 92.)

Renata Tonks Forste

To let the Lord guide us, we first must let go of our biases or false traditions as we conform our will to the Lord's. (In *BYU Speeches*, 29 July 1997, 343.)

Ruth Hardy Funk

You have to give up your own independence and become totally dependent on the Lord to maximize your ultimate blessings. . . . I cannot do what I need to do or must do until I finally come to [the Lord] in total dependence. (In *Keepers*, 117.)

Michaelene P. Grassli

As we submit "even as a child doth submit to his father" (Mosiah 3:19), we can accept callings that may seem beyond our capacity, knowing he will make us able. We can dismiss the judgments of others, knowing his is the only will to please. We can be more humble because our submission has stripped us of pride. We can become in-nocent because we follow the Savior's example. We can be kind because in a child of Christ there is no jealousy, malice, or unkindness. (*What I Have Learned*, 120.)

Ardeth Greene Kapp

Experience teaches us that our Heavenly Father knows what is best and that all we need or want to know is his will. (*Joy of the Journey*, 84.)

Vilate M. Kimball

I try to submit all things into the hands of God. (In *Their Own Words*, 139.)

Elaine Sorensen Marshall

We cannot heal from life's pain, much less aspire to become godly, only by knowing and obeying commandments on a checklist. We must move one step further to submission to the Savior and acceptance of his gift of grace. (In *Women in the Covenant*, 265.)

Virginia H. Pearce

Our ongoing responsibility is to keep offering ourselves and everything that we have and are to Him. (In *Best of Women's Conference*, 435.)

When we submit voluntarily and joyfully, far from being passive victims, we become victors, because we have accepted a partnership with an all-powerful and all-loving Being. (In *Best of Women's Conference*, 435.)

LOUISE Y. ROBISON

May we live in the principles of the Gospel of Jesus Christ, that we shall be able to feel and say, as the Prophet of old, "O God, thou art my God." Then peace will come no matter what the conflict in the world; then joy and happiness, development and eternal progress will be ours. (In *Relief Society Magazine*, Nov. 1936, 718.)

TESSA MEYER SANTIAGO

If we are to become women of Christ, we must learn to embrace the will of God. (In *Best of Women's Conference*, 473.)

MARY ELLEN SMOOT

When we choose to serve the Lord, we choose to submit our will to his and to respond to the promptings of the Spirit. (In *Best of Women's Conference*, 514.)

ELIZA R. SNOW

In order to render life desirable, we must cultivate feelings of submission and cherish in our own bosoms that peace and tranquillity which will enable us to rejoice in whatever situation we may be placed. (*Personal Writings*, 84.)

M. CATHERINE THOMAS

Let us observe that Jesus could not have been who he was had he not made his life all obedience, all prayer, all working by the gift and power of his Father. (*Spiritual Lightening*, 99.)

It is when God's will becomes my will that power begins to break like the sunlight in the morning, that the daystar arises in the heart. (*Spiritual Lightening*, 98.)

Just as the Father was the doer of all Jesus' deeds and the speaker of all his words, so the Lord Jesus offers the same essential relationship to each of us, and that relationship is indeed the only way to sanctification. (*Spiritual Lightening*, 99.)

SHIRLEY W. THOMAS

When we have come to [the] point of belief that we can trust in whatever the Lord is going to ask of us, without questioning, we have opened our lives to the powers of heaven. Our Father can [then] provide us with the particular experiences our growth requires and not just what we will accept. (In *Wisdom's Paths*, 5.)

WENDY L. WATSON

Made-to-measure ironies are part of each woman's compressed, personalized curriculum of life. . . . Diligently searching for more light and responding to these ironies with humility and resiliency allows us to live fully the perpetually unexpected life. (In *Every Good Thing*, 41.)

HELEN MAR WHITNEY

Subduing our *wills* and the pride of our hearts is the *deepest* and *hardest lesson* that mortals have to learn. (*Woman's View*, 192.)

Pride

ANYA BATEMAN

Getting in touch with our childlike joy in learning helps us eliminate pride from our lives. (*Talent Race*, 47.)

SUSAN EASTON BLACK

Preventing pride from taking its creeping parasitic grip on us requires surrounding ourselves with the armor of God, so that we will be protected from pride now and in the future. (*Finding Christ*, 65.)

Pride robs us of the humility we need to acquire Christlike attributes to enjoy a happy life. (*Finding Christ*, 65.)

HEIDI S. SWINTON

Pride stands in the way of hearing the voice of the Lord. (In *Best of Women's Conference*, 531.)

Humor

JANENE WOLSEY BAADSGAARD

Feeling joy and finding humor can be learned, practiced, reinforced, and internalized just like any other skill. Humor is not just telling jokes but a way of looking at life and responding to it positively. When we decide to respond to life this way in spite of our circumstances, it's easier to find the silly or absurd around us. (In *Clothed with Charity*, 79.)

LOUISE DURHAM

With humor, our shortcomings are no longer debilitating weaknesses but common bonds that link us together. Think about it. The one trait we all share is imperfection. If we laugh at them, the flaws aren't threatening. (In *Clothed with Charity*, 75.)

MARY ELLEN EDMUNDS

Humor is learning to laugh at ourselves and circumstances, but never at that which is sacred. Humor is a way to deal with life's inconsistencies without irreverence. (*Happiness*, 136.)

Humor for me is often two parts love and three parts courage. (*Happiness*, 135.)

Humor can be—and should be—gentle and kind, bringing down walls that may separate us, but never used as a "weapon" to hurt or humiliate. (*Happiness*, 135–36.)

Studies show that when people laugh hard, the heart rate speeds up, the circulatory system is stimulated, and the muscles go limp. The body's immune system is stimulated, and more endorphins—which are natural pain-relieving substances in the brain—are produced during laughter. So much for the science and body chemistry of it. Now for life. In my life, humor has helped me cut down on competition and envy. Humor increases peace. (In *Women Steadfast*, 149.)

Laughing together is similar to crying or weeping together: it's unifying, it's a tenderizer, and I believe it helps us be more *real* with each other. (In *Women Steadfast*, 153.)

Humor has a way of leveling—of helping us experience equality. When the same thing touches or amuses two people, it reaches across a lot of artificial walls and even cuts through language and other communication barriers. (In *Women Steadfast*, 153.)

AMY HARDISON

Laughter is a coping mechanism. It helps us deal with the physical and mental stress we encounter on a daily basis. We feel physically and mentally better for having laughed. (*How to Feel Great*, 84.)

EMILY BENNETT WATTS

I don't have problems that require a wailing wall. What I need is more like a whining wall. Little things build up. It's not the great big problems that are most troubling, because I know enough to seek the Lord in those times, but the little accretions of every day just glom onto me, building up even when I don't quite realize it's happening. . . . Those are the times when an appropriate sense of humor would help. (In *Arise*, 190.)

Influence

PAMELA J. ATKINSON

Remember that our lives may be the only scriptures that some people read. (In *Hearts Knit Together*, 136.)

DONNA LEE BOWEN BARNES

We are responsible for ourselves and can guarantee no one else's exaltation. . . . We can only help and guide; we cannot determine another's eternity. (In *As Women of Faith*, 74.)

LINDA J. EYRE

Maybe we should quit worrying so much about trying to change the people around us and worry more about changing ourselves. (*I Didn't Plan to Be a Witch*, 140.)

SHARLENE WELLS HAWKES

A faithful member of the Church living out in the world can be a beautiful example and a point of reference for those who are drifting without direction. By serving as spiritual beacons, such members can help steer those who are otherwise lost to the safety found in the welcoming arms of Christ. (*Living*, 3–4.)

ELAINE L. JACK

To live heroically is to understand that there is a difference between making a difference in the world and making a splash. (*Eye to Eye*, 115.)

ARDETH GREENE KAPP

How we look and act, what we say and do, may be the only message some people will receive. (In *Best of Women's Conference*, 246.)

ANN N. MADSEN

There is a right way to influence others. It is called righteousness. And righteousness does influence others. (In *Best of Women's Conference*, 315.)

ELAINE SORENSEN MARSHALL

Often we may choose the path of least resistance—but occasionally we catch a glimpse of our own divine nature and realize that our influence can be limitless. (In *Ensign*, Mar. 1983, 31.)

JAN UNDERWOOD PINBOROUGH

We accomplish most in our relationships when we focus more on what we *can* control—our own attitudes and behavior—and less on what we *can't* control—the attitudes

and behavior of the other person. (In *Ensign*, Sept. 1990, 51.)

We do the most good for our friends, spouses, and children when we concentrate less on controlling them and more on being available to them. (In *Ensign*, Sept. 1990, 51.)

Letting go of the belief that we can control another person's behavior does not mean that we cease to care about that person. Instead, it means that we trust that the Lord loves that person and knows better than we do how to help him. Our task then becomes being open to the Spirit's promptings in our relationships. (In *Ensign*, Sept. 1990, 51.)

CAROLYN J. RASMUS

You can help light the way for others with every Christlike act, every kind word spoken, every good thought, every honest act, every righteous choice, every scripture read, every prayer offered, every act of forgiveness, every effort to lift another. By making these choices, you can become a righteous influence and a courageous example for others. (In *Living the Young Women Values*, 52–53.)

BARBARA B. SMITH

We can strive to be a model of righteousness. Children learn what life is by observing and doing. (In *LDS Women's Treasury*, 277.)

LEAH D. WIDTSOE

The Lord intended that His people should be leaders in all that is righteous—more virtuous, if possible, more helpful and understanding than the world who do not choose to follow in His footsteps. (In *Improvement Era*, Apr. 1938, 221.)

ZINA D. H. YOUNG

Let us show the world that we have something better than they have by living righteous lives. (In *Woman's Exponent*, 1 Oct. 1887, 70.)

Jesus Christ

Jesus Is the Light of the World

SHERI L. DEW

The antidote to the distractions of the adversary is Jesus Christ. Light *is* stronger than darkness. Jesus Christ illuminates our vision of who we are and why we are here and gives us courage to move forward in the journey toward our heavenly home. (In *Best of Women's Conference*, 137.)

XANTHE K. FARNWORTH

When innocent blood dropped to the ground in Gethsemane and Jesus gave his all on Calvary, our source of power was insured. By doing the will of the Father, he overcame the world. The paths of truth lead both to him and from him, bring together the past, present, and future. He is the light of the world. (In *Thy Word Is a Lamp*, 48.)

VIRGINIA U. JENSEN

There are all kinds of darkness in this world: darkness that comes from sin; darkness that comes from discouragement, disappointment, and despair; darkness that comes from loneliness and feelings of inadequacy. . . . The light of Jesus Christ is stronger than any darkness we face in this life, *if* we have faith in Him, seek after Him, and obey Him. (In *Ensign*, Nov. 2000, 62.)

SHARON G. LARSEN

Christ is your light and He will show you the way through the happy times and the mists of darkness. You *never* need to feel alone or forsaken. (In *Ensign*, May 1999, 90.)

CHIEKO N. OKAZAKI

Our spiritual requirement for light is just as desperate and as deep as our physical need for light. Jesus is the light of the world. (In *Women and Christ*, 8.)

[Jesus] is the light of the world. That's what will really bring light into our lives. (In *Women and Christ*, 5.)

We know that this world is a dark place sometimes, but . . . the people who walk in darkness can have a bright companion. We need

[Jesus], and he is ready to come to us, if we'll open the door and let him. (In *Women and Christ*, 8.)

VIRGINIA H. PEARCE

Our sign of life, our key to life in all of its majestic and meaningful simplicity, is Jesus Christ. He fits every door, every life experience, every death experience that any mortal can possibly encounter. . . . He stands as the fountain in ancient times as well as today. . . . He is the light and the life. (In *May Christ Lift Thee Up*, 3.)

Christic Is Our Model

DONNA LEE BOWEN BARNES

If we recognize Christ's greatness and what he does for us, we can only respond in humility, hoping to deal with others with the same Christlike generosity. (In *Women Steadfast*, 278.)

SUSAN EASTON BLACK

The pattern is clear. Christ extends his tender mercies. He pleads. He teaches. He assists. He challenges. He chastises. He corrects. He blesses. He waits and hopes for our repentance. As followers of Christ, we need to be as he is. . . . It is not enough to know or even to do. We must be as he is. (*Finding Christ*, 58.)

ELAINE CANNON

Christ is our model. . . . He labeled loving others as the great commandment and warned that because of iniquity the love of many would "wax cold." To keep our own love from waxing cold, we can strive to be more like him. (*Gatherings*, 138–39.)

KAREN LYNN DAVIDSON

We see most often represented in verse, in music, and in paintings . . . the gentle side of Christ. . . . On the other hand, no one who has ever lived has shown more strength, more courage, more perseverance, more willingness to stand up for truth or rebuke wrong, even at tremendous cost, than has the Savior. . . . He had the strength to stand alone. He had absolute confidence in himself and in his Father—confidence to lead out in what was right. (In *Best of Women's Conference*, 113.)

JANET G. LEE

Our Savior is the perfect image for us to visualize as we strive to be successful. We need to tape his image on the pages of our lives so that we may visualize his perfect life as we lift ourselves up from our failures. (In *BYU Speeches*, 14 Sept. 1993, 12.)

MARGARET D. NADAULD

The trend in the world is to demand our rights, to accuse others, and to excuse ourselves. The Savior taught us to care for others, to bless their lives, to understand their needs, and to be humble and meek, merciful and kind. (In *BYU Speeches*, 2 Nov. 1997, 52.)

IDA SMITH

Some women complain that they have no strong role models in the scriptures. That is not true. . . . Our main model is the same as for men—the Savior. (In *Woman to Woman*, 46.)

Nowhere does the Lord say that tenderness, kindness, charity, faithfulness, patience, gentleness, and compassion are female traits and should be exemplified by women only. And nowhere does he say that courage, strength, determination, leadership, and a willingness to fight—and, if necessary, die—for what is right should be the exclusive prerogatives of men. (In *Woman to Woman*, 46.)

MARTHA H. TINGEY

[Christ's] life . . . was one round of sorrow, trial and suffering, yet with characteristic self-sacrifice He buried His sorrows deep in His own bosom, and went forth administering comfort and happiness on every hand. Let us imitate His noble example, and in seeking to cheer, comfort and bless others, we shall receive peace and consolation to our own hearts. (In *Young Woman's Journal*, Jan. 1890, 117.)

Our Relationship with Christ

PAULA CARLSON

[Jesus] knew how it was to deal with . . . hard things because he has dealt with hard—much harder—things himself. But he chose to do those hard things so he would know how to help us, to support us, to sustain us. And his bottom line for doing it was simply that he loves us. (In *Thy Word Is a Lamp*, 18.)

DIXIE R. CLIFFORD

Some people speak of personal Gethsemanes that we endure, yet we can be certain that our experiences do not begin to approach those of our Master. Christ is our Savior, our exemplar, and our model. . . . His experience in Gethsemane when he embraced the Atonement and took upon himself the sins and inequities of the world was for all of us. (In *Thy Word Is a Lamp*, 110.)

SHERI L. DEW

There is a direct relationship between how we feel about Jesus Christ and how we see ourselves. We cannot increase our devotion to the Savior without also obtaining a greater sense of purpose, identity, and conviction. (In *Ensign*, Nov. 1997, 92.)

RUTH HARDY FUNK

Jesus Christ is our Savior, our brother, our friend. He is as near as we allow him to be. Our only ultimate joy and happiness is predicated upon our relationship with him. Our only peace, through disappointments, sorrow, and challenges, will come as we draw nearer unto him. . . . His love for us is a gift beyond price. (In *Ensign*, Nov. 1978, 106.)

VIRGINIA U. JENSEN

[Jesus'] knowledge of you goes beyond a catalog of your deeds. He knows you individually and completely. (In *Best of Women's Conference*, 234.)

ARDETH GREENE KAPP

We know about our Savior, but it is often in our adversities that we truly find him and know him and love him. (*Rejoice!* 44.)

SHARON G. LARSEN

Christ's presence with us is the gift he offers. His constant succoring, forgiveness, and encouragement not only make our burden light but increase our own capacities. (In *Arms of His Love*, 24.)

ANN N. MADSEN

Knowing who we really are allows us to live with light. Sometimes we forget that we are children of a living God. Jesus knows perfectly our eternal relationship to himself and our Father. We are actually his brothers and sisters. Once we are sure of who we are, we understand our eternal family relationship, and we are able to feel loved. (In *Redeemer*, 44.)

Our careful instruction [by Jesus] has been an ongoing process that spans eternity. He has proved his love for us, which includes his right to educate us in heavenly matters. He has promised he will take all the time necessary to help us understand. We have his word that

not one of us will miss the opportunity for learning. (In *Redeemer*, 69.)

We had a closeness with the Lord before we came here. We are not establishing, but reestablishing, that relationship. He is no stranger to us. (In *As Women of Faith*, 149.)

CHIEKO N. OKAZAKI

Think what it means to be a son or daughter of Christ. . . . Our baptismal covenant enables us to enter into a new relationship with the Savior, to have new claims on his mercy, and to experience his grace and love in new ways. (*Sanctuary*, 95.)

I'm not going to tell you to read the scriptures, fast and pray, keep the commandments, attend the temple, and attend your meetings as ways of coming to know Christ. . . . All of them will improve and strengthen our relationship with the Savior, but they are not the relationship itself. . . . The relationship I'm talking about is a sense of presence, a sense of companionship, a sense of closeness. It's a relationship not with an idea or a historical image but with a living individual. When we have the feeling of the Savior as a real person, there's a new awareness of what it means to take his name upon us, almost of being clothed in his name, of seeing with his eyes and of feeling his work being done with our hands. (*Aloha!* 66–67.)

In the preexistence . . . we assumed the burden of freedom because we loved Christ so much.

And he assumed the burden of being our Savior because he loved *us* so much. (*Cat's Cradle*, 163.)

WENDY L. WATSON

As we increase our interactions with the Savior, as we really draw close to him, he will become an increasing reality in our lives. And as we seek to understand the power of the Atonement, that it can be applied to our sins, our deficiencies, our pains, our frustrations, it can be the greatest reality in our lives. (In *May Christ Lift Thee Up*, 51.)

The Power of Christ

HANNAH BREYTON

[Jesus] is the only one who can change our hearts. He is the only one who can take away the hurt. He is the one who bears all offense. He is the only one who can show us the way. He is the only one who can bring us to forgiveness. He waits for us to turn our hearts over to him; then he performs the healing, changing, finishing miracles. . . . He waits patiently for our hearts to be ready. (In *As a Woman Thinketh*, 76–77.)

SHERI L. DEW

The Savior isn't our last chance; He is our only chance. (In *Ensign*, May 1999, 66.)

Satan *is* the god of Babylon, or this world. Christ is the God of Israel, and His Atonement gives us power to overcome the world. (In *Ensign*, Nov. 1999, 98.)

MARY ELLEN EDMUNDS

Jesus has more than enough power and love and experience to understand, succor, comfort, sanctify, rescue, heal, bless, and save. He knows what we feel and why. He has more than enough power and love and experience to be our Brother, our Everlasting Friend, our Savior, King, Redeemer, Prince of Peace, and Good Shepherd. He's knocking. Let Him in. (*Happiness*, 94.)

KIMBERLEY BURTON HEUSTON

The Lord is mindful of you and your situation and the limitations under which you are laboring. If you ask for help in faith and singleness of heart, he will reach out to you and assist you in ways that are personally meaningful and even miraculous. (*Single Parenting*, 64.)

MARJORIE P. HINCKLEY

The light of Christ brings peace to the troubled mind, rest to the weary, solace to those in sorrow, and joy to those who walk uprightly. (In *Glimpses*, 19.)

PATRICIA T. HOLLAND

When we can finally trust our lives, our hearts, our whole souls to the Great Physician, then he not only heals what was but goes one better and makes all things new. . . . He gives us a new strength of soul, a new birth, a new heart—holier and happier, healthier than it ever was before. (In *Arms of His Love*, 373.)

ARDETH GREENE KAPP

In our times of trial, if we will turn to him, the Spirit bears witness that our Savior not only can but will ease our burdens. (*Rejoice!* 44.)

MARGARET D. NADAULD

[Our Savior] feels what we feel; He knows our heart. It was His mission to wipe away our tears, cleanse our wounds, and bless us with His healing power. He can carry us home to our Heavenly Father with the strength of His matchless love. (In *Ensign*, May 1998, 64.)

CHIEKO N. OKAZAKI

[Jesus] could part the Red Sea before us or calm the angry storm that besets us, but these would be small miracles for the God of nature. Instead, he chooses to do something harder: He wants to transform human nature into divine nature. (*Sanctuary*, 157.)

JEANNE KANE PUTNAM

For me the balm of Gilead is like the oasis breeze that surrounds and soothes a parched soul. It is the unction of redemption from pain. It anoints with healing, soothes physical aches, and calms worried hearts. It is the ointment of oneness with the healing hand of Jesus Christ, ever-ready to reach out. . . . The balm of Gilead is peace. (In *Balm of Gilead*, 54.)

M. CATHERINE THOMAS

We are invited to exceed our telestial bounds through making a connection with the laws and powers of Jesus Christ. (*Selected Writings*, 14.)

Feeling Joy in Christ

STACE HUCKS CHRISTIANSON

What enables us to live righteously is not our devotion to the commandments, but our devotion to Christ. If we love and desire to serve him, keeping his commandments is a joy and not a task. (In *Living the Legacy*, 30.)

SHERI L. DEW

As we increase our interaction with Him, we learn for ourselves that He will never betray us, never turn away, never change His criteria for coming unto Him. His attention is riveted on us, His brothers and sisters. (In *Ensign*, Nov. 1997, 92.)

CHIEKO N. OKAZAKI

The Savior loves us. He promises us joy and rejoicing. . . . The message of the gospel isn't that we're miserable sinners. It's that we're unique and beloved children of our Father in Heaven. (*Disciples*, 243.)

Once we have learned to recognize the Savior, I think we realize that he is our companion, even as we fly through a list of demands, distractions, and duties. He is a help, an anchor. (*Aloha!* 35.)

Our truest sanctuary is a heart steadfastly fixed upon the Savior. That is a place of safety that requires no walls or doors. (*Sanctuary*, 9.)

BARBARA B. SMITH

The Lord . . . invites, not commands, us to follow him. . . . He provides us with opportunities to serve and to learn. . . . He describes our mission in this life and in the life to come. And he gives us the power to do his work and invites us to use the powers of heaven in our daily lives. (*Grandmothering*, 114.)

EILEEN N. WHITAKER

Not only *may* I depend upon my Savior whenever I need him but I *have* to depend upon him. (In *To Rejoice As Women*, 94.)

Realizing how completely dependent upon the Lord we are can bring tremendous peace. Our fears, our achings, even our unanswered questions and prayers can all be all right. (In *To Rejoice As Women*, 94.)

Every living being on this earth depends upon [Christ] for their every breath, for their very life. The tragedy is that few realize it. (In *To Rejoice As Women*, 94.)

Come unto Christ

DONNA LEE BOWEN BARNES

When we approach Christ, we can use no facades, no stereotypes, no labels, for we approach him as his sisters, as children of God. (In *Women Steadfast*, 278.)

ELAINE CANNON

In Christ's day, people were pressing heavily about him on one occasion. A woman in trouble reached out to touch him in faith. . . . He knew her touch was different. She had connected. He responded by healing her. . . . Our touch must be different. Rather than merely moving about Christ, wanly waiting for his blessings, we must reach out and connect—in faith. (In *Ensign*, Nov. 1978, 108.)

SHERI L. DEW

The gospel, with its sanctifying and redeeming power, is available to all. . . . There are no qualifiers relative to age, appearance, intellect or talent, marital status, ethnicity, social standing, or Church calling. . . . He has invited *all* of us to come unto him, to learn to hear his voice, to attach and commit ourselves to him, and to ultimately enter his presence. (In *Best of Women's Conference*, 133.)

When I think of the times in my life that I have felt excluded— because I didn't have the right marital status, or the right look, or the right social connection—it comforts me to know that the Keeper of the ultimate gate, the Host whose guest list I most want to be included on, has placed no limitations on my accessibility to him. (In *Best of Women's Conference*, 133.)

The Lord places no limits on our access to him. But we, unfortunately, often do. We limit ourselves when we sin, when we are lazy spiritually, when we fail to ask and seek. (In *Arms of His Love*, 393.)

If we don't come unto Christ, meaning that we never turn our lives over to Him, we will go through our probation here on our own rather than experiencing what the Savior promised when He said, "Come unto me, all ye that labor and are heavy laden, and I will give you rest." (In *Ensign*, Nov. 1997, 93.)

The only way that *we* may overcome the world is by coming unto Christ. And coming unto Christ means walking away from the world. It means placing Christ and Christ only at the center of our lives so that the vanities and philosophies of men lose their addictive appeal. (In *Ensign*, Nov. 1999, 98.)

CINDY BISHOP GRACE

Our Shepherd, the Savior Jesus Christ, sweat beads of blood and then laid down his life for us that we might escape the bonds of death and return to him someday. He loves us. He knows each of us by name. If we will learn to recognize and follow his voice, he will lead us home. (In *Living the Legacy*, 70.)

Even though there are millions of people in the world, just as in a flock of hundreds of . . . sheep, the shepherd knows them individually.

It is our responsibility to learn to recognize his voice through praying, studying the scriptures, and following his example. (In *Living the Legacy*, 67.)

ELAINE L. JACK

We must seek to know Jesus Christ, for this is knowledge that is singular and everlasting. . . . Seeking Jesus feeds our spiritual soul and at the same time prompts us to feed others. We do it in small ways, and these efforts make a big difference. . . . Seeking Jesus is learning to balance what we feel in our hearts with what we know to be true in our minds, and show through our actions that we understand that balance. (In *Ensign*, Nov. 1994, 89.)

If I could offer but two words of counsel, they would be "Seek Jesus!" (In *Ensign*, Nov. 1994, 89.)

ARDETH GREENE KAPP

When we feel a need to pull away, let us reach out to [the Savior]. Instead of feeling the need to resist, let us submit to his will with a broken heart and a contrite spirit. (In *Arms of His Love*, 8.)

CAMILLA EYRING KIMBALL

We seek to follow the Savior, adhering to his teachings, emulating his virtues, enduring whatever burdens may be placed upon us, bearing his name, accepting his great sacrifice, and calling upon his grace. We then have hope that he will reach out and draw us to him, making us more than we have made ourselves. (*Writings*, 25.)

CHIEKO N. OKAZAKI

How can the burden be light? Because the yoke is a double one, designed for two. Jesus wants to be our yoke-fellow. . . . The Savior wants to share that burden, and we need to let him. (In *Women and Christ*, 2.)

We need to know [Jesus]. Not just concepts about him. Not just lists of things he wants us to do. Not just stories from the scriptures or from other people's testimonies, but our very own stories. (In *Women and Christ*, 5.)

We must give our hearts to the Savior so that he becomes the light of our lives and the touchstone by which we measure every relationship, every action, every word, and every thought, whether it is worthy of him or not. (*Sanctuary*, 71.)

What I would wish for every sister in the Church [is] a gift so powerful that it will sustain us into the eternities, so personal that only you can understand how completely it matches who you are and what you need, so joy-producing that you will feel like shouting hallelujah. That gift is a true knowledge of our Savior, Jesus Christ. (In *Women and Christ*, 5.)

We do not need to wait for ideal circumstances before Jesus can enter our lives. Jesus came to save people who were not perfect, to heal people who were not already healthy, to show a better way to people who had gone astray. He will enter our homes, too, even though they are not perfect, if we open our doors to him. (*Aloha!* 8–9.)

Jesus Christ is our loving Savior. He is not some distant person in robes and sandals. . . . We can share our whole lives with him. . . . I want to tell you that Jesus wants our whole hearts. He knows our whole lives. (*Disciples*, 93.)

The Savior has already given us all of his love. We don't need to earn it. But I think it takes our whole lives to make that boundless love real in our limited perspective, to really believe in unconditional love with our very conditional minds and hearts. (*Sanctuary*, 10.)

The death of the body is nothing —for Christ's Resurrection guarantees our own—but He cannot rescue us from the death of the spirit unless we choose to ally ourselves with Him, with His hope, with the inexhaustible and irrepressible life that is His. (In *Ensign*, Nov. 1996, 90.)

Strengthen yourselves by seeking the source of true strength—the Savior. Come unto him. He loves you. He desires your happiness and exults in your desires for righteousness. Make him your strength, your daily companion, your rod and your staff. Let him comfort you. There is no burden we need bear alone. His grace compensates for our deficiencies. (In *Ensign*, Nov. 1993, 96.)

Do not feel that you need to be at the chapel to be in the presence of the Savior. He is with us as we talk to our children, as we wash our dishes, as we hurry to the market, as we greet others at our place of work. He understands the things that hurt us and worry us. He is with us when we grieve, just as he is with us when we rejoice. He understands when burdens become too heavy and when we become discouraged and exhausted. He understands that there are seasons when we must rest from our labors, like the winters, and seasons when our lives seem vigorous and new, like the spring. Do not walk away from him. Let him come with you. (*Cat's Cradle*, 178.)

I hope that all of us begin our day by spending some time with the Savior, feeling his Spirit and enjoying his love for us. (*Aloha!* 35.)

VIRGINIA H. PEARCE

We always have the right to accept the Savior and his atonement, which restores to us a wholeness that our mistakes or the mistakes of others have temporarily destroyed. (In *To Rejoice As Women*, 37–38.)

No one can keep us from coming to the Savior. . . . No matter what our circumstances, we do have the power to move toward him ourselves. (In *To Rejoice As Women*, 37.)

MARY ELLEN SMOOT

Invitations from the Lord are vital. They guide us back to our Heavenly Father and lead us in the way of truth and righteousness. Truly they acknowledge our infinite worth as daughters of God. They are so lovingly personalized. They come from our Heavenly Father. He speaks to us in a language of invitations: "Come unto me," "Follow me," "Come ye." (In *Ensign*, Nov. 1998, 89.)

We can come unto Christ, again and again—for strength, guidance, and forgiveness. We need only live His laws to receive His blessings. (*Sweet Is the Work*, 11.)

MARIAN JEPPSON STODDARD

By seeking and following [revelation from Christ], we will pass from faith to knowledge, from knowledge to exaltation, by his grace and love and our obedience and faithfulness. His word is sure and will not fail. (In *Thy Word Is a Lamp*, 176.)

WENDY L. WATSON

Life-giving, life-changing relationships are created as we come unto the Savior. Even the sweet experiences of life, if not grounded in the Savior, are as cotton candy, sweet for a moment and then gone. (In *May Christ Lift Thee Up*, 50.)

When we want to live closer to the Lord than we ever have, closer to him than to anyone else, he brings us closer to everyone else. (In *Arise*, 173.)

Journals and Family Records

JANET BRIGHAM

The act of *writing in a journal can help a person deal with emotional pressures.* Some people who don't intend to keep journals—and some who don't even want to—find themselves writing as they try to cope with difficulties. (In *Ensign*, Dec. 1980, 57.)

ELAINE CANNON

Our posterity has a right to know their roots without scrounging for them and perhaps uncovering only part. Keeping records can assure them of this. Writing our life story can help them know their parents. Knowing brings understanding, and understanding strengthens love. (*Gatherings*, 21.)

We who would give our children everything, would even sacrifice our lives for them if need be, must consider the importance of keeping records that can enrich their lives beyond description and reach them beyond our voice. (*Gatherings*, 21.)

The day will come for each of us, . . . when we will value the incredible experience of reading the records of someone dear to us. (*Count Your Blessings*, 52.)

A big difference between the Nephites and Lamanites is that the Nephites kept records so that the children could learn and value the traditions of their fathers. (*Count Your Blessings*, 53.)

JESSIE L. EMBRY

If family members talk to you about your life stories, I hope you will remember these keys: Be yourself, share your emotions, tell stories, and be honest. Then your posterity will not put you on a pedestal and have to reach for the impossible heights they thought you had set. And historians like me will bless you. (In *Women in the Covenant*, 209.)

CAMILLA EYRING KIMBALL

If we keep a personal journal, we can expect to be held in honorable memory by our descendants, who will learn from our experiences and testimony. (*Writings*, 24.)

Family history is a kind of scripture if it records how individuals have dealt with the challenges of life and how God has played a role in their lives. . . . When we have received knowledge of the past, we have obligation to use it, to perpetuate it, and to enlarge it. (*Writings*, 35.)

EILEEN GIBBONS KUMP

[A] creative activity that breeds optimism and self-knowledge and shapes our lives is journal-keeping. . . . It is a crucial assignment . . .

necessary and beyond value. Why? Because daily recording forces us to confront ourselves daily. (In *Woman's Choices*, 106.)

CAROL CORNWALL MADSEN

Like our books of scripture, [pioneer trail journals] read like sacred texts and are a latter-day testament of God's dealings with his covenant people. . . . It has been wisdom that these latter-day records have been preserved. We can claim them as our own sacred history. (In *BYU Speeches*, 29 Sept. 1998, 26.)

JEANIE MCALLISTER

We are counseled to keep journals. They help us remember faith-promoting experiences from the past, giving light and hope when neither seems to be shining brightly before us. (In *LDS Women's Treasury*, 333.)

LOUISE PLUMMER

Many of us do not write about ourselves . . . because we think our lives are boring. We don't appreciate the fabric of our own life, the details of it, the repetition of it. We don't understand that our experience as ordinary human beings is valuable. We don't understand that just by being alive we are unique. . . . It is through the journal that we record our uniqueness. (*Grasshopper*, 87.)

Unlike essays or critical writing, journal writing enables you to write authoritatively, without proof, evidence or footnotes. Your life is the

proof. No one can argue with your experience, with your unique view of the world. (*Grasshopper*, 88.)

If anyone down the line is remotely interested in my life, I'd rather have them read it from my voice than from the voice of a grandson or granddaughter who knew me only as an old lady. (*Grasshopper*, 112–13.)

BELLE S. SPAFFORD

From the past we inherit not only patterns and standards, but vision, strength, insight, faith and courage. (In *Relief Society Magazine*, Dec. 1945, 751.)

The past has passed on to us . . . as a part of our heritage, its unfulfilled dreams and desires and bids us keep faith with it in regard to these, for these, too, are a part of its contribution to advancement and progress. (In *Relief Society Magazine*, Dec. 1945, 751.)

KAREN SEDGWICK STONE

Perhaps we'll never know how important [record keeping] is until we move to our third estate and can there perceive in spiritual dimensions what we're simply not capable of here. Maybe there we will recognize the importance of the written word, its relationship to the sealing power of Elijah, and its ultimate connection to Deity itself. (In *Wisdom's Paths*, 76.)

As the literal children of God, perhaps we'll someday recognize not only that our histories are priceless and a tribute to him who made us but also that our very writing of them is part of the process by which we are written into the Lamb's Book of Life. (In *Wisdom's Paths*, 77.)

The Lord places such a high value on records, and their place as the very foundation of righteous society, that he sanctioned the removal of Laban as being a better alternative "that one man should perish than that a nation should dwindle and perish in unbelief" (1 Nephi 4:13). (In *Wisdom's Paths*, 74.)

SUSAN L. WARNER

My father . . . was a living testimony to me throughout his life. But near the end of his life he also wrote his personal history in order to bear record not only to his children and grandchildren but to all of his posterity for generations to come. Nothing he could have left his family is more precious than the record of his testimony and love. (In *Ensign*, Nov. 1998, 66.)

Joy and Happiness

Happiness Is the Object of Our Existence

JANENE WOLSEY BAADSGAARD

Life's so hard so it can also be so wonderful. I believe we exist to feel joy. But the fact is, we don't experience joy on a smooth straight highway. To experience joy, we have to experience its opposite. Without sorrow and pain like the uphill climb on the roller coaster, there is no hill to descend, no thrill or reward, no true joy. (*Families Who Laugh*, 163.)

JAROLDEEN ASPLUND EDWARDS

In bad times and good, joy is the great companion our Heavenly Father intended us to have. (*Celebration!* 3.)

The Lord's plan is a plan of happiness; clearly, he does not intend happiness to be inaccessible. He wants us to be joyful now, in the midst of mortal stress, adversity, and sorrow. (*Celebration!* 7–8.)

PATRICIA T. HOLLAND

God wants us to be happy! He is eternally committed to our well-being and wants us to be committed to our ultimate happiness as well. (In *To Rejoice As Women*, 97.)

Attitudes of Happiness

LINDA R. ARCHIBALD

Joy—sunshine in your heart— carries a responsibility to stretch. (*Sunshine in My Soul*, xiii.)

Without question there are those beyond the scope of our mortal vision—Satan and his legions—who have no sunshine in their hearts and who will do everything they can to pull us into their discouraging circle. . . . We have the power to dispel their influence, the seeds of pessimism and despair, if we but begin the quest for sunshine. (*Sunshine in My Soul*, xiv–xv.)

Joy is initially a personal choice, a desire and a decision to put in sufficient effort to face the light regardless of external circumstances. Afterward, . . . our joy can be increased, becoming more brilliant and secure each day as we, through the help of the Spirit, learn to live this important principle. (*Sunshine in My Soul*, xiv.)

Pessimism can be habit-forming, and the doldrums of self-pity can provide artificial protection from life's unexplored seas, allowing us to row aimlessly in circles around our comfort zones. (*Sunshine in My Soul*, xiii.)

MILDRED BARTHEL

Happiness is a conscious choice, not an automatic response. (In *Ensign*, Apr. 1987, 43.)

ELAINE CANNON

Imagine the spread of happy contagion if people focused on all the wonderful things that have happened to them in a week or a lifetime. More than blessing-counting, this could be a remembrance of happenings that set your heart to pounding and caused your shoulders to relax, your arms to fold about you, your eyes to glisten with tears, your voice to soften. (*Sunshine*, 41.)

Enough of negativism! There has been too much recounting of trials and highlighting of personal martyrdom. On with remembering that life is about gladness, too. Yes! Find the joy! (*Sunshine*, 41.)

LUCY GRANT CANNON

Happiness comes from within; it is a state of mind. (In *Keepers*, 65.)

KAREN LYNN DAVIDSON

As Latter-day Saints, we tend to be oriented toward goals and results. The thought of a joyful future sustains us. . . . The trouble is, in our preoccupation with the future, in looking forward to results and goals, we forget to enjoy the process of getting there. (In *Women and the Power*, 19.)

AFTON J. DAY

Quite possibly the difference between a person who is consistently happy and successful and one who is happy only when his lofty demands are met is an ability . . . to roll with the punches, to redefine his goals. (*Coming Up*, 49.)

Harbor high hopes, dream delightful dreams, and, in general, expect the best. Happy, successful people live that way. (*Coming Up*, 49.)

MARY ELLEN EDMUNDS

"Be of good cheer" is a commandment, not a suggestion. (In *Women Steadfast*, 149.)

JAROLDEEN ASPLUND EDWARDS

Celebration is the conscious decision to live our lives with joy. (*Celebration!* 3.)

SUSA YOUNG GATES

When it is almost second nature to see the bright side of things, then indeed you are ready to become a dispenser of sunshine to all your associates. Your own heart will swell and glow in the delight which is bestowed upon others. (In *Young Woman's Journal*, Apr. 1900, 186.)

Be cheerful at home, and you cannot fail to be cheerful abroad. Be cheerful in prosperity, for riches enable you to dispense many temporal blessings. Be cheerful in sickness, for in no other way can you learn more valuable lessons of faith and trust. Be cheerful in poverty, for thus has God tested and tried His best and truest Saints. Be cheerful in your labor, in your pleasure, your privation, and in your struggle; storms feed the precious roots of the growing tree. God moves in an atmosphere of peace and sunshine; let your heart learn to reflect His bright glory. (In *Young Woman's Journal*, Apr. 1900, 186.)

AMY HARDISON

Happiness does not come from things but from the thoughts we choose to think. If we fail to make this distinction, we build our happiness on a very wobbly foundation. And when we lose our things or when their newness wears off and we tire of them, the foundation of our happiness crumbles and we cease to be happy. (*How to Feel Great*, 72.)

JEANNE BRYAN INOUYE

The delights of childhood are good. They are a first taste of the deeper joys of Christ's gospel, to be fostered and remembered. (In *Behold Your Little Ones*, 106.)

An important aspect of nurturing children is helping them to feel joy and to choose the ways of happiness. (In *Behold Your Little Ones*, 106.)

LUCILE JOHNSON

Happiness is a choice. . . . If we fantasize that, somehow, someplace, sometime, we will have the affluence and perfect circumstances that will make us happy, then we are fooling ourselves. (*Sunny Side Up*, 128.)

Happiness is both a state and a trait. The *state* of happiness is a mood that comes and goes. The *trait* of happiness is a predisposition to a feeling of well-being. . . . If you have developed a happiness trait, you will be happy most of the time in spite of unpleasant circumstances in your life. (*Enjoy the Journey*, 9.)

If we constantly live for the future, there will come a day when we will discover we have missed the joy that could have been ours all along the way. (*Sunny Side Up*, 128.)

You have a tremendous ability to influence not only the people in your home, but all the people on the periphery of your life, when you smile. (*Sunny Side Up*, 150.)

It has been said that some people are like sunshine; it is as if they have been plugged into the sun. The world beats a path to such people because they are a joy to be with and to look at. We need to be plugged into the sun. (*Sunny Side Up*, 150.)

Be a smiler, not a downer. . . . Downers are people whose mouths turn down and their eyes turn down, their whole face seems to turn down. We have to fight the law of gravity all the time because it's constantly pulling everything we have down. The way to overcome the law of gravity, and the natural tendency to be grim and down in the mouth, is to be a smiler. A smiler is beautiful, and the world needs uppers. (*Sunny Side Up*, 150.)

BARBARA BARRINGTON JONES

In any person or situation, we can choose to dwell either on the negative or the positive. . . . We can all find greater happiness if we look for [it]. (In *Feeling Great*, 82.)

CAMILLA EYRING KIMBALL

The happy life is not ushered in at any age to the sound of drums and trumpets. It grows upon us year by year, little by little, until at last we realize we have it. (*Writings*, 143.)

You do not find the happy life. You make it. (*Writings*, 143.)

JILL C. MAJOR, LAUREN C. LEIFSON, AND HOLLIE C. BEVAN

In order for us to spread happiness to others, we first must be of good cheer. To be able to bear our testimonies, we must first build our own testimonies. (*Encircled by Love*, 3.)

COLLEEN H. MAXWELL

If we understand the Atonement, the plan of salvation, and the glad tidings of the gospel, then we have reason to be of good cheer. If we are of good cheer—if we portray optimism and hope—others around us will know the tilt of our soul and that it is positive. The spiritual radiance we may have can carry over to daily life. (In *Arms of His Love*, 384.)

BROOKIE PETERSON

A woman can elect to be happy or sad. If she resolves to have more compassion for herself and to avoid labeling herself with self-defeating adjectives . . . she is surely opting to be happier. (*Woman's Hope*, 35.)

IDA SMITH

Happy people shed their own sunlight, warming others as they warm themselves. (In *As Women of Faith*, 210.)

KATHRYN S. SMITH

People who give in to negatives are choosing to be unhappy.

Choosing to be positive is power. (In *Feeling Great*, 35.)

EMMA LOU THAYNE

It is intelligent to be happy—not as a mood, but as a mode. (In *Arise*, 197.)

The best thing I have to offer anywhere is a happy person. Unhappy, . . . I become part of the problem instead of part of the answer. (*As for Me*, 27.)

BARBARA W. WINDER

Developing a cheerful disposition can permit an atmosphere wherein one's spirit can be nurtured and encouraged to blossom and bear fruit. (In *Ensign*, Nov. 1987, 96.)

Being pessimistic and negative about our experiences will not enhance the quality of our lives. A determination to be of good cheer can help us and those around us to enjoy life more fully. (In *Ensign*, Nov. 1987, 96.)

Sources of Joy and Happiness

NORMA B. ASHTON

Enjoyable days come from enjoying and working with what we have today instead of yearning for different circumstances. (In *Best of Women's Conference*, 22–23.)

JANENE WOLSEY BAADSGAARD

Joy comes when I pay attention to all the things I'm grateful for instead of all my problems. (In *Best of Women's Conference*, 27.)

ELAINE CANNON

A happy person is one who is full of love. (*Love You*, 40.)

CATHERINE CHRISTENSEN

True joy can be born of painful experience. The atonement of Jesus Christ makes this joy possible. (In *Balm of Gilead*, 48.)

SUZANNE LITTLE DASTRUP

Our happiness does not depend on our circumstances or things around us or people we live with; it depends on something internal. (In *Women in the Covenant*, 56.)

Often our happiness depends on worldly things. . . . When these externals are jerked away one way or another—when we lose our health, lose our money, lose our spouse, lose our kids—then we have to find peace internally. (In *Women in the Covenant*, 56.)

SHERI L. DEW

In this world, the only true joy comes from the gospel—the joy that radiates from the Atonement and from ordinances that transcend the veil, and from the Comforter that salves our souls. (In *Ensign*, Nov. 2000, 95.)

MARY ELLEN EDMUNDS

As Saints we *can* be happy, . . . we *ought* to be happy, and . . . in a very real sense, we are the creators of our own happiness. Happiness is within us—that's where it's *found,* and that's where it's *kept.* And from there, that's where it's *shared,* too. (*Happiness,* 205.)

Perhaps the height of happiness—the ultimate in joy and peace—is pleasing God, having His will become ours, and ours His. (*Happiness,* 11.)

I know there will always be many people who have much, much more than I do— . . . but there will also always be millions who have much, much less than I do, and in many situations much, much less than they need. . . . It is not what I have, but what I enjoy, that brings real happiness. (In *LDS Women's Treasury,* 352.)

JAROLDEEN ASPLUND EDWARDS

When we recognize the minute gap that separates ordinary accomplishment from accomplishment that gives satisfaction and joy, we can feel a tremendous surge of hope, because we understand that by seeing our lives with new eyes, we can identify little things that can lift our spirits, our memories, and our ability to rejoice in work nobly completed. (*Celebration!* 60.)

Everyday occasions can be transformed into experiences of joy. The power of improving the delight of our lives is not an enormous thing—it is a small proportion of all the hundreds of things we are already doing right. (*Celebration!* 60.)

To feel joy . . . requires a decision on our part—a chosen approach to life, a chosen attitude, a constant awareness. This decision is the necessary beginning to recognizing, feeling, and developing the joy with which Heavenly Father has filled our creation. (*Celebration!* 3.)

MICHAELENE P. GRASSLI

The more well developed we are spiritually, the more joy we find in simple pleasures. (*What I Have Learned,* 82.)

I believe that if we can enjoy the simple pleasures of life as adults, we can be more appreciative of our Heavenly Father and his creations and the gifts he has given us. I think it increases our spiritual sensitivities. (*What I Have Learned,* 82.)

AMY HARDISON

"Which comes first, the smile or the happiness?" . . . The answer is simple: both. At times, happiness stimulates the smile. At other times, the smile stimulates the happiness. The same is true for singing and whistling. Frequent smiling, singing, or whistling can help us establish the happiness habit. (*How to Feel Great,* 86.)

PATRICIA T. HOLLAND

The safety and surety of making covenants with God is anchored in the fact that he has prepared them for our exquisite joy. (In *To Rejoice As Women*, 97.)

Joy comes from loving and being loved. When this divine attribute is at work in our feelings for our family, our neighbors, our God, *and ourselves*, we feel joy. (In *LDS Women's Treasury*, 96–97.)

CAMILLA EYRING KIMBALL

Happiness comes of the capacity to feel deeply, to enjoy simply, to think freely, and to be needed. It comes from conforming our lives to those things which set our minds at rest and our hearts at peace. (*Writings*, 143.)

JENNIE B. KNIGHT

Let us get joy and happiness out of the things that God has given to us to enjoy. (In *Relief Society Magazine*, June 1927, 310.)

Life is much more joyful and satisfying to one who is compassionate, forbearing, tender, lenient, gentle, mild, forgiving, and appreciative. (In *Relief Society Magazine*, Jan. 1940, 56.)

EILEEN GIBBONS KUMP

Happiness lies so much in knowing that what is happening may be earthshaking, not just in being there and moving on. (In *Woman's Choices*, 108.)

From where I sit I can see . . . three high school students. My senses are alive. The family is coming home! . . . My Israel is gathering, and as soon as Dad and the other girl arrive, we will all be under one roof. This happens almost every day, yet it is a highlight of my life. I am overwhelmed with a sense of its importance. Such fleeting moments need our attention and thought. (In *Woman's Choices*, 108.)

JANET G. LEE

Life does not have to be perfect to have moments of perfect happiness. They come with the smile of a child, the kindness of a co-worker, the satisfaction of a job well done, or the appreciation of a sunset, a blossom, a familiar melody, or even a well-scrubbed sink. (In *Best of Women's Conference*, 285.)

COLEEN K. MENLOVE

It is knowing and feeling the pure love of Christ that brings exquisite joy to our souls. It is knowing that forgiveness for our mistakes is possible. It is through the Atonement of the Savior, who satisfied the demands of justice and offers us mercy, that hope and joy are possible. (In *Ensign*, May 2000, 13.)

CAROLINE EYRING MINER

I want to sweep out the cobwebs that have hidden the joyousness that the gospel, pure of slander and selfishness, offers my life. (In *Ensign*, Mar. 1980, 29.)

JOANN OTTLEY

If my musical involvement ended tomorrow, I would probably

shed some tears and it would be painful, but my overall joy would remain intact because I know . . . that while music is a great joy, it is only a delicious fragment of a greater joy, even a promised fullness of joy. (In *Woman's Choices*, 98.)

TESSA MEYER SANTIAGO

Satan, the author of confusion, would have us believe that an "easy way" is one of quick, instant gratification. But pleasure is not the purpose and goal of our existence. Joy is. . . . Satan wants us to confuse the two. (In *May Christ Lift Thee Up*, 205.)

BARBARA B. SMITH

When we can respect not only the differences in others but also their accomplishments, we begin to experience some of the joy the Lord intended. There is so much more of happiness to be had when we can rejoice in another's successes and not just in our own. (In *Ensign*, May 1982, 97.)

IDA SMITH

We all at one time or another make a big mistake in thinking we are, or can be, responsible for the happiness of others. No person can make another person happy. (In *As Women of Faith*, 210.)

ELIZA R. SNOW

Surely happiness is not altogether the product of circumstances—our Father who watches over his children's welfare will order all things for good if we will put our trust in him; we need not fear. (*Personal Writings*, 133.)

BELLE S. SPAFFORD

Service to others is essential to joy in living. We cannot live selfishly and be completely happy. (In *Relief Society Magazine*, Nov. 1970, 806.)

Happiness is an infallible by-product of service. (*Today's World*, 211.)

M. CATHERINE THOMAS

We don't need ideal relationships in order to be happy; we can live happily with less than ideal because each relationship can be enriched with that spirit of at-one-ment which so greatly improves the quality of our personal emotional lives. (*Spiritual Lightening*, 84.)

HELEN MAR WHITNEY

I believe that we have been and are still the happiest people living, for the Holy Spirit has assisted us, and *that* with a clear conscience is of more worth than the whole world without it. (*Woman's View*, 130.)

BARBARA W. WINDER

Joy, it seems, is not only happiness, but the resultant feeling of the Holy Ghost manifest within us. (In *Ensign*, Nov. 1987, 96.)

Joy is knowing that through the atoning sacrifice of Christ we can receive a remission of our sins. (In *Ensign*, Nov. 1987, 97.)

Kindness

ELAINE CANNON

One of the beautiful compensations of life is that no one can be genuinely gracious to another without being blessed himself. (*Count Your Blessings*, 63.)

MARJORIE P. HINCKLEY

There is no such thing as a small act of kindness. (In *Glimpses*, 214.)

ELAINE L. JACK

Sometimes kindness means we should keep quiet or leave a situation. Sometimes kindness requires us to remain and try to make things right. (In *Ensign*, July 1995, 53.)

Kindness doesn't mean we have to be submissive to others, but kindness does require of us that we measure our own responses against a righteous standard. We must be submissive to the Spirit of the Lord. (In *Ensign*, July 1995, 53.)

Being kind is nothing more than reaching out with gentleness and understanding. How desperately that is needed in this brash, coarse, insensitive world! (*Eye to Eye*, 21.)

Few things are as healing as simple kindness—a gentle touch, a pat on the arm, an encouraging word, patient silence, a probing question when something is obviously wrong, a withholding of judgment until all the facts are known. If we are sincere about being followers of Christ, if we really mean it when we partake of the sacrament on Sunday or attend a temple session, we will be kind. (In *Ensign*, July 1995, 53.)

As we increase our kindness, we add charity to our storehouse and we are strengthened. (In *Ensign*, Nov. 1996, 91.)

BETTY JO JEPSEN

We are made kind by being kind. (In *Ensign*, Nov. 1990, 91.)

Kindness has many synonyms—love, service, charity. But I like the word *kindness* because it implies action. It seems like something you and I can do. (In *Ensign*, Nov. 1990, 91.)

JO ANN LARSEN

Kindness's benevolence . . . constitutes a golden chain, the links of which, ever so delicately, tenderly interlace and interlock God's creatures, one to another. (*Heart of Goodness*, 240.)

CHIEKO N. OKAZAKI

We must choose kindness as the way in which we lead our lives—but without a spiritual foundation, we simply will not have the strength and will to sustain our desire to be kind. (*Aloha!* 171.)

Kindness is an addiction nobody would want to cure. Kindness multiplies and strengthens. It's like a chemical reaction—a good one—that doesn't stop, once it's set in motion. (*Sanctuary*, 79.)

BELLE S. SPAFFORD

Friendliness and human kindness are universal needs of mankind. Without them one is lonely and embittered, with them one's spirit is light and he rises above the things that would defeat him. (*Today's World*, 55–56.)

Courtesy and Good Manners

ELAINE CANNON

Good manners are . . . an outward expression of our inner feelings toward others. (*Bell Ringer*, 91.)

SYDNEY SMITH REYNOLDS

Good manners are a matter not just of which fork to use but of civility and respect for all our Father's children. (In *Clothed with Charity*, 262.)

BELLE S. SPAFFORD

Good manners involve the art of adjusting our behavior to all. They transcend the habits of clique, caste, or period of time. (*Today's World*, 127–28.)

Genuine courtesy comes from the heart and is based on morality, decency, and consideration. (*Today's World*, 127.)

Human felicity is produced not so much by great pieces of good fortune as by little considerations every day. (*Today's World*, 127.)

Using good manners . . . is the suiting of our behavior to the greatest benefit, comfort, and ease of others. (*Today's World*, 127.)

Knowledge and Truth

Education

KAREN LYNN DAVIDSON

We should never be so proud, so smug, that we think we have learned enough. (In *Women and Christ*, 27.)

God never wastes education. When we are teachable, we are always learning—from books, from experiences, from observation. This education is never wasted on us individually; we become more appreciative, more alive. (In *Women and Christ*, 27.)

SUSA YOUNG GATES

Education is gained by study, of books, yes, but also by study of men, and of nature in all its forms. Books are merely the opinions of men who have studied things out in various ways. (In *Relief Society Magazine*, Sept. 1921, 498.)

There is no pleasure on earth like that given by a refined and cultivated intellect, lit up by the glorious rays of the spirit of the living God. (In *Women's Voices*, 327–28.)

CAMILLA EYRING KIMBALL

No learner has ever run short of subjects to explore. (*Writings*, 13.)

ELAINE SORENSEN MARSHALL

True education is a process of life and not a means to an end. (In *Woman's Choices*, 29.)

ANNE OSBORN POELMAN

Formal educational degrees . . . are relatively unimportant from the eternal point of view. The personal qualities that the educational process enhances are not. . . . While the earthly medical degree I worked so long and hard to attain has permitted me to render a very special type of service, perhaps even more important are the qualities of compassion, intellectual discipline, decision-making, analytical skills, and faith that were honed and enriched by that rigorous professional training. These are portable, eternal qualities that can and will rise with us in the resurrection. (In *Joy*, 49.)

ELLIS R. SHIPP

How happy must be [an] . . . educated person, for even the cur-

sory knowledge I have gained . . . has opened to my view depths and heights of which I had never dreamed. (*While Others Slept*, 219.)

BELLE S. SPAFFORD

True education to the Latter-day Saint is education that builds faith and promotes righteousness. Education that fails to do this cannot be considered as aught but inferior education. (*Woman's Reach*, 36.)

A golden tomorrow can only be assured if the highly perfected products of science are utilized by highly perfected personal character. (*Woman's Reach*, 40.)

The laboratories of citizenship—the home, the school, the church, and the community—must be as patient, tireless, and intelligent in the production of fine character as is science in the products of its laboratories. (*Woman's Reach*, 40.)

LEANN P. WHEELER

Education is a vital part of the plan of salvation, the plan to perfect us, to open our understanding and to prepare us to return to live in the presence of an eternal Father in Heaven. (In *To Rejoice As Women*, 232.)

How shortsighted . . . if we regard education as merely a mortal stepping-stone. . . . Education is a long-term process, an eternal process, not an end in itself. Losing sight of its ultimate purpose can result in frustration, if not a sense of futility. (In *To Rejoice As Women*, 232.)

Barbara W. Winder

Learning is a gradual process of growth, each step building upon the other. It is a process whereby the learner organizes and integrates not only facts but attitudes and values. (In *BYU Speeches*, 16 Aug. 1988, 4.)

Education . . . is not merely gaining knowledge or skills helpful toward productive work. . . . Rather it is a replenishment and an expansion of the natural thirst of the mind and soul. (In *BYU Speeches*, 16 Aug. 1988, 4.)

Seeking Knowledge

Marilyn Arnold

The wise books that bring joy and stability to our lives are the books that carry knowledge and truths that endure in language worthy of them. (In *Best of Women's Conference*, 9.)

All books are not created equal, . . . all books are not rooted in principles that lead us to understanding and stability. (In *Best of Women's Conference*, 9.)

Marilyn S. Bateman

The purpose of our learning effort is eternal in nature. Secular learning is important, . . . but there is a danger when one takes pride in one's scholarship, when one does not couple scholarship with discipleship. (In *Wisdom's Paths*, 117.)

Ultimately, any person who seeks truth will be led to the gospel of Jesus Christ, for it contains all truth. (In *Wisdom's Paths*, 104.)

Jaroldeen Asplund Edwards

Here are some guidelines to help distinguish between intellectualism and knowledge:

Knowledge never builds barriers between us and others. . . . Intellectualism considers itself superior to others.

Knowledge gives us vision and supports and reinforces spiritual truth. . . . Intellectualism deliberately obfuscates. . . .

Knowledge ponders and is obedient. . . . Intellectualism defies direction and desires constant rethinking. . . .

Knowledge teaches how much we have yet to learn. It teaches us the value of the Spirit and the ideas of others regardless of their education. Knowledge makes us truly humble.

Intellectualism makes us proud and causes us to jealously guard what we know to use against others to convince, control, or win. It causes us to have faith in the learning of man rather than in the Spirit of the Lord.

Finally, true knowledge fills the countenance with truth and light and makes us more approachable, open, and understanding—more loving. (*Celebration!* 98–99.)

Ruth May Fox

Opportunities are not lacking these days for intellectual advancement. All roads are open, thank God, to the humble poor, as well as to others of greater needs. . . . Remember that all good things are yours for the seeking, and that genius is often nothing more than well-directed energy. (In *Improvement Era*, Aug. 1912, 922.)

Man's intellect is God-given, and is a spark of that eternal intelligence which governs all things. Through its proper training man may reach to the highest possible culture, or through its misdirection may descend to the very dust. (In *Improvement Era*, Aug. 1912, 921.)

Man grows in intelligence as he grows in good works. So it is not altogether what he knows that counts, but what he does, or, how he uses the talents with which God has blessed him. (In *Improvement Era*, Aug. 1912, 921.)

SUSA YOUNG GATES

Let the youth who places his feet upon the threshold of learning say once and forever to his own soul, "I know that every principle of the Gospel is true, and by that iron rod will I measure everything which comes before me." (In *Young Woman's Journal*, Feb. 1895, 335.)

Books and teachers give us help in crossing over from the land of ignorance to the land of learning. (In *Relief Society Magazine*, Sept. 1921, 498.)

The world that an individual lives in is as large and no larger than is his mental geography. The world is always bounded, for us, by what we do not know. (In *Young Woman's Journal*, Nov. 1900, 523.)

MARJORIE P. HINCKLEY

The rewards for intellectual curiosity are many. The world will always be your pumpkin, full of magic, full of wonder. You will be interesting to your friends, to your husband, and a joy to your children. You will have perpetual youth. (In *Glimpses*, 106.)

ELAINE L. JACK

Light and truth are not obscure terms. Truth is basic to the gospel. The more we seek to know, the better we are able to distinguish between a foolish notion and a wise idea. From such wisdom, we find truth. (In *Ensign*, Nov. 1994, 89.)

Being able to read enables us to seek further light and truth. Light is more than being able to see with eyes. It includes revelation of things as they are, as they were, and as they are to come. Light brings definition out of darkness. (In *Ensign*, Nov. 1994, 89.)

CAMILLA EYRING KIMBALL

Learning is not just for one set of people or for one time of life. It is a basic activity for all mankind. (In *Heritage of Faith*, 7.)

We are on earth to learn, first of all the principles of salvation, and then the secrets of the world, to subdue it and make it fruitful, and to delight the mind. (In *Heritage of Faith*, 7.)

The Lord fosters beauty, and there is beauty in all knowledge, not just in music and painting, but in biology and geology and mathematics, too. (In *Heritage of Faith*, 7.)

LINDA HOFFMAN KIMBALL

Ours is a gospel that teaches believers to seek for further light and knowledge. That means that some sentences that seem to have periods on the end really need ellipses. Dot Dot Dot . . . Stay tuned! More to come! To be continued! (In *Women in the Covenant*, 189.)

JOAN B. MACDONALD

Questions have answers, and if young people are humble and seek their Heavenly Father's help, they can allow ideas that are too simple or too naïve to die, knowing that God is with them and will help them reach new levels of understanding. (*Holiness of Everyday Life*, 26.)

HOLLY METCALF

There is more danger in filling my head and heart indiscriminately than there is in filling my stomach indiscriminately. (In *As a Woman Thinketh*, 119.)

CAROLINE EYRING MINER

Curiosity keeps adults from feeling old and helps children and young people become mature. (In *Relief Society Magazine*, Mar. 1965, 223.)

BARBARA B. SMITH

When true learning takes place, we realize how much there is yet unknown and feel the thrill of accepting the challenge to pit ourselves against the unknown. (*Love*, 65.)

The pursuit of knowledge, the learning little by little—one step at a time—and the setting of the mind to the ongoing excitement of learning is part of what we should do with our lives. It is an adventure. (*Love*, 65.)

There is something to learn from everyone and from every experience. (In *Ensign*, Apr. 1976, 68.)

MARY ELLEN SMOOT

Truth endures and liberates, whereas fallacy falters and imprisons. Truth carries with it power, whereas falsehood yields only unfulfilled expectations. (In *BYU Speeches*, 10 Feb. 1998, 171.)

BELLE S. SPAFFORD

Parents are urged to take a long-range view of the needs of their children. . . . Their future welfare and the strength of the nation are in large measure bound up with the wise use of school opportunities. If our children are to be equipped for tomorrow, they should go to school today. (In *Relief Society Magazine*, Sept. 1944, 509.)

Spiritual Knowledge

SUSAN EASTON BLACK

Truths [of the gospel] are not new but eternal. . . . But for me and for you, individually, the truths need to be discovered anew to reach an understanding of who we are in the eyes of deity and why Jesus loved us so much he would atone for our sins that we might return to our Father in Heaven. (In *BYU Speeches*, 22 Nov. 1994, 68–69.)

JUTTA BAUM BUSCHE

The truth that makes one free is twofold: the truths of the restored gospel, which provide a map of eternal realities, and the skill of being truthful with oneself and others, which leads to genuine repentance and integrity. (In *Women and the Power*, 23.)

ELAINE CANNON

Personal opinions may vary. Eternal principles never do. (In *Ensign*, Nov. 1978, 107.)

SUSA YOUNG GATES

Some day people will learn that material things do not bring happiness and are of little use in making men and women creative and powerful. Then . . . the world will turn . . . to the study of God and prayer and the spiritual forces which as yet have hardly been scratched. When this day comes, the world will see more advancement in one generation than it has seen in the past four. (In *Improvement Era*, Apr. 1930, 407.)

ARDETH GREENE KAPP

Glimpses of understanding come line upon line, precept upon precept. Our Father is anxious to feed us just as fast as we can handle it, but we regulate the richness and the volume of our spiritual diet. (In *Best of Women's Conference*, 240.)

Everything we do takes time, and our time is our life. Some give their life for little or nothing and then it is gone. But if our life is spent in learning and teaching truth, used in righteousness, then the investment is good. It is worth the price because the acquisition of that knowledge is transportable. (*I Walk by Faith*, 96.)

If a person chooses to set aside the things of the Spirit while pursuing only academic endeavors, the outcome is predictable. . . . At a later date, as graduates with degrees, such individuals may stack their acquired academic knowledge against the thin threads of a faith that has been weakened through neglect. Their spiritual strength may have remained at . . . an elementary school level. And when they endeavor to make judgments of things of the Spirit that come only by faith, the great reservoir of truth into which they could have dipped will be shallow, discolored, or stagnant. (*I Walk by Faith*, 98–99.)

CAMILLA EYRING KIMBALL

With all the other knowledge that enriches our lives, let us not forget to include the knowledge of the gospel of Jesus Christ. (*Writings*, 86.)

AMY BROWN LYMAN

Believing that the Glory of God is intelligence, Latter-day Saints have always fostered education; and believing in a life beyond the grave where we take with us all that we learn here, they have sensed the importance of placing emphasis on those things which are spiritual in nature and permanent in value. (In *Relief Society Magazine*, Nov. 1936, 699–700.)

ANN N. MADSEN

Truth. Jesus taught shining truths. He knew that our knowing the truth would free us to be exalted. He knew that truth would attract us, like a miraculous magnet, and would contribute to our happiness and peace. He knew that we would be enlivened and empowered by it. (In *Redeemer*, 47.)

DEBORAH ELDREDGE MILNE

Looking through my spiritual eyes rather than my physical eyes, I am better able to distinguish true ideas from false ideas. I can avoid sources that destroy my inner peace. . . . By nourishing our souls as well as our minds, we can enjoy a rich harvest of testimony, spirituality, and peace. (In *Ensign*, Apr. 1996, 61.)

BARBARA B. SMITH

We must love the truth—love it enough to seek for it, love it enough to understand it, love it enough to live it. (In *BYU Speeches*, 9 Feb. 1978, 15.)

Bring the light of truth. Do it through your senses, through your reason, and most significantly through the Spirit. . . . The light of truth is there waiting to be discovered, and, being discovered, waiting to illuminate the life of each child of God. (In *Ensign*, Nov. 1981, 101.)

M. CATHERINE THOMAS

The urge to know the mysteries of godliness is not necessarily an idle curiosity; rather, it is a divine drive to acquire that level of godly power modeled by Christ and others of his holy order. (*Selected Writings*, 154.)

The whole gospel is a collection of mysteries—truths pertaining to salvation that would not be known by men in the mortal probation if God did not reveal them. (*Selected Writings*, 84.)

WENDY L. WATSON

The Lord generously manifests to us those things we are seeking— just as soon as he perceives we are ready. (In *Arise*, 171.)

ZINA D. H. YOUNG

Obedience and humility brings to us the grandest knowledge on earth and opens the door of Heaven to us. (In *Woman's Exponent*, 15 Oct. 1894, 199.)

Latter-day Saints

MILDRED CHANDLER AUSTIN

Being picked out of a crowd as a Mormon should be a compliment, because it shows our willingness to set an example in all things. Mormons *should* look like Mormons. (*Divine Destiny*, 43.)

JANETTE HALES BECKHAM

Our stakes and wards can provide a place removed from worldly influences. The ward is such an important place for every member of the Church. It can be an environment of trust where every member can feel loved, understood, respected, and able to contribute. (In *BYU Speeches*, 7 Aug. 1994, 193.)

MICHAELENE P. GRASSLI

We mustn't fall into the trap of equating the human differences of our brothers and sisters with weakness in the Church or in the gospel. The gospel of Jesus Christ is true and perfect. We mortals in his church— all of us—are just learning how to live it. (*LeaderTalk*, 62.)

BEPPIE HARRISON

If Jesus Christ were to return tomorrow (and he might), would I be doing anything differently today? And if so, why? (*Plain and Precious*, 140.)

We have to be prepared for Christ's coming. Our preparations make sense if the recognition that the way we prepare ourselves is to be living the best life of which we're capable and if we're doing that, it doesn't greatly matter if Christ comes tomorrow or if we live a long life and have our reunion with him only when we pass to the other side. Either way we are living as he would have us live. (*Plain and Precious*, 314–15.)

MARJORIE P. HINCKLEY

We are in a time when the winds of adversity and sophisticated criticism and bitter attack have become the order of the day. . . . Those of us who have inherited a firm foundation from the faithful ones who preceded us [must] build the kingdom, while others may wear out their lives trying to destroy it. (In *Best of Women's Conference*, 181.)

CAMILLA EYRING KIMBALL

We are of royal birth. Realizing this, we should strive to develop to our highest potential. (*Writings*, 82.)

We assume a tremendous responsibility when we take upon ourselves the name of our Savior. As members of his church we are his representatives here on the earth, and we have the responsibility to represent him faithfully. (*Writings*, 82.)

I always tried to teach our children that people are not perfect, but that the gospel plan is perfect. I told them never to be let down by what an individual does. If a [person] makes a mistake, that has no effect on the truthfulness of the gospel. (*Writings*, 88.)

SHARON G. LARSEN

It is not an easy matter to undertake to be a Latter-day Saint, nor is it possible at the same time to keep that summer home in Babylon. (In *Arms of His Love*, 34.)

AMY BROWN LYMAN

The gospel is so high in its ideals that we should not represent it unless we have high ideals. (In *Relief Society Magazine*, June 1922, 324.)

PATRICIA P. PINEGAR

Being involved in building the kingdom will require us to move out of our comfort zone. One of the great purposes of earth life is to help us change and become more Christlike. That requires us to stretch and grow. (In *BYU Speeches*, 7 Mar. 1999, 165.)

Being a kingdom builder is a wondrous opportunity. . . . I believe, because we are the spirit children of God the Father, because we have taken upon ourselves the name of Jesus Christ, because we have received the gift of the Holy Ghost, within our souls there is a yearning to serve, to be kingdom builders. (In *BYU Speeches*, 7 Mar. 1999, 165–66.)

The Lord does not require that you have exceptional gifts or abilities. He asks that you be humble, trusting, sincere, and willing to serve. Then He can guide you to do important work in His kingdom. (In *BYU Speeches*, 7 Mar. 1999, 164.)

ROSE MARIE REID

I learned that other people respect us and are proud to know us and want us . . . to live up to our standards. So, . . . tell everyone you meet that you are a Mormon, and then live your religion to the utmost of your ability. As sure as you do, the most wonderful blessings will follow as automatically as day follows night. (In *BYU Speeches*, 1 June 1953, 4.)

LOUISE Y. ROBISON

We are not pessimists but people of faith, faith in ourselves and in our country—faith in the living God who strengthens the cause of right and we are going to set our hands to the task that lies before us. (In *Relief Society Magazine*, Mar. 1932, 154.)

BARBARA B. SMITH

Many problems are severe and debilitating. They cause fear and guilt and heartache. Often, the difference in people's finding their way or discovering solutions is the kindly, understanding friendship we can provide for them in our priesthood and Relief Society meetings or other

Church settings. (In *Ensign*, Nov. 1982, 82.)

The Savior . . . counsels, "Behold, I come quickly." (Rev. 3:11.) We must live with constant anticipation of his coming. Being ready to receive him is the position of our greatest strength. Let this be our bulwark against temptation or slothfulness. Let it cause us to read the Savior's words, to search our hearts, and to try to live every principle of righteousness he taught. (In *Ensign*, Nov. 1983, 85.)

MARY ELLEN SMOOT

As I have traveled and met new converts, their eyes ablaze with the joy and peace their newfound faith has brought them, I have seen them make great sacrifices to join the fold. We must honor their sacrifice by loving them and strengthening them. (In *Ensign*, Nov. 1997, 12.)

BELLE S. SPAFFORD

The individual behavior of each person who claims to be a Mormon affects the reputation of the Church as a whole, and influences the opinions of people with regard to the general desirability of the religion and its effectiveness in the lives of Church members. (In *Relief Society Magazine*, Aug. 1942, 550.)

Latter-day Saints can remain composed, they can calm the frenzy of others, they can . . . purposefully direct their lives and intelligently adjust to whatever comes if they place confidence in their leaders, if they study the word of God and do his bidding, if they commune with him often, both in their homes and in the house of worship. These are the sources from which we may draw courage and strength to meet these precarious times. (*Today's World*, 62.)

The terms "brother" and "sister," so universally used in the Church are symbols of the fellow feeling that should characterize us upon all occasions and under all circumstances as The Church of Jesus Christ of Latter-day Saints. There is no organization more concerned with the well-being and happiness of mankind. (*Today's World*, 57.)

All Latter-day Saints now have unusual and abundant opportunity to teach the Gospel in the most impressive and effective way—by living according to Church standards every day under all circumstances. (In *Relief Society Magazine*, Aug. 1942, 551.)

PEGGY ST. CYR

Commitment is difficult; it demands involvement and activity on an emotional and a physical level. But commitment is necessary if we are to stay close to the Lord, if we are to live the life we chose for ourselves when we were baptized as members of his church. (*Conversion to Commitment*, 5.)

M. CATHERINE THOMAS

As [Jesus] drank the cup his Father gave him, so the Saints drink what the Lord Jesus gives them. The Savior's cup was not that he be ministered to but to minister and to give his life as a ransom for many. (*Selected Writings*, 152.)

In the midst of the worst trials ever known among the children of men, the Saints will finish up the work of this dispensation under the direction of the Lord Jesus Christ. (*Selected Writings*, 39.)

We will have to be a people who understand personal revelation. We will have to live in direct contact with the temporal world, but we will have to know how to be guided by the heavenly, unseen world. (*Selected Writings*, 40.)

Leadership

MICHAELENE P. GRASSLI

Whether or not we are born leaders, sooner or later most of us in the Church lead someone sometime. When we think of our eventual state or condition, we know we all have the potential to be leaders in the eternities. This means we can be wonderful leaders now. It's there inside us just waiting to be developed. (*LeaderTalk*, 3.)

To be a leader, you must lead. Leaders are out in front, setting the pace and showing the way. Leaders get problems solved as they help others learn and grow. They don't do it alone, but their leadership sets the climate in which others serve and the standard others will strive for. (*LeaderTalk*, 2.)

ARDETH GREENE KAPP

Leaders must be strong, consistent, and stable under pressure. People, especially youth, find security in leaders who stand by correct principles, uphold them, and teach them by example. (*Lead*, 48.)

A leader with vision is like a light in the darkness. A leader with vision can motivate people to do things they would not otherwise do, turning dreams into reality by effectively enlisting others in a good cause. . . . Your own vision and conviction can help others begin to see, feel, and believe in what is yet to be realized. (*Lead*, 22.)

Recognizing, feeling, and following the promptings of the Spirit should be the matter of greatest importance in all leadership responsibility. (*Lead*, 74.)

Goals help leaders become results oriented instead of task oriented. (*Lead*, 55.)

Consider both ministering and administering, with emphasis on ministering. *Administering* tends to focus on programs, activities, and meetings. *Ministering*, on the other hand, focuses on people and principles first, and then programs are considered in the context of how best to serve the people and teach the principles. (*Lead*, 65.)

The key to being effective is planning with a purpose. We simply ask the question, "What do we . . . want to have happen?" Once that goal is clearly understood, effective planning can begin. (*Lead*, 54.)

Leadership requires studying, preparing, seeking, asking. Inspiration is available to those called to lead—women as well as men—when we seek it earnestly, ask prayerfully, and work diligently. And having prepared in mind and heart, we speak up in the spirit of the work. (In *Thy People*, 15.)

CHIEKO N. OKAZAKI

We face a turbulent future, one in which the hunger for leadership will rise to famine proportions. . . . Make the choice to be a light-bringer to dark places. Have the humility to reflect the greater light rather than to rely only on your own resources. (*Disciples*, 188.)

Sometimes I think we see programs. We count the Lord's sheep instead of feeding them. We check to see how many chairs are filled, not who is filling them and—even more important, who is missing. We see groups instead of individuals. We see cases instead of the person. (*Cat's Cradle*, 24–25.)

LOUISE Y. ROBISON

The challenge is here for us today. The person who is willing to make the effort—and it requires effort—to study and understand the principles of the Gospel, plus the courage to live its principles, will become a leader, and leaders are needed in every country. (In *Relief Society Magazine*, Aug. 1934, 463.)

Love

Love Is the Greatest Need

ELAINE CANNON

Love is the most used, misused, understood, misunderstood, simple yet profound word in our language. It is the most poignant, powerful, beautiful, fulfilling concept placed in the heart of man. Love is a thought given by God to man so that man might become like God. (*Love You*, 40.)

Love is life's great gift. And if ever, perchance, you have felt unloved, vow never to let that happen to any other person you know. (*Count Your Blessings*, 153.)

Deanna Edwards

I have never met anyone who was too old, too hurt or too tired to be loved. (*Grieving*, 156.)

Joy F. Evans

Having compassion on those who are hurting for whatever reason and then translating the response of the heart into the needed act is truly ministering as God would have us do. (In *Ensign*, May 1989, 73.)

Susa Young Gates

We must love one another. Only so can our long years of toil and struggle reach full reward and we be crowned with life everlasting. (In *LDS Women's Treasury*, 403.)

Suzanne L. Hansen

We all crave love, just like plants crave water. (In *Sharing the Light*, 69.)

Elaine L. Jack

Nothing is more central to a true Christian life than demonstrating love for others. (*Eye to Eye*, 153.)

If our work is not based on love, it won't matter what it is based on. (*Eye to Eye*, 153.)

Wendy L. Watson

When I ask myself, "What is the biggest difference between a life-giving relationship and a life-grieving relationship?" the answer is love. (In *May Christ Lift Thee Up*, 42.)

Love Is a Gift of God

Elaine Cannon

With all things being possible through Christ, love can happen. It doesn't come with a snap of the fingers but rather through countless acts of kindness and a mind set on establishing choice relationships. . . . We have but to put our heart in Christ's and reach for renewal and a healing in love. (*Love You*, 2.)

Patricia T. Holland

Perfect love, the kind that brings real peace, is bestowed. It is a gift given from our Father in heaven in answer to the prayer of faith. (*On Earth*, 32.)

Elaine L. Jack

When Christlike love becomes our main motivator, when we really get serious about truly demonstrating our love for the Lord, good things happen. (In *BYU Speeches*, 2 June 1991, 129.)

Camilla Eyring Kimball

Cheerfully express the love you . . . feel and go to your Heavenly Father and ask him for more. (*Writings*, 129.)

Wendy L. Watson

Without the love of the Savior in our lives, no other love can fill the void of being out of his presence. (In *Arms of His Love*, 200.)

Charity—the Pure Love of Christ

ELAINE CANNON

To love as God loves is to believe in the spark of the divine in all men and to value God's gifts or principles for relating to others. (*Love You*, 148.)

MARILYN JEPPSON CHOULES

The Savior's nature is characterized by [kindness]. It is a basic component of the pure love of Christ. (In *Behold Your Little Ones*, 94.)

AILEEN H. CLYDE

Understanding charity or being charitable is not easy. And our scriptures have not indicated that it would be. Even "charity suffereth long" requires our thoughtful interpretation. The suffering that may come from loving is the result of our great caring. It comes because another matters to us so much. (In *Ensign*, Nov. 1991, 77.)

MARY ELLEN EDMUNDS

If we really have charity, with all that it means, then peace happens, and *Zion can* be a reality. (In *Knit Together in Love*, 50.)

Charity—the pure love of Christ—is the greatest force on this earth, and one of the *only* things powerful enough to change all the trouble in this world. (In *Knit Together in Love*, 34.)

Charity is a condition of the heart, and a conditioning of the heart. (In *Knit Together in Love*, 42.)

Charity is not only the "act," the "doing," but that which compels us to act and to do. (In *Knit Together in Love*, 42.)

I have come to know that the gospel of Jesus Christ is full of beautiful words, all related to the word *charity*. Words such as *feed*, *hug*, *mourn*, *serve*, *forgive*, *lift*, *succor*, *comfort*, *share*, *visit*. Love is what makes us *whole*. Love perfects us. (In *Knit Together in Love*, 50.)

If we could really figure out how to love, how to exercise charity, we wouldn't need a whole lot of other commandments. (In *Knit Together in Love*, 47.)

LINDA J. EYRE

You can have all the traits necessary to develop the greatest quality of all: charity—the pure love of Christ. (*Joyful Mother*, 125.)

MARIE K. HAFEN

Whereas cooperation involves mostly our own power to love, charity is a combination of our own desires and energies coupled with the Spirit and the healing power of God. Whereas cooperation may be action-centered, charity is motive-centered. (In *Clothed with Charity*, 45.)

PATRICIA T. HOLLAND

We have been created to become like the Gods. That means we

already have inherent within us godly attributes, the greatest of which is Christlike charity. And the key to emotional health is charity—love. (In *LDS Women's Treasury*, 96.)

Charity is the greatest of all talents, gifts, and virtues. (In *Ensign*, June 1984, 52.)

ELAINE L. JACK

Love—charity—is an eternal law of such magnitude that the prophets have told us if we don't possess it, little else matters. (*Eye to Eye*, 153.)

Charity is so important that we must have it in our lives. It is not just nice to possess charity; it is essential. (In *BYU Speeches*, 10 Mar. 1992, 87.)

Charity is love—not just earthly love or temporary love, but the pure love of Christ. (In *BYU Speeches*, 10 Mar. 1992, 87.)

Charity helps us maintain our footing when all around us are skidding about. (In *Ensign*, May 1994, 16.)

Charity is the ability to rejoice in the accomplishments and the gifts of others, to forget about competing. (In *Clothed with Charity*, 51.)

Charity—mature, pure Christlike love—is an arm that reaches out to encircle and reassure; it is a willingness to forgive—and forget . . . ; it is the faith that we can do what the Lord has asked; it is the humility to

take direction and the strength to lead. (In *Clothed with Charity*, 51.)

LUCILE JOHNSON

We need to decide in our marriage and in all relationships that it is never too late to be charitable. We must decide we will try the hardest when it is the hardest to do. (*Enjoy the Journey*, 186.)

ARDETH GREENE KAPP

In expressing true love, we must dip into the reservoir of divine love, the love of Christ. We share in part the pure love of Christ, the fountain of all love. (*My Neighbor*, 118.)

AMY BROWN LYMAN

Charity seeks to build up rather than to tear down character; it refrains from unkind or unfair criticism. It helps those who are weak to rise and then assists in sustaining them. (In *Relief Society Magazine*, Jan. 1915, 6.)

Charity does more than give to the needy—it sympathizes with those in distress, comforts those who mourn, forgives those who do wrong. (In *Relief Society Magazine*, Jan. 1915, 6.)

CHIEKO N. OKAZAKI

We may be ordinary people—vessels made of ordinary clay. But when we experience even a touch of that pure love of Christ, we also experience that promised purity. (*Lighten Up!* 128.)

Christ was born, he lived, and he died to teach us how to love one another and to love our Heavenly Father. The gospel that he taught was one of love. The cause of Christ is to increase the amount of love in the world today—the amount of love in our hearts, the amount of love in our homes, the amount of love in our offices and businesses, the amount of love in our communities, the amount of love in our chapels, the amount of love in our nation, and the amount of love on our planet. (*Cat's Cradle*, 162–63.)

CAROLYN J. RASMUS

Charity . . . is the kind of love that allows us to give of ourselves, to reach out to other people, to build them, and to really love them. The real gifts are gifts of listening and caring and sharing. (In *BYU Speeches*, 16 June 1981, 108.)

[Charity] is not always sweet and nice and agreeable and accommodating. It is, however, always honest and truthful. Love—true love—requires that we ask hard questions and sometimes do hard things. (In *BYU Speeches*, 16 June 1981, 106.)

BARBARA B. SMITH

Charity, or the pure love of Christ, is not synonymous with good deeds or benevolence. But kind, thoughtful, loving acts are the way Jesus has directed us to express our love—both our love for him and our love for others. (In *Ensign*, Nov. 1980, 103.)

If we are thoughtful, warm, and caring to those who are sick, those who mourn, those who are fatherless, those we love, *and* those who despitefully use us, then we have charity, for we are moved to act with compassion. (In *Ensign*, Nov. 1980, 103.)

As we serve with the single desire to nurture all life, we come to know what charity means. (In *Ensign*, Nov. 1980, 103.)

MARY ELLEN SMOOT

Charity is more than a plate of cookies or a scheduled visit. It's a plate of cookies prepared *with love*; it's visiting and teaching *with love*. Charity is a love that never fails, the kind of love we all need—the kind of love we all need to share. It is pure religion. (*Sweet Is the Work*, 39.)

SHIRLEY W. THOMAS

It is not enough that we love; we must also come to a knowledge of the truth and pray with all the energy of our hearts that we may be filled with that love which is called charity, the pure love of Christ, so that when He comes again, we shall be like Him. (In *Woman's Choices*, 23.)

DWAN J. YOUNG

Charity is the power which changes human life. It is the power which soothes the aching heart and restores the soul. (In *Ensign*, Nov. 1983, 86.)

Characteristics of Love

MARILYN ARNOLD

Love is a softening of the heart; pride is a hardening. (In *Hearts Knit Together*, 184.)

MARY ELLEN EDMUNDS

Love requires courage. To share in Christ's way is a courageous undertaking. Do it. Do it now. Respond to promptings that come. (*Love Is a Verb*, 3.)

You can serve without love . . . but I don't think you can have genuine love without serving. . . . Love is thus a powerful, peaceful force for good. (*Love Is a Verb*, 1.)

BEPPIE HARRISON

When you truly love, you are spilling yourself outward. There's no way for irritation or anger or jealousy or insecurity to worm their way against that flow into your heart. . . . There is only warmth and, rising from it, the serenity of harmony. (*Plain and Precious*, 120.)

ELAINE L. JACK

Nothing enriches the soul as much as loving someone else enough to put them first. (*Eye to Eye*, 152–53.)

Perhaps the major reason the Lord told us to love one another is that only through the experience of loving someone can we begin to understand the Lord's love for us. (*Eye to Eye*, 152.)

ARDETH GREENE KAPP

Love grows from risking, taking down the protective covering, and opening our inner thoughts and feelings, sharing our very self. (*Miracles*, 11.)

JO ANN LARSEN

In one sense, letting go can be an unselfish act, a realization that "letting go" may be equivalent to "loving," for when one truly loves, one does not cling to another but gives room for that person to choose his or her own life circumstances. Letting go, then, sometimes represents a formidable test of genuine love. (*Heart of Goodness*, 60.)

Love has a soft touch and a quiet voice. It expresses itself through smiles, through tender words, through friendly eyes, and through warmth that radiates from the soul. (*Heart of Goodness*, 33.)

To love is to give without thought of receiving; it is to consider the safety, growth, and happiness of another to be as significant as that of our own; and it is to offer quiet understanding, loyalty, and forgiveness. To love is . . . to extend the readiness to be inconvenienced and to unselfishly dedicate time to—and to share resources with—another. . . . To love is to courageously share the hidden parts of ourselves, complete with our fears and follies, and to unconditionally accept the complexities and irrationalities of another. (*Heart of Goodness*, 11.)

ELLIS R. SHIPP

'Tis sweet to love, I think indeed it is those who love most who are most Godlike. (*While Others Slept*, 218.)

ELIZA R. SNOW

Everything connected with our affections is engraven on the heart. (*Personal Writings*, 86.)

LEAH D. WIDTSOE

Love grows by expression, not by hiding it under a bushel. (In *Relief Society Magazine*, July 1958, 424.)

Sympathy, Empathy, and Compassion

KATHLEEN RAWLINGS BUNTIN

Empathy says, "I love you. I care. I'm with you." Empathy is encouraging. It is recognizing that grief is a natural process of confronting and adjusting to death and that each person holds the keys to his or her own healing. Empathy is walking a moon in someone else's moccasins. . . . Empathy lifts. (*All Alone*, 107–8.)

CHRISTINE DURHAM

Peacemakers discern beyond the language that we sometimes hear, beyond the actions we sometimes observe; they discern the needs of other human hearts. (In *Every Good Thing*, 336.)

MARY ELLEN EDMUNDS

I don't think it's possible to feel compassion without being *compelled* to do something to help. (In *Knit Together in Love*, 34.)

JOY F. EVANS

It is said that love is tested and proved in the fire of suffering and adversity. How sensitive we should be to those who are suffering or hurting. . . . What we do or say is not as important as that we do or say something—"I care about you," or "Let me help." Where love is, heart will respond to heart and burdens will be lightened. (In *Ensign*, May 1989, 75.)

ELIZABETH HANSEN

Compassion is a deep awareness of the suffering of another *coupled with the wish to relieve that suffering.* (In *Hearts Knit Together*, 31.)

MARY B. JOHNSTON

Compassion, a wind that blows down walls, whispers away prejudice, and cools anger. Compassion, a magic alloy that builds bridges and creates inseparable bonds. (In *Women Steadfast*, 185.)

Think of all the forces that have had the power to separate us from each other: religion, race, class, age, political persuasion, nationality. The list is painfully long. With compassion, these differences do not need to separate or threaten us but instead can provide an opportunity to feel the love of God fill [us]. (In *Women Steadfast*, 185.)

Jo Ann Larsen

Caring opens up its ears as well as its heart to discover and embrace the inner soul of another. And thus caring commits to listening to the words and actions of others and goes in search of their feelings. (*Heart of Goodness*, 339.)

As one person sees through the eyes of another, that person experiences *compassion*. (*Heart of Goodness*, 132.)

Barbara B. Smith

Many times it is the sympathetic arm around the shoulder and the encouraging smile that give to the distressed hope and to the downtrodden courage to try again. We can help them know that others wrestle with problems, too; but strength of family and of character, developed through living gospel principles, has enabled them to rise above life's difficulties. (In *Ensign*, Nov. 1982, 82.)

Emmeline B. Wells

Sympathetic expression is the beautiful gift of some people, but ofttimes the tender handclasp, the silent embrace, or the gentle kiss, speak more than words to those in sorrow and express the love of an overflowing heart. (In *Relief Society Magazine*, Jan. 1915, 4.)

Elizabeth Ann Whitney

We learn to understand human nature by being brought into close connection with each other, and more especially when under trying and difficult circumstances; and we seldom think more unkindly of persons from gaining an insight into their real hearts and character. (In *Their Own Words*, 203.)

Benefits of Love

Ruth E. Brasher

There is an integral relationship between loving our Father in Heaven, loving our neighbors, and loving ourselves. Love in these realms gives perspective to all of the laws and the commandments. (In *BYU Speeches*, 12 July 1983, 159.)

Elaine Cannon

Both the one loved and the one loving benefit from the joy that happens when something wonderful is done out of love—for one particular loved one or for the human race. (*Love You*, 126–27.)

Bear each other's burdens, the gospel teaches, and we come to love God more. (*Love You*, 127.)

Love should be considered an action word, with people moving out to spread joy in today's world. (*Love You*, 127.)

When the heart isn't locked up in self-centeredness it is open to God's influence and sweetening spirit. (*Love You*, 98–99.)

Countless people have testified about the wonder that fills their hearts and minds and the joy that fills their lives as they conscientiously try to love all people. A change actually occurs in them. A miracle happens. (*Love You*, 96.)

Thinking love, feeling love, sharing love, being grateful to God for love's warm healing and comforting spell actually bring a change in one's physical appearance, behavior, and general health. (*Love You*, 23.)

[Love] is like the sun shining over the whole earth—through love everything is seen in its best beauty. With love dictating the gentle, wondrous responses to God, nature, and all mankind, life has an awesome luster. (*Gatherings*, 147–48.)

When we show forth love toward God with all our heart, might, mind, and strength and in the name of Jesus Christ serve him by loving and teaching and helping others, we will be filled with God's love. We will be changed. (*Gatherings*, 153.)

The withholding of love because of grief, envy, fatigue, self-pity, anger, lust, or sin is a mighty loss in life. . . . It is to deny ourselves the opportunity of drawing near enough . . . to bask in His lifting Spirit, to be inspired by His example, to be touched by His compassion. (*Gatherings*, 148.)

DEANNA EDWARDS

Love affirms another person's right to be and to feel what he feels. (*Grieving*, 156.)

Love breaks up the terrible anonymity of loneliness. Thomas Wolfe said, "Love is the ultimate expression of the will to live." (*Grieving*, 156.)

BEPPIE HARRISON

The best sensitivity training comes when we turn away from contemplating our own sensitivities and pay attention to somebody else's. (*Plain and Precious*, 156.)

LUCILE JOHNSON

When we nurture others, we in turn are nurtured. When we give support and time, when we lift and love, it will return. It's a principle of the universe. . . . Some day, some hour, we will receive the same kind of blessing. (*Enjoy the Journey*, 151.)

CAMILLA EYRING KIMBALL

In love alone—the love of God and the love of man—will be found the solution of all the ills that affect the world today. (*Writings*, 82.)

If you can give warmth, love, kindness, and encouragement, if you can sincerely share your plans, hopes, and dreams with others, you will forge bonds of friendship that will endure, and you will be the one most blessed in the end. (*Writings*, 128–29.)

JO ANN LARSEN

In a full, loving relationship, each person's spring of love feeds the other. (*Heart of Goodness*, 13.)

When love is active, healthy, and shows itself often, it is as though it flows from a wellspring deep inside a person, having no end. (*Heart of Goodness*, 13.)

JILL C. MAJOR, LAUREN C. LEIFSON, AND HOLLIE C. BEVAN

Learn to express your love and do it often. It will brighten cloudy eyes, turn up the corners of a downcast mouth, and scatter shadows of loneliness. When you communicate love, you will find that miracles will bloom all around you. (*Encircled by Love*, 72.)

CHIEKO N. OKAZAKI

When we choose mercy, love, and pity, we are choosing order over chaos, life over death. (*Lighten Up!* 128.)

No act of compassion is ever futile or wasted. Each choice to act from tenderness feeds our own spirits and becomes a conduit by which the pure love of Christ can spill into a world hungry for such transforming, abounding, infinite love. (*Lighten Up!* 128.)

ESTHER RASBAND

Unconditional love eliminates the insatiable need for recognition. (*Confronting the Myth*, 56.)

BARBARA B. SMITH

Where love is, life begets life and love begets love, and in all its compounding there is born a quality of immortality. (In *BYU Speeches*, 14 Feb. 1984, 64.)

M. CATHERINE THOMAS

Is it possible that much of the emotional pain we have doesn't come from the love we weren't given in the past, but from the love we ourselves aren't giving in the present? (*Spiritual Lightening*, 85.)

WENDY L. WATSON

Love invites the Spirit, and the Spirit invites love. (In *May Christ Lift Thee Up*, 43.)

EMMELINE B. WELLS

Love withheld brings vain regrets, whilst love bestowed brings sweet content. (In *Relief Society Magazine*, Jan. 1915, 4.)

LEAH D. WIDTSOE

Oh, it is such fun to love—it gives one such inner warmth and glow and lends such glamor and joy to every moment of life. To love gives one the power to spread happiness and sunshine to everyone around the loved one. (In *Relief Society Magazine*, July 1958, 422.)

ZINA D. H. YOUNG

[Love] . . . is a little word of only four letters, yet how potent, how powerful, and with it comes our liberty or bondage. (In *Woman's Exponent*, 1 Mar. 1885, 149.)

Love of God Comes First

JUTTA BAUM BUSCHE

When we truly learn to love God, we learn to love all things—others, ourselves, all creation, because God is in all, with all, and through all. (In *Best of Women's Conference*, 72.)

MARY ELLEN EDMUNDS

The sweeter our relationship with God, the more we will long to serve and love Him and to make ourselves ready for anything He needs us to do. (*Love Is a Verb*, 7.)

BARBARA DAY LOCKHART

Instead of wanting to measure up to the world's hollow, constantly fluctuating expectations, we will be motivated in all that we do by our love for our Father in Heaven, by our trust in his love for us, and by our desire to do his will. (In *Ensign*, June 1995, 51–52.)

SHIRLEY W. THOMAS

We [must] love the Lord. If we do, [he] can make all things work together for our good and become blessings. In light of these truths, we all have reason to be happy and optimistic. (In *Ensign*, Feb. 1982, 62.)

WENDY L. WATSON

Our closeness to the Savior fills us with love, increasing our ability to love others and to feel love from others. (In *Arms of His Love*, 199.)

Love Thy Neighbor As Thyself

MARILYN ARNOLD

People who love the Lord also love each other. (In *Hearts Knit Together*, 184.)

ELAINE CANNON

Let us learn to give love to others whether they return the feeling or not. We will be better for the giving. (*Love You*, 128.)

When people esteem others as themselves they are quick to reach and lift and praise and rejoice in another's success and weep over another's heartbreak. (*Love You*, 98.)

AFTON J. DAY

Life is so simple when you learn to allow others to be inadequate! (*Coming Up*, 96.)

JOY F. EVANS

We must take seriously our responsibility to reach out in love to those among us who may be lonely or unhappy—who are struggling with problems or temptations. They will find friends somewhere; they will find comfort somewhere. What is our failure if they find it elsewhere because we were not there, were not welcoming? (In *Ensign*, May 1989, 74.)

BEPPIE HARRISON

Tolerance means looking at people, even people as close and dear to you as your very own children, and giving them room to be different without your hassling them about it. (*On Being a Parent*, 40.)

Tolerance doesn't mean simply ignoring our differences. Tolerance means coming to accept them and recognize the different strengths we bring to each other. (*On Being a Parent*, 51.)

PATRICIA T. HOLLAND

We can choose love and experience peace, or choose fear and experience conflict. (*On Earth*, 26.)

I firmly believe that if we did nothing else but faithfully practice love for our neighbor, we would have found our ability and success in accomplishing all else. (In *Best of Women's Conference*, 198.)

To be anybody, you must love everybody. (In *Ensign*, June 1984, 52.)

ARDETH GREENE KAPP

Expressions of love, like manna from heaven, need to be gathered every day. Love isn't something we store up. We draw it fresh from God each day. The love that we express can feed the soul of both the one who gives and the one who receives. (*My Neighbor*, 118.)

CAMILLA EYRING KIMBALL

Learn to think of love and warmth as something you give, not something you get. (*Writings*, 129.)

KATE L. KIRKHAM

If we do not *care* much for ourselves, then to love our neighbor as ourself doesn't mean much. (In *BYU Speeches*, 19 May 1987, 148.)

Loving ourselves can magnify our charity toward others. If we overvalue or undervalue ourselves, we are less able and ready to learn from others. (In *BYU Speeches*, 19 May 1987, 148.)

AMY BROWN LYMAN

It is difficult to love our neighbors as we love ourselves. . . . It is difficult to do unto others as we would be done by, to return good for evil, to love our enemies; difficult to forgive; difficult not to judge. However, the nearer we can live according to these teachings, . . . the nearer we will be to the goal to which all good Christians aspire. (In *Relief Society Magazine*, May 1941, 345–46.)

JILL C. MAJOR, LAUREN C. LEIFSON, AND HOLLIE C. BEVAN

Temporally or spiritually, we cannot feed the hungry if our table is empty. We cannot offer water from an empty well to one who is thirsty. We cannot take in a stranger if we have no roof over our head. Nor can we clothe the naked, feed the sick, or visit those in prison, if we ourselves are without clothes, unable to lift our heads from bed, or caged behind prison bars. (*Encircled by Love*, 3.)

We spiritually nourish others when we learn to value them for who they really are. We must look beyond outward appearances . . . or considerations of what they can do for us, and recognize their inherent worth as sons and daughters of God. (*Encircled by Love*, 27.)

It is of paramount importance that we learn to care for ourselves so that we can more fully care for others. (*Encircled by Love*, 3.)

We cannot truly love ourselves without loving our neighbors, nor can we truly love our neighbors without loving ourselves. We are inseparably linked to each other as brothers and sisters. (*Encircled by Love*, 1.)

NEILL MARRIOTT

To rejoice honestly in one another's achievements, our *hearts* must become unselfish and Christlike. (In *Hearts Knit Together*, 122.)

Unclouded understanding and an attitude of rejoicing for others comes from our spiritual Father and our Savior through the Holy Ghost, for they can lift us out of our selfishness to rejoice in others as they do. (In *Hearts Knit Together*, 124–25.)

ESTHER RASBAND

When we are loved, we learn that to the person who loves us, *it doesn't matter whether we are lovable or not*. . . . The source of love—our security base—is utterly dependable, notwithstanding our weakness. (*Confronting the Myth*, 51.)

ELIZA R. SNOW

Alas! that Saints of God can be so full of selfishness as to sacrifice the source of others' happiness to gratify their own enthusiastic notions. (*Personal Writings*, xix.)

DONLU DeWITT THAYER

No other success can compensate for failure to love. (In *Women and Christ*, 142.)

WENDY L. WATSON

One major issue that affects relationships is the ability to show love to the other person in a way that means love to him or to her. (In *Arms of His Love*, 198.)

Friendship

ELAINE CANNON

Time makes friendship valuable —time filled with countless small favors, efforts, demands, and moments of being there. Chemistry, too, of course. Friends, however, need not have all that much in common, except each other. (*Gatherings*, 114.)

LUCILE JOHNSON

To have a friend is to have one of the sweetest gifts; to be a friend is to experience the solemn and tender education of the soul from day to day. (*Enjoy the Journey*, 124.)

Like every other worthwhile thing in life, desire, time, and effort are required in order to have friends and maintain friendships, but friends add priceless enrichment to our lives here, and now, and forever. (*Enjoy the Journey*, 124.)

ARDETH GREENE KAPP

Love and friendship are not a social matter. They are a deeply religious matter. . . . When we are striving to exert ourselves in the cause of spiritual growth for another, we discover that genuine love is self-replenishing and, in turn, nurtures our own spiritual growth. (*Joy of the Journey*, 26.)

CAMILLA EYRING KIMBALL

My choice of friends has helped keep me straight. I have had friends who expected me to be good, and I have tried not to disappoint them. (*Writings*, 125.)

JO ANN LARSEN

In interweaving our own lives with others, we can enrich and fortify each other. (*Heart of Goodness*, 4.)

BROOKIE PETERSON

One of the finest ways of accomplishing [God's] work is through friendships. All involved are uplifted and happier. We can roll back and forth between helping each other as our needs and trials come and go. (*Woman's Hope*, 95.)

SANDRA ROGERS

Christ's ideal of friendship requires that we be friends on a high moral and spiritual level. Under his divine guidance and discipline . . . our affection and friendship can mature into charity, the pure love of Christ, and we can be Zion, a people with one heart. (In *Arms of His Love*, 195–96.)

An obligation of friendship, even at the risk of losing that friend, is to give wise counsel. (In *Arms of His Love*, 196.)

Charity elevates friendship to a plane that will endure through the years and all eternity because such friendship is bound by ideals that are themselves eternal. (In *Arms of His Love*, 196.)

BARBARA B. SMITH AND SHIRLEY W. THOMAS

A true friend is a treasure to be cherished, and all can be true friends. (*Words for Women*, 98.)

ELIZA R. SNOW

The more endearing the . . . friendship—the more implicit the confidence; the more painful is the separation. (*Personal Writings*, 83.)

BELLE S. SPAFFORD

Friends are the savor that brings flavor and sweet refreshment to life. (In *Elect Ladies*, 162.)

EMMELINE B. WELLS

In days of loneliness how pleasant it is to think, we have had friends who loved us for ourselves, and fully estimated all our goodness. (In *Woman's Exponent*, 1 May 1877, 177.)

Forgiving Others

JOYCE BACA

I will always treasure a prayer sent by my sister at a time when my heart was full of anger and pain. Living this prayer became my goal: Thank you, Heavenly Father, for those people in my life who have wronged me. How else can I learn to forgive? (*Divorce*, 117.)

HANNAH BREYTON

Whether we have been talked about, have been judged unfairly, have suffered in marriage because of a faithless spouse, or have been physically abused; whether we've been forgotten, ignored, criticized, lied about—whatever the offense, we are to be like Christ. We are to forgive our enemies. We even are to love them. Fortunately, with God nothing is impossible. (In *As a Woman Thinketh*, 79.)

AFTON J. DAY

Forgive your enemies. Feelings of hatred, distrust, disdain, hostility, jealousy, and the urge for revenge play havoc with your insides and rob you of the serenity you need to order your life. When you get rid of those feelings it is possible for the Spirit to work in your behalf. (*Coming Up*, 34.)

MARY ELLEN EDMUNDS

Few things can lighten burdens more dramatically than the miracle of forgiveness. Our burdens are certainly lightened when we are forgiven, and oh, how they are lifted and lightened when we do the forgiving! (*Happiness*, 45.)

Our willingness and ability to forgive others is one of the greatest acts of love we can show to one another. (*Happiness*, 45.)

SUZANNE L. HANSEN

How do you begin to forget an evil someone has done? I find it helps if I am able to look at the person who has hurt or offended me with my *spiritual eyes*. It makes a difference if you can see the person as a child of God. . . . By looking at them with love and compassion rather than anger and judgment—and by praying sincerely that your heart will be softened—angry, bitter feelings will leave you; old grudges will crumble. Forgiving then will become more natural, and forgetting the hurt inside will be easier. (In *Joy in the Journey*, 113.)

PATRICIA T. HOLLAND

Forgiveness is the key to peace in personal relationships. If you can somehow wipe the slate clean and see everyone as blameless, you will begin to see yourself as blameless. (In *Ensign*, June 1984, 52.)

LUCILE JOHNSON

Inner peace can be reached only when we practice forgiveness. It can help us to let go of our judgments, grievances, and fears. (*Enjoy the Journey*, 107.)

SHERRIE JOHNSON

Forgiving those close to us for faults in our relationships is possibly the most difficult kind of forgiveness. But it is an important key to a happy life and is absolutely essential to eternal progression. (In *Ensign*, Jan. 1985, 59.)

JENNIE B. KNIGHT

To those who have been sorely tried and bitterly offended, remember it requires a prayerful, generous, and merciful heart coupled with a strong will to forgive, but remember also, an unforgiving heart places a barrier between itself and God's forgiveness. (In *Relief Society Magazine*, June 1924, 309.)

VIRGINIA H. PEARCE

Nobility suggests that even when we receive injury, we refuse to seek petty revenge. We may seek to right a wrong, but revenge is another story. (In *Best of Women's Conference*, 432.)

ANNE OSBORN POELMAN

How others handle their mistakes is their problem; it is between them and the Lord. But how *we* respond to their transgressions is our own responsibility. (*Amulek Alternative*, 115.)

M. CATHERINE THOMAS

The Lord has forbidden getting even, paying back, taking vengeance—in any form (e.g., see Mormon 3:15). He requires us to try to act continually in a forgiving mode, being kind to those who, by the telestial way of thinking, don't deserve even a pleasant word from us. (*Spiritual Lightening*, 88.)

WENDY L. WATSON

Unforgiveness increases suffering. Unforgiveness is lethal. Bitterness, resentments, and malice, like dark words, lodge in our minds, hearts, cells, and souls and wreak havoc, causing more mental and emotional pain, more physical and spiritual agony, than even the initial sin brought about. (In *Every Good Thing*, 46–47.)

To forgive in our hearts involves a deep spring-cleaning of our souls, even a change of heart so that all the acid constraints of unforgiveness are gone and can never come back. (In *Every Good Thing*, 47.)

Judging Others

LINDA R. ARCHIBALD

The Lord is quite clear about people who judge. When Moroni sensed that the Gentiles might make fun of his writing and mock him and his people, he was told that it would be the fools who would mock (see Ether 12:26). Ah! So the person who is trying, no matter the outcome, is not the fool after all. The fool is the one with the pointing finger. (*Sunshine in My Soul*, 22.)

SHERI L. DEW

It is wonderful to talk about principles, which apply equally to each of us, but it is rarely helpful to suggest how those principles should be applied. . . . We could do more good by encouraging each other to develop our spiritual sensitivities so that we can receive inspiration about our own lives. The need for spiritual acuity is universal, for the Lord is in the best position to give advice. (In *Best of Women's Conference*, 134.)

MICHAELENE P. GRASSLI

We all have faults, but our job in life is to identify and correct our own faults, not those of others. (*Leader-Talk*, 49.)

Our neighbors, our co-workers, and our church associates don't always agree with us. Sometimes people offend and even conspire against us. . . . We need to leave the judging and sentencing to civil or Church authorities or to the Lord. Of us it is required to love unconditionally. (*What I Have Learned*, 51.)

CLARE HARDY JOHNSON

When we don't know the circumstances in people's lives—what the Lord is doing with them and what he is asking them to do—we cannot judge whether their decisions are made righteously or with the inspiration of the Lord. . . .

We only know that we are responsible for finding out what *we* ourselves should do and for asking the Lord for his blessings to sustain us in our righteous endeavors. (In *Journal of Collegium Aesculapium*, Spring 1994, 27.)

CHIEKO N. OKAZAKI

We need differences. . . . Remember, the way of love is to draw a circle that includes, not one that excludes. Differences are okay. If we can lighten up about them we'll find that differences are delicious and delightful, not dangerous and damaging! (*Cat's Cradle*, 58.)

When we set aside the burden of judgment, then our hands and hearts are free to serve others with joy. Such service is truly the way of the Christian. (*Aloha!* 111.)

EMMA LOU THAYNE

We're all basically paddling to stay afloat the best way we know how. With no two of us ever mustering in the same way, how we do it is more to be understood than criticized. (*As for Me*, 46.)

Love Thine Enemies

ANITA R. CANFIELD

To harbor anger or hate or bitterness toward any individual is to canker the soul. An unforgiving mind is like an open wound which burns, throbs, stings with pain. . . . Usually, the person who is hated doesn't even know how bitter and strong the hatred against him (or her) is. . . . The damage comes to the one who hates. (*Self-Esteem*, 46.)

ARDETH GREENE KAPP

Love is the strongest force in the world, and when it is blocked, pain results. We can kill the love so that it stops hurting, but then, of course, part of us dies too. Or we can ask God to open up another route for that love to travel. (*Miracles*, 15.)

M. CATHERINE THOMAS

Abrasive people in our lives are friends in disguise. They are there to teach us to perfect love in ourselves, not to perfect them. (*Spiritual Lightening*, 84.)

HELEN MAR WHITNEY

We ought not to feel angry at our persecutors but pity their ignorance. (*Woman's View*, 61.)

LEAH D. WIDTSOE

Hate hurts worse the one who hates, not the one who is hated. (In *Relief Society Magazine*, July 1958, 422.)

Marriage

Marriage Is a Sacred Institution

SUSA YOUNG GATES

The vows which we take upon us at the altar of marriage, especially those which are sealed by the Priesthood of God, and in His holy temple, are most holy. Sacred, pure, and God-ordained, they should be regarded as of the solemn and binding character. (In *Young Woman's Journal*, Sept. 1896, 563.)

PATRICIA T. HOLLAND

Marriage is the highest and holiest and most sacred of human relationships. (In *BYU Speeches*, 15 Jan. 1985, 61.)

LUCILE JOHNSON

Marriage is ordained of God. Marriage is not a result of the laws of man, the state, the military, or the government. The principle of marriage preceded all of these and was given to us by God. (*Enjoy the Journey*, 257.)

ARDETH GREENE KAPP

We are not two but three—thee and me and God for eternity, a most sacred triangle, a relationship of which we are each a part. (*My Neighbor*, 121.)

CAMILLA EYRING KIMBALL

[Heavenly Father] has designed that we, as men and women united by the bonds of eternal marriage and strengthened by the bonds of love and companionship, can build a family unit and thus carry out the Lord's design for the fulfillment of the destiny of the human race. (In *BYU Speeches,* 9 Sept. 1980, 119.)

LOUISE Y. ROBISON

Marriage for eternity [is] more than a physical union—it is a spiritual union. . . . In such a union there should be love and companionship—spiritual companionship—which would endure as long as the spirit endures. (In *Improvement Era,* Apr. 1936, 216.)

BARBARA B. SMITH

Marriage is a sacrament entered into by two people and it is designed by the Lord to be eternal in nature. (*Love,* 68.)

When a man and woman make marriage covenants in the holy temple, they begin a new, eternal family unit. . . . Such a union is dedicated to the sacred purpose of the Lord. (In *Ensign,* Nov. 1981, 83.)

M. CATHERINE THOMAS

Eternal marriage . . . is both a type and a function of at-one-ment. It is a type in that it constitutes two separate, fallen beings—a man and a woman—brought into oneness with each other and with God through the grace and power of Jesus Christ. It is a function of atonement in that, through the divine enabling power of the Atonement, a man and woman make their marriage eternal. (In *Women and Christ,* 90.)

Temple Marriage Is Essential for Exaltation

MARILYN S. BATEMAN

Marriage is a holy and sacred covenant that we have made together. We need each other, and we need to be committed to each other. No man or woman can reach perfection and exaltation in God's eternal kingdom alone. (In *Arms of His Love,* 343.)

GENEVIEVE DeHOYOS

We find that exalted man cannot be without a wife, and exalted woman cannot be without a husband, as entrance to the highest degree of glory must be achieved by couples who have dedicated their lives to the Lord, magnified their callings, gained God-like qualities, and learned to live the celestial law of the proper order of the family. (*Stewardship,* 103.)

MARIE K. HAFEN

[Eternal marriage] . . . is not available to a worthy holder of the priesthood unless he is sealed . . . to a woman who is as worthy as he is. How significant it is for our understanding of the interdependence and equality of men and women in the eyes of God to know that neither can achieve exaltation alone. (In *Ensign,* Mar. 1987, 8.)

Among the greatest of the priesthood blessings is the temple ordinance of eternal marriage.

Unless we enter into this priesthood ordinance in this life or in the hereafter, we cannot receive exaltation. (In *Ensign*, Mar. 1987, 8.)

SHERRIE JOHNSON

In God's eternal plan neither the woman nor the man can receive exaltation alone. To reach exaltation each female must unite with a male and each male must unite with a female in celestial marriage. The couple sealed together as a unit can then progress to Godhood. (*Man, Woman, and Deity*, 23.)

Love in Marriage

BEPPIE HARRISON

One of the comforts of marriage is discovering that you can be reasonably fond of each other in February and passionately in love in July and get along okay in September and have the passion flare back up for no [apparent] reason to warm you in a bleak and windy November. (In *LDS Women's Treasury*, 203.)

LUCILE JOHNSON

The principles by which we become one with our spouses are the same ones by which we become one with God. Love is the heart of our relationship with him, so it must also be at the heart of our relationship with our spouses. (*Enjoy the Journey*, 183.)

BARBARA B. SMITH

The longing of the human heart is often for someone who will treat tenderly the devotion one has to give. (In *Ensign*, Nov. 1981, 83.)

In [Proverbs 31:11] we discover a remarkable description of marriage. It reads: "*The heart of her husband doth safely trust in her.*" This memorable line discloses, first, that the husband has entrusted his heart to his wife, and second, that she safeguards it. They seem to understand an important truth, that every man and woman who covenant to establish a family must create a safe place for their love. (In *Ensign*, Nov. 1981, 83.)

BELLE S. SPAFFORD

Husbands and wives should be inclined to love one another with a deep, a sacred, and an enduring love. (In *Relief Society Magazine*, Nov. 1958, 717.)

LEAH D. WIDTSOE

Marriage is just the beginning and not the end of courtship and romance. The honeymoon should never cease; it may and should last through life and throughout eternity. (In *Relief Society Magazine*, July 1958, 424.)

Responsibilities of Marriage

AFTON J. DAY

We must determine what goals in marriage are worthy ones. A

happy home, a Christlike atmo-sphere, an environment conducive to growth and progress—these are all acceptable and deserve much time and effort. (In *Building a Love*, 122.)

MARIE K. HAFEN

Both of the partners in an eter-nal marriage "sustain the priesthood" that sealed them by striving always to be faithful to each other and to the Lord. (In *Ensign*, Mar. 1987, 8.)

NEDRA HARDY

A marriage is a commitment between two people that is designed to last for eternity. One person can-not carry that commitment to fruition alone. When it is not being upheld by both parties, it ceases to be eternal. (In *Women in the Covenant*, 55.)

BEPPIE HARRISON

Marriage takes all the possibili-ties and problems of all the rest of human relationships and compresses them into a nutshell. (In *LDS Women's Treasury*, 205.)

Among all the other things mar-riage gives us is the unavoidable opportunity for service. It is only in service that we discover who our truest selves are, that we gain our greatest dignity. (*Needles*, 43.)

PATRICIA T. HOLLAND

God expects a *marriage*, not just a temple-sanctioned understanding or arrangement, not a live-in wage earner or housekeeper. . . . It is not marriage unless we literally share each other, the good times and the bad, the sickness and the health, the life and the death. (In *Ensign*, June 1986, 31.)

LUCILE JOHNSON

Part of the [marriage] covenant is that we will love and cherish our spouse. The covenant does not guar-antee the righteousness of either party through the mere performance of the ordinance, nor does it state that we may love our spouse only when it is convenient or when we feel good about our marriage. (*Enjoy the Journey*, 257.)

SHERRIE JOHNSON

Husband and wives should help each other to obtain the best gifts and should realize that they will be held accountable if they hinder their spouse from developing spiritual gifts or talents. (*Man, Woman, and Deity*, 32–33.)

Each man and woman should pray and ponder and seek the Spirit to know what the duties of his or her mission in life are and then seek the gifts that will best help him or her to perform that mission. Every husband and wife should also pray and ponder and seek the Spirit so that he or she will understand the duties of his or her spouse. Only with such under-standing can we truly assist our counterparts to best perform their missions in life. (*Man, Woman, and Deity*, 33.)

To maintain order in the kingdom, God established a system of government. To his sons God gave the stewardship over the life-giving ordinances of the priesthood. To his daughters God gave the stewardship over life. Both are great gifts. Both are tremendous responsibilities. Both are necessary for salvation. (*Man, Woman, and Deity*, 36.)

As a wife gives herself to her husband and he receives her she is a gift to him and the responsibility for the welfare and care of the gift falls to the receiver. It stands to reason that at some point an accounting must be made as to how the gift was cared for. Thus the eternal destiny of every man's soul . . . will in part be determined by how he treated his wife. (*Man, Woman, and Deity*, 63.)

BARBARA B. SMITH

Growth can come for both partners when husband and wife develop the kind of love that allows the other to turn potential into perfection and talent into testimony. (In *Ensign*, Nov. 1981, 83.)

A strong marriage takes strong individuals equally committed to calling forth the best in themselves as well as in their eternal partner. A husband must give his support if a wife is to adequately use the gifts God has given her. A wife must give her support if her husband is to lead the family. (In *Ensign*, Nov. 1981, 83.)

Marriage is not an outlet nor an escape from the realities of life. Marriage is a schooling of oneself and a giving of loving service. (*Love*, 69.)

LEAH D. WIDTSOE

Marriage is successful only when both partners understand their mutual obligations as well as their privileges and use wisdom and intelligence in making their united lives a bit of heaven on earth. (In *Improvement Era*, May 1938, 317.)

A successful marriage is always the result of daily effort (enjoyable, if at times difficult) on the part of two well-mated individuals who unselfishly seek to please and appreciate the other more than self. . . . Each must understand the other and plan for daily happiness. (In *Improvement Era*, Apr. 1938, 220.)

In homes where the man honors his Priesthood and performs fully his Church duties I have always found the greatest happiness. You help him and in turn he will help you to do your duty. (In *Improvement Era*, Apr. 1938, 221.)

CLARISSA S. WILLIAMS

There is no holier union than that of marriage, and . . . it takes the Spirit of the Lord and the spirit of self-sacrifice in order to make complete [that] union. (In *Relief Society Magazine*, June 1925, 324–25.)

Specific Responsibilities of Wives

AFTON J. DAY

Honoring the priesthood is a lifestyle. It includes being at peace with yourself, being in tune with the Lord, and being willing to make the first move as often as is necessary to show acceptance of and appreciation for the man at the head of your family. (*Perfect Wife*, 31.)

BEPPIE HARRISON

Women . . . are the keepers of relationships and have the responsibility of the home. We are the child-bearers and nurturers and the earliest teachers of our children. Our attitudes establish the emotional tenor of the places we and our families live. (In *LDS Women's Treasury*, 195.)

MARJORIE P. HINCKLEY

We have a great responsibility to our husbands. . . . [Develop] the kind of love and friendship that will be delightful and enduring. . . . Encourage him. Be kind. . . . Be cheerful. Don't be a whiner. (In *Glimpses*, 75.)

CAMILLA EYRING KIMBALL

Take an interest in your husband's problems and successes. Be quick to praise and encourage and very slow to criticize. (*Writings*, 114.)

BROOKIE PETERSON

Surely the way to build your husband is not to remind him of his shortcomings but rather to see and prize the things he does well or tries to do well. Your compliments, if genuine and specific, will have a greater effect on his self-esteem, as well as on his accomplishments, than anything he hears from anyone else in this world. (*Woman's Hope*, 40.)

Showing appreciation is a way to cherish your husband. Your verbal approval and commendation will lift and help him. . . . Seek every day for something on which to sincerely compliment him. (*Woman's Hope*, 40.)

ANN S. REESE

A wife can determine the mood of a home. . . . A woman can create happiness, or unhappiness, for those within her sphere of influence. . . . What better gift can we give our partner than a joyful and loving relationship where praise is given instead of criticism, and encouragement instead of disparagement? (In *Ensign*, Sept. 1984, 58.)

MARTHA H. TINGEY

Let woman prepare herself to stand side by side, shoulder to shoulder with her husband in all the affairs of life, to be a wise counselor and helpmeet unto him, as her Creator designed she should be. (In *Young Woman's Journal*, Sept. 1893, 549.)

Strengthening Marriage

Joyce Baca

In the marriages that work, I see couples that find "our" way to do things instead of two people who rigidly adhere to "my" way. (*Divorce*, 87.)

If, as M. Gawain Wells claimed, a secure relationship with Deity is perhaps the best preparation for marriage, then working on that relationship now is vitally important. As we develop that relationship and become more Christlike and obedient, we are also preparing to live with God. (*Divorce*, 109.)

Elaine Cannon

Even the smallest effort put forth in marriage can often bring immediate rewards. This may be because we aren't alone in working toward the goal. (*Gatherings*, 15.)

Janath R. Cannon

We do emphasize the family a lot in the Church, and rightfully so, but the family unit is headquartered in the husband and wife. There are times when husbands and wives need to be [alone] together. (In *Ensign*, June 1978, 20.)

Carole Osborne Cole

Being sealed in the temple for all eternity does not eliminate the need for talking and listening to each other, laughing and crying together, and generally nourishing a marriage. (In *Building a Love*, 26.)

We *make* the time for one another that is necessary for our marriage to be the vital, growing, lively contact we need to be happy. (In *Building a Love*, 27.)

Afton J. Day

A goal that involves remaking your mate's personality to suit your specifications is not in keeping with the Savior's plan and almost certainly will result in lessening love and mutual respect, two musts in a celestial relationship. (In *Building a Love*, 122.)

"United but Unique." Couldn't that phrase describe a happily married couple? (*Coming Up*, 21.)

Kathy England

The necessary vision of who your partner really is—the ability to see beyond an irritating moment into the eyes and heart of the person you love—makes the sorting-out process easier; it becomes a strengthening, bonding experience instead of a weakening drag on your relationship. It requires accepting the other and choosing to interpret his or her actions and intentions with love, not doubt. (In *Building a Love*, 4–5.)

Curious, romantic beings that we are, we build many expectations before marriage. . . . We begin to sketch in our minds a picture of the perfect marriage. Yet our picture may be slightly, even dramatically, different from our companion's. And when those different expectations start surfacing—right after the honeymoon—it takes both vision and commitment to sort out a realistic blueprint both partners can live by. (In *Building a Love*, 4.)

BEPPIE HARRISON

Marriage—real marriage—goes way past politeness. It progresses deep into the territory of love, which includes dealing with the realities of irritation and exasperation and genuine disagreement and sacrifice. (*Plain and Precious*, 152.)

Marriage is constructed for getting through problems. You can deal with difficulties today because you have tomorrow to enjoy the rewards. (*Plain and Precious*, 194.)

Marriage is meant to be a relationship that transcends the whole issue of equality, a relationship in which one and one add up to something greater than the sum of the parts. It might not always be easy, but there's no other way to get to where we want to go. And if we get it right, the potential is breathtaking. (*Needles*, 44.)

PATRICIA T. HOLLAND

A good relationship is not one in which perfection reigns; rather, it is one in which a healthy perspective simply overlooks the faults of others. (In *Ensign*, June 1984, 53.)

ELAINE L. JACK

The art of living together happily is perhaps one of the greatest of all arts. (*Eye to Eye*, 163.)

LUCILE JOHNSON

There is a healing power when we respond positively and nurture others rather than criticize. We, in turn, are nurtured. There is a healing power when we give love and support and lift others. We then receive love and support and are lifted! (*Enjoy the Journey*, 186.)

Marriage is a key to the celestial kingdom, a key to eternal life. When you have taken that step and have been obedient to that commandment, are you guaranteed love and happiness? No, only the *opportunity* to pursue those things. (*Enjoy the Journey*, 258.)

As a couple makes the Lord their partner, each marriage partner can be strengthened. (*Enjoy the Journey*, 257.)

Spirituality is the keystone of significant relationships, especially the marriage relationship. (*Enjoy the Journey*, 257.)

The greatest help we have for truly loving our companion, nurturing our love in the family, and overcoming conflict is to first love God. (*Enjoy the Journey*, 260.)

In order to be successful, we need more than techniques. We need

Jesus Christ and his divine help. That is the real secret of a happy marriage. (*Enjoy the Journey*, 260.)

SHERRIE JOHNSON

A man who demeans womanhood or motherhood in any way will incur the displeasure of God. A woman who demeans manhood or priesthood in any way will incur the displeasure of God. Mutual respect is a necessary foundation for a good marriage relationship. (*Man, Woman, and Deity*, 36.)

CAMILLA EYRING KIMBALL

Marriage is an equal partnership between husband and wife. Each has specific roles that the potential of man or woman can fulfill most effectively. (In *BYU Speeches*, 9 Sept. 1980, 119.)

BARBARA B. SMITH

Some marriage relationships are little more than an amicable truce; but if such couples were to lay the foundation stones of commitment and trust, of consecration and love, they could build a safe place where individuals can be heard, and where love can grow and can encompass and integrate differing points of view. (In *Ensign*, Nov. 1981, 84.)

Where trust is, love can flourish. Then add to love consecration, the dedication of two lives to a holy purpose. (In *Ensign*, Nov. 1981, 83.)

[Marriage] requires the best efforts of the man and the woman if it is to be a successful venture, one sufficiently sound in camaraderie, in mutual support and trust, and in love to last beyond mortality. (In *BYU Speeches*, 9 Feb. 1978, 18.)

Counsel for Troubled Marriages

AFTON J. DAY

The first step to positive action [in dealing with problems in marriage] is to recognize what we can and should do and what would infringe upon the other's agency. (In *Building a Love*, 122.)

KARLA C. ERICKSON

Keep your family business at home and never, *never* talk to other people about each other or your problems and disagreements. Any problems should be settled privately between the two of you. Few things destroy faith in a marriage quicker than discovering that your private matters are not private. (*Dandelions*, 82.)

NEDRA HARDY

A hopeless marriage need not be forever; an abusive situation need not be tolerated. You can still have worth as a person with an unsuccessful marriage. (In *Women in the Covenant*, 55.)

BEPPIE HARRISON

The intimacy of marriage means that husbands and wives know

enough about each other to know exactly what words will stop the other dead in his or her tracks. This terrible ability to hurt each other is the sinister other face of our ability to comfort each other—and a lot of the bitterness of divorce rises out of the fact that that weapon of knowledge is the one that was ultimately wielded. (*Day at a Time*, 69–70.)

SHERRIE JOHNSON

If a marriage is no longer full of love, the answer is not necessarily divorce; the answer could very well be repentance. (*Man, Woman, and Deity*, 106.)

BARBARA B. SMITH

In a marriage relationship that is secure, differences need not lead to discord. They can be openly considered until a satisfactory solution is reached because the premises are agreed upon: both the husband and wife are committed to love one another, to build the kingdom of God, and to establish an eternal family unit. (In *Ensign*, Nov. 1981, 83.)

Missionary Work

The Importance of Missionary Work

JOANNE B. DOXEY

We can have a positive influence on everyone with whom we come in contact. . . . We need to radiate the happiness we have found in the gospel of Jesus Christ. (In *Ensign*, Apr. 1995, 60.)

CAMILLA EYRING KIMBALL

We are all missionaries, wherever we go, whomever we meet. We are committed to seek after everything "virtuous, lovely, or of good report," and we can bring to the Church either respect or scorn. (*Writings*, 82.)

AMY BROWN LYMAN

If preaching the Gospel is the most important work in the Church, and we are told emphatically that it is, let us continue to support it vigorously. (In *Relief Society Magazine*, Nov. 1938, 760.)

CAROLE MIKITA

Spreading the gospel is not something that we do; it's simply who and what we are. We must live our beliefs every day, then be prepared, be knowledgeable, and live with the Spirit to alert us to the opportunities. (In *Arise*, 283.)

DOROTHY L. NIELSEN

The Lord urgently appeals to [older couples] to help. The

experience of a mission for a mature couple is retirement with a purpose, a divine purpose. (In *Ensign*, Oct. 1993, 36.)

LEAH D. WIDTSOE

Truth and brotherly love alone may save the world from utter degeneration and darkness, and yours is the privilege to spread the Light. (In *Improvement Era*, June 1935, 384.)

Blessings and Challenges of Missionary Service

SUSA YOUNG GATES

Don't pity yourself because your bed is hard, your food poor, or your physical surroundings unpleasant. Forget yourself and rejoice, and be exceeding glad that you are chosen a weak instrument to do and suffer a little of what your Savior suffered so much. (In *Improvement Era*, May 1905, 504.)

MARY ELLEN EDMUNDS

Based on my experience . . . of working with senior missionaries . . . I have come to the conclusion that missionary work can actually add years to your life *and* life to your years. And I think the secret lies in service and sacrifice. (In *Ensign*, July 1984, 14.)

AMY BROWN LYMAN

The greatness of those men who first crossed the mighty deep to carry the Gospel to England and other European countries was equalled by the ability, bravery, and fortitude of the women of that day who were associated with them. (In *Improvement Era*, July 1937, 416.)

ANN N. MADSEN

What an inspired program, sending missionaries all over the world where we confront personally different languages, often different dress, different customs, and different food. We arrive as strangers and foreigners, uncomfortable and very much aware of differences, but with a precious message of restored truth to deliver. That message motivates us to look beyond the differences, and, as we teach these strangers who they are, the children of our Heavenly Father, our own brothers and sisters in an eternal family, differences give way to kinship. (In *BYU Speeches*, 20 July 1982, 185.)

BELLE S. SPAFFORD

[A missionary] has been called by the Lord by his chosen and appointed leaders. He will go forth proud in the cause he represents, sure of the truths he teaches. He will plant the gospel in the hearts of those who will listen. He will teach people to obey its divine mandates and to be governed by its sacred truths. There is no more important work in which a young man could be engaged. (*Today's World*, 450.)

Money and Resource Management

JANENE WOLSEY BAADSGAARD

If you want to get where you're going, in a financial sense, you have to choose your destination and be willing to pay the price to get there. The road will probably be full of potholes and twists of fate, but you'll still get there if you stay on the right road long enough. (*Family Finances*, 33.)

Generally, when we are out of control of our spending, we have a much deeper-seated problem and are using spending to replace something that is missing in our lives. (*Family Finances*, 48.)

MARIAN R. BOYER

Many homes throughout our Church could be made happier and more secure if the homemakers would resolve never to let their yearnings exceed their earnings. (In *Ensign*, Mar. 1976, 75.)

KARLA C. ERICKSON

A family must learn how to keep everyday expenses within their income. Since each family's income is as varied as each family's needs, learn how to live within *your* income in order to survive money mania. (*Make Time Count*, 55.)

"Going without" certainly can be a blessing. Restraint teaches us that too often what we consider necessary for happiness is nothing more than clutter to our minds. (*Make Time Count*, 63.)

LINDA J. EYRE

Simplify—what a great key this word is in coping with stress! There is a way to simplify everything. Try turning things around and thinking in terms of how little, not how much, you can get along with. (*Joyful Mother*, 65.)

PATRICIA T. HOLLAND

One of the great laws of heaven and earth is that your expenses need to be less than your income. (In *BYU Speeches*, 15 Jan. 1985, 60.)

You can reduce your anxiety and your pain and your early marital discord—indeed, you can reduce your *parents'* anxiety and pain and marital discord right now!—if you will learn to manage a budget. (In *BYU Speeches*, 15 Jan. 1985, 60.)

AMY BROWN LYMAN

We should study our own resources and family, and try to live the best we can within our possibilities. (In *Relief Society Magazine*, May 1932, 298.)

Debt, whether national or personal, is bondage. (In *Relief Society Magazine*, May 1939, 343.)

Thrift is considered by wise philosophers as a great asset, and as one of life's greatest character builders. (In *Relief Society Magazine*, Nov. 1941, 767.)

Barbara B. Smith

Women and children should know that, no matter how important or how worthwhile an item might seem to be, if they cannot afford it, it is an unwise expenditure. (In *Ensign*, May 1981, 83.)

Living on a budget is not a chore. It need not even be a deprivation. Budgeting should be a great learning experience. (In *Ensign*, May 1981, 83.)

Savings in food budgets come by pennies, not only by dollars. Clothing budgets are cut by mending— stitch by stitch, seam by seam. Houses are kept in good repair nail by nail. Provident homes come not by decree or by broad brushstroke. Provident homes come from small acts performed well day after day. (In *Ensign*, Nov. 1980, 86.)

Let us see what creativity can do to heighten the standard of our living, not reduce it—to be provident without becoming penny-pinching, miserly, or ungenerous. (In *Ensign*, Nov. 1980, 85.)

Self-reliance comes by complying so completely with the principles of the gospel that each individual and family are added upon by the Lord's strength, making them able to stand strong against the blows of adversity and the changing winds of time and growth. (In *Ensign*, Nov. 1981, 85.)

Belle S. Spafford

Everyone has a responsibility as a citizen to exercise restraint in his spending and to save as much as possible. Saving stores up purchasing power for the future, and has a national, as well as personal, significance. (In *Relief Society Magazine*, Feb. 1944, 631.)

Kathleen E. Voorhees

Saving money should bring feeling of security and satisfaction, like the feeling you have when you know that down in your basement you've got food storage. Money in the bank and food in the basement are preparations for the future. (In *Every Good Thing*, 232.)

Leah D. Widtsoe

One is very much more apt to spend unwisely if one can say "charge it" than when putting down the great big silver or paper dollars which are so hard to earn and which go so quickly. (In *Improvement Era*, May 1938, 269.)

Wealth

Janene Wolsey Baadsgaard

Most of us waste our lives trying to make the right amount of money, have the right title, drive the right car, or wear the right clothes. But we can never get enough of the things we don't need. What we don't need can never satisfy. (*Families Who Laugh*, 81.)

There is enough sweetness for everyone, if we don't mind sharing. It's hoarding what we believe we own that kills our spirit and gives material possessions the right to possess us. (*Families Who Laugh*, 121.)

What we have will never be enough if we can't give it freely away. (*Families Who Laugh*, 121.)

Money will enable us to buy just about anything in the world. But the things we can buy with money are always of this world. Things of this world don't last. (*Family Finances*, 7.)

Most of us, whether we earn a little or a lot, allow money to make far too many of our important decisions. We allow it to limit our hopes and dreams and determine our life choices. Money simply doesn't deserve all this respect—it's not an accurate yardstick or compass. We are the masters of our choices. (*Family Finances*, 8.)

We are never truly prosperous until we are able to give away our money and our time. (*Family Finances*, 54.)

Money can be your servant or your master—and it makes a lot more sense to force it to be a servant. To be master over your money, you have to be master over yourself. Money mastery is really self-mastery. Self-mastery is self-discipline, or your

ability to control the thoughts that lead to your actions. (*Family Finances*, 30–31.)

SUSAN EASTON BLACK

To acquire material things in this world but not to [take] pride in what we acquire becomes our challenge. If we indulge ourselves in personal accumulation, we deny ourselves the blessings of righteous living, of becoming as he is. (*Finding Christ*, 65.)

The underlying principle of keeping the commandments and enjoying prosperity is plain: that which you freely give to bless the life of another will bless your own life. (*Finding Christ*, 70.)

KARLA C. ERICKSON

Not relying on buying "things" to supply life's excitement puts a person in tune with more important matters. (*Make Time Count*, 61.)

CAMILLA EYRING KIMBALL

In an affluent and competitive society we should ask ourselves how little can we get along with, not how much can we get. (*Writings*, 140.)

MARY ANN RASMUSSEN

Greed not only keeps us from giving of our economic resources but may also start corrupting our sense of honesty. We may come to value money to the exclusion of integrity. (In *Women Steadfast*, 162.)

IDA SMITH

A bird in a gilded cage—no matter how opulent the cage—is still in prison. (In *As Women of Faith*, 209.)

BELLE S. SPAFFORD

Lavish spending at any time is neither good taste nor good judgment. (In *Relief Society Magazine*, Nov. 1944, 631.)

SUSAN L. WARNER

Materialism is pride, pride is sin, and sin destroys. Though all suffer, materialism destroys the souls of the "haves" more than the souls of the "have-nots." (In *Women Steadfast*, 182.)

The means by which we live will, without our realizing it, become our ends. (In *Women Steadfast*, 178.)

LEAH D. WIDTSOE

Unfortunately, many people have come to think of the accumulation of wealth as the real end of existence. (In *Improvement Era*, Aug. 1936, 470.)

Mortality

Purposes of Mortality

LINDA R. ARCHIBALD

One of [life's] purposes is to cause us to strengthen our relationship with our Father and His Son as we turn to Them for help with our specific problems. (*Sunshine in My Soul*, 62.)

FRANCINE R. BENNION

We have existed without beginning and . . . we are here because we chose to come. We are here not just because God decided it would be a good idea and made it happen, not just because Adam and Eve fell and we automatically followed, but because we chose to come. (In *Heritage of Faith*, 64.)

DIXIE R. CLIFFORD

Mortality is that fragile, vulnerable slice of time sandwiched between what was and what will be. Mortality is a school in which we can learn from our experiences and become more Christlike. Mortality is God's gift to humankind with promises of greater glory when we prove valiant. Mortality is now. (In *Thy Word Is a Lamp*, 111.)

SUSA YOUNG GATES

The great test . . . of your souls, is that you shall live in this life by faith, knowing by faith your lofty birth, realizing by faith your important mission upon earth, and living by faith in accordance with the laws of eternal life. (In *Young Woman's Journal*, May 1892, 378.)

JOAN B. MACDONALD

Heavenly Father did not send us to earth just to mark time until we could return to him. He sent us here to learn to make choices; take responsibility; create order, purity, and beauty; and gain knowledge and understanding. (*Holiness of Everyday Life*, 29.)

LOUISE Y. ROBISON

This earth was planned by a wise and loving Father as the best environment for His children at their present stage of development to build for joy, fulness of life, and lasting happiness. (In *Improvement Era*, Apr. 1936, 215.)

BARBARA B. SMITH

No one should accept any despondent view of mortality. Eternal progress is linked to this sojourn on earth where the spirit is subject to the flesh. Mortality allows each individual the opportunity to learn to walk by faith, to use his or her agency to choose right from wrong. . . . We cannot, in good conscience, write this experience off with a negative, dejected, unresponsive waiting out of time. (*Love*, 11.)

M. CATHERINE THOMAS

Life is not granted to *please* us or to *satisfy* our telestial ideas of what life should be; but rather it is given and arranged to *develop, refine,* and *reveal* to us what remains in the sanctifying process. (*Selected Writings*, 152.)

EMMELINE B. WELLS

We are here for a purpose, every one of us; here to prove our integrity before high heaven; here to develop the faculties which have been implanted in our natures, and to make good use of our time in doing our Father's work. (In *Woman's Exponent*, 1 Jan. 1876, 114.)

GAYLA WISE

We left home so we could mature through experience and achieve our divine inheritance. We came so that we could return with honor and receive glory. Jesus Christ lights our way back home to glory. (*Sign of the Son*, 116.)

DWAN J. YOUNG

Mortality is the time to learn to walk by faith. . . . It is the time to learn to be doers of the word, not hearers only. . . . It is the time to gain knowledge and master some wisdom. It is the time to realize that it is not enough to know; we must also act on knowledge with wisdom. . . . It is the time to learn how to love one another. (In *Ensign*, Nov. 1983, 87.)

There is purpose in living. That purpose is for each of us to learn those Christlike attributes which will make us worthy of eternal life. (In *Ensign*, Nov. 1983, 87.)

Conditions of Mortal Life

JANETTE HALES BECKHAM

Just as Adam and Eve had to leave the Garden of Eden, spiritual maturity requires that we have experience in this world. It is experience that helps us know good from evil. It is experience that helps us recognize the promptings of the Spirit. (In *Ensign*, Nov. 1997, 75.)

FRANCINE R. BENNION

I think suffering on this earth is an indication of God's trust, God's love. I think it is an indication that God does not want us to be simply obedient children playing forever under His hand, but wants us able to become more like Himself. (In *Heritage of Faith*, 71.)

If we are to be like God, we cannot live forever in fear that we may meet something that will scare us or that will hurt us. We have to be able, as He is able, to meet what comes of others' agency, and of living in a lawful universe that allows creation of a habitable planet only when it allows also the difficulties that come in natural operations of such a planet. (In *Heritage of Faith*, 71–72.)

We exist now as adolescents between ignorance and full truth, with real interactions among ourselves and the universe more numerous and complex than we yet observe or comprehend. It is within this context that I trust God and His commandments. (In *Heritage of Faith*, 72.)

DIANE BILLS

For those who have lived righteously, when their purposes in this life are fulfilled, they will be called home to participate in the great and glorious work on the other side of the veil. (*Trust in the Lord*, 27.)

Every person alive has a purpose on this earth. (*Trust in the Lord*, 27.)

SHERI L. DEW

It's not living the gospel that's hard. It's *life* that's hard. (In *Ensign*, Nov. 1998, 94.)

Life is a test. But divine assistance is available to help us successfully complete this most critical examination. (In *May Christ Lift Thee Up*, 193.)

JOANNE B. DOXEY

A loving Heavenly Father knew we would need help to learn again the basic things we had once been taught in the heavenly councils. So He gave us the gift of the Holy Ghost to bring all things to our remembrance, and living prophets to direct us. He also provided scriptures to teach us, commandments to help us become like the Savior, and covenants to remind us of our solemn responsibility to remember Him. (In *Ensign*, Nov. 1989, 89.)

KATHRYN KAY HARRIS

We feel that religion is an important part of life. But rather, isn't it that life is an important part of religion? (In *BYU Speeches*, 15 Dec. 1958, 5.)

ELAINE L. JACK

Before we came to this earth, we shouted for joy at the opportunity to take this leap of faith in our eternal progression. (In *Ensign*, May 1994, 15.)

MARGARET D. NADAULD

We're on this earth to have experiences. Those experiences aren't always the ones we would choose for ourselves, but we're more likely to fulfill Heavenly Father's purposes and our goals if we develop the faith to know that after all we can do, he will bless our experience to our good. (In *BYU Speeches*, 2 Nov. 1997, 58.)

CHIEKO N. OKAZAKI

Experience *is* for our good. Good experience, bad experience, happy experience, painful experience—it's all for our good, and we can accept it, deal with it, come to terms with it, and learn from it because it is part of why we came here. . . . We cannot have an experience that will destroy us unless we choose to let it. (*Aloha!* 165–66.)

ANNE OSBORN POELMAN

There are celestial compensations and earthly challenges in every circumstance. (In *Joy*, 50.)

LOUISE Y. ROBISON

Our Heavenly Father is ever giving us opportunities to prove ourselves, to learn if the Gospel of Jesus Christ has made us stronger in overcoming temptation; if we have greater faith to sustain us in defeat and to inspire us to further endeavors; if it has given us the power of patience, of endurance and the assurance of final victory. (In *Relief Society Magazine*, Nov. 1936, 717.)

BARBARA B. SMITH

Mistakes are a part of learning. The greatest tragedies come only when we willfully do what we know is wrong or if we do nothing at all. (*Love*, 11.)

SANDRA TANNER

We can learn what eternal law is and then function from a position of increased knowledge and truth. I believe this learning often requires the breaking of our hearts. (In *Clothed with Charity*, 206.)

If we imagine that the problems we face will be fixed quickly and permanently, we will not be satisfied with what life really gives us to learn from. (In *Clothed with Charity*, 206.)

Effects of Premortal Life on Mortality

ARDETH GREENE KAPP

The lessons we were taught in the premortal existence included the plan for our salvation. The small promptings or inklings of memory we carry into this life are like a lighthouse in the harbor that beckons us home through stormy seas. (*Rejoice!* 86–87.)

M. CATHERINE THOMAS

A loving Father shapes, even now, our path according to a prearranged, premortal covenant. (In *BYU Speeches*, 7 Dec. 1993, 50.)

We are born without a conscious memory of [premortal] promises, but the Lord has supplied scripture and personal revelation to restore in some measure our premortal memories so that we act in faith in his mortal probation as we did in the premortal world. (*Selected Writings*, 9.)

Learning that we are members of the house of Israel because we were invited into that lineage tells us a good deal about ourselves in the former world. (*Selected Writings*, 21.)

Guidelines for Mortality

JANENE WOLSEY BAADSGAARD

We're all the authors of our own life stories. We're all given personal restrictions and deadlines. But we're free to find inner joy in the process of living, forgiving ourselves, and finding the courage to keep writing in spite of setbacks. (*Families Who Laugh*, 119.)

DONNA LEE BOWEN BARNES

Inherent in this mortal slice of the divine order is the idea that we are given roles, duties, and the agency to decide how we will respond. (In *As Women of Faith*, 73.)

JOY F. EVANS

We must recognize that life is a precious gift . . . , that trust and tenderness are fragile, that we must love and serve one another, must encourage one another, forgive one another—all this not once, but over and over again. Then perhaps we shall be remembered among those on the right hand of the Lord when he shall come in his glory. (In *Ensign*, May 1989, 75.)

RENATA TONKS FORSTE

We sometimes disregard certain options in life because we question our own ability to succeed—instead of telling the Lord what we will not do, we tell him what we cannot do. At times the Lord can prompt us to follow a certain path, and we must have the faith to overcome our weaknesses and do the Lord's will. (In *BYU Speeches*, 29 July 1997, 343.)

MARJORIE P. HINCKLEY

Somehow I have the feeling that life is so short that unless we begin now to organize and plan, it is going to slip away in bits and pieces with nothing ever realized. (In *Glimpses*, 105.)

PATRICIA T. HOLLAND

If our desires and works are directed toward what our heavenly parents have intended us to be, we will come to feel our part in their plan. We will recognize the "full measure of our creation," and nothing will give us more ultimate peace. (*On Earth*, 4.)

It seems clear that our greatest task is to live worthily enough to know step by step what the Lord's will is regarding us, remembering that occasionally what we may want to do . . . may not be what we covenanted to do long ago. (*On Earth*, 50.)

We must live close to the Spirit through prayer, study, and righteous living in order to avoid the distractions and more selfish goals that might frustrate the Lord's design for us and cause us to forsake it. For when that occurs, I believe, we will feel frustrated and forsaken and not feel the peace and security that can come only from fulfilling the mission that is ours. (In *LDS Women's Treasury*, 304.)

LUCILE JOHNSON

This mortal life is a place for trials and tests, hope and sorrow, pain and peace. Don't wish your life away waiting. Enjoy the journey. (*Enjoy the Journey*, 266.)

Don't imagine that one day everything is going to be perfect. If you are waiting for that perfect day, that perfect life, that perfect marriage, you will have a long wait. (*Enjoy the Journey*, 266.)

HELEN M. PLUNK

Heavenly Father does not put us here on earth to fail. He wants us to succeed and to return to him. He wants all of his children back home. He gives us the tools and the promises. It is our choice to use them or not to use them. (In *Balm of Gilead*, 36.)

ANNE OSBORN POELMAN

The rhythm and pace, the "times and seasons," of each individual's life are different. The critical thing is to discover what our own times and seasons are and to make the most of them, not yearn to follow someone else's timetable. *Heavenly Father has a plan*, not just for his children collectively but for each one of us individually. (*Simeon Solution*, 90.)

EMMA SMITH

First of all that I would crave as the richest of heaven's blessings would be wisdom from my Heavenly Father bestowed daily, so that whatever I might do or say, I could not look back at the close of the day with regret, nor neglect the performance of any act that would bring a blessing. (In *Elect Ladies*, 17.)

M. CATHERINE THOMAS

Only God has the overview of the journey, and only God knows what will be needed along the way.

He offers everything each one needs to succeed in the quest. (In *Doctrines of the Book of Mormon*, 186–87.)

EMMELINE B. WELLS

Let us . . . make the best of life and not go about sorrowing and mourning, lamenting our cruel fate, our unhappy future; for, when we deplore our own existence, we are guilty of the sin of ingratitude, and injustice to our Divine Creator. (In *Woman's Exponent*, 15 Sept. 1874, 55.)

Worldliness

MICHAELENE P. GRASSLI

Let us choose to live each day free from activities and decisions that would rob us of our innocence. (*What I Have Learned*, 20.)

PATRICIA T. HOLLAND

This world is not our ultimate home; and while we do have to live here, and live here constructively, we are not ever, as Christians, really of this world. And we do not seek its praise. (*On Earth*, 55.)

If we can be patient with [God's] process—which simply means having faith—if we can commune personally and often with him, we can spare ourselves the emptiness and frenzy we feel if we are "conformed to the world": fainthearted, impatient, troubled by envy or greed or pride of a thousand kinds. We can

keep our minds fixed enough on eternity to remember that God's ways are not our ways. (In *Clothed with Charity*, 4.)

ELAINE L. JACK

Are we willing to leave behind the world to become like God? Worldly comforts may temporarily minimize the impact of our struggles here on earth; they may give us comfort and a sense of importance, even a measure of success. But such reliance on material possessions deprives us of reliance upon our Heavenly Father and his saving grace. (In *Ensign*, Aug. 1994, 66.)

ARDETH GREENE KAPP

If we value a position or title more than an opportunity to serve, perhaps we are adopting the world's criteria for worth. (*Lead*, 159.)

AMY BROWN LYMAN

Much of the trouble in the world today, and much of the need for changes is due to wrong methods of operation in the world affairs based upon wrong ideas, all of which have developed as a result of human selfishness, greed and love of power. (In *Relief Society Magazine*, May 1935, 297.)

As Latter-day Saints we have much to depend upon, much to hold to. The Lord has spoken in this dispensation, and has instructed us how to live; and if we live fully according to His laws and His teachings, we can still be serene and happy and even helpful in a troubled and changing world. (In *Relief Society Magazine*, May 1935, 298.)

JOAN B. MACDONALD

Jobs, housework, school—secular activities all, associated with the world and worldliness; yet this is the context within which the gospel must be lived. (*Holiness of Everyday Life*, 29.)

BARBARA B. SMITH

If we choose to live in shaky, immoral environments, we have to recognize that the nature of the soil upon which we build will bring about our destruction. (In *Best of Women's Conference*, 497.)

SUZANNE TRUBA

We are here to say no to the adversary, and yes to life, yes to eternal life. (In *Arms of His Love*, 299.)

LEAH D. WIDTSOE

There are countless things in life of more value than dressing in the latest fashion or going to a "movie" every night. Yours is the life that could and should bring earth's deepest satisfactions—it depends upon your attitudes and understanding of things most worthwhile in life. (In *Improvement Era*, Aug. 1936, 472.)

BARBARA W. WINDER

Satan . . . would lead us to believe that gospel standards which we know to be good—virtue, honesty, morality, courtesy, industry, cleanliness of mind and body—are no longer important. . . . The Lord's eternal values are still true. The ways of the world may have changed, but the commandments of our Heavenly Father, given for our welfare, are still in force, and true joy comes only from doing his will. (In *LDS Speaker's Sourcebook*, 508–9.)

The world today presents a different set of values from that taught by the gospel of Jesus Christ. Eternal values never change while those of the world are transitory and are usually, or often, inconsistent with gospel standards. (In *BYU Speeches*, 12 Nov. 1985, 44.)

Music

ELAINE CANNON

Universally, music brings gladness as it opens hearts one to another. Music can do this, not so much because of the particular instruments being played or the tone of a certain human voice, but because of the emotion evoked by the melody, that miraculous series of sounds. (*Sunshine*, 22.)

KARLA C. ERICKSON

Music can be the springboard to memories, flooding the mind with warm, happy thoughts. (*Make Time Count*, 13.)

SUSA YOUNG GATES

Music is a part of religious worship; it was before we came to earth and will be after we leave, and yet we pay little attention to the details of that worship. (In *Relief Society Magazine*, June 1921, 330.)

Words arouse thought, but music stirs emotion, and if the words are poetry they also arouse emotion. That is what song is for. (In *Relief Society Magazine*, June 1921, 333.)

The art that goes right into eternity with us is music and poetry. (In *Relief Society Magazine*, June 1921, 334–35.)

ARDETH GREENE KAPP

Music has a very powerful and wonderful influence in establishing feelings and moods that can lift and elevate your thoughts and your actions. But because it is so powerful, it is cleverly used by the adversary to stimulate your thoughts, feelings, and moods, to pollute and poison your mind and cause you to do things you would not otherwise consider doing. (In *Ensign*, Nov. 1990, 94.)

CAMILLA EYRING KIMBALL

If something worries me so that I cannot sleep, I just start singing the hymns in my mind. I find it the most successful way to dispel my worries. (*Writings*, 142.)

GLADYS KNIGHT

Too much music plays into the power of the adversary and it's unfortunately making its mark. (In *Arms of His Love*, 143.)

Music is like being quickened; it gets you close to the Lord right away. (In *Arms of His Love*, 143.)

Music has power, so we must be very careful with the music we put into our spirits. If we choose the right music, we definitely experience a good power in our lives. (In *Arms of His Love*, 143–44.)

To liken joy in the Spirit to having a song in your heart is a perfect analogy because of the role music plays in our lives. We all should carry a song in our hearts. (In *Arms of His Love*, 143.)

JOANN OTTLEY

I believe music exists for the purpose of joy in a tough world, healing, blessing, and lifting lives. (In *Woman's Choices*, 95.)

[Music's] power is so great . . . that we can easily be swayed to make it an object rather than a tool of worship. (In *Woman's Choices*, 96.)

JANICE KAPP PERRY

As we allow it, the Spirit of the Lord does soften and tune our hearts through worthy music. (In *Best of Women's Conference*, 447.)

Music can help us in thousands of ways. Our hymnbook is as scripture to us, and our beautiful hymns can shield us. (In *Best of Women's Conference*, 454.)

Music enhances every situation of our lives. During difficult times, music makes the burden easier. In happy times, music enhances our happiness. (In *Best of Women's Conference*, 447.)

BROOKIE PETERSON

A song on our lips can make a difference. . . . Whenever I'm happy I sing. (*Woman's Hope*, 9.)

In times of strain or stress . . . the songs I sing can help bring the happy feelings back. (*Woman's Hope*, 9.)

Obedience

Necessity of Obedience

JANET D. GOUGH

The commandments were given to protect us from hurt and danger here on earth as well as prepare us to live with Heavenly Father again. (In *Living the Young Women Values*, 77.)

BEPPIE HARRISON

Obedience to God's laws is necessary because it is through the daily, small choices we make to comply with eternal law that we become the sort of beings who will be able to come home. (*Plain and Precious*, 101.)

ARDETH GREENE KAPP

Principles are commandments or laws that the Lord has provided to serve as a sure compass and pilot us through stormy seas until we arrive safely home. (*Lead*, 51.)

CAMILLA EYRING KIMBALL

A vital thing for us to understand is that all the commandments of God are for our best good. They are not made arbitrarily to be a deterrent to joy and happiness, but are designed to help us avoid mistakes that will bring sadness and misery. (*Writings*, 82.)

SHARON G. LARSEN

[Christ's] commandments are not rigid laws to catch us when we mess up. They are an instruction sheet for the great plan of happiness. It's like following the instruction pamphlet to put together a bicycle piece by piece and then rolling down the road with the wind in our hair and the soft, warm rain on our face, singing as we go. (In *Arms of His Love*, 24.)

CAROLINE EYRING MINER

Our condemnation and eternal sorrow . . . may well be the knowledge within ourselves that we failed to do the things we knew to be right. (In *Relief Society Magazine*, May 1962, 351.)

LOUISE Y. ROBISON

When our Father in Heaven speaks or when His Prophet tells us the mind and will of God, it is our privilege and our solemn obligation to heed the instruction. To the extent that we ignore this principle we cut ourselves off from the blessed security of having His Spirit with us. (In *Relief Society Magazine*, Mar. 1938, 147.)

LUCY MACK SMITH

The angel showed [Joseph] . . . the difference between good and evil, and likewise the consequences of both obedience and disobedience to the commandments of God, in such a striking manner, that the impression was always vivid in his memory until the very end of his days; . . . not long prior to his death, he remarked, that ever afterwards he was willing to keep the commandments of God. (*History of Joseph Smith*, 81.)

SANDRA TANNER

God's power is grounded in knowledge of eternal law. He knows that if you plant carrot seeds, you get carrots. The same principle holds true in all spheres of being. Eternal laws govern outcomes. (In *Clothed with Charity*, 206.)

The Spirit of Obedience

RUTH E. BRASHER

The limits we personally set should go beyond what we think is required. They should be limits that enhance our commitment and conformity to eternal truths. (In *BYU Speeches*, 30 May 1995, 201.)

JUTTA BAUM BUSCHE

One great stumbling block to our progress in faith is rule-keeping that does not spring from an honest heart. (In *Women and the Power*, 23.)

Too many people imply in their attitude toward others that our Heavenly Father expects a perfect conformity to established rules. But Jesus Christ never condemned the honest in heart. (In *Women and the Power*, 23.)

SUSA YOUNG GATES

It is easy to take pleasure, but hard to do our duty, until, indeed, the day comes when it is a pleasure to do our duty. (In *Young Woman's Journal*, Apr. 1900, 185.)

MARJORIE P. HINCKLEY

Do what needs to be done, when it needs to be done, with a cheerful heart. (In *Glimpses*, 77.)

MARY ELLEN SMOOT

When obedience becomes a quest, it is no longer an irritation. (In *Ensign*, Nov. 2000, 91.)

DWAN J. YOUNG

We can all do what Christ asks us to do. He has a plan that will bring us happiness. As he whispers through the Spirit, he tells us how to follow his plan. (In *Ensign*, Nov. 1984, 95.)

EMMELINE B. WELLS

To do a good action is noble in itself, but to do it in a graceful and pleasing manner adds very much to it. (In *Woman's Exponent*, 15 July 1879, 30.)

HELEN MAR WHITNEY

If we could but realize the great loss that we are sustaining by disobeying any of the commandments of God and remember that we have got to render up to Him a strict account for every act, word, and even every idle thought, we would certainly do different. (*Woman's View*, 316.)

Fruits of Obedience

RUTH E. BRASHER

Consider the personal strength that ensues from *choosing righteous limits over license, leeway, and laxity.* (In *BYU Speeches*, 30 May 1995, 201.)

SUSA YOUNG GATES

The buoyant, exalted feeling which comes to the spirit who has obtained a victory over the flesh and its appetites and passions, is worth whatever of sacrifice may be involved. (In *Young Woman's Journal*, Nov. 1894, 76.)

JANET D. GOUGH

Independence doesn't come by ignoring or breaking commandments. It comes by obedience to them. (In *Living the Young Women Values*, 77–78.)

Obedience proves we can be trusted, and that trust is rewarded by greater freedom. (In *Living the Young Women Values*, 78.)

Integrity—the process of making our actions consistent with our knowledge of right and wrong—is developed when we keep the commandments. (In *Living the Young Women Values*, 78.)

BEPPIE HARRISON

The widespread belief that obedience to the commandments is restrictive is one of Satan's greatest triumphs. (*Plain and Precious*, 86.)

When we place our lives in accord with the commandments of our Father in Heaven, then and only then are we able to be our best, our freest selves. (*Plain and Precious*, 86.)

We cannot be free without obedience. (*Plain and Precious*, 86.)

ARDETH GREENE KAPP

When we keep the commandments, we are clean; and when we are clean in our thoughts, our words, and our actions, we can hear the whisperings of the Holy Ghost. In answer to your prayers, you will feel what is right and you will be able to discern between good and evil. (In *Ensign*, Nov. 1990, 94.)

JENNIE B. KNIGHT

Obedience as taught by Jesus forms a strong foundation for desirable personality. (In *Relief Society Magazine*, Feb. 1939, 128.)

HELEN M. PLUNK

We have beautiful promises from the Lord if we will but do what he asks of us. And though that isn't always easy and we will not always succeed, as long as we keep trying our best, the promises are sure. (In *Balm of Gilead*, 36.)

MARY ELLEN SMOOT

Our ability to hear the voice of the Spirit is dependent upon our willingness to keep the commandments, for "when we obtain any blessing from God, it is by obedience to that law upon which it is predicated" (D&C 130:21). If we want to experience the inexpressible joy of gospel living and feel of Christ's atoning mercies, obedience to all, and not just a select few, of God's commandments is the only way. (In *Ensign*, Nov. 2000, 90–91.)

BELLE S. SPAFFORD, MARIANNE C. SHARP, AND GERTRUDE R. GARFF

As we cling fast to the word of God, the spirit of God will attend us. (In *Relief Society Magazine*, Jan. 1946, 3.)

SANDRA STALLINGS

I draw strength when I remember that first comes obedience to the Lord's commandments and faith in his promises, and then come the blessings, proportionate to the degree of faith and sacrifice. (*Ensign*, Apr. 1987, 34.

WENDY L. WATSON

The more laws we know, and more important, the more laws we live, the more joy and peace we experience. (In *Arise*, 167.)

HELEN MAR WHITNEY

Could we always be obedient, or even willing to repent and humble ourselves like a little child, how much less sorrow and suffering we would have in this life. (*Woman's View*, 53.)

BARBARA W. WINDER

Through obedience we build spiritual strength that sustains us during times of adversity. (In *Ensign*, Nov. 1985, 96.)

As we obey the commandments, we have the evidence of blessings, feelings of accomplishment, and inner peace. (In *Ensign*, Nov. 1985, 96.)

Parenthood

Attitude toward Parenthood

JANENE WOLSEY BAADSGAARD

Children will free us from our selfishness if we let them. (*Family Finances*, 16.)

If we don't have children because we don't want to give up our privacy, we may find ourselves alone when we don't want to be. Sometimes we have to give up the things we think we want in order to obtain the things we truly need. (*Family Finances*, 16.)

There is no higher calling in this life, or in the next, than being a parent. The God of us all asks us to call him simply *Father*. (*Life after Birth*, 19.)

JAROLDEEN ASPLUND EDWARDS

If we wish away the moments, they will be gone. The things we have wanted to leave—the mess, the noise, the obligations—will be gone, but so will the children! This is true of every moment of life. If we do not see its joys, if we do not make the most of it, it will pass—and so will its opportunities. (*Things I Wish I'd Known*, 65.)

LILLIE TUCKET FREEZE

The Prophet Joseph Smith . . . said the time would come when none but the women of the Latter-day Saints would be willing to bear children. (In *Young Woman's Journal*, Nov. 1890, 81.)

PATRICIA P. PINEGAR

[Parents,] be aware of Satan's influences. Where do the feelings come from that make you feel that your efforts in the home are not fulfilling or important? Where do the feelings come from that make you feel unappreciated? (In *Ensign*, May 1997, 13.)

Parenting is a godly responsibility necessary for the salvation of Father's children and important for our preparation for eternal blessings. (In *Ensign*, May 1997, 13.)

Look to parenthood; prepare and plan for it. Prepare to be worthy fathers and mothers. The thoughts of your future children can keep you in the right way. . . . Your eternal reward can be an eternal family. (In *Ensign*, May 1997, 14.)

SYDNEY SMITH REYNOLDS

Parenthood is a most valuable responsibility. It is, in fact, a core value of the gospel. (In *Ensign*, Mar. 1984, 20.)

BARBARA B. SMITH

No training you will ever receive will be as revealing to you as your parenthood. (In *BYU Speeches*, 9 Feb. 1978, 19.)

Keys to Child Rearing

SUSAN NOYES ANDERSON

Take time to fill yourself up and replenish your strength daily, for good self-care is a key ingredient of effective parenting. (*End of Your Rope*, 26.)

JANENE WOLSEY BAADSGAARD

Surviving parenthood may well mean knowing which notes or activities you can leave out and which still keep the music going well enough to get by. When life moves too fast, it's best to start saying no, even to good choices. (*Families Who Laugh*, 114.)

AFTON J. DAY

The ability to listen *completely* is of great importance. If you want to encourage your child to talk, . . . [don't be] interrupted by the urgency of your household tasks in the middle of a heart-to-heart talk. Do whatever you can to assure your ability to keep your mind on the conversation. These little talks will possibly mean more to your present and future relationship with your child than all the cookies you will ever bake or all the family outings you will ever plan. (*Perfect Wife*, 71.)

Since we can't possibly listen intently *all the time*, it is important that we make sure we listen intently and completely to each of our children *some time* during each day. (*Perfect Wife*, 71.)

LINDA J. EYRE

Maybe we should quit worrying about some of our children's idiosyncrasies and worry just enough about their safety to do something positive to combat possible pitfalls. (*I Didn't Plan to Be a Witch*, 140.)

BEPPIE HARRISON

This is the child your Heavenly Father has sent to you, and one way or another, the two of you have to cope with each other. Hard as it may be sometimes to figure out, there is a reason the two of you were given to each other. You have lessons to teach each other, and once you've weathered the process, you will each be more of what your Heavenly Father knows you are capable of being. (*Needles*, 52.)

KIMBERLEY BURTON HEUSTON

Many of us assume total responsibility for our children's success and happiness, when in fact our children select from many voices as they begin to build their own lives. (*Single Parenting*, 107.)

MARJORIE P. HINCKLEY

You have to trust children. I tried hard never to say "no" if I could possibly say "yes." I think that worked well because it gave my children the feeling that I trusted them and they were responsible to do the best they could. (In *Glimpses*, 55.)

JO ANN LARSEN

[Join] your children wherever they happen to be and [savor] the moment with them. When you do this, your behavior and actions say, "I, as an adult, take you seriously. What you are doing or saying matters to me. I like you and I want to be with you." Kids blossom in the glow of such messages. (*I'm a Day Late*, 39.)

EMMA RAY MCKAY

The art of rearing children peacefully and pleasantly is the art of becoming a child again, of growing up with them. (In *Motherhood*, 66.)

CAROLINE EYRING MINER

There must be time to stand and stare at anything of beauty—the sunset, the flowers forming and fading. One must take time to stare at ants drying out their food store after a spring rain, or spiders spinning their webs back and forth. Children must follow butterflies, birds, and frogs in complete abandon from time to time. (In *Ensign*, July 1981, 49.)

JANICE MADSEN WEINHEIMER

Children will go just as far as you'll let them, but they're much happier when you set . . . limitations and stick to them. (*Families Are Forever*, 71.)

Receiving God's Help in Child Rearing

TRACI CUTLER BLACK

The Lord counsels me to remember that [our] little ones are incapable

of sin, which makes it easier for me to bear my burden of reminding them, over and over again, of rules and tasks to be done. . . . I become more patient in my instruction when I realize how patient the Lord is when he has to remind me again and again. (In *Thy Word Is a Lamp*, 73.)

EARLENE BLASER

Probably the most important part of communicating in parenting is listening to the Holy Ghost. Respecting the gift of the Holy Ghost and acting upon those promptings is like developing spiritual muscles. The more you use it, the easier it is to recognize the help it offers for each of us. (In *Emotional First Aid*, 67.)

RUTH MAY FOX

Remember that your child is God's child and that He is interested even more than are you in his welfare and He will help you. (In *Relief Society Magazine*, Oct. 1931, 566.)

Mothers, be encouraged. The children of the Latter-day Saints have a mission to perform. They are destined to lead the world out of darkness. Do your part; God will do His, and your dreams for your children will yet come true. (In *Relief Society Magazine*, Oct. 1931, 566.)

KIMBERLEY BURTON HEUSTON

Our children need us. But we are not all that they need. . . . When I have done all I know how to do and there is still need, I prayerfully turn that part of [my] child's training over to the Lord. (*Single Parenting*, 107–8.)

CAMILLA EYRING KIMBALL

Wise indeed is the mother who has found the source of divine aid through prayer. (*Writings*, 75.)

KATHLEEN "CASEY" NULL

When our children puzzle us, at least fourteen times a day, it's comforting to know we can have a relationship with someone who knows them very well. (*Where Are We Going?* 41.)

Our children, at least until they become teenagers, grant us godlike qualities and abilities. And so we turn to the Creator, knowing where those qualities and abilities truly are to be found. (In *As a Woman Thinketh*, 116.)

PATRICIA P. PINEGAR

What are some things that we can do to improve [as parents]? I believe that seriously studying how our Father cares for His children can help us. Everything we know about our Heavenly Father is connected with His parenthood and His loving care for our souls. (In *Ensign*, May 1997, 13.)

ZINA D. H. YOUNG

Mothers need the assistance of the Lord; . . . the platform of faith and obedience is for the mothers to rest on. (In *Woman's Exponent*, 1 Nov. 1887, 85.)

Parental Example

JANENE WOLSEY BAADSGAARD

Sooner or later all parents are forced to admit they have very little control over anyone but themselves. The hardest part of parenting lies in the fact that children seldom model character they don't observe in action. Parents simply can't be undisciplined disciplinarians with any degree of success. (*Families Who Laugh*, 97.)

KARLA C. ERICKSON

Our children hear and watch us ask the Father for guidance and direction, and we hope that they will incorporate this into their lives. (*Dandelions*, 61.)

Whether we like it or not, we are teachers to those young people who have come to live with us. By our thoughts, words, actions, we are teaching them patience or impatience, love or dislike, compassion or apathy. (*Make Time Count*, 97.)

LINDA J. EYRE

It has been said that children never stop learning, even for a moment. But *what* they are learning is not always what we think we are teaching. We teach by example every day, and sometimes children learn things that we'd rather not have them know. (*Joyful Mother*, 240.)

RUTH MAY FOX

In this age of the world people must live what they teach. A mother should be "armed so strong in honesty" that her children will never doubt her word. (In *Relief Society Magazine*, Oct. 1931, 565.)

MICHAELENE P. GRASSLI

Some women decline to serve in responsible positions in the Church because they wrongly assume that to be successful in a Church calling means they risk being neglectful parents. Although the risk is there, wise leaders can rear their children responsibly while they give effective Church service. The service we give can be a demonstration to our children of our dedication both to them and to the Lord. It is one of those unspoken messages about the faith of a parent that children never forget. (*LeaderTalk*, 11.)

ELIZABETH HUNTINGTON HALL

Some of our most sacred and important times as a family have come when our children have shared their revelations with us. You feed them and feed them when they are tiny, and then they begin to feed you, and that food is some of the sweetest and most delicious that exists in the universe. I am sure it mingles with the fruit of the tree of life. (In *To Rejoice As Women*, 204.)

If from their early childhoods you learn to share with your children your own moments of spiritual insight and experiences with the scripture, you will be rewarded in ways you could never foresee as your children begin to share theirs with you. (In *To Rejoice As Women*, 204.)

BEPPIE HARRISON

Goodly isn't perfect. Goodly is real: I would guess myself that the best practical definition of "goodly parents" is parents who are doing their best the great majority of the time. (*Plain and Precious*, 183.)

SHARLENE WELLS HAWKES

The home where family prayer is the pattern—and where fasting, the payment of tithes, scripture reading, and faith and devotion are taught—usually produces children who can resist temptations. (*Living*, 181.)

When parents provide an environment that is free of profanity or physical, verbal, or sexual abuse, and when the home is a place where Sabbath observance is taught and practiced, where the Word of Wisdom is lived, and where the parents live to be worthy of their temple recommends, children can grow up fortified against the world. (*Living*, 181.)

CARROLL HOFELING MORRIS

Parents who are willing to reveal themselves to their children give them a great gift. They give them examples of what it's like to be human, to hurt, to strive, to triumph, to grieve, to err, to laugh, to love, and even to be outrageous now and then. They give them the freedom to be themselves and to express their uniqueness. (*"Why Do I Hurt?"* 46.)

Children [who] do not see their parents in helpful parenting models . . . may learn codependent behavior themselves. For instance, children who do not see their parents resolve differences of opinion or conflict through communication and compromise may not learn how to handle disagreement except by denying it. (*"Why Do I Hurt?"* 78.)

PATRICIA P. PINEGAR

We must love children enough to bear testimony of the truth. Our actions and our words bear record of the Savior and his gospel. (In *Arms of His Love*, 285.)

SYDNEY SMITH REYNOLDS

When we show our children a consistent example of wholehearted faith, they will likely follow that example. Even if they temporarily experiment with another set of values, or are momentarily distracted by an exciting theory, they will usually return to the sound teachings of their parents. (In *Ensign*, Mar. 1984, 20.)

What do we say to our children if by our words or actions we express the idea that the only place we can get fulfillment, the only place we can be happy, is out of the house? As we raise our children, we ought to teach them by our example that we find ultimate worth in being with them, teaching them, and nurturing them. (In *Ensign*, Mar. 1984, 20.)

BELLE S. SPAFFORD

A lack of restraint and self-discipline on the part of the parents can outweigh all their good precepts and adversely affect children throughout their entire lives. (*Today's World*, 278–79.)

Through her training, example, and watchcare, a mother *can* implant moral principles in a child so that when his influence is extended into public life, there will be no winking at unscrupulous or dishonorable behavior, but a steadfast adherence to right. (In *Relief Society Magazine*, Nov. 1968, 809.)

ANNE G. WIRTHLIN

We teach first what we are—and those are the impressions that live in the minds and hearts of our children. (In *Ensign*, Nov. 1995, 82.)

When our children feel our love for the Lord and our unconditional love for them, then our example becomes a meaningful guide to them as they develop their own spiritual strength. (In *Ensign*, Nov. 1995, 81.)

We cannot teach truth to our children apart from the trusting, caring relationships that we have with them. (In *Ensign*, Nov. 1995, 81.)

[Children] will grow in their devotion to the Lord as they see our devotion to Him. They will understand the power of prayer as they hear us pray to a loving Heavenly Father who is there listening and answering our prayers. They will understand faith as they see us live by faith. And they will learn the power of love by the kind and respectful ways that we relate to them. (In *Ensign*, Nov. 1995, 81.)

When first we love the Lord with all our hearts, then we can lead our children to Him in all of our interactions. (In *Ensign*, Nov. 1995, 81.)

DWAN J. YOUNG

In spite of the excellent teachers that the Church provides, and in spite of the wonderful programs that we spend so much time giving to our youth, parents still have the greatest impact on [a] boy. This force for good or bad . . . is the strongest influence on the moral and spiritual values of the child. (In *Woman's Choices*, 44.)

Parental Responsibilities

SUSAN NOYES ANDERSON

If an error has been made in our parenting, the best course is to recognize it, correct it, and move forward, grateful that repentance is available and aware that perfect parents do not exist. (*End of Your Rope*, 44.)

JANENE WOLSEY BAADSGAARD

I've been told that the childhood you think your children are having isn't what they're experiencing at all. Well, the parenthood my children think I'm having isn't what

I'm experiencing either. They think I assume I'm in charge. (*Families Who Laugh*, 16.)

BONNIE L. GOODLIFFE

I believe we do our children no favor by waiting on them. Service is a fine principle, but children should not think of their parents as servants. (In *Hearts Knit Together*, 205.)

MICHAELENE P. GRASSLI

We need to discover who our children really are. We need to know what interests them, what worries them, and what they would do if they had their fondest dreams come true. Nearly always, their fondest dreams are wonderful. (In *Ensign*, Apr. 1994, 62.)

BEPPIE HARRISON

There's little doubt that the responsibility of being a mother or a father is a fast, high road to learning lessons that most of us would valiantly resist learning any other way. (*On Being a Parent*, 15.)

PATRICIA T. HOLLAND

Do we labor spiritually to deliver our children from evil to the degree that we labored to bring them into the world? (*On Earth*, 17.)

AMY BROWN LYMAN

When a parent looks into the face of a little child believing that its spirit is immortal, that it will go on and eternally progress, there comes into his soul a feeling of reverence for the life and personality of this little being whom God has entrusted to his care. (In *Improvement Era*, Mar. 1933, 291.)

To Latter-day Saint parents generally the most important thing in life, aside from the gospel itself, is their children and children's children. (In *Improvement Era*, Mar. 1933, 290.)

CHIEKO N. OKAZAKI

We can pray that our children will develop faith in the Savior, and we can testify of our own faith, but we cannot give them our faith. (*Sanctuary*, 15.)

PATRICIA P. PINEGAR

Parenting is a godly responsibility necessary for the salvation of Father's children and important for our preparation for eternal blessings. (In *Ensign*, May 1997, 13.)

JANICE MADSEN WEINHEIMER

Children need parents who have time—time to listen, time to play, time to understand, time to love. (*Families Are Forever*, 86.)

Parents' Responsibility to Teach

MARIAN R. BOYER

So few years are allowed us to teach and train our children that every experience with them becomes a precious teaching moment. (In *Ensign*, Mar. 1976, 75.)

JOANNE B. DOXEY

Parents are their children's first and most influential teachers. (In *Ensign*, Nov. 1987, 90.)

The responsibility of teaching proper values and sacred truths cannot be successfully delegated to anyone else. We must remember the sanctity of [our] children; they do not belong to us; they are children of our Father—his spirit children come to earth. (In *Ensign*, Nov. 1987, 90.)

LINDA J. EYRE

Contrary to what you might sometimes like to think, school and church do not teach your children all that they need to know. Parents are really the prime source of a child's education. (*Joyful Mother*, 240–41.)

PATRICIA P. PINEGAR

Satan rejoices in our confusion and frustration, and his influences surround us. . . . Sometimes Satan's influences are more subtle. I have asked myself . . . : Do I leave my children exposed to danger when I don't teach them the truths of the gospel? Do I neglect their souls when I don't help them recognize the promptings of the Spirit and the guidance they can receive? Do I leave my children exposed to danger when my example is not the same as my words or when I don't share my love in such a way that each child feels it deeply? (In *Ensign*, May 1997, 13.)

DWAN J. YOUNG

Parents are the responsible party to teach—not the bishop, the Primary president, the home teacher, the priesthood advisor, or the seminary instructor. They can help supplement, but we must teach the principles. (In *Woman's Choices*, 43.)

It is in a gospel-centered home, with father and mother setting the example, that family members grow in faith, centering their lives in Christ and on His teachings. (In *Woman's Choices*, 43.)

We need to be fortified ourselves, to study and to prepare, and then we can be filled so that we can teach our children. (In *Woman's Choices*, 43.)

What Should Parents Teach?

ELAINE CANNON

Mothers, teach proper manners for smoother personal relationships and acceptable behavior in a crowded, stress-filled world. Teach moral values and provide vivid understanding about the wisdom in God's commandments so that resistance against temptation holds. Teach right from wrong, and also teach best from better. Teach repentance, faith, and forgiveness. Teach patience. Teach cleanliness and

refinement. Teach correct principles of the gospel of Jesus Christ. Teach prayer. It is through prayer—closeness to Heavenly Father—that spiritual discernment and security in life's situations come. (*Mothering*, 81.)

KARLA C. ERICKSON

If we can teach our children self-denial in worldly belongings, it is easier for them to comprehend the higher law of self-denial and obedience concerning temptations. Mastering self-control permits true freedom. (*Make Time Count*, 62.)

DARLA HANKS

What a child believes to be real *is* reality to him; and what a child comes to believe about himself determines his actions. (In *Ensign*, Apr. 1973, 25.)

KIMBERLEY BURTON HEUSTON

Parents who teach their children to have faith in themselves are teaching them ways to feel at home with themselves. Children need to be taught that they can trust their perceptions and feelings. (*Single Parenting*, 84.)

SHERRIE JOHNSON

Gaining the companionship of the Holy Ghost and then abiding by the promptings of the Spirit is the single most important thing we can do to become spiritually centered mothers. It is also the most important thing we can teach our children to do. (*Spiritually Centered*, 85.)

If we make our children dependent upon us we will fail, but if we teach them to be dependent upon their Father in Heaven, Jesus Christ, and the influence and guidance of the Holy Ghost, they can be helped at any time, at any place, in any situation, according to their needs. (*Spiritually Centered*, 85.)

CAROLINE EYRING MINER

As mothers, we should keep curious and eager ourselves in learning and asking questions. We should develop an inquiring atmosphere in our homes. Considering a child's question sacred, important, and helping him to find answers, is a worthwhile parental goal. (In *Relief Society Magazine*, Mar. 1965, 223.)

SYDNEY SMITH REYNOLDS

We need to make sure our children know . . . that there are some things they *cannot* be and still be strong in the faith. (In *Ensign*, Mar. 1984, 20.)

We have the responsibility to make our homes a gospel learning center where the scriptures, the doctrines, and the teachings of the prophets are taken seriously. Our doing so will bless our children with a strong core of values that will provide a basis from which they will be able to operate successfully when they meet the world. (In *Behold Your Little Ones*, 4.)

We can never warn our children against every specific evil they may encounter in this life, nor should we try. What we can do is help them become familiar with the Holy Spirit themselves. . . . If they keep the commandments and learn to hear the voice of the Spirit, they can weather any storm. (In *Ensign*, Mar. 1984, 20.)

LOUISE Y. ROBISON

If there is in our hearts a burning testimony that Jehovah has spoken in our dispensation, is there anything in the world that we can do that is of more importance than to teach this truth to our children, and help them to know that the Gospel is true? (In *Relief Society Magazine*, Nov. 1937, 739.)

Do you ever take time to teach your children honesty? You cannot begin too early. (In *Relief Society Magazine*, May 1934, 292.)

BARBARA B. SMITH

It is the fortunate child whose parent teaches him the value of doing a job well. (In *Ensign*, Nov. 1981, 84.)

Family members can . . . learn to have regard for work through being given significant tasks for which they must assume responsibility. The home is a safe place for children to learn how to work because mistakes can be corrected before they become serious, and they can be forgiven. (In *Ensign*, Nov. 1981, 84.)

BELLE S. SPAFFORD

Fortunate indeed is the child whose mother, at times, kneels with him in prayer to petition the Father for help in meeting his little individual problems which may appear to him to be large and vexatious. (In *Relief Society Magazine*, Nov. 1959, 720.)

Important as are our obligations to family prayer, so also must we be conscientious in teaching our children, as individuals, to petition the Father in prayer in the silence of their own rooms for needed blessings, and to acknowledge his goodness unto them. (In *Relief Society Magazine*, Nov. 1959, 720.)

Just as we must teach our children the true personality of God, and that he is a kind and loving Father, so also must we teach them that he is omnipotent, unlimited in power, ability, and authority, and that they are accountable to him for their every act. They must be taught that they are in very deed his children. (In *Relief Society Magazine*, Nov. 1959, 719.)

Myra Tollestrup

One of the best ways to encourage pondering is to take the time to help your child develop a store of beliefs and ideas against which to examine new thoughts he may encounter. (In *Arms of His Love*, 349.)

Leah D. Widtsoe

If children have the right training in their homes and their schools, they are prepared for their own great responsibilities as parents. We train

them for every other profession, why not for the greatest one of all—that of making worthy homes and becoming wise parents? (In *Relief Society Magazine*, July 1958, 420.)

How Should Parents Teach?

Susan Noyes Anderson

Every effort should be made to sustain a friendship with our children, especially during hard times. (*End of Your Rope*, 106–7.)

When we are disappointed in our children, it is more effective to empathize than to criticize. (*End of Your Rope*, 107.)

We have everything to do with our own success and much to do with encouraging the success of our children, yet any real control of their outcome is limited. . . . All we can control is ourselves and our parenting, and even that is not easily accomplished. (*End of Your Rope*, 23–24.)

Jaroldeen Asplund Edwards

I wish I had known from the first moment of parenting what my father-in-law taught me. "Let 'yes' be your natural response rather than 'no,'" he counseled. I would like to have learned earlier to want to serve more as my children's "facilitator" and less as their "controller." (*Things I Wish I'd Known*, 48.)

KARLA C. ERICKSON

The most important lesson we teach our children by communicating with our family through prayer is to call upon their Heavenly Father when they need help. (*Dandelions*, 61.)

LINDA J. EYRE

For some reason, many of us think that our job description as parents is mostly to find things that children are doing wrong and correct them. . . . Actually, the very opposite strategy works 110 percent better. If we can just wait for our children to do something right and then immediately tell them about it, the change in their behavior is almost miraculous. For years, Richard and I have had this motto: "Catch them doing something right—then use effusive praise." (*I Didn't Plan to Be a Witch*, 144.)

MICHAELENE P. GRASSLI

Sometimes we are so busy regulating children that we don't take time to listen to them. If we would listen more, we could discover how to be successful with them. They are more likely to listen to us when they know they are listened to and understood. (In *Ensign*, Apr. 1994, 62.)

BEPPIE HARRISON

It can be a surprise to discover that there are things about our children we can't change. They arrive, as we did, with individual temperaments that might mesh and blend with our own or might not. . . .

Our children are so young and so vulnerable, and what we say to them about themselves forms such a large part of what they think about themselves. (*Needles*, 51.)

As we adjust our expectations closer to reality, we find that even if the ultimate reward of raising a child we are proud to lead back to our Heavenly Father still shimmers in the distance, we can relax more and enjoy what's happening now. (*Needles*, 58.)

We might still leave a lot to be desired when it comes to perfection, and so may the kids, but when we take it easy and don't tie ourselves into knots about it, there are still golden moments, and hours, and even long happy days when practically everything goes right and everyone charitably overlooks the rumples that don't. (*Needles*, 58.)

KIMBERLEY BURTON HEUSTON

Ideally, parents act as a kind of mirror, reflecting children's actions and ideas back to them so that they feel heard and understood. (*Single Parenting*, 84.)

It takes years of nurturing before faith bears its sweet fruit. So it is important that we as parents do everything we can to ingrain habits of faith into the normal routine of daily life. (*Single Parenting*, 116.)

As parents we should be sensitive to . . . ways in which we are teaching our children the Lord's character. Our children use their experiences in our families as a guide to their experience with the Lord. (*Single Parenting*, 113.)

Children . . . need to experience first-hand the blessing of lives dedicated to service. They need to be touched by those who are living with the pure charity of Christ. (*Single Parenting*, 116.)

PATRICIA T. HOLLAND

A faculty member at Brigham Young University said to me one day, "Pat, parenting has almost nothing to do with training. It has everything to do with your heart." (*On Earth*, 22.)

I wonder if reaching and teaching our children requires becoming more childlike ourselves? Shouldn't we share our deepest fears and pain with them, as well as our highest hopes and joys, instead of simply trying to lecture and dominate and reprove them again and again? (In *Ensign*, June 1985, 14.)

CAROLINE EYRING MINER

I tremble to think of the "sung sermons" some of our children are getting from television and radio without supervision. Maybe, as parents, we had better start singing more sermons of our own. (In *Relief Society Magazine*, May 1962, 266.)

PATRICIA P. PINEGAR

As we bear testimony of our love for our Heavenly Father and the Savior, our very young children will gain language to express the spiritual feelings that are so evident in their young lives. Being able to recognize and identify those feelings and then being able to verbalize their love for Heavenly Father and the Savior will give them power to make righteous choices. (In *Arms of His Love*, 282.)

SYDNEY SMITH REYNOLDS

Parents can never internalize values *for* their children. But I think we can help by making sure that we understand those values thoroughly ourselves and make them a part of our own lives. When our teaching is honest, it has a good chance of being effective. (In *Ensign*, Mar. 1984, 20.)

How can we teach children to be responsible for their own decisions if we won't let them make decisions to be responsible for? (In *Arms of His Love*, 351.)

BARBARA B. SMITH

We can strive to be a model of righteousness. Children learn what life is by observing and doing. (In *Ensign*, May 1982, 81.)

We can learn to become like him as we use his ways to teach our children: establishing regular communications with them; listening, guiding, prompting; watching over them always; protecting but not manipulating; allowing them to learn by experience; correcting them in such a way that they learn to obey—not because it is our will, but because they have learned to do what is right to do to grow in wisdom. (In *Ensign*, May 1982, 81.)

We can plan our lives and, to the degree that it is possible, determine the end from the beginning by building upon God-given principles to provide the security of truth. (In *Ensign*, May 1982, 81.)

When children are treated fairly, there is no cause for jealousy because there is no partiality. (In *Ensign*, Nov. 1981, 84.)

Parenting should be done with love and great care and . . . it is never permissible behavior to allow one's children to run wild—undisciplined and uncared for. (In *Ensign*, Apr. 1976, 68.)

MARIAN P. SORENSEN

It takes a lot of soul-searching and personal prayer to know the needs of each child in the family. If a mother has prepared herself in this way, she might be able to see the reason for misbehavior and have the patience to be understanding during a difficult time. (In *Ensign*, May 1973, 34.)

[A mother] can help her child to gain a vision of the purpose of this life if she will take the child to a private place where the two of them can pray together for the needs of the troubled one. She can show her love for this child when in the spirit of prayer she is able to express the feelings that are so difficult to put into words. (In *Ensign*, May 1973, 34.)

MYRA TOLLESTRUP

As mothers we need to encourage our children's propensity to ponder and reflect by ensuring that our time and theirs is available for meaningful conversation. Conversations, not lectures from us nor lessons in school, lead children to become reflective. (In *Arms of His Love*, 349.)

SUSAN L. WARNER

In a society of unstable values and confusing voices, testimony can be the means by which parents give children an anchor for their faith. (In *Arms of His Love*, 282.)

JANICE MADSEN WEINHEIMER

The Lord doesn't want us to force our children to do what's right. He wants us to love them into the right way. We should be gentle and kind when we're trying to be persuasive, never dogmatic and abusive. (*Families Are Forever*, 91.)

Parents should never argue with children. With little children, we need to quietly and respectfully insist they obey, but not beg them to do it. They soon learn to recognize the voice of authority and are much happier when they know they have to be obedient. (*Families Are Forever*, 72.)

Motherhood

JANENE WOLSEY BAADSGAARD

My generation was perhaps the first advised not to waste ourselves on home, husband, and children.

We were told to venture out into the world and make a difference. But as the years have gone by, I've discovered that any real difference in the world begins at home. I've come to know that all real daring begins within. My children are the catalyst for that inward journey. (*Families Who Laugh*, 31.)

JAROLDEEN ASPLUND EDWARDS

My wonderful conclusion on [a] long-ago night . . . as I put my children to bed, kissed them goodnight, and looked at my rumpled, bumbling house full of things to do . . . was that I had not missed my prime . . . my own personal, wonderful, wouldn't-change-it-for-the-world prime. I had been living it every day all through the years. . . . To me all the years, even the hard ones, had been prime. Better than prime: choice. (*Things I Wish I'd Known*, 20–21.)

It is an irony that motherhood is the one profession that a dedicated and educated adult can practice for a decade and still not be considered an expert. . . . I have chosen [motherhood]; it does not master me, I master it. I am not its victim, I am its recipient. (*Things I Wish I'd Known*, 34.)

LINDA J. EYRE

One of the most glorious things about being a mother is the potential for personal growth. (*Joyful Mother*, 125.)

AMY HARDISON

It never dawned on me that there would be times I would feel overwhelmed, exhausted, and inadequate. But neither did I imagine the joy of holding my own baby, the delight of listening to a three-year-old's imaginative play, or the pride of watching my own kindergartener in a school Christmas play. . . . The expectations of motherhood are not always fulfilled, but often they are surpassed. (*How to Feel Great*, 13.)

We . . . need to make allowances for "almosts." We can be very successful mothers if we are almost always attentive . . . loving and patient. . . . Motherhood is not a matter of absolutes. If we have not completely met our expectations, it doesn't mean we have failed. . . . It is quite possible to both fall short of and exceed our expectations of motherhood. (*How to Feel Great*, 12–13.)

MARJORIE P. HINCKLEY

There is no such thing as the perfect mother. . . . We just do the best we can with the help of the Lord, and who knows, these children who are struggling to be free may someday rise up and call us blessed. (In *Glimpses*, 61.)

PATRICIA T. HOLLAND

Mother is one of those very carefully chosen words, one of those rich words—with meaning after meaning after meaning. We must not, at all costs, let that word divide us. I believe with all my heart that it is first and foremost a statement about our nature, not a head count of our children. (In *Ensign,* Oct. 1987, 33.)

Amy Brown Lyman

Those who create always suffer greatly when the fruits of their creation are endangered or are in peril. Then what of the mother who produces life . . . ? She only, who has produced human life, knows the cost and the value of human life, and therefore she has . . . profound reverence and regard for it. (In *Relief Society Magazine,* Apr. 1943, 237.)

Kathleen "Casey" Null

There is some kind of special power that seems to leak from beyond the veil at the time when mothers are the conduit from there, bringing forth their newborns. It gets all over mothers and gives them a special vision. (*Where Are We Going?* 54.)

Ellis R. Shipp

It is to me the crowning joy of a woman's life to be a mother, and to feel that love welling from the heart that is a joy both to the giver and the receiver. What nobler mission in life than to be a *faithful mother.* (*While Others Slept,* 264.)

Only He the Eternal Giver could know and grant unto me the most sincere prayer of all of my life to be a perfect mother. . . . to nourish, to cherish, to rear and mold and guide unto all the highest, holiest,

exalted possibilities of earthly achievement. What sacred mission for mortal woman to fill! (*While Others Slept,* 47.)

Barbara B. Smith

Mothering is not given only to children . . . , but mothering can be given to parents, or to husbands, or to the next person one sees who needs someone to care who will care more about them at that moment than about herself. (In *Wisdom's Paths,* 237.)

Barbara B. Smith and Shirley W. Thomas

Mother is a title that belongs to every woman by lineage from our earliest mother, Eve, and also by an eternal destiny. Every woman can learn how the designation fits her life and how to find glory in it. (*Words for Women,* 81.)

Belle S. Spafford

The Latter-day Saint mother knows that hers is a divine calling; that she was created and placed on earth to be the mother of spirits that were created by our Heavenly Father. . . . She knows that this is her great and all important mission. (In Relief Society Magazine, Nov. 1958, 720.)

Wendy C. Top

The pain that bears down relentlessly upon a mother as she brings forth life is, in a small measure, symbolic of the infinite weight of the Atonement that bore down unremittingly upon our Lord in Gethsemane as he brought forth eternal life. Further, the birth of a precious and pure new baby is a type and shadow of the justified and sanctified "new creature" who is born again in Christ (see 2 Corinthians 5:17). (*Getting Past the Labels*, 58.)

LEAH D. WIDTSOE

Every mother should sing to her babies in her home, and especially should she sing in her heart for the great gift of motherhood. (In *Relief Society Magazine*, Mar. 1942, 180.)

The Love of Mother

AILEEN H. CLYDE

Maternal-type love, while tender and compassionate, also has a toughness and tenacity that outlasts awful disappointment. . . . It parallels the love our Savior offers unconditionally by his grace. This love has nothing to do with deserving and everything to do with divine compassion meeting human need. (In *Hearts Knit Together*, 177.)

BEPPIE HARRISON

One of the truths about motherhood we all discover is . . . the lesson the Lord means us to learn about love and service: the deeper the space we hollow out by unselfish service to others, the greater the area available to be filled with the love that is our mortal link with divinity. (*Needles*, 50–51.)

LUCILE JOHNSON

Those of us most difficult to love, most abrasive, need love the most. (*Sunny Side Up*, 112.)

Arrogant, hard to manage, mouthy children that wound our egos by their rebuffs, need in a very large measure, our continuing verbalization of love and appreciation and our hanging in there with them. (*Sunny Side Up*, 112.)

Every child needs to know that you would love him, seek for him, go wherever it is necessary to go, because you love him. (*Sunny Side Up*, 112.)

JENNIE B. KNIGHT

We want our mothers to be so fortified with workable knowledge of mothercraft that the instinctive love will be but a beginning of the greater love. (In *Relief Society Magazine*, June 1926, 316.)

DWAN J. YOUNG

In the soft and gentle arms of a mother's love, children can come to know the voice of the Lord. (In *Ensign*, Nov. 1983, 87.)

The Importance and Influence of Mother

JANENE WOLSEY BAADSGAARD

Being a parent is a tremendous responsibility and an unequaled joy—a lifelong, exhilarating/exhausting, exuberant/exasperating task. But I'd rather make a home than a fortune. I'd rather bow for the tender kisses of my children than before millions of fans. All that is right with the world must begin with me and that tiny babe in my arms. (*Families Who Laugh*, 42.)

FLORA AMUSSEN BENSON

Being a mother may begin with bringing a child into mortal life, but it reaches through the continuing responsibility of preparing that child for immortality and eternal life. (In *Women of Devotion*, 3.)

Mothering, of the kind we hope for, means perpetuating righteousness through generations of our Heavenly Father's children. (In *Women of Devotion*, 3.)

MARIAN R. BOYER

It is the homemaker who must build the spirit of the home. Here she reflects the basic spiritual qualities she would teach her family. (In *Ensign*, Mar. 1976, 76.)

ELAINE CANNON

Acts of love have been done by women in many situations—angels for a day, season, or lifetime in the holy business of nurturing and warming . . . of mothering. (*Mothering*, 41–42.)

A mother not only serves Heavenly Father in coaching precious human beings along life's climb but also brings the Father and his Beloved Son right into the picture,

thus vividly teaching the reason for living and growing, the promise for future joy, the cause for hope in the midst of life's inevitable struggle and despair. (*Mothering*, 22.)

With her hand in God's a mother carries the unselfish burden of receiving spirit children of his eternal family and showing them the possibilities a physical body can provide them during their turn on earth. (*Mothering*, 22.)

RUTH MAY FOX

People must live what they teach. A mother should be "armed so strong in honesty" that her children will never doubt her word. (In *Relief Society Magazine*, Oct. 1931, 565.)

SUSA YOUNG GATES

Do you know there are people in this world who need *just mothering* more than they need any other possible thing? (In *Motherhood*, 253.)

MARJORIE P. HINCKLEY

How marvelous are mothers who are nurturing and strengthening the children of today. How valiant they are in making their homes a refuge from the evils that could otherwise engulf them. (In *LDS Women's Treasury*, 284.)

There are few things as powerful in the world as the examples of righteous mothers and dedicated women. (In *LDS Women's Treasury*, 284.)

CLARE HARDY JOHNSON

There is a great generation held in the heavens and reserved to come to earth this very hour. Never has there been a more important generation to be raised in righteousness. I believe the Lord has given this calling to women, not by default, but because of honor and because of his trust in their competence and faithfulness. (In *Journal of Collegium Aesculapium*, Spring 1994, 27.)

ARDETH GREENE KAPP

Has anyone ever read the inspiring account of Helaman's two thousand stripling warriors from the Book of Mormon without pondering the question, "What did their mothers know?" (*Stripling Warriors*, 12.)

The sacrifice and service of a mother is a quiet labor, often unrecognized until the time of the harvest. But without her gentle, tender, continuous nourishment, the seeds of faith planted in the hearts of her children may lie dormant. Even with her best efforts, fruit may not appear for many seasons. (*Stripling Warriors*, 74.)

CAMILLA EYRING KIMBALL

A true mother's objective is to teach and train wisely until she can say with assurance, "My children are strong enough to walk alone with faith as their guide." (*Writings*, 76.)

LOUISE Y. ROBISON

A singing mother makes a happy home. (In *Women of Covenant*, 273.)

BARBARA B. SMITH

When a mother provides an example of joy, the children's world is one of happiness. When she makes wise choices, she helps them to learn discernment, and she brings to her home the refining quality that is such an important element in worthwhile progress. (In *Ensign*, May 1982, 81.)

Learning from the Lord a Christlike love, [a mother] can manifest [a] . . . selfless care that will bless her home and at the same time show her children how to love. (In *Ensign*, May 1982, 81.)

BARBARA B. SMITH AND SHIRLEY W. THOMAS

Coming to earth, a newborn baby turns a pristine page in his book of life. His mother has the first opportunity to affect its contents—establishing continuity with the past, influencing direction for the future. (In *Women of Devotion*, 1–2.)

LUCY MACK SMITH

I have never prayed for the riches of this world . . . , but I have always desired that God would enable me to use enough wisdom and forbearance in my family to set a good example before my children. (*History of Joseph Smith*, 88.)

BELLE S. SPAFFORD

To contemplate [a mother's role] leaves one impressed that no other work to which she might set her hand could be so broad and inspiring, so filled with interest, and so demanding of intelligence and ability. (*Today's World*, 110.)

Regardless of the greatness of our religious, educational and social institutions, the most important lessons of life are still learned at the mother's knee. (*Today's World*, 286.)

The genuine mother reaches beyond her own, sensing her responsibility to all children. (*Today's World*, 291.)

Every mother's job is to transmit the ideals and dreams of life to her children, and to influence them righteously. (*Today's World*, 286.)

Intelligent mothering realizes that the child's future to a large extent is measured in the mother's ability to influence and direct wisely. (*Today's World*, 291.)

Mothers, in large measure, set the family patterns. They create the tone and spirit of the home. They establish the traditions that have meaning in the lives of their children. Theirs is the most potent influence in determining whether the home is a good home which will influence aright the homes of future generations and favorably affect children for time and eternity. (*Today's World*, 232–33.)

HEIDI S. SWINTON

If we as women, sheltering the family from the adverse effects of a haphazard and misguided life-style, can keep our own perspective, we can make a most remarkable impact. (In *As a Woman Thinketh*, 40.)

The Lord placed women in the middle of the family on purpose. It's the one place where we have the chance to touch everyone around us, to lead and be led. (In *As a Woman Thinketh*, 36.)

Visibility does not necessarily mean influence, while a woman's place in the family is undeniably significant. (In *As a Woman Thinketh*, 40.)

JANICE MADSEN WEINHEIMER

The emotional climate of the home is really up to the mother. (*Families Are Forever*, 78.)

ZINA D. H. YOUNG

Mothers have a great work to do and a great mission to fill. . . . Our children who are obedient to the Gospel are a great and shining light, and we should be very careful to set a good example before them, so that they may walk in our footsteps. (In *Woman's Exponent*, 15 Feb. 1889, 143.)

Responsibilities of Mother

FLORA AMUSSEN BENSON

A mother has a feeling of partnership with our Heavenly Father when her child is born, and there is also a desire to be one with whom he can be pleased. (In *Women of Devotion*, 3.)

MARIAN R. BOYER

It is the homemaker who must build the spirit of the home. Here she reflects the basic spiritual qualities she would teach her family, such as honesty, truthfulness, self-control, loyalty, compassion, kindness, courage, and devotion to the gospel. Here by precept and example she helps to build faith in the hearts of her children to fortify them against the forces of evil which pull at them from every side. Here she teaches them to seek after those things of eternal consequence. (In *Ensign*, Mar. 1976, 75.)

SALLY PETERSON BRINTON

It is well known that the early years are the most important in forming a child's character and abilities. A mother's love and example are critically important at this time in her children's lives. (In *Woman's Choices*, 85.)

Judicious mothers realize that they hold a powerful position for good. (In *Woman's Choices*, 84.)

AFTON J. DAY

Common sense, woman's intuition, mother love—whatever it is called, each of us has a reservoir of good judgment and inspiration that is ours to help us in making those on-the-spot decisions or preventing impending disaster. (*Perfect Wife*, 54.)

GENEVIEVE DEHOYOS

Woman is given motherhood, which makes her responsible to help her children gain salvation so that in the process, she may gain God-like qualities and salvation. (*Stewardship*, 103.)

LINDA J. EYRE

If we as mothers believe that our relationships with God and our families are our highest priority in life, if we regard our children as people that Heavenly Father entrusted to us to nurture and teach and prepare for their own parenting, then we must approach our position as being of the highest importance. It is an awesome responsibility. (*Joyful Mother*, 4.)

Take time to . . . think about one child at a time. . . . It is so easy for a little child to get lost in the crowd! (*Joyful Mother*, 97.)

MARIE K. HAFEN

There is no career more meaningful, no calling more divine, than being a person who truly *makes* a home in the sense of creating and maintaining an environment of human warmth, intellectual stimulation, and spiritual strength. (In *Ensign*, June 1992, 52.)

BEPPIE HARRISON

Rocking a baby, walking hand-in-hand with a preschooler, watching your eight-year-old son chase your car up the driveway, his face alight with joy at having you home again, an after-midnight talk with your adolescent daughter struggling into her own womanhood—those will be the moments you will unfold and remember once the children are grown and launched on lives of their own. It seems only fair that we should enjoy them and give ourselves the time to enjoy them, while they're going on. (*Needles*, 60–61.)

Maybe . . . mothers are the ones who need the quality time the most. We need those times when we can savor the sweetness of our children to sustain us through the rest of the times when the workload seems overwhelming and the end of the tunnel infinitely far. (*Needles*, 60.)

The hours pass at the same steady pace, however we spend them. A certain number of them, in the inescapable nature of things, will get used up vacuuming and dusting and doing the grocery shopping and weeding the garden, but we must keep some of them for us and our children. The children need them, true enough. But we need them more. (*Needles*, 61.)

Virginia U. Jensen

Focus on what you can do as a mother in the time that you have. You can't do everything. (In *Arms of His Love*, 313.)

Clare Hardy Johnson

Great and comforting promises have been made to mothers in special circumstances where they are required by necessity or where they are moved by true personal revelation from the Lord to place their children in the care of others. This is

what I might call being thrown into the lions' den. We have to remember that there is a difference between being thrown into the lions' den and expecting the protection of the Lord and choosing to enter into the lion's den out of curiosity and interest and presuming all will be well. There is a very great difference. (In *Journal of Collegium Aesculapium*, Spring 1994, 27.)

Ardeth Greene Kapp

One faithful and somewhat idealistic mother reportedly . . . announced that the next person who spoke an unkind word would have his or her mouth washed out with soap. . . . In response to the question of whether or not she followed up, she admitted, "Yes, I did, and it tasted terrible." (*My Neighbor*, 101.)

Mothers of stripling warriors sense the sacred role of motherhood and the eternal significance of every physical and spiritual experience that molds, shapes, refines, and prepares the body and the spirit of a child. . . . Lessons often begin before daybreak and continue long after nightfall. . . . The time is ever so brief. There is so much to accomplish in so short a time, with so much opposition from the world in which we live, and so much at stake. (*Stripling Warriors*, 19–20.)

Mothers see far beyond the evidence of immaturity, messy rooms, poor grades, and, sometimes, wrong choices. They see their sons and daughters not as they are, but as they are becoming. (*Stripling Warriors*, 29.)

MARILYNNE TODD LINFORD

As we look around at other mothers, it is easy to see the best and finest in them. Then we compare that seemingly perfect person with ourselves at our worst. It often appears that no one else has problems. But everyone does. . . . Don't shackle your forward progress by negative thoughts. (*Mother's Self-Esteem*, 106.)

Being imperturbable means being calm and serene, even in times of stress. It means having a reasonable degree of self-control. . . . No human can be totally imperturbable. But the more calm, cool, and collected a mother is in daily experiences, the healthier her self-esteem will be. (*Mother's Self-Esteem*, 16.)

CHIEKO N. OKAZAKI

The principle behind motherhood is that we as women have the great responsibility and the wonderful blessing, ideally in partnership with our husbands, of teaching our children the gospel. Our Heavenly Father entrusts most of us with other precious spirit children who aren't quite as far along as we are in terms of mortal experience. (*Lighten Up!* 23.)

KRISTEN D. RANDLE

It falls to the mother to do the basic, sturdy construction of family fabric—to the mother who stays home and interacts with her children on a regular, fundamental basis. . . . And so the scriptures, if they are going to be part of the goodly garment, have to start in the mother's hands. (In *My Soul Delighteth*, 83–84.)

LOUISE Y. ROBISON

The path is clear for mothers to follow. We must live the Gospel in our homes in such a way that our children will have confidence in our teaching. We must feel that no effort is too great to teach our children that there is a Father in heaven, and that he does hear our prayers. (In *Conference Report*, Apr. 1930, 144–45.)

TESSA MEYER SANTIAGO

If we mother well, we wear out our lives bringing to pass the lives of others. (In *Best of Women's Conference*, 481.)

ELLIS R. SHIPP

How few mothers know how to take care of the children, the delicate plants entrusted to their care. Truly it is time that woman should shake off this lethargy and awaken to the responsibilities of motherhood and educate and prepare for those responsibilities. (*While Others Slept*, 210–11.)

How necessary for mothers to cultivate the purest, mildest and most ennobling emotions, for her child will partake of every sensation of her being. (*While Others Slept*, 213.)

BELLE S. SPAFFORD

A firm and unwavering testimony is of first importance to a mother, not for her sake alone, but also because of her key position in the home and the potency of her influence upon her children. She is peculiarly situated to implant faith and build testimony, or to cause doubt and discount truth. (In *Relief Society Magazine*, Nov. 1953, 719.)

A personal testimony in the mind and heart of the mother is the beginning place in the establishing of it in the mind and heart of her child. (In *Relief Society Magazine*, Nov. 1953, 719.)

JANICE MADSEN WEINHEIMER

If we hate housework, it's because we choose to hate it—we always have another choice. So we might as well make up our minds to be good mothers and housewives and enjoy what we do. We'll be much happier, and so will everyone else. And the bonus feature is that we'll accomplish much more. (*Families Are Forever*, 50.)

EMMELINE B. WELLS

Mothers, cling to your boys, do not send them out from you to see, hear and learn all the evils that prevail in this fast age, before their minds are capable of comprehending right from wrong. (In *Woman's Exponent*, 15 Nov. 1873, 94.)

LEAH D. WIDTSOE

If every mother were to impress upon her young and growing child that to love is so much more fun than to hate, that men are essentially good and are intended to love righteousness, and that everyone's difficulty may be settled by finding out what is right and then doing it—if that could be done, then wars would be impossible. (In *Relief Society Magazine*, Mar. 1946, 148.)

Single Parents

SUZANNE LITTLE DASTRUP

If you are to survive as a single parent, you must learn to lower your expectations about things that aren't so important and not feel depressed and guilty about what you don't get done. (In *Women in the Covenant*, 58.)

KIMBERLEY BURTON HEUSTON

Put your own life in order so that your children feel free to move on to form their own families. Teach them what you have learned: that the best guarantee of a happy marriage is two happy, strong individuals who have learned to love themselves, their families, and their God, and now are ready to love someone else—and if doing all that takes time, well, they've got eternity. (*Single Parenting*, 105–6.)

JANET KENT

The single most important lesson I've learned as a single mother is to *rely on the Lord*. . . . If we are worthy, working diligently to solve our problems and fulfill our duties, the

Lord will be there for both spiritual and temporal blessings, if we will exercise our faith. (In *Ensign*, Apr. 1985, 44–45.)

In a happy, two-parent family, the romantic love and companionship between the parents is the well from which the whole family can drink. . . . A single parent must somehow find the creative and emotional resources to provide his or her family this food for the heart and spirit. (In *Ensign*, Apr. 1985, 48.)

Barbara B. Smith

We are confident that the Lord is particularly mindful of [single parents] and that, while their role is an unusually challenging one, they can succeed. But they too must make their decisions in the light of the principles and purposes of the Lord, in that faith which is truly the substance of things hoped for. (In *Ensign*, May 1982, 81.)

Wayward Children

Susan Noyes Anderson

Only our children can make the choices that will lead them back to our Father in Heaven. They have their agency, and watching them abuse it can be terrifying. (*End of Your Rope*, 24.)

Mildred Chandler Austin

Even though the devil may win a battle, those who follow the Lord's battle plan will win the war. (*Divine Destiny*, 69.)

Anita R. Canfield

When our loved ones reject our love and help, if we serve diligently to help others, our sacrifices will be sanctified. There will come into the lives of our loved ones those who will water the seeds we have planted. (*Perfect Brightness*, 91.)

Wendy Evans Ruppel

Heavenly Father never ever takes away our agency. We always have choices in our lives, and our children do, too. (In *Clothed with Charity*, 179.)

Janice Madsen Weinheimer

We are never alone in our suffering. Our Father in heaven will seek to soften the hearts of our wayward children so they can see the errors of their ways, but we must have unending faith and courage. We must fast and pray often for these special spirits who have momentarily gone astray. Above all, we must never lose hope. We must never give up, for nothing is really lost until we quit trying. (*Families Are Forever*, 126–27.)

Ruth B. Wright

As parents, we should keep our desire to do our best, constantly show our love, and not blame ourselves if our children choose another way. (In *Ensign*, May 1994, 84.)

Peace

Peace Is a Gift of God

FRANCINE R. BENNION

Our God knows us. God looks with compassion on us and our hopes and fatigues, and in a thousand ways invites us to come to Him, to joy and peace. (In *Behold Your Little Ones*, 38.)

NADINE Q. COOK

Heavenly Father has pronounced eternal peace to be one of the choicest blessings that he has available for his children. . . . This blessing of peace, then, should be a prime goal in our lives. (In *As a Woman Thinketh*, 90.)

JANET G. LEE

The Lord can speak peace to our minds wherever we are. (In *Best of Women's Conference*, 292.)

The Lord . . . offers to all the gift of peace. (In *Every Good Thing*, 10.)

KRISTEN SHUMWAY

Peace is the promise of the Lord. It is his calling card, his enticement, his confirmation, and his congratulations. It is his gift to those who love him and seek him. And I know, if the Lord is pleased with me, he will always send peace. (In *Balm of Gilead*, 21.)

[Bad days] have taught me . . . peace is a daily activity. It's not necessarily a daily struggle, but it has to be a daily priority. That is because peace is a particular blessing and doesn't happen by default. Peace is not merely the absence of noise and turmoil but the presence of the Spirit. (In *Balm of Gilead*, 20.)

I used to think [that] peace came when I completed my checklist of righteous things to do as if it were a gumball that dropped out with the payment of the correct change. But now I think that when I am obedient, I have stronger faith that the Lord wants to bless me with peace. And when I ask for peace with that kind of faith, he can grant it to me. (In *Balm of Gilead*, 21.)

M. CATHERINE THOMAS

As God is at peace in spite of our choices, so may we be at peace in spite of anyone else's choices. (*Spiritual Lightening*, 72.)

EMMELINE B. WELLS

O my poor, aching heart. Where shall it rest its burden? Only on the Lord, only to Him can I look, every other avenue seems closed against me. O help me, Father in heaven, to overcome. (In *Women's Voices*, 298.)

Blessings of Peace

ELAINE CANNON

Find peace with God, and one can't rest until wrongs are righted at home. Then that place becomes a heaven on earth, and all who sit at the table are as if at the Lord's Supper. (*Gatherings*, 13.)

Peace usually begins at home and advances to reconciliation with God. (*Gatherings*, 13.)

NADINE Q. COOK

We cannot be exalted in the celestial kingdom unless we are peacemakers. (In *As a Woman Thinketh*, 90.)

MARY ELLEN EDMUNDS

Peace is a critical ingredient of happiness. (In *Arms of His Love*, 215.)

MICHAELENE P. GRASSLI

Peace in the Lord can give . . . freedom from self-doubt, freedom from fear, freedom from the confinement of . . . environment, freedom from enslaving habits. (*What I Have Learned*, 105.)

JANET G. LEE

Sometimes peace comes dramatically, like the calming of a raging sea. . . . Most of the time, however, peace comes quietly, as a subtle feeling of wellness, a renewed sense of God's omnipotent power, and the still, small voice whispering God's messages: words of comfort, thoughts of hope, feelings of strength, and a reassurance of love—the language of peace. (In *Every Good Thing*, 10–11.)

It is the gift of peace that brings joy, surety, and solace—the kind of peace that can never be taken away. (In *Best of Women's Conference*, 292.)

KRISTEN SHUMWAY

Peace is the staple of a successful day, as necessary as air. (In *Balm of Gilead*, 20.)

Obtaining Peace

FRANCINE R. BENNION

If our children believe peace exists only where there is no war, pain, disagreement, confusion, injustice, or loneliness, they will not taste peace in this world where lions do eat lambs and asps bite. (In *Behold Your Little Ones*, 38.)

If we look with compassion on our own young ones and lead them toward peace, wherever we are with them can become a fruitful haven, a watered garden, whatever their current hard ground, weeds, and drought. (In *Behold Your Little Ones*, 38.)

Personal peace is difficult for persons constantly surprised that things are not as they had hoped. It is important not only to hope for the ideal but also to study and meet present realities. (In *Behold Your Little Ones*, 40.)

DIANE BILLS

As we put our lives in alignment with the Lord's will and spend our time doing what he wants us to do, we will experience increasingly greater amounts of peace. As we raise our voices, our thoughts, and our hearts to heaven, the powers therein will comfort us and calm our fears. (*Trust in the Lord*, 81.)

MARY ELLEN EDMUNDS

Peace is knowing that the One in charge of everything is our Father and that he not only knows everything but he understands, and his plan is called the great plan of happiness! (In *Arms of His Love*, 215.)

ELAINE L. JACK

The beauty of the world, the majesty of good literature, fine art, and music can soften the jangle of daily living. (In *Best of Women's Conference*, 210.)

JANET G. LEE

If I spend too much time thinking about the past or the future, I will miss the peace that comes from the present. (In *Best of Women's Conference*, 288.)

MARILYNNE TODD LINFORD

We do not have . . . power over the elements, but we do have the power to calm, perhaps, our own

nerves, a crying baby, contentious children, a disheartened sister, or an over-worked husband. It is within our power to find solutions, to work through difficult situations, to be peacemakers. (*Woman Fulfilled*, 111.)

DIANE L. MANGUM

When I think of peace, in my mind I see calm water, stillness. . . . But I'm learning that stillness is an impossible illusion. It doesn't work any more than holding on tight to just one secure place on the iron rod will get you to the tree of life. There is no escalator under our feet that will transport us to peace. We have to do the moving ourselves. (In *Balm of Gilead*, 104.)

DEBORAH ELDREDGE MILNE

If I can't physically visit a safe place, I can cultivate inner peace, wherever I am, in my own mind by calling upon God. (*Reflections*, 40.)

VIRGINIA H. PEARCE

We like very much to please others—sometimes seeking approval so frantically that we become torn and confused by the conflicting needs of those around us. Concentrating on pleasing Heavenly Father brings peace, a respite from fear and anxiety. (In *Ensign*, Nov. 1992, 91.)

ESTHER RASBAND

Peace is not in self-esteem or even in self-awareness at all. Peace is in mercy. Peace is in calling upon God to receive our strength and keeping the commandments. Peace is in enduring to the end. Peace is diametrically opposed to self-focus. (*Confronting the Myth*, 42.)

The route to peace is through humility to repentance to finding mercy. It is a function of the heart. (*Confronting the Myth*, 89.)

LOUISE Y. ROBISON

We shall never have a nation of peace and justice until we have individual peace and justice founded upon love of man as well as love of God, and taught in the homes and in the schools. (In *Relief Society Magazine*, Jan. 1939, 4.)

MARY FIELDING SMITH

I feel but little concern about where I am, if I can keep my mind staid upon God; for . . . in this there is perfect peace. (*Mary Fielding Smith*, 99.)

HEIDI S. SWINTON

Peace is not a place; it is a state of mind. It is knowing that the Lord's promises are true and then living worthy to receive them. (In *Best of Women's Conference*, 531.)

EILEEN N. WHITAKER

Inner turmoil is one of the greatest deterrents to spiritual communication. If we can be still, we can feel the complete peace that comes without complete understanding, and it is sufficient. (In *To Rejoice As Women*, 94.)

LEAH D. WIDTSOE

When the chain of world peace is forged, it can be no stronger than the men and women who have come from homes such as yours and mine with their determination, or lack of it, to be truly "men of good will." (In *Relief Society Magazine*, Mar. 1946, 149.)

MERCEDES WIEDERHOLD

Peace and fear cannot abide in the same space. Anxiety, anger, and the inability to forgive are the antitheses of peace and joy. (In *Balm of Gilead*, 28–29.)

Perfection

Developing Perfection

ANITA R. CANFIELD

Perfection is a long, slow process. Perfection is not an event! (*Young Woman*, 66.)

SHERI L. DEW

The Savior . . . sees us as works in progress. . . . It is purity, rather than perfection, that we are seeking at this stage of our eternal quest. (In *Best of Women's Conference*, 136.)

MICHAELENE P. GRASSLI

All of us will make mistakes in our lives, but although perfection is our ultimate destination, righteousness, or goodness, is the chariot to carry us there. (In *Ensign*, Nov. 1988, 90.)

KATHLEEN BUSHNELL JENSEN

If we had been capable of perfection on our own, we wouldn't need a Savior. Jesus came to help us make up the difference between what we can do at our best and what we aspire to become. (In *Best of Women's Conference*, 220.)

Many times we think we have to be perfect instantly and perfect in everything: that's what causes us to run faster than we have strength. (In *Women and Christ*, 54.)

BETTE S. MOLGARD

There is a distinct difference between striving for excellence and requiring perfection. Excellence is something every one of us can reach for. Perfection is impossible without the Savior's grace. (*Everyday Battles*, 69.)

The adversary has whispered directions inviting us to strive to perfect ourselves, leaving the Savior's atonement completely out of the picture. (*Everyday Battles*, 72.)

CARROLL HOFELING MORRIS

We are all caught up in perfectionism to one degree or another. But some who adopt this standard become obsessed by the need to perfect themselves and others around them. They act as if they have forgotten the Atonement, as if they have forgotten that Jesus said, "For *I* am able to make you holy" (D&C 60:7; italics added). (*"Why Do I Hurt?"* 64.)

CHIEKO N. OKAZAKI

To me being perfected in Christ means accepting the atonement of Christ by relying on the Savior's love and abiding in the path of prayer to let that atonement work in me. (*Aloha!* 128.)

ANNE OSBORN POELMAN

In our individual and collective quest for perfection, it is not the sprinter, the saint whose spirituality is only momentarily incandescent, who wins the eternal prize. Like running a marathon, to finish, to endure to the end, is to win. (In *Joy*, 46–47.)

LOUISE Y. ROBISON

The Gospel teaches us that the way to perfection is going from one small degree to another, from one small capacity to a greater one. (In *Relief Society Magazine*, Nov. 1938, 734.)

BARBARA B. SMITH

The gospel instructs us to develop our talents and to strive continuously for their perfection. (*Love*, 11.)

GAYLA WISE

Our personal path to perfection is simple: "Be thou humble; and the Lord thy God shall lead thee by the hand." (D&C 112:10.) Where do we suppose he will lead us? The answer is irrefutable—home to glory. (*Sign of the Son*, 116.)

Imperfections

AFTON J. DAY

It's all right to be imperfect; but it's not all right to settle for imperfection. (*Perfect Wife*, 6.)

SHERI L. DEW

The adversary would have us hung up on perfection and stymied by the commandment to become perfect. He wants this glorious potential to loom as a giant stumbling block rather than the promise of what is ultimately possible. (In *May Christ Lift Thee Up*, 198.)

The Savior doesn't want us to be paralyzed by our errors but to learn and grow from them. He sees us as works in progress. (In *Best of Women's Conference*, 136.)

MICHAELENE P. GRASSLI

As I have studied the word righteousness, I have found nothing that indicates that being righteous is being perfect. (In *Ensign*, Nov. 1988, 90.)

BEPPIE HARRISON

We're supposed to be working on perfection, not beating ourselves up for not being there yet. (*Plain and Precious*, 183.)

PATRICIA T. HOLLAND

We must have the courage to be imperfect while striving for perfection. (*On Earth*, 86.)

When you dwell on your limitations excessively, to the point that they affect your inner view and strength, you mock God in his very creation. You deny the divinity within you. You resist the gift of Christ on the cross. So be patient in your pursuit of perfection. (In *BYU Speeches*, 6 Sept. 1988, 25.)

JO ANN LARSEN

As fallible creatures, imperfect in our nature, we are always in the process of becoming—always accumulating wisdom and experience. . . . It is out of our errors that much of our learning takes place. In fact, making mistakes is absolutely essential to the growth process. (*I'm a Day Late*, 125.)

ELLIS R. SHIPP

I feel most forcefully the necessity of improvement and above all I desire to overcome, and I know this can be accomplished save but one way—by the power and spirit of my Father and God and this I will seek for with all my might, mind and strength. (*While Others Slept*, 86–87.)

Perspective

NORMA B. ASHTON

Our challenge is to learn and not be defeated by the package life hands us or by our attitude about that package. (In *Women of Wisdom*, 19.)

Whatever our circumstances, we must learn the lessons of life. (In *LDS Women's Treasury*, 145.)

JANENE WOLSEY BAADSGAARD

Let's quit viewing life as a long, hard, uphill ride to the ultimate destination of heaven. I'm sure heaven will be wonderful, but so is life right now. (In *Clothed with Charity*, 83.)

Let's not put off living and loving and laughing. The joy of life is in the ride. So stop waiting. (In *Clothed with Charity*, 82.)

There is more joy and wonder right here in our own lives than we are willing or able to enjoy. Just think . . . all this and heaven, too! (In *Clothed with Charity*, 83.)

There is a bit of heaven here on earth. Listen for tinkling ice, smell the pungent spice of rich, sweet pines, and glance out your back window to watch your children at play. (*Families Who Laugh*, 80.)

CONNIE L. BLAKEMORE

If your beliefs are based on gospel perspectives, your glasses or belief window will allow you to see eternity from a celestial kingdom perspective. On the other hand, if your belief lenses are made from a non-gospel or worldly prescription, you will see just the opposite and earn your place for eternity in one of the lower kingdoms. So, what you see is what you get—literally. (In *BYU Speeches*, 28 July 1998, 324.)

ELAINE CANNON

Heavenly Father wants you to succeed and to be happy. He wants you to come home to him after you have lived and learned enough to dwell in his presence. (*Bell Ringer*, 2.)

Personal progress is what this life is all about. We must begin at once to work our plan of life, deciding to whom and what we will give our fullest attention, our highest loyalty, our deepest commitment. (In *Ensign*, Nov. 1979, 107.)

We all must . . . move steadily forward in ultimate faith that the end can be better than the beginning, wherever we may start. (In *Ensign*, Nov. 1979, 107.)

AILEEN H. CLYDE

There is a constant struggle to balance our knowledge of light against the error and fear that are among the hallmarks of our world. (In *Ensign*, May 1995, 26.)

CHRISTINE DURHAM

The point of getting up every morning is not to rush through to the end of the day—or at least it shouldn't be. There are days like that, of course; we all have days when we get that first foot on the floor, and we feel like we've started a foot race that is not going to end until midnight. I suggest that when we are living our lives that way, we've lost track of . . . doing what we do, thinking what we think, saying what we say, experiencing what we experience with *intentionality*, with focus, with the ability to remember who we are and what God wants of us. (In *Every Good Thing*, 334.)

RUTH HARDY FUNK

I marvel as I look back at the divine orchestration of my life. I really do believe that the Lord customizes our experiences according to our needs. (In *Keepers*, 117.)

SUSA YOUNG GATES

Enthusiasm is beautiful, godlike and glorious, but unless it is tempered with judgment and common sense, as we call it (Solomon termed it understanding), we are most apt to be led astray. Keep your head among the stars if you will, but guard your feet lest they stumble on the earth. (In *Improvement Era*, Oct. 1905, 912.)

MICHAELENE P. GRASSLI

Every day—every minute—is a new, blank page of life. Regardless of our past, we can have a fresh start at any moment and write on that page what we choose. We are empowered in that by the Savior, in whom all becomes new. (*What I Have Learned*, 18.)

SHARLENE WELLS HAWKES

We *can* live in the world, walk side by side with the rest of the world in a search for better ways to exist and coexist, but yet we can keep our minds, our hearts, and our spirits consistently focused on ultimate success and acceptance in a very different world . . . a celestial one. (*Living*, 240.)

MARJORIE P. HINCKLEY

It's a valuable exercise to close your eyes every once in a while and think, "What is the most wonderful moment I have lived through during the past year?" (In *Glimpses*, 89.)

ELAINE L. JACK

The gospel assures you that your value is not dependent on your looks or material possessions. . . . Part of what it means to be a Latter-day Saint is to know within your soul your eternal worth, who you really are, and why you are here on earth. (In *Ensign*, Nov. 1989, 88.)

Sometimes I fear we have expectations that the good life is the life being led by someone else. The truth is that the good life is the life you have, for it is the only one you can lead. (In *Ensign*, July 1995, 51.)

VIRGINIA U. JENSEN

If we could thrust aside the veil and get an inkling of who we were before we came to earth, we would be that much closer to knowing ourselves as Christ knows us. (In *May Christ Lift Thee Up*, 38.)

LUCILE JOHNSON

Live in this day, this hour, this moment. We never know what will come tomorrow. (*Sunny Side Up*, 127.)

ARDETH GREENE KAPP

To have vision is to be future oriented and to see and believe in something that, with the help of others, you can make happen. It is to move into the unknown with faith, not fear, because of what you see and feel in your mind and heart. (*Lead*, 22.)

MARY B. KIRK

The mere fact that we are *alive today* is holy in itself. (In *Clothed with Charity*, 116.)

We chose to participate in mortality. So let's "rejoice and be glad" in it, and acknowledge our stewardship over each day, and *feel* each day's potential for holiness. (In *Clothed with Charity*, 116.)

Eternal life doesn't start at the Savior's second coming, . . . it's right now. Our relationship with God and Christ goes back all the way and it goes forward all the way and today is part of it. (In *Clothed with Charity*, 116.)

EILEEN GIBBONS KUMP

Mortality should be an adventure, not a burden. (In *Woman's Choices*, 100.)

JO ANN LARSEN

To have patience is to slow down enough to notice the people and problems in our lives, observations that often save the day. (*Heart of Goodness*, 383.)

SHARON G. LARSEN

Every day and every decision determines the next. In time we will look back at what may seem like disconnected, independent pieces of our lives and better understand what God is trying to make of us. (In *Arise*, 303.)

MARILYNNE TODD LINFORD

Celebrating life for what it is rather than clinging to the dream of what it isn't works best for me. (*Woman Fulfilled*, 77.)

ELAINE SORENSEN MARSHALL

[Life] *is* a process, moving through time, offering interesting insights, challenges, and pleasures along the way. It is not a quick, straight shot to heaven and perfection. (In *Every Good Thing*, 238–39.)

We hear the generic "life is a journey" metaphor. . . . If that metaphor has lost its power for you, try a different word: Your life may be an expedition, an adventure, an assembly line, a book in progress, a pilgrimage, an excursion, a parade—whatever image best conveys the process for you. (In *Every Good Thing*, 238.)

KATHLEEN "CASEY" NULL

We are ages old. We are ageless. We can't mark our beginning, so we can't attach a number to our existence. . . . Our earthly bodies are earthly. In this pre-immortal state they were meant to serve us only for earth life. But the essential "me" does not break down or sag. I was built to soar. (*Where Are We Going?* 30.)

ANNE OSBORN POELMAN

The eternal perspective brings our choices and challenges into sharp, clear focus. . . . The tasks at hand and those that lie ahead are gargantuan only if we fail to see that ordering these very activities, putting them in proper perspective, is indeed part of our mortal learning process. (In *Joy*, 43, 45.)

LOUISE Y. ROBISON

We are living in eternity. Though this life is but a part of the great eternity it is of as much significance as any part. (In *Improvement Era*, Apr. 1936, 215.)

To those who have caught, in part, the comprehensiveness of the gospel plan, life takes on new beauty and purpose. (In *Improvement Era*, Apr. 1936, 215.)

BARBARA B. SMITH

There is an urgent need for each of us to love life, to live fully, and to reject the multiple philosophic views that relegate us to an existence filled only with tedium, never-ending nothingness, devoid of hope. (*Love*, 10.)

Making long-range plans brings us the pleasure that comes with expectation and progress that is the result of purpose. But other essential growth and a more profound joy can often come from adjusting our hopes to an altered and perhaps eternal plan. (In *BYU Speeches*, 16 Feb. 1982, 94.)

EMMA LOU THAYNE

I cannot go back. Neither can I make up for deficiencies in the past by wishing or guilt in the present. (*As for Me*, 46.)

DWAN J. YOUNG

As you review the last year or the last ten years, what is the best day you remember? . . . The best day may really have been the one when life's events forced you to your knees to communicate with your Father with new intent; it may have been a day that wasn't convenient or even happy, but you became a bigger and better person when you faced a problem with courage. (In *Ensign*, Nov. 1986, 87.)

Prayer

Importance of Prayer

JILL TODD BANFIELD

Considering the endless blessings that are freely showered upon us each day, we should be anxious for the occasion to thank God. (*Draw Near unto Me,* 19.)

The concept of knowing God implies developing our relationship with him as our Heavenly Father. Essential to this development is our experiencing daily two-way communication in prayer. (*Draw Near unto Me,* 83.)

ELAINE CANNON

It is important to pray. The Lord has told us to pray to Heavenly Father in his name, that is, in the name of Jesus Christ. This is the way you communicate with your Heavenly Father. . . . He loves you. . . . He is interested in how you are doing. Prayer is your way to talk it over with him. (*Bell Ringer,* 111.)

JOANNE B. DOXEY

We can't put off establishing the practice of speaking intimately with the Lord. . . . As we pay the price, the rewards will come. (In *Ensign,* Apr. 1987, 32.)

PATRICIA T. HOLLAND

If we listen too often to the voices of the world, we will become confused and tainted. We must anchor ourselves in the spirit and that requires daily vigilance. (In *Ensign,* July 1980, 27.)

CAMILLA EYRING KIMBALL

Our Father loves us, and he is as near to us as we will let him be. We should constantly seek his inspiration through prayer. If we ever have a feeling that he is far away, it is because we have moved away from him. (*Writings,* 84.)

JENNIE B. KNIGHT

It is a woeful thing not to be on speaking terms with our Father in heaven. (In *Relief Society Magazine,* June 1929, 325.)

AMY BROWN LYMAN

Fortunate is the individual who has learned to seek the Lord in secret prayer, when hearts may be freely unburdened and solace and strength received. This is a precious privilege denied to no one. (In *Relief Society Magazine,* June–July 1943, 366.)

CHIEKO N. OKAZAKI

If your relationship with the Lord is not all that you would like it to be, I encourage you to spend more time with him in prayer. (*Aloha!* 109.)

BELLE S. SPAFFORD

The scriptures . . . tell us that our prayers shall ascend to our Heavenly Father as from a holy altar. (*Today's World*, 29.)

We need to pray, our children need to pray, that we may constantly be reminded that a Supreme Father rules over all, that life has purpose and direction. (*Today's World*, 35.)

[Prayer] is a choice privilege granted by a kind and loving Father through which his children may obtain promised blessings. (In *Relief Society Magazine*, Nov. 1959, 717.)

Blessings of Prayer

JILL TODD BANFIELD

In developing our relationship with God, we must devote time to meaningful communication with him. . . . This communication helps to prepare for eternal life by coming to know God better and by becoming more comfortable in his presence. (*Draw Near unto Me*, 83.)

As we experience successful prayer each day, our desire and ability to live a Christlike life will increase. Each is expanded by the other. (*Draw Near unto Me*, 16.)

Prayer need not be a resounding siren for the Lord to lift our yokes or ease our burdens. Rather it can be a constant relationship prepared early in times of prosperity and depended upon in times of famine. (*Draw Near unto Me*, 21.)

Prayer should serve as a peak event to enhance our day. It should draw us out of the world for a few minutes so that with our Father's love, strength, and motivation we may prepare ourselves to meet the day's activities. (*Draw Near unto Me*, 16.)

DIANE BILLS

Prayer is the key to knowing who we are and what God expects of us. (*Trust in the Lord*, 13.)

MARY ELLEN EDMUNDS

God loves to hear from us. He's our Father. . . . He asks us to share our innermost thoughts with him so that we can understand better what we're thinking and feeling. (*Happiness*, 180.)

DEANNA EDWARDS

When there is nothing else that can be done, we can pray, and prayer can bring physical, as well as spiritual healing. (*Grieving*, 195.)

Prayer seems to provide an active kind of energy that helps people cope with loss. (*Grieving*, 195.)

LINDA J. EYRE

Prayer is the key to many things. It can give us peace and calmness of heart and mind. It helps us to make hard decisions. . . . Prayer can help us resolve dilemmas and overcome bad feelings toward others, and can guide us in our relationships with husbands and children. (*Joyful Mother*, 22.)

MICHAELENE P. GRASSLI

Nothing softens hearts and unifies like praying together. (*Leader-Talk*, 50.)

BEPPIE HARRISON

Prayer transcends geography and the laws of physics. Prayers from anywhere can be heard and answered. It may seem easier to us to pray from our most sacred places, and we can feel our Lord's presence there, but so can our brothers and sisters worshipping all over the world at exactly the same time. (*Plain and Precious*, 46.)

PATRICIA T. HOLLAND

If in my heart I go to God the moment I feel even the slightest intimation of fear (or darkness or worry) instead of waiting to let it accumulate, if I speak to God even as my most trusted friend, my wisest counselor, and stay there in my heart or on my knees talking to him long enough, I can always see a ray of light at the edge of . . . dark shadows. (*On Earth*, 40.)

VIRGINIA U. JENSEN

The changes prayer effects in our homes are multiple. It restores peace and gives hope. It lightens heavy hearts and heals the wounds of sin. It restores perspective, allowing us to recognize our blessings even in the midst of our trials. (In *Ensign*, Nov. 1997, 90.)

ARDETH GREENE KAPP

This daily source of strength [prayer] makes the steep and steady climb upward in this life one of adventure and hope, not of despair and discouragement. (*Joy of the Journey*, 135.)

CAMILLA EYRING KIMBALL

If at the close of the day we can kneel and sincerely thank [our Father] for a good day, . . . there will be a spirit of peace and well being in our heart. (*Writings*, 84.)

SHARON G. LARSEN

Prayer is what makes the connection with God's power, which leads to loving and serving, sacrificing, and enlarging your own capabilities. (In *Ensign*, May 1999, 90.)

MARILYNNE TODD LINFORD

Prayer, the natural inclination of a child to talk to his father, is one of our Heavenly Father's kindest gifts to us. (*Mother's Self-Esteem*, 52.)

KATHLEEN "CASEY" NULL

Growth is enhanced by effective communication. If we are to learn to communicate well in our relationships, we can take lessons during prayer. Communicating well with our Father in Heaven provides a solid foundation for communicating with others. (*Where Are We Going?* 27.)

CHIEKO N. OKAZAKI

You're not praying for [someone else] because they need it. You're praying for [them] because you have a prayer to give. The prayer does not exist because of their poverty. It exists because of your richness. (*Sanctuary*, 134.)

Think of the power of . . . prayer. It's as if you lift someone with loving hands and hold him or her up in remembrance before God. That person is in your memory, in your heart, in your thoughts. And now you have brought his or her name before God in joyous, sympathetic remembrance. What a wonderful gift of plenitude! (*Sanctuary*, 134.)

VICKEY PAHNKE

Prayer does not provide a quick fix or represent a shortcut in a world of problems and complexities, but . . . it is a sure way to obtain truth in a world of falsehoods; it is a means of becoming more humble and teachable, so that our lives conform more to the Lord's will. That makes us happy. And it makes Heavenly Father happy. (In *Living the Legacy*, 165–66.)

BERTHA S. REEDER

Prayer becomes the compass that charts a true course back to our Father in heaven. (In *Relief Society Magazine*, Sept. 1956, 575.)

ELLIS R. SHIPP

My heart continually ascends to Heaven for that divine aid that I know is never withheld from those who ask in faith. (*While Others Slept*, 69.)

Though often the cloud looks dark and my heart feels like it would break, . . . thank Heaven there is one source of consolation—*Prayer*. (*While Others Slept*, 92.)

BARBARA B. SMITH

Heavenly power can help us understand and relate the timeless to our immediate concerns. (In *Ensign*, Nov. 1983, 84.)

What Should We Pray For?

ELAINE CANNON

A crushing desire to believe fosters prayer. (*Gatherings*, 262.)

DEANNA EDWARDS

It is time to begin to teach our children to pray, not just for fairness all the time, or for constant protection of our loved ones, or that pain will never come into our lives. Perhaps we must learn to pray for the internal strength to cope with loss when it does come, for the capacity to forgive ourselves and others, and for the faith to accept God's love even in the midst of pain and destruction. (*Grieving*, 195.)

PATRICIA T. HOLLAND

Our prayers ought to be to see as God sees, to flip the switch in our minds so we may see things eternally. (In *Ensign*, July 1980, 27.)

JANET G. LEE

Often, my prayerful requests are for feelings of peace, understanding of others, forgiveness, and patience. Through prayer combined with a sincere desire to receive these blessings, I have often felt a change of heart almost immediately. (In *Wisdom's Paths*, 43.)

ANN N. MADSEN

Ask in a prayer what to say in a prayer. (In *Clothed with Charity*, 96.)

KATHRYN S. SMITH

As you open your heart to instruction from the Spirit, it will flow more and more freely. Soon it will come unbidden, even in the middle of the day and moment by moment. If you pray every morning for instruction, and then at night you "report back in" with the result of your actions, and ask for further instruction, your partnership with God will build. (In *Serving with Strength*, 232–33.)

There is nothing irreverent about using paper and pencil to record impressions received during your prayers. (In *Serving with Strength*, 233.)

Answers to Prayer

ELAINE CANNON

A suggestion to the struggler longing to hear Jesus is to come to know that he is and that he cares. . . . Listen deep within your soul for a still, small voice. Then you can know (*know!*) that he is talking to you, mindful of you, aware and concerned about your special problems and needs. (*Gatherings*, 124.)

When you turn to the Lord in need and in increasing faith, the comfort always comes. It has never proven otherwise. That is the thing to remember. And when he has helped you, you quickly turn to help others. (*Gatherings*, 122.)

We all have been blessed in so many needful, small ways that we know Christ is in our midst. Look for the small miracles. (*Sunshine*, 95.)

JOANNE B. DOXEY

Only God knows our individual possibilities and limitations. He blesses us according to his plan for us, consistent with our need to grow. We must be sensitive to the whisperings of the Spirit, which often come in peaceful, unexpected ways. (In *Ensign*, Apr. 1987, 33.)

One . . . principle in the prayer process is patience. The Lord's time is not our time. (In *Ensign*, Apr. 1987, 32.)

WINNIFRED C. JARDINE

As we come to our knees spiritually and petition the Lord in righteous prayer, we are cleansed and are given, perhaps not what in our limited sight we have asked for, but enduring gifts of living water. The Lord knows what we do not. And he wants us purified. (In *As a Woman Thinketh*, 52.)

LUCILE JOHNSON

Receiving inspiration and revelation through prayer is one of the greatest achievements of man, and to expect that blessing without effort is contrary to the order of heaven. (*Sunny Side Up*, 16.)

ELLIS R. SHIPP

God had given men the fulfillment of His promise to hear and answer prayer. Great was my faith, frequent my prayers, and marvelous my blessing. (*While Others Slept*, 48.)

BARBARA B. SMITH

When Joseph Smith knelt in the Sacred Grove and asked his question, it was for each of us. The answer he received provides a sure foundation of fundamental truths upon which we should structure our lives. He also demonstrated that through personal prayer eternal truths answer individual needs. (In *Ensign*, Nov. 1983, 84.)

The Manner of Prayer

MARILYN ARNOLD

Prayer is not to be simply a worldly wish list; it must engage the very soul. (*Sweet Is the Word*, 171.)

Prayer should be a habit of mind, a consciousness of the Lord's presence even when formal invocation is not on the lips. (*Sweet Is the Word*, 171.)

JILL TODD BANFIELD

As we begin [a] prayer a marvelous truth is laid before us. Of all the titles applicable to God, he has asked that when we approach him in prayer we call him Father. (*Draw Near unto Me*, 13.)

ELOUISE BELL

Prayer is less a deed than a condition, less something we do than something we are. (In *Women Steadfast*, 30.)

Silence can lead to stillness, which facilitates meditation or reflection. Reflection leads often to prayer. Prayer of the most useful sort . . . leads to receptivity, to attending, to waiting on the Lord. (In *Women Steadfast*, 30.)

ELAINE CANNON

Pray in your secret places! Pray in sincerity, for a prayer admits gratitude for the joy and gladness in life, for the wonders of creation, for the amazing goodness and beauty of

God's children, for comfort and strength, and for supportive "other" blessings that come even when prayers are answered in a way different from what we had in mind. (*Sunshine*, 105.)

JOANNE B. DOXEY

We cannot afford to be casual in our communications with Him who is our guide and stay. (In *Ensign*, Apr. 1987, 32.)

MARY ELLEN EDMUNDS

Remember to make your communication with your Heavenly Father real and meaningful. Let it become the blessing and privilege it is meant to be. (*Happiness*, 180.)

BEPPIE HARRISON

Keeping in touch with Heavenly Father can be done anytime and anywhere, but . . . a relationship with the Lord is unlikely to thrive if all we devote to it are absentminded spare minutes here and there. (*Day at a Time*, 30.)

PATRICIA T. HOLLAND

Stop what you are so frantically doing and go into your private wilderness. Shut the door, turn out all earthly lights, set aside all earthly sights. Position yourself calmly, quietly in humble serenity until your prayer flows naturally, lovingly. When you feel God's presence, when you feel he is with you, you will be filled with a wonderful strength that will allow you to do anything in

righteousness. (In *Clothed with Charity*, 12.)

In some sense, prayer may be the hardest work we will ever be engaged in, and perhaps it should be. (In *Best of Women's Conference*, 197.)

CHIEKO N. OKAZAKI

Prayer is an endlessly refreshing and delightful dialogue that can be carried on, even without words, between the heart in tune and the Spirit of the Lord. (*Aloha!* 109.)

BELLE S. SPAFFORD

When we offer prayer, our hearts must be right before him. As we are humble, fervent, submissive, yielding ourselves to the will of the Lord, we shall have his Spirit to guide us and our prayers will be heard and answered by an all-wise Father for our greatest ultimate good. (*Today's World*, 29.)

DWAN J. YOUNG

Your prayer can take many forms. It can be sung in a hymn, or whispered, or even thought. It can be as short as one word—"help!"— or it could be as long as Enos's prayer that lasted all night and all day. (In *Ensign*, Nov. 1985, 92.)

Pray often, talk to Heavenly Father, seek his counsel so that he can guide you. When you draw near to Heavenly Father in prayer, he will draw near to you. (In *Ensign*, Nov. 1985, 91.)

Pray Always

JILL TODD BANFIELD

The idea that man can speak with God, the Creator and power of the universe, is boggling to the mind, yet he has commanded us to approach him often. Unlike speaking with great men on the earth, speaking with God requires no official appointment or special position. This privilege is offered to all. (*Draw Near unto Me*, 13.)

ELOUISE BELL

To most of us, prayer means asking for something or expressing thanks for something. But there is, of course, more. We are told to pray always. We read of the Savior praying throughout the night. Are we talking here about endless repetition of requests, pleading and repeating our petitions? Or does "pray always" mean to be ever receptive, ever attending, listening, waiting? (In *Women Steadfast*, 30.)

ARDETH GREENE KAPP

Our Heavenly Father has told us to pray anytime. Have you ever thought how available he is to us? No appointments, no waiting periods, no scheduling, no callbacks. He is always available. (*Joy of the Journey*, 169.)

CHIEKO N. OKAZAKI

Think of the line in the Lord's Prayer, "Give us this day our daily bread." Why does the prayer say the bread of "this day" and not the bread of "tomorrow"? Could it be because God wants us to come to him tomorrow likewise? If we already had tomorrow's bread, is it possible that we would fail to ask Heavenly Father for it? (*Sanctuary*, 36.)

Prayers are not little set speeches that we deliver at stated times during the day or rituals for opening and closing meetings. Think of prayer as a sustained, ongoing conversation that you have with God during the whole day. (*Aloha!* 108.)

VICKEY PAHNKE

Where do we pray? This is a given. Pray anywhere and everywhere. . . . Pray when you are working and when you are playing. Pray when you are prompted and pray when you are tempted—particularly when you don't feel like it at all. (In *Living the Legacy*, 166.)

M. CATHERINE THOMAS

It is when we move from sometimes-praying to nearly all-times-praying that things change perceptibly. (*Spiritual Lightening*, 98.)

MARGARET J. WHEATLEY

Life is so much nicer, so much easier, so much more fun when we call upon the Lord in our moments of pleasure, when we call upon the Lord for companionship, for enjoyment, when we call upon the Lord for every little need, not just the big ones. (In *Women and Christ*, 43.)

Communication in Prayer

JILL TODD BANFIELD

Prayer is like a ladder. As we make the effort to climb each step, the Lord opens to our view new horizons of progress and knowledge. (*Draw Near unto Me*, 85.)

It is through prayer that we learn to approach and converse with God, acquire the ability to listen to him, and develop the skill of understanding and working with his Spirit. (*Draw Near unto Me*, 85.)

In striving to establish two-way communication with God we must not become so busy diagnosing our personal circumstances and seeking the advice of others that we fail to ask and listen for God's vital instructions to us. (*Draw Near unto Me*, 41.)

We need to discipline ourselves and demonstrate our knowledge and desire to hear the Lord's will by listening carefully for his directions. (*Draw Near unto Me*, 41.)

ELAINE CANNON

Blessings and answers are commensurate with effort, agency, agenda, and God's will. (*Sunshine*, 100.)

The person who cries out frantically for handouts from heaven but has not personally prepared may indeed be disappointed. (*Sunshine*, 100.)

Effective praying—that is, actually reaching God through a one-on-one communication and experiencing a feeling of an exchange of love with him—happens according to law, formula, recipe, pattern, principles. (*Sunshine*, 100.)

JAMIE GLENN

The way we develop a close relationship with anyone is by sharing our feelings and communicating openly and often. The same is true for our relationship with Heavenly Father. (*Walk Tall*, 53.)

PATRICIA T. HOLLAND

Find a private place and kneel comfortably and calmly in the center of the room. For a few moments say nothing, just think of [Heavenly Father]. Just kneel there and feel the closeness of his presence, his warmth, his peace. With humility, express your gratitude for every blessing, every good thing you enjoy. Share with him your problems and fears. Talk to him about each one and pause long enough to receive his counsel. I promise that you will learn his shoulders are broad enough for your burdens. (*On Earth*, 37.)

WINNIFRED C. JARDINE

Praying . . . is like sinking roots into the earth in search of water—living water. Sometimes the moisture level is close to the surface and easy to reach, and prayers are quickly and obviously answered. Sweet relief! But oh, how often I have to push prayer roots down through hard layers of stubborn clay, deeper and deeper to find that nourishing water. (In *As a Woman Thinketh*, 51.)

CHIEKO N. OKAZAKI

When it comes to prayer, let's have no more empty statements and insincere but polite phrases. Be honest. If you're mad, say so. If you're confused, say so. And don't think anything is too small for the Savior's loving attention. (*Lighten Up!* 184.)

CAROLYN J. RASMUS

Active listening is as critical as asking. (*In the Strength of the Lord*, 65.)

Priesthood

DONNA LEE BOWEN BARNES

The priesthood is a means to funnel the power of God to us on this earth. It is the means by which order is imposed, by which the steps are established that we must follow to return to the Lord. (In *As Women of Faith*, 72.)

JANETTE HALES BECKHAM

It was in [a] prison setting that God taught Joseph Smith about priesthood power. . . . Priesthood power is used to minister, to preach, to teach, to baptize, to ordain, to heal, to seal, to restore, to bless, to prophesy, to testify, to do good. (In *Ensign*, Nov. 1995, 11.)

ELAINE CANNON

The hands that pass the sacrament, baptize a child, or hold a girl's ought to be clean. (*Not Just Ordinary*, 38.)

HORTENSE H. CHILD

Priesthood operates on a standard of righteousness. When one undertakes to cover sins, gratify pride or vain ambition, or exercise control or dominion or compulsion upon another soul in any degree of unrighteousness, the Spirit withdraws and the priesthood cannot operate. (In *BYU Speeches*, 29 July 1975, 193.)

RUTH MAY FOX

To receive a blessing under the hands of one holding the holy Priesthood to do certain work is no small thing. No women outside of the Latter-day Saint Church have such a privilege. (In *Relief Society Magazine*, Dec. 1936, 751.)

MARIE K. HAFEN

All my experience teaches me that as I seek to sustain the priesthood, whether through loyalty to my husband, to my appointed leaders, or to my Savior, the priesthood sustains me, for the priesthood is the power of Him who will not forsake me. (In *Ensign*, Mar. 1987, 8.)

When we sustain the priesthood . . . we are doing more than respecting the Lord's servants who administer the ordinances, important as that is. We are also honoring our sacred priesthood covenants and feeling profound gratitude for our priesthood blessings. (In *Ensign*, Mar. 1987, 8.)

ELAINE L. JACK

In the Doctrine and Covenants we are told that the Melchizedek Priesthood holds "the keys of all the spiritual blessings of the church" (D&C 107:18). I know it is God's power and authority on earth to bless our lives and help us bridge our earthly experiences to the eternities. When we receive the blessings of the priesthood, we are drawing on the power and grace of God. (In *Ensign*, Nov. 1996, 76.)

SHERRIE JOHNSON

The man presides to assure order, but with that comes the burden of responsibility. . . . The call to preside is a call to serve. It is a call of responsibility to assure that all is done in righteousness and that order prevails. (*Man, Woman, and Deity*, 27.)

LOUISE Y. ROBISON

Let us not forget that God is always on the side of right. When we are working earnestly, under the direction of His Priesthood for the benefit of His children, a power greater than our own is with us. (In *Relief Society Magazine*, Nov. 1938, 767.)

M. CATHERINE THOMAS

Priesthood is the great governing authority of the universe. It unlocks spiritual blessings of the eternal world for the heirs of salvation. The power to play a saving role is the most sought-after power among righteous priesthood holders in time or in eternity. (*Selected Writings*, 85.)

A righteous priesthood holder can work by faith to provide great benefits to his fellow beings (Mosiah 8:18). He can, in fact, exercise great faith in behalf of others of lesser faith, "filling in" with faith for them; thus a prophet and a people together can bring down blessings for even a whole community. (*Selected Writings*, 86–87.)

LEAH D. WIDTSOE

To use a well-known simile, we may liken the Priesthood to electricity which brings light and power unto every home that wills to use it. It may be installed in any and every home to benefit the entire family if they will pay the price and make the proper connections. But the connections must be made correctly and by one who is authorized to do so or the house will remain in darkness. (In *Relief Society Magazine*, Nov. 1940, 738.)

Respect the Priesthood in every way and that will give you power to become the leader in your home and truly successful in all the undertakings of your life. (In *Improvement Era*, May 1938, 269.)

Women and the Priesthood

HORTENSE H. CHILD

One of the greatest works and missions of women is first to live by a standard of righteousness themselves and be able to influence priesthood bearers—fathers, brothers, husbands and sons, friends—to live righteously. Then the rights of the priesthood which are connected to the powers of heaven can be controlled in her behalf. (In *BYU Speeches*, 29 July 1975, 194.)

SHERI L. DEW

From an eternal perspective we know little about the reasons specific assignments were given to men and women. Because of that, the adversary seeks to create confusion about something that need not be confusing. What we do know is that the Lord has declared his will on this matter, and for reasons known to him, our assignments as sisters do not require that we be ordained to the priesthood, though the assignments of worthy men do require ordination. This difference in the stewardship between the sons and daughters of God need not concern us. We should feel secure about the manner in which the Lord administers his kingdom. (In *Arms of His Love*, 399–400.)

RUTH HARDY FUNK

Women of the world can gain the liberation they seek only by recognizing within themselves the gifts of womanhood, the gifts of motherhood, and satisfying them in the natural and divine role as found within the priesthood and as provided through those vessels of the Lord who are the bearers of the priesthood. This is the only key to our identity—the role we play in the priesthood of God. (In *New Era*, Nov. 1973, 9.)

SUSA YOUNG GATES

When the key was turned in the opening portal of sky and earth to admit men once again in life's sacred courts, men were endowed with the power and majesty of the Holy Priesthood; and all its blessings, gifts, and powers are shared and shared alike by man and his true mate. (In *Improvement Era*, Apr. 1920, 543.)

Woman is admitted not only into public courts of worship and activity, symbolically and equally in religious and civic affairs, but in temples, which are the most sacred places maintained by the Church, side by side with . . . her husband, she is given her place and position in all sacred ordinances. Indeed, to receive his highest blessings a man must be accompanied by his wife. Women share the gifts, blessings and labors of the priesthood, within and without the temple. (In *Improvement Era*, Oct. 1927, 1102–3.)

ELAINE L. JACK

It is significant to me that the women were organized under the authority of the priesthood. We sustain the priesthood and are sustained by its power. The sisters of the Church . . . treasure our opportunity to be full partakers of the spiritual blessings of the priesthood. (In *Ensign*, Nov. 1996, 76–77.)

SYDNEY SMITH REYNOLDS

Our challenge as women is ultimately the same as our brothers' challenge as men; that is to live the gospel, to become Christlike, and to achieve our fullest potential—namely, immortality and eternal life. (In *Ensign*, Oct. 1979, 67.)

M. CATHERINE THOMAS

Women . . . have right and access to all the gifts of the Spirit.

No difference in spiritual power and potential is implied by giving priesthood authority to men only. Spiritual power is based on personal sanctification, faith, and thorough submission to righteousness. These gifts are not gender specific. (*Spiritual Lightening*, 50.)

LEAH D. WIDTSOE

When the women of this Church learn to understand and to magnify their relationship to the Priesthood, greater blessings than any yet dreamed of will be their portion. (In *Relief Society Magazine*, Nov. 1940, 740.)

Priorities

ELAINE CANNON

You can't maintain a heavy schedule unless your heart is in the right place, or you'll end up with broken hearts. (In *Keepers*, 126.)

There are at least two critical areas to concentrate on—for all of us . . . The first is to strengthen self. The second is to serve the Lord by serving others. (In *Ensign*, Nov. 1978, 107.)

JANATH R. CANNON

The principle of free agency and choice is laid upon us by the Lord. Every day he sets before us choices—

not only choices between good and evil, which are easy for most of us to make, but choices between good and good. . . . We *cannot* seek after *all* of them at the same time. To everything there is a season. (In *Ensign*, Apr. 1976, 70.)

Put successful personal relationships, especially with those dearest to you, near the top of your list of priorities. (In *Ensign*, Apr. 1976, 70.)

The work of the Lord should have precedence over other pursuits in our search for excellence. (In *Ensign*, Apr. 1976, 70.)

Always . . . set your priorities by inspiration and by hearkening to the living prophets of the Lord. . . . Through obedience and love, by studying, praying, and hearkening, we can receive inspiration to set our particular priorities in our pursuit of excellence. (In *Ensign*, Apr. 1976, 70.)

SHERI L. DEW

How often are we so focused on pursuing the so-called good life that we lose sight of eternal life? It is the fatal spiritual equivalent of selling our birthright for a mess of pottage. (In *Ensign*, Nov. 1999, 97–98.)

KARLA C. ERICKSON

It is not always important to accomplish many tasks during the day. What counts is touching people around us. (*Make Time Count*, 97.)

ELAINE L. JACK

Being engaged in many causes does not necessarily mean we are engaged in the best causes. (*Eye to Eye*, 119.)

There are many good things vying for our attention, but the good and the better need to be subjugated to the best. (*Eye to Eye*, 119.)

Focusing on our eternal purposes can ease our burdens and make our lives happy and more productive. Indeed, we often can do less and have it mean more. (In *Ensign*, May 1994, 16.)

VIRGINIA U. JENSEN

The adversary would like to confuse us and divert our attention from what matters most. But we are blessed, for we know that faith and family matter most. (In *Ensign*, Nov. 2000, 93.)

ARDETH GREENE KAPP

If possible, the adversary would keep us busily engaged in a multitude of trivial things in an effort to keep us distracted from the few vital things that make all of the difference. (*Joy of the Journey*, 4–5.)

SHARON G. LARSEN

When we've set our course, the Lord will help us set our priorities. (In *Arise*, 306.)

ANNE OSBORN POELMAN

One of the great learning experiences of this life is not only to make the right decisions, but also to sequence them properly. . . . In order to experience the joy of a balanced life we need to sequence our priorities . . . from the eternal point of view. (In *Joy*, 43.)

LOUISE Y. ROBISON

In budgeting life we must remember that there are three big fundamentals, the physical, the mental and the spiritual. (In *Relief Society Magazine*, June 1925, 315.)

Priorities of Women

NORMA B. ASHTON

Can you choose to take a class instead of sewing all your children's clothes . . . ? On some days can you throw the covers up quickly on the bed so you can . . . play tennis because you decide you need exercise more than a perfectly made bed? Can you use your agency in these seemingly insignificant ways without feeling weighed down with guilt? If so, you are living well today. (In *Woman to Woman*, 22.)

JANENE WOLSEY BAADSGAARD

[If a woman] can remember full-time homemaking is her *choice*, not her confinement, then life in the home will take on a whole new perspective, one that will allow her to see this time of her life as only part of a great whole. (*Life after Birth*, 19.)

SUSAN EASTON BLACK

The family unit is basic to mortality and will exist among the righteous in eternal realms. When a woman ignores her familial responsibility, frustration will become apparent in her divine nature—for a woman is to be a daughter, a wife, and a mother. A woman cannot reject any of these divine roles without rejecting the essential process of womanhood. (In *LDS Women's Treasury*, 18.)

JAROLDEEN ASPLUND EDWARDS

It is important to see choices as opportunities, not as frustrations. (*Things I Wish I'd Known*, 20.)

We cannot do everything, all the time, all at once. We can, through the years, do many things, at different times, one at a time. (*Things I Wish I'd Known*, 19–20.)

PATRICIA T. HOLLAND

We can become so sidetracked in our compulsive search for identity and self-esteem that we really believe it can be found in having perfect figures or academic degrees or professional status or even absolute motherly success. Yet, in so searching externally, we can be torn from our true internal, eternal selves. (*On Earth*, 86.)

KATHLEEN BUSHNELL JENSEN

[One] way to keep perspective is to remember that "to every thing there is a season." (Ecclesiastes 3:1.) . . . My advice is be content where you are. If you have young children, enjoy them! . . . Don't wish away your toddlers and bright-eyed pre-schoolers. They will never be yours at that age again. Don't rush your seasons. (In *Women and Christ*, 51–52.)

VIRGINIA U. JENSEN

On a Monday evening not long ago, I was walking past a playground where a young family was choosing up sides for a game. I overheard one of the children call out, "Mom, choose me." As I walked on, these words rang in my ears. Life in today's world places a multitude of demands on a woman's resources of time and energy. We can choose to apply our talents in more arenas than ever before, but there are only a few of those places in which our influence is irreplaceable. I can imagine children the world over saying, "When you decide where to spend the time and the gifts that God has given you, Mom, choose me." (In *Ensign*, Nov. 1997, 90.)

Prominence does not equal priority, nor can the world's paycheck equal that of our Heavenly Father's, who knows the importance of a woman's devotion to the salvation of souls. (In *Ensign*, Nov. 2000, 93.)

ARDETH GREENE KAPP

When the lights have gone out and the curtain is closed on our second act, the opinions of others, the acceptance and applause of the crowd, will be a haunting echo if our Father's approval is in question. It won't matter if we play center stage or in the wings if our Lord and Savior is at the very center of our life. (*My Neighbor*, 7.)

Even as we endeavor to play our various parts in their appropriate seasons, there . . . are those who would attempt to revise, rewrite, and restructure the script, changing the sacred roles of men and women, modifying the scenes and seasons, adjusting the morals and models where possible, and even altering the main stage, the home, in which the most important drama of life should unfold. (*My Neighbor*, 7.)

JENNIE B. KNIGHT

Our aim is to serve and in that service find joy in this life, and eternal life in the world to come. (In *Relief Society Magazine*, June 1924, 307.)

MARILYNNE TODD LINFORD

If we always respond to the *shoulds* in life, weariness will be our mode. *Could* is a soft, kinder word. *Could* means you are a free agent who makes good choices and decides what to do now and what can wait. (*Woman Fulfilled*, 51.)

LOUISE Y. ROBISON

If we are such excellent housekeepers that we cannot spend one moment in spiritual development, what is the price we are paying? (In *Relief Society Magazine*, June 1925, 314.)

What are the satisfactions of pride or social popularity when it means lowering our standards and destroying our children's confidence in the principles of the Gospel? Women of Relief Society, set your standards high. We do not make better friends by disloyalty to principle. (In *Relief Society Magazine*, Mar. 1938, 147.)

IDA SMITH

Our first priority must always be ourselves and our relationship with

God. If that core relationship is good, we will somehow manage to accomplish what we must regardless of our circumstances. (In *As Women of Faith*, 215.)

BELLE S. SPAFFORD

Not what we *have*, but what we *are* should be the watchword of womankind. (In *Relief Society Magazine*, Nov. 1968, 810.)

HEIDI S. SWINTON

When we define ourselves by what we do rather than by how we live, we lose our eternal perspective. (In *As a Woman Thinketh*, 36.)

Progression

MARGARET HAFEN ARCHIBALD

In trying to do our best as mothers and fathers, we are developing traits that make us better people. We grow by leaps and bounds every time we strive for patience, kindness, love, service, humility, and being in tune with the Spirit. . . . The rewards are not measured in earthly terms. (In *Emotional First Aid*, 111.)

JANETTE HALES BECKHAM

Have you thought about what it means to be damned? It means that our progress is stopped; our growth is stopped. (In *BYU Speeches*, 7 Aug. 1994, 191.)

Getting ahead will be of little value if it is not connected to principles of righteousness. (In *BYU Speeches*, 7 Aug. 1994, 191.)

SUSA YOUNG GATES

We will in every little fault as well as virtue of our individual nature either go up with much greater rapidity than ever before in our lives, or we will go down with as great rapidity. (In *Young Woman's Journal*, May 1893, 376.)

MICHAELENE P. GRASSLI

We are limited only by our own degree of desire, resolve, or commitment. Circumstances may seem to limit us, but circumstances are only incidental to people determined to succeed. (*What I Have Learned*, 18.)

ELAINE L. JACK

When we are on the path, we can feel it. The fruits of eternal progress are manifest in joy, peace, love, hope, and increased confidence in the Lord. (In *Ensign*, May 1994, 16.)

So often we go around in a circle, spinning our spiritual wheels while only our temporal treads hit the road. (In *Ensign*, May 1994, 15.)

Our eternal progression is the very essence of our earthly existence. (In *Ensign*, May 1994, 15.)

ARDETH GREENE KAPP

Whenever we are weighed down with concerns that keep us from the spirit of the Lord, we are in a real sense in bondage, burdened with a load that keeps us from progressing as we might. (*Rejoice!* 55.)

CHIEKO N. OKAZAKI

God's patience with us means that we have all the time we need, as long as we're trying. We can start over as many times as we need. Life isn't a race. God isn't waiting at some mythical finishing line, tapping his foot, glancing at his stopwatch, and muttering, "Hey, get a move on, will you?" As long as we're moving in the direction of sainthood and are sincerely trying, he's happy. In fact, far from waiting at the finishing line, he's there, right beside us, encouraging us and sometimes even lifting us over the rough spots. (*Aloha!* 205.)

VICKEY PAHNKE

Don't allow someone else's actions—however innocent—to keep you from progressing. (In *Joy in the Journey*, 126.)

If your desires . . . are good and your goals worthy, you CAN succeed. You can go forward, even in a backward world. (In *Joy in the Journey*, 126.)

ANNE OSBORN POELMAN

Exaltation is not an instant process. Life is not leaping tall buildings at a single bound. It is more like carefully pacing ourselves, marshaling our precious energy and spiritual resources so that we *can* mount those steps one at a time. (In *Joy*, 50.)

MARIAN JEPPSON STODDARD

We end one calling and begin another. . . . Even the successful completion of this life is the doorway to beginning eternal growth and glory. (In *Thy Word Is a Lamp*, 175.)

MARY WILSON UMOREN

The great thing in this world is not so much where we stand but in what direction we are moving to reach that port in heaven. Sometimes we must stand with the wind and sometimes against it. But we must sail and not drift or lie at anchor. (In *Thy Word Is a Lamp*, 39.)

LEAH D. WIDTSOE

It is wise to plan that life shall be so lived from day to day that one is increasingly just a little nearer the source of light and truth instead of farther away. (In *Relief Society Magazine*, Mar. 1942, 177.)

It is impossible for one to stand still intellectually or spiritually or to always be content with things as they are. If we are not climbing upward, growing, learning, improving ourselves, we are bound to be on the downward track. (In *Relief Society Magazine*, Mar. 1942, 177.)

Prophets

JANETTE HALES BECKHAM

As each of us listens to the prophet and responds to his message, if we are in tune we can carry his message with us. Others will feel the prophet's message because of the way we act. . . . Isn't that exciting to think about? We can make his message be a force for good in our own lives, but also in our homes, in our neighborhoods, and at school. (In *Ensign*, May 1996, 85.)

JANATH R. CANNON

The word of the Lord through his living prophets has priority over any of our own ideas, however excellent they may seem to us. (In *Ensign*, Apr. 1976, 70.)

VIRGINIA U. JENSEN

There aren't many guarantees in this life. . . . But . . . the Lord has given some marvelous guarantees without any disclaimers. And this is one of them: He will choose the prophet, and He will never let that man lead us astray. Imagine for a moment the impact of that promise. (In *Ensign*, Nov. 1998, 13.)

If we listen to the voices of the world, we will be misled. But if we listen to the voice of the Lord through His living prophet and follow his counsel, we will never go astray. (In *Ensign*, Nov. 1998, 13.)

BETTE S. MOLGARD

We . . . have easy access to the words of prophets, both past and present, that we know represent words of comfort, hope, and peace from our Heavenly Father. That faith and confidence in our prophets can replace many fears. Study their words. When coupled with your faith in the calling of a prophet, their words are filled with peace. (*Everyday Battles*, 39.)

BELLE S. SPAFFORD

If we truly believe in prophets and their divinely ordained calling as we claim to do, we impose upon ourselves a responsibility of strict obedience to their teachings. (*Woman's Reach*, 64.)

A prophet is one chosen and inspired of God to speak in God's name regarding the future happenings pertaining to the church on earth and also to the well-being of God's children. . . . He is the living oracle of God—God's mouthpiece on earth. (*Woman's Reach*, 63.)

PEGGY ST. CYR

Only one man on earth has the authority to lead the entire Church any one time, and that is the President of The Church of Jesus Christ of Latter-day Saints. If we adhere to his guidance, we cannot err. (*Conversion to Commitment*, 79.)

The Prophet Joseph Smith

LUCY DIANTHA MORLEY ALLEN

I've seen the Prophet wrestle, and run, and jump, but have never seen him beaten. In all that he did he was manly and almost godlike. . . . The only words that express his looks and actions are: "Surely he was a man of God." (In *Young Woman's Journal*, Dec. 1906, 537–38.)

SUSA YOUNG GATES

To bear testimony that Joseph Smith was a prophet, is but a new declaration that there is a God, and that he came with his Son once more to earth, to usher in a new dispensation, or to restore the gospel in its fulness and purity. (In *Improvement Era*, Mar. 1907, 347.)

MARY ALICE CANNON LAMBERT

I knew him the instant my eyes rested upon him, and at that moment I received my testimony that he was a prophet of God, for I never had such a feeling for mortal man as then thrilled my being. . . .

The love the Saints had for him was inexpressible. They would willingly have laid down their lives for him. If he was to talk, every task would be laid aside that they might listen to his words.

He was not an ordinary man. Saints and sinners alike felt and recognized a power and influence which he carried with him. It was impossible to meet him and not be impressed by the strength of his personality and influence. (In *Young Woman's Journal*, Dec. 1905, 554.)

MARY A. NOBLE

In the spring of 1834, . . . was the first time I ever beheld a prophet of the Lord, and I can truly say at the first sight that I had a testimony within my bosom that he was a man chosen of God to bring forth a great work in the last days. His society I prized. His conversation was meat and drink to me. . . . Never did I hear preaching sound so glorious to me as that did. I realized it was the truth of heaven. (In *They Knew the Prophet*, 15–16.)

JANE SNYDER RICHARDS

The first time I ever saw Joseph Smith I recognized him from a dream I had had. He had such an angelic countenance as I never saw before. He was then thirty-seven years of age, of ordinary appearance in dress and manner, a childlike appearance of innocence. His hair was of a light brown, blue eyes and light complexion. His natural demeanor was quiet; his character and disposition was formed by his life work. He was kind and considerate, taking a personal interest in all his people, considering every one his equal. (In *Their Own Words*, 172.)

BATHSHEBA W. SMITH

My first impressions were that he was an extraordinary man, a man of great penetration; was different from any other man I ever saw; had the most heavenly countenance; was genial, affable and kind; and looked the soul of honor and integrity.

I know him to be what he professed to be—a true prophet of God. (In *Juvenile Instructor*, 1 June 1892, 344–45.)

LUCY MACK SMITH

My son Joseph has had revelations from God since he was a boy, and he is indeed a true prophet of Jehovah. (In *Early Mormon Documents*, 1:220.)

"Am I indeed the mother of a prophet of the God of heaven, the honored instrument in performing so great a work?" I felt that I was in the purview of angels, and my heart bounded at the thought of the great condescension of the Almighty. (*History of Joseph Smith*, xxxii.)

ELIZA R. SNOW

I had ample opportunity of judging of [Joseph Smith's] daily walk and conversation, and the more I made his acquaintance, the more cause I found to appreciate him in his divine calling. (In *Women of Mormondom*, 65.)

Though his expansive mind grasped the great plan of salvation and solved the mystic problem of man's destiny—though he had in his possession keys that unlocked the past and the future with its succession of eternities, in his devotion he was as humble as a little child. As a philanthropist, his soul was broad as eternity. In the cause of truth and righteousness—in all that would benefit his fellow man, his integrity was as firm as the pillars of heaven. . . . He . . . proved himself true to every heaven-revealed principle—true to his brethren and true to God, then sealed his testimony with his blood. (In *Woman's Exponent*, 1 Jan. 1847, 117.)

EMMELINE B. WELLS

[When I first saw Joseph Smith], his majestic bearing, so entirely different from anyone I had ever seen (and I had seen many superior men) was more than a surprise. It was as if I beheld a vision; I seemed to be lifted off my feet, to be as it were walking in the air, and paying no heed whatever to those around me. . . . Then I saw this man . . . shaking hands with all the people, men, women, and children. . . . When he took my hand, I was simply electrified—thrilled through and through to the tips of my fingers, and every part of my body, as if some magic elixir had given me new life and vitality. I am sure that for a few minutes I was not conscious of motion. I think I stood still, I did not want to speak, or be spoken to. I was overwhelmed with indefinable emotion. (In *Young Woman's Journal*, Dec. 1905, 555.)

He was beyond my comprehension. . . . His expression was mild and almost childlike in repose; and when addressing the people, who loved him it seemed to adoration, the glory of his countenance was beyond description. At other times, the great power of his manner, more than of his voice (which was sublimely eloquent to me), seemed to shake the place on which we stood and penetrate the inmost soul of his hearers, and I am sure that then they would have laid down their lives to defend him. (In *Young Woman's Journal*, Dec. 1905, 556.)

EMILY D. PARTRIDGE YOUNG

Joseph was a prophet of God, and a friend of man. His was a noble character. All who knew him can testify to that assertion. He was all that the word *gentleman* would imply—pure in heart, always striving for right, upholding innocence, and battling for the good of all. (In *They Knew the Prophet*, 173.)

ZINA D. H. YOUNG

We . . . honor the name [of Joseph Smith] because of his integrity to God and the principles of light and truth which he was the instrument of restoring to the earth for our salvation, and that of the whole human family if they will but accept of the glad message. (In *Woman's Exponent*, 1 Apr. 1892, 140.)

Relief Society

The Organization of Relief Society

AMY BROWN LYMAN

There is something greater in the Relief Society than any one of these activities or than all of them, and it is the spirit of the work, the great, dynamic spiritual force which has been with the Society from the beginning. And what is this force? It is the spirit of the Lord with which the organization has been blessed since the Prophet Joseph Smith turned the keys to women. (In *Relief Society Magazine*, Dec. 1928, 667.)

In all our labors, we try to keep in mind always that the most priceless thing in the world to us is the gospel of Jesus Christ, and our testimony of the gospel. These we value above everything else. We realize that it is through our knowledge of the gospel and its laws, through our belief in the rights and powers of the Priesthood and the authority of the Priesthood and through our testimonies, that we are held together, and that we survive as an organization. (In *Relief Society Magazine*, Aug. 1927, 396.)

BARBARA B. SMITH

When Joseph Smith turned the keys in behalf of women in Nauvoo . . . light and knowledge from heaven began to flow down upon women not only in the Church, but everywhere; and the wheels of progress provided women with more and more opportunities to take the responsibility for their own lives, and thus work out their own salvation and make contributions to the work of society. (In *Ensign*, May 1983, 90.)

EMMA SMITH

We are going to do something extraordinary. . . . We expect extraordinary occasions and pressing calls. (In *Elect Ladies*, 3.)

BELLE S. SPAFFORD

Relief Society was divinely inspired and is a greatly blessed organization for women, being organized under the priesthood and after a pattern of the priesthood—the only women's society so organized in the world today. (In *Improvement Era*, Nov. 1956, 838.)

The elements which make any organization successful are good beginnings or a solid foundation, a purposeful and worthy program, a capable leadership, and a devoted membership, Relief Society has all of these. (In *Relief Society Magazine*, May 1945, 280.)

The constancy of its purposes, their suitability to the needs of each succeeding and changing era, the consistency with which its basic programs have furthered and accomplished its purposes, attest the divine inspiration attendant upon the [Relief] Society. (In *Relief Society Magazine*, Nov. 1953, 716.)

Relief Society is great because of the greatness of its birth. Under divine inspiration, a Prophet of God, one chosen to be the instrument through which the gospel was to be restored to earth, gave to latter-day women this Society, and he personally taught them correct procedures and what their several activities would embrace. (In *Relief Society Magazine*, Mar. 1947, 148.)

Relief Society is not just another woman's organization. It was divinely founded. It is an auxiliary of the only true Church on the face of the earth today. (*Today's World*, 347.)

The Mission of Relief Society

AILEEN H. CLYDE

Charitable, compassionate service is the central mission of our Church's Relief Society organization. (In *Ensign*, Nov. 1991, 77.)

SHERI L. DEW

Relief Society can help us turn away from the world, for its express purpose is to help sisters and their families come unto Christ. . . . We no longer have the luxury of spending our energy on anything that does not lead us and our families to Christ. (In *Ensign*, Nov. 1999, 98.)

For all the good it has done in the past, Relief Society has yet to help move this latter-day work forward as it must. Sisters, the time has come to unleash the power of righteous happiness that exists among women of God. The time has come for us to be anxiously engaged in the work of saving souls. The time has come for the sisters of Relief Society to stand with and for the prophet in helping build the kingdom. The time has come for us each to stand tall and to stand together. (In *Ensign*, Nov. 2000, 95–96.)

Regardless of time or place, Relief Society has meant sisters lifting one another spiritually, loving and taking care of one another, and absorbing insight and inspiration from other women headed in the same direction. (In *Ensign*, Mar. 1992, 51.)

ELAINE L. JACK

The purpose of the Relief Society organization of the Church, stated in our handbook, is to help women and their families come unto Christ. This means bringing the influence of Jesus Christ into our homes. It means we focus on his gospel and we find joy in living his commandments. (In *Ensign*, Nov. 1995, 92.)

The very name "Relief Society" describes our purpose: to provide relief. (In *Ensign*, Nov. 1995, 91.)

VIRGINIA U. JENSEN

The first objective of Relief Society is to build faith in Jesus Christ and to teach one another the doctrines of the kingdom of God. (In *Ensign*, Nov. 1998, 92.)

Within the organization of the Relief Society we have all of the tools and resources we need to soothe a single soul or to heal a troubled world. (In *Ensign*, Nov. 1998, 92.)

The spiritual strength and secure testimonies of the women of the Church are absolutely vital—to themselves, to their families, to their branches and wards, and to the world itself. (In *Ensign*, Nov. 1998, 92.)

AMY BROWN LYMAN

No matter how interesting their educational and cultural programs have been, Relief Society women have never been satisfied with mere self-improvement. They have realized the need of contributing to something outside themselves. They have had a feeling that life was incomplete unless through their work and themselves they were able to make a contribution toward the welfare of others. (In *Relief Society Magazine*, Nov. 1941, 727.)

The Relief Society . . . is interested, at all times, . . . in promoting and enriching family life, in helping individuals to achieve their best, and in establishing and maintaining fine community standards. (In *Relief Society Magazine*, May 1932, 296.)

LOUISE Y. ROBISON

The type of service may not be the same today as in the beginning, for we have homes and schools and churches, but there are aching hearts to be comforted; there are the discouraged and the sorrowing who need us to carry the too heavy load, and help them plant their feet again on the firm foundation of faith and hope and high standards. (In *Relief Society Magazine*, June 1936, 348.)

It is the human personality which Relief Society is trying to develop; it is seeing beyond the service the real heroes and heroines and meeting them with love and patience. (In *Relief Society Magazine*, May 1939, 346.)

Cherry B. Silver

As members of this worldwide organization called Relief Society, our mission is clear. In all our diversity we combine our strengths to bless each other and to do the work of the Lord. (In *Knit Together in Love*, 18–19.)

Barbara B. Smith

With the organization of the Relief Society came the Lord's program for his daughters. The cornerstone of that work was to become deeply engaged in relieving suffering among his children. (In *Ensign*, Nov. 1978, 109.)

A fundamental reason for organizing the Relief Society was so that the sisters could act together to extend the work of the bishop in caring for the Saints and thus help build the kingdom of God on earth. (In *Ensign*, Nov. 1979, 83.)

As sisters in Relief Society, we have a noble heritage, a present challenge, and a vision of greatness to be. (In *Ensign*, Nov. 1978, 109.)

While individually learning and striving toward righteousness, [women] are collectively adding their strength toward establishing the kingdom of God here upon the earth. (In *Ensign*, Mar. 1983, 23.)

Bathsheba W. Smith

The Relief Society is a help to the work of the Gospel . . . [in] every . . . labor that pertains to the work of God on the earth. Let our works correspond with our teachings and set a good example before the growing generation; let us pass over our trials and keep hold of the iron rod, let us be humble and faithful to the end. (In *Woman's Exponent*, 1 Oct. 1890, 68.)

Emma Smith

[It is the duty of Relief Society sisters to] seek out and relieve the distressed . . . [to] be ambitious to do good. (In *Elect Ladies*, 21.)

Mary Ellen Smoot

Relief Society can achieve what the Lord has proposed, but only as we work in harmony with our priesthood leaders. Truly, we are all working together to bring men and women and families to Christ. (*Sweet Is the Work*, 160.)

The time has come for the members of Relief Society to realize fully the magnitude of its mission and to represent the Lord and his leaders to the women of the world. The time has come to raise our heads and fly the banner of righteousness. (In *Best of Women's Conference,* 508.)

If we desire to walk in the light of the Lord, we put one spiritual foot in front of the other. We follow the path of spiritual preparedness as it is set forth in scripture and by our living prophets. We take full fellowship in the Relief Society organization. This society, established and directed by our prophets through divine inspiration, is not just a Sunday meeting. It is an organization to bring sisters and their families unto Christ. (In *Ensign,* Nov. 1998, 89.)

ELIZA R. SNOW

[We] should be a select society, separate from all the evils of the world, choice, virtuous, and holy. (In *Women of Nauvoo,* 124.)

BELLE S. SPAFFORD

With the spirit of the Gospel permeating all that is done, Relief Society will continue to be a sustaining influence in the lives of its members, and the new season will offer rewards commensurate to the effort put forth. (In *Relief Society Magazine,* Sept. 1942, 641.)

Relief Society is pre-eminent among women's organizations because it is God's organization for his daughters here upon earth. (In *Relief Society Magazine,* Nov. 1954, 719.)

Relief Society women are women embarked in the service of God, and it follows that they are embarked in the service of their fellow men. Ours is not a man-made society—a higher power is operating to bring about the fulfillment of the purposes of Relief Society. (In *Relief Society Magazine,* Nov. 1954, 719.)

Relief Society was organized "under the Priesthood after a pattern of the Priesthood," not only for "the relief of the poor, but for the accomplishment of every good and noble work." Inspiration has guided its destiny, and intrinsic worth has characterized its activities. (In *Relief Society Magazine,* July 1944, 386.)

To search after objects of charity and administer to their needs, to pursue study along lines of thought and action that tend toward the elevation, development, and advancement of women, to enlarge homemaking talents and increase homemaking skills, to implant and nourish testimonies of the divinity of Jesus Christ and the divine mission of Joseph Smith—these are the fundamental purposes of Relief Society. (In *Relief Society Magazine,* Nov. 1953, 716.)

Throughout its history, the [Relief] Society has been guided, directed, and protected by the influence of that sacred power given to men holding the Holy Priesthood. (In *Relief Society Magazine,* Mar. 1947, 148.)

[The Relief Society's] membership has been made up of devoted, self-sacrificing, hard-working women, rendering free-will service because of an inner conviction of the truth of the gospel and the importance of caring for the children of our Father and of contributing to the Master's work. (In *Relief Society Magazine*, Mar. 1947, 148.)

BELLE S. SPAFFORD, MARIANNE C. SHARP, AND GERTRUDE R. GARFF

Ours is a healing mission requiring the larger heart, the kindlier touch, the steadier will; it is a work of many skills, requiring the alert mind, the measured judgment, the trained hand. Ours is not easy work—it was never intended to be so; but it is work, the bountiful fruits of which are joy, satisfaction, and growth. (In *Relief Society Magazine*, Jan. 1947, 3.)

CLARISSA S. WILLIAMS

No matter where you are, you are a part of that great body of women who are working for the betterment of women and children and communities. (In *Relief Society Magazine*, Dec. 1925, 632.)

BARBARA W. WINDER

The work of Relief Society is focused on the pure and simple part of the gospel, to develop faith and bear testimony; to render compassionate service as we care for the needy; to strengthen our families here and in eternity; and to work with our "hearts knit together in unity and love one towards another" (Mosiah 18:21). (In *Ensign*, May 1990, 76.)

Relief Society Strengthens the Home

LOUISE Y. ROBISON

Sisters of the Relief Society! The office given to you is the opportunity to grow in intelligence and to gain that knowledge which will give you "advantage in the world to come." The degree of success depends upon your effort. The reward justifies your best endeavor. "Welcome the task that makes you go beyond yourself, if you would grow." (In *Relief Society Magazine*, Mar. 1939, 148.)

BARBARA B. SMITH

Relief Society teaches women to build a home based on gospel principles. This kind of home—as possible for the woman who lives alone as for a woman with a family—becomes a place of warmth and renewal for all who enter. (In *Ensign*, Mar. 1979, 24.)

BELLE S. SPAFFORD

Mothers are intimately involved in the attitudes and patterns of life adopted by their families in the homes. Relief Society, therefore, has the responsibility to guide, teach, and train the mothers in these fundamentals of good living. This, to me, is a vital welfare service of the Society. (In *Relief Society Magazine*, Aug. 1967, 567.)

It is a fundamental duty of Relief Society to help mothers to have the proper concept of the eternalness of the family relationship; to awaken in them high ideals in their daily living; to inspire them with the greatness and joy of their mission as mothers and homemakers; and, continually, to give unto them constructive help in meeting the daily obligations of motherhood and homemaking. (In *Relief Society Magazine*, Nov. 1959, 716.)

The Relief Society, since its inception, has accepted as one of its major responsibilities the task of guiding, directing, and training its members in their vital role of mother and homemaker. In fact, to develop within the members a firm and abiding testimony of the gospel, and to make of them good mothers and homemakers is one of Relief Society's first concerns. (In *Relief Society Magazine*, Nov. 1949, 727.)

Shirley W. Thomas

Love, work, service, stewardship, self-reliance and consecration . . . are the foundation stones upon which all welfare services are built. Relief Society . . . teaches the Christlike qualities of pure love, or charity; teaches that work sustains, that service gives work its meaning, that stewardship brings accountability, and that self-reliance allows a freedom to focus on another's needs, and that consecration is to give all one has. (In *Ensign*, May 1980, 87.)

Serving As Relief Society Sisters

Marian R. Boyer

The emotional support and strength that you Relief Society sisters can provide one another can be as important, or more so, than food or shelter. (In *Ensign*, Nov. 1981, 103.)

Sheri L. Dew

In the days ahead, a casual commitment to Christ will not carry us through. (In *Ensign*, Nov. 1999, 98.)

Elaine L. Jack

We can soothe a suffering heart when we can't eliminate the trouble. (In *Ensign*, Nov. 1995, 91.)

Our strength as Relief Society sisters in the gospel is most visible and most critical at home. Women are the heart of the home. Whatever your circumstance, you are the heart of your home. (In *Ensign*, Nov. 1995, 92.)

Virginia U. Jensen

As Relief Society sisters we can bring light into the lives of those we serve along with the loaves of bread we bake and the casseroles we share. We can give hope, we can lift, and we can inspire. We can teach of Christ and help others find peace and comfort within His light. (In *Ensign*, Nov. 1998, 92.)

AMY BROWN LYMAN

What can we do, as Relief Society women, to help out? We can teach the Gospel, and bear testimony to its truthfulness; we can live the Gospel, conform to all its standards, and thus show that such a life is rich, satisfying and bears good fruit. (In *Relief Society Magazine*, June 1931, 347.)

In all phases of work . . . which have been undertaken by [Relief Society women], they have shown courage, vision, resourcefulness, efficiency, earnestness of purpose, and great capacity for leadership. (In *Relief Society Magazine*, Mar. 1944, 138.)

CHIEKO N. OKAZAKI

Concentrate on the joy, not the job. We can do great good when we work as a united sisterhood, as long as we don't burden ourselves with unrealistic expectations that rob us of the joy of achievement. (*Aloha!* 21.)

LOUISE Y. ROBISON

Although our records are well kept, there is no human power which can give account of the deeds of loving kindness performed by our Relief Society members. (In *Relief Society Magazine*, Mar. 1931, 143.)

Love expresses itself in service and Relief Society gives opportunity for such service. (In *Relief Society Magazine*, Mar. 1938, 148.)

BATHSHEBA W. SMITH

Seek to bind your society with hoops of love and union. (In *Woman's Exponent*, 1 Jan. 1902, 67.)

LUCY MACK SMITH

We must cherish one another, watch over one another, comfort one another and gain instruction, that we may all sit down in heaven together. (*LDS Women's Treasury*, 474.)

MARY ELLEN SMOOT

Love must undergird everything we do. As sisters of the Relief Society, we love the Lord, we love our families, we love life and learning, and we love one another. (In *Ensign*, Nov. 2000, 91.)

Sisters . . . *we must prepare for our time because our time has come.* We must possess the spiritual strength to overcome our challenges, laying our faults on the altar and giving our lives to the Lord. We must focus our priorities on contributing, as we are able, to the building of the kingdom of God through service in the Relief Society. (In *Ensign*, Nov. 1997, 87.)

As a devoted Relief Society sister, you will see miracles happen in your own lives—and in the lives of those you serve. Under its banner, impossible dreams can come true. (In *Best of Women's Conference*, 508.)

Every visit, every act of service, every phone call we make as Relief Society sisters can be done in an attitude of love. That is what charity means. (*Sweet Is the Work*, 39.)

ELIZA R. SNOW

Tell the sisters to go forth and discharge their duties in humility and faithfulness and the Spirit of God will rest upon them, and they will be blest in their labors. Let them seek for wisdom instead of power and they will have all the power they have wisdom to exercise! (In *Ensign*, Sept. 1973, 62.)

We must have the Spirit or we cannot remain organized. (In *Women of Covenant*, 63.)

BELLE S. SPAFFORD

Leaders exercise spiritual leadership, not leadership by the sheer weight of position and authority but leadership by a depth of insight into the purposes of the organization [of the Relief Society], and into the personalities with whom they are working. Then by perfected techniques in meeting the women at the point of their needs, interests and abilities, growth opportunities are provided. (In *Relief Society Magazine*, Nov. 1938, 741.)

Compassionate service is according to the nature of woman. (In *Relief Society Magazine*, Mar. 1947, 149.)

Relief Society women today must guard their trusts carefully. They must not let the hours and days slip by, unmindful of time's swift passing until their day shall be done,

insensitive to the needs and the opportunities about them, unheeding the dangers lurking ahead. But, walking in the paths marked out for them by our latter-day prophets, holding fast to gospel truths, strengthened and reinforced by the knowledge and intelligence gained through the educational opportunities of the Society, they must advance the fundamental purposes for which this Society was established. (In *Relief Society Magazine*, Mar. 1947, 150.)

Just as all of our righteous efforts return to bless us and make us glad, so will the efforts of Relief Society women . . . return to bless them and bring to them joy in full measure. They may experience the satisfaction that comes from a task well done. They may feel assured of the approbation of our Heavenly Father. They may enjoy that deep sense of happiness and contentment that comes from doing one's part in a great and worthy cause. (In *Relief Society Magazine*, Nov. 1948, 726.)

The Lord will come unto Relief Society; he will make his abode with us, and the blessings of heaven will rest upon our beloved society so that it will continue to move forward in a glorious manner if we who make up its membership will but love the Lord and keep his commandments. (In *Relief Society Magazine*, Mar. 1949, 150.)

A review of the history of Relief Society leaves one deeply impressed with the foresight, the courage, the judgment, and the progressive action of our early-day leaders. Imbued with the spirit of the gospel, eager to bring about righteousness and the well-being of their fellows, counseled and directed in their activities by the Priesthood, they not only advanced the cause of Relief Society, but they stepped to the fore in such fields as nursing, medicine, industry, and the arts, winning for themselves a place among the noteworthy. (In *Relief Society Magazine*, Apr. 1953, 216.)

[Relief Society women] . . . are women of spiritual grace, womanly charm, poise, uprightness, and stability of character. They are women who are working together to build for themselves and others a life of glorious fulfillment. (In *Relief Society Magazine*, Nov. 1955, 718.)

Relief Society is a mature, experienced, adult organization. It was founded under divine inspiration and it has had inspired counsel and direction [ever since]. We must not be content with standards of performance that are in any way short of the best. (In *Relief Society Magazine*, Nov. 1960, 727.)

Relief Society work is a joyous, enlightening, satisfying experience for any woman who devotedly enters into it. Nonetheless, it is a serious and responsible work which calls for humility, faith, prayer, and the intelligent application of our energies and talents to our respective assignments. . . . Relief Society must measure up to its full responsibilities as an auxiliary of the Church. (In *Relief Society Magazine*, Nov. 1960, 784.)

LEAH D. WIDTSOE

In Relief Society . . . we are helping fulfill the righteous purposes of our Father regarding the welfare of His children on earth. It is not enough to love Him, . . . we must try to uplift our neighbors as well as ourselves. Relief Society gives us that opportunity. (In *Relief Society Magazine*, July 1943, 367.)

The world is starving for understanding, for sympathy. The greatest help that can be given by our Relief Society sisters is the spiritual uplift for men and women who have to struggle against adversity. (In *Relief Society Magazine*, May 1934, 276.)

CLARISSA S. WILLIAMS

The spirit of love and of sympathy and of humility which characterized every act of the life of our beloved Savior can be exemplified in the lives of the women of the Relief Society. (In *Relief Society Magazine*, June 1923, 291.)

Blessings of Relief Society

MAUREEN URSENBACH BEECHER

The essential element of the Relief Society, the only immutable part, is its spiritual core, maintained by shared sisterhood and confirmed by divine daughterhood. (In *Women Steadfast*, 59.)

AMY BROWN LYMAN

The achievements of Relief Society women, both in public life and in the home, stand today as a monument to the power of their faith and service and as a challenge to the coming generations. (In *Relief Society Magazine*, May 1940, 181.)

In the process of saving and rescuing human beings, both those who help and those who are helped are stimulated, lifted up, purified and spiritualized. (In *Relief Society Magazine*, Nov. 1936, 700.)

CHIEKO N. OKAZAKI

In Relief Society, women should feel accepted and cherished just for being there. . . . They are accepted and acceptable just because of who they are and where they are. (*Disciples*, 74.)

LOUISE Y. ROBISON

Relief Society was organized to help women find the true values of life. Each lesson studied, each act of loving service performed, each friendship made, broadens our horizon and gives us a desire to more nearly walk in obedience to the commandments. (In *Relief Society Magazine*, Mar. 1938, 148.)

When the gospel was restored, and our Father in heaven graciously gave that revelation through the Prophet Joseph Smith for Emma Smith and the women of the Church [to organize], seems to me that it opened the door for women in every direction. (In *Relief Society Magazine*, June 1929, 311.)

Relief Society offers elevating, beautiful friendships. The sweetest friendships of my life have been found in Relief Society work. (In *Relief Society Magazine*, Dec. 1945, 741.)

BARBARA B. SMITH

This organization offers relief from spiritual and intellectual ignorance, relief from poverty and suffering, relief from sorrow and loneliness, relief from the evils of the world, relief from cynicism and doubt. (In *Ensign*, May 1982, 111.)

Most important is the continuing gift of discernment which the inspiration of heaven provides to us through Relief Society. We can see more clearly today than ever before how great the challenge is for us to build strong homes and provide loving care for the children who come to our care. It really is not now and never has been a question of either a rich and full life for women or a strong and loving home. A Relief Society home must meet the challenge of both positions. (In *Ensign*, May 1982, 111.)

MARY ELLEN SMOOT

If we will catch the vision of [Relief Society], its potential influence can reach the world. We each have challenges in our lives, . . . but one thing is certain: *The truths of the gospel of Jesus Christ apply perfectly to your challenges and circumstances as well as to mine if we have patience and faith.* Each of us was born to face and overcome our challenges of a time such as this. (In *Ensign*, Nov. 1997, 88.)

BELLE S. SPAFFORD

Service in Relief Society gives to a woman competence in the management of her home and wisdom in guiding and directing her children. It blesses her with an understanding heart and develop within her a testimony that becomes a deep and abiding comfort and sustaining influence as long as life lasts. It makes of her a woman who does justly, who loves mercy, and who walks humbly with the Lord. These are rewards of the highest order. (*Today's World*, 321.)

To the woman who serves in Relief Society there comes understanding, enlightenment, and a truer evaluation of her own problems and a wish to solve them in all righteousness. (*Today's World*, 321.)

Few organizations in all the world have so comprehensive a program as does Relief Society. There is not a worthy interest or a woman's talent that cannot be nourished in this wonderful society. Relief Society reaches into every avenue and touches every aspect of a woman's life. (In *Relief Society Magazine*, Nov. 1954, 720.)

There is within this society a great life-giving element—a spirit which reaches out to women . . . binding together women of all nationalities into a great sisterhood, unifying them in purpose and impelling them on to worthy accomplishment. This life-giving spirit is the spirit of the gospel; it is this which makes Relief Society different from other women's organizations the world over. (In *Relief Society Magazine*, Mar. 1949, 148.)

Blessed indeed were the women of the Church when the Lord gave to them an organization through which their humanitarian impulses might find expression in an organized and divinely directed way. . . . In founding Relief Society and assigning to it a humanitarian and compassionate service, the Lord's plan was not alone for the relief of the distressed and the amelioration of human woes, but for the soul growth and life enrichment of all of his daughters. (In *Relief Society Magazine*, Nov. 1960, 714.)

The women of the Church will find wisdom and treasures of knowledge, they will develop an innate goodness to help them in their divine calling as mothers and homemakers through active affiliation with Relief Society. (In *Relief Society Magazine*, Nov. 1961, 720.)

Visiting Teaching

JOHANNA FLYNN AND ANITA R. CANFIELD

We are special, particular, and we should bother to be at our best when we are going out about our Father's business. (*Visiting Teaching*, 42.)

Women have the ability, mind, and heart to literally pour out love to each other. (*Visiting Teaching*, 42.)

When you build and raise others [through visiting teaching], you build and raise yourself! (*Visiting Teaching*, 43.)

ELAINE L. JACK

[In visiting teaching] we cannot always lift the burden of one who is troubled, but we can lift her so she can bear it well. (*Eye to Eye*, 149.)

Hands often speak as voices can't. A warm embrace conveys volumes. (*Eye to Eye*, 149.)

Visiting teaching is not a perfunctory task. . . . It is a matter of building a personal relationship. This is a much harder thing to do. It is also a much more rewarding thing to do. (*Eye to Eye*, 146.)

We must nurture, protect, defend, support, cheer, and love one another. As long as we feel this concern and love, visiting teaching will be a successful and important part of who we are as Latter-day Saints. (*Eye to Eye*, 142.)

CAMILLA EYRING KIMBALL

I feel I really know a woman only when I enter her home. In this way I can serve her person-to-person. (In *Women of Covenant*, 359.)

ARDETH GREENE KAPP

Visiting teaching . . . is so much more than a social visit; we are carrying buckets of living water to many who are thirsting. Even the smallest gestures in expression of love can help spread this life-giving substance. (*Rejoice!* 131.)

JENNIE B. KNIGHT

Let us try to take happiness into the homes we go to as teachers— . . . we must preach happiness and joy and satisfaction; that is our mission. (In *Relief Society Magazine*, June 1927, 310.)

LOUISE Y. ROBISON

To be a successful Visiting Teacher one must have a testimony of the Gospel and be diligent in upholding Church standards. One can never teach any principle successfully which that person does not believe and try to live. (In *Relief Society Magazine*, Nov. 1938, 740.)

It is one of the most important callings that can come—to be a visiting teacher who will take a vital message into the homes, who will stimulate the women who have not the spirit to lead better lives, and to those who are doing well to further inspire them to go on. (In *Relief Society Magazine*, Nov. 1933, 649.)

BARBARA B. SMITH

Visiting teaching is a tool given to us by the Lord. Properly used it is a great source of inspiration, strength, and comfort. . . . In an urban world that is often filled with loneliness, in the midst of a crowd, visiting teachers are essential. They are the Lord's way of helping us keep in touch with each other, and I think they are his recognition of the sanctity of each home. (In *Ensign*, Nov. 1980, 103.)

MARY ELLEN SMOOT

My desire is to plead with our sisters to stop worrying about a phone call or a quarterly or monthly visit, and whether that will do, and concentrate instead on nurturing tender souls. (In *Ensign*, Nov. 1997, 12.)

Our responsibility is to see that the gospel flame continues to burn brightly. Our charge is to find the lost sheep and help them feel our Savior's love. (In *Ensign*, Nov. 1997, 12.)

BELLE S. SPAFFORD

Not only must we strengthen homes through watchcare over material needs but we must contribute to the spiritual well-being of the home. (*Today's World*, 367.)

Life is strenuous and our people are not without need. With all we enjoy, there are still those who are brushing elbows with poverty. There are still the insecure, the heartbroken, the frustrated, the disconsolate; there are the sick, the lonely, the homebound aged. There are those whose faith is weak. . . . The strains and pressures of life today call for the

exercise of sisterhood as fully as at any time in the history of the [Relief] Society. (*Today's World*, 359.)

We must not lose sight of the fact that when a pair of visiting teachers call at a door they offer not the lone services of two good women, competent and sisterly as they may be, but behind them is a great and powerful Church auxiliary concerned with the home and ready to serve it. (*Today's World*, 367.)

The importance of the work of the visiting teachers today calls upon them to look to themselves, that they may grow in spiritual strength and perception so as to sense the needs and have the inspiration to meet them. If there is a kind word that should be spoken, may they speak it. If there is a soul that needs encouragement, may they give it. If there is a temporal need that cannot be met alone, may it be revealed to them. If there is need for a testimony to be borne, may they bear it. (In *Relief Society Magazine*, Mar. 1958, 175.)

[Visiting teaching] involves conscientious study, prayer, countless hours of time, unselfish effort, and the strict regulation of their individual lives in order that they more fully may meet the requirements of the calling. Regardless of the demands made of them, however, these sisters go forth devotedly on their mission of love and mercy. (In *Relief Society Magazine*, Mar. 1969, 171.)

Repentance

The Need for Repentance

VIRGINIA U. JENSEN

We can all find ourselves in places of darkness from time to time. We may wander into dark, spiritual caverns when we make foolish choices, admit harmful influences into our lives, or turn away from the light of the gospel to embrace the world just a little longer. . . . Let us bask in the warm and illuminating light provided by the gospel of Jesus Christ. Let the Savior's kindly light lead us one step at a time. Let covenants and commandments keep us safe as we follow the gospel pathway to our heavenly home. (In *Ensign*, Nov. 2000, 63.)

ARDETH GREENE KAPP

If any of you are burdened with sin and sorrow, transgression and guilt, then unload your wagon [as the pioneers unloaded theirs] and fill it with obedience, faith, and hope, and a regular renewal of your covenants with God. (In *BYU Speeches*, 13 Nov. 1990, 50.)

ANN N. MADSEN

We will find the Lord if we prepare ourselves to feel comfortable in His presence. No unclean thing can enter the Lord's presence. We must truly repent, truly forgive: two sides of the same coin. We must purify our own lives without procrastinating or finding excuses to avoid this mighty change. (In *As Women of Faith*, 157.)

We must trust in the Atonement. Our only real affirmation of the Atonement is our own repentance. Otherwise, we mock God. (In *Best of Women's Conference*, 319.)

CHIEKO N. OKAZAKI

If there's darkness in your life, don't grapple with it, don't dwell on it, don't stay involved in it. Get to the light switch! (*Lighten Up!* 201.)

SHIRLEY W. THOMAS

Anytime is a good time to step back and look objectively at ourselves, but it is especially good when we yet have opportunity to make course corrections. (In *Wisdom's Paths*, 10.)

Repentance Is a Glorious Principle

MARY ELLEN EDMUNDS

One of the most vicious and destructive lies concocted by the father of all lies (the devil) is that there is no return from mistakes and sin. He would have us believe that there are no U-turns allowed. This is *wrong.* We *can* turn around, change our minds, change our hearts, and come unto Christ. (*Happiness,* 42.)

If we did some repenting, some returning to the Source of love, we would be able to discern promptings faster and better. (*Love Is a Verb,* 7.)

BEPPIE HARRISON

The tool of repentance is there all the time, within our reach. It won't make what happened disappear, but it will lift the burden of our guilt and hopelessness from our shoulders. We can start over, wiser because of what we have learned but not continually burdened by it. (*Day at a Time,* 88–89.)

WENDY L. WATSON

As we take responsibility for our wrong choices, experience sincere remorse, and deeply desire to turn away from our sins . . . —choosing instead to keep the commandments and devote time to building up the kingdom—we each can experience the Savior saying, "Daughter, be of good comfort; thy faith hath made thee whole." (In *Best of Women's Conference,* 584.)

DWAN J. YOUNG

Repentance makes it possible to return to the straight and narrow path and become as pure as we were at baptism. (In *Ensign,* Nov. 1984, 95.)

Understanding Repentance

MARILYN ARNOLD

Both repentance and baptism are . . . perpetual rather than one-time, discontinuous events, and the counsel to repent and to be baptized is applicable, even essential, throughout our lives. (*Sweet Is the Word,* 250.)

We often speak of the sacramental ordinance as one in which believers reconfirm their baptismal covenants. If the ordinance is in some sense, then, a symbolic rebaptism or renewal of baptism, repentance appropriately precedes the partaking of the sacramental emblems. (*Sweet Is the Word,* 250.)

JUTTA BAUM BUSCHE

Jesus preached that through repentance we become free from sin; however, only as we become honest, do we feel the necessity of repentance. (In *Best of Women's Conference,* 69.)

MARIE K. HAFEN

Planning to sin and then repent is an affront to the Savior because it assumes that we control our own forgiveness. While we must do all we can do to be worthy of Christ's grace, we cannot turn that miraculous power on and off like a water faucet. He loves us no matter what we do, but he forgives only the honest in heart—and on his terms, not on ours. (In *BYU Speeches,* 9 May 1995, 172.)

BEPPIE HARRISON

Doing something wrong is like failing a test. Repentance is the process of going over what went wrong very carefully, figuring out what your mistake was, fixing it (if it's fixable), and then moving past it. . . . You've learned that lesson, and you don't need to carry the bad grade any longer. Sometimes the Lord gives us the same test again, just to check; sometimes, I guess, he can tell we got it. (*Plain and Precious*, 332.)

If you could just waltz off in a new direction without a second glance or a single twinge, it wouldn't be repentance. It would simply be deciding to do something else. There's a difference. (*Plain and Precious*, 341.)

ELAINE L. JACK

Repentance means turning the heart and the will to God. It denotes a change of mind, a fresh view about God, about oneself, and about the world. It is a cleansing process. It *is*

the way back. (In *Ensign*, Nov. 1989, 88.)

MARY ELLEN SMOOT

Each of us makes mistakes and wanders off the track from time to time. We all need to make course corrections, and when we clearly know what it is we want to get back to—what the standard is—we can more easily make those changes that lead us back to God. (*Sweet Is the Work*, 4.)

WENDY C. TOP

Repentance is a lifelong state we must be in, not a place we just visit occasionally when we really mess up and commit big sins. (*Getting Past the Labels*, 35.)

WENDY L. WATSON

Guilt—if used well—is exactly the help most of us need to stop sinning and start toward full repentance. (In *Best of Women's Conference*, 583.)

Revelation

MILDRED CHANDLER AUSTIN

The Lord has given us very clear guidelines to follow, and then has invited us to ask him for more personal direction. If we stumble because of a lack of information, it is only because we haven't turned on the light—gospel light. Extra light

for our specific problems is available to us; the switch is pressed by the bended knee. (*Divine Destiny*, 1.)

MARJORIE P. HINCKLEY

Our greatest quest is to live worthy to know what the Lord's will is regarding us—what we are meant to do. (In *Glimpses*, 240.)

PATRICIA T. HOLLAND

Whatever our role is, we must seek it through righteous living and personal revelation. We must not lean on the arm of flesh nor the philosophies of men—or women. We must have our own personal Liahona. (In *LDS Women's Treasury*, 304.)

With simple, traditional, tried-and-true principles, such as earnest prayer, serious scriptural study, devoted fasting, compassionate service, and patient forbearance, the blessings of heaven distill upon us even to include the personal manifestations of the Son of God himself. (*On Earth*, 18.)

KATHLEEN BUSHNELL JENSEN

Often we forget that we're entitled to inspiration in our lives, if we just ask for it. If we are being led by the Spirit, we don't have to feel guilty or ashamed of our choices and circumstances. (In *Best of Women's Conference*, 218.)

LUCILE JOHNSON

Personal revelation is evidence of [God's] love and is an important means through which our Father in Heaven reveals his love for us. Personal revelation is the love of God working in our lives. (*Enjoy the Journey*, 153–54.)

ARDETH GREENE KAPP

It is while one stands undecided, uncommitted, and uncovenanted, with choices waiting to be made, that the vulnerability to every wind that blows becomes life threatening. May we find ourselves doing less and less drifting as we make right choices based on personal revelation. (In *Church News*, 9 Feb. 1980, 13.)

What is it that distinguishes us from others? The distinction is that we profess to be guided by revelation. It is because of this principle that we are peculiar, since all of our actions can be under divine guidance. (In *Best of Women's Conference*, 246.)

AMY BROWN LYMAN

There is a spirit in man and the inspiration of God giveth it understanding. (In *Relief Society Magazine*, May 1936, 295.)

TESSA MEYER SANTIAGO

We are entitled through our noble birthright as daughters of God to personal revelation and inspiration concerning our circles of influence. And we are duty-bound to work to obtain that inspiration. (In *Best of Women's Conference*, 485.)

BARBARA B. SMITH

Revelation from the Lord is the great foundation stone of all happy, productive living. (In *Best of Women's Conference*, 497.)

LUCY MACK SMITH

The word of God shall be my guide to life and salvation, which I will endeavor to obtain if it is to be had by diligence in prayer. (*History of Joseph Smith*, 50.)

SUSAN CHAMPION SOMMERFELDT

The study of revelation . . . becomes the invitation for further revelation. (In *Thy Word Is a Lamp*, 169.)

MARIAN JEPPSON STODDARD

Before the world was, Christ was the Word, the messenger of salvation, and his words will light our way through, given by the Spirit to our own hearts, by his servants to our individual needs, by record for our own reading and study, and by eternal ordinances in his house. (In *Thy Word Is a Lamp*, 175–76.)

HEIDI S. SWINTON

Impressions may come in the car, in the kitchen, or on our knees. We may "hear" in a crowded room or in the middle of a cluttered day. Time and place are really only mortal terms. Revelation reaches through the veil, reminding us of who we are and where we want to go. (In *Best of Women's Conference*, 528.)

We have been guided, encouraged, shielded, and taught by the voice of the Lord. When we choose to have ears to hear, we step forward on the path that leads all the way home. (In *Best of Women's Conference*, 528.)

Satan

LINDA R. ARCHIBALD

Evil . . . loves darkness rather than light (joy). [Satan] has no light, no joy, and [he] desires only to make us as miserable as he is (see 2 Nephi 2:27). [He] pulls and pushes us into the shadows. He distracts us with foreboding black clouds of despair while he plunges in daggers of discouragement. Then he keeps twisting the knife. He is a wholesale distributor of blindfolds and earplugs, which, if we accept his wares, leave us with neither ears to hear the music and laughter nor eyes to see the sunshine. Then the dark one

dances in delight at our dejection. (*Sunshine in My Soul*, 108.)

MARILYN S. BATEMAN

We were born to succeed. One of Satan's aims is to distract us from being successful. He would have us believe that success is something that it really is not. Satan's plan is full of half-truths, and he tries to lure us into accepting his counterfeit interpretation of life. (In *BYU Speeches*, 9 Sept. 1997, 11.)

JANETTE HALES BECKHAM

Satan does not support those who follow him. He can't! It is the

Lord who sustains; the Spirit sustains; righteousness sustains. That sustenance is not Satan's to give. . . . The Spirit sustains those who try to live by faith. When adversity comes, and it does come, the Spirit seems stronger. (In *BYU Speeches*, 16 Mar. 1993, 89.)

VIVIAN R. CLINE

In life, for everything of great value and lasting beauty, Satan has cleverly disguised a cheap imitation, something he would convince us would make us happy and bring us joy but in truth will not. (In *High Fives*, 55.)

SHERI L. DEW

Satan . . . lies. He shades and obscures truth. He makes evil look good and good look unenlightened and unsophisticated. He will try anything to obscure the truth about who we are, where we are, and what's really important. (In *Arms of His Love*, 388.)

The adversary . . . is intent on obstructing our vision and undermining our faith. He will do anything and everything to confuse us about who we are and where we're going because he has already forfeited his privilege of going there. (In *Best of Women's Conference*, 125.)

[Satan] loves it when we seek for security in bank accounts, social status, or professional credentials when ultimate security and peace of mind come only from a connection with the Lord Jesus Christ. (In *Best of Women's Conference*, 137.)

[Satan] claims victory when we rely on others for spiritual strength—on husbands, leaders, friends, family members. He doesn't want us to find out how intimate our connections with our Father and Elder Brother can be and how palpable and sustaining their love is. (In *Best of Women's Conference*, 137.)

If the adversary can keep us so distracted that we never really seek, embrace, and commit ourselves to the Lord, then we will also never discover the healing, strengthening, comforting power available because of the Atonement. We will never know that because of the Savior we have access to everything we need to pass this test. (In *Best of Women's Conference*, 137.)

Satan baits us with perishable pleasures and preoccupations—our bank accounts, our wardrobes, even our waistlines—for he knows that where our treasure is, there will our hearts be also. (In *Ensign*, Nov. 1999, 97.)

MARY ELLEN EDMUNDS

It is interesting that Satan, who voted for "no opposition," has become the main source of it! (In *LDS Speaker's Sourcebook*, 407.)

XANTHE K. FARNWORTH

Satan is the great counterfeiter. I was taught that he is so successful not because he's smart but because he's old and experienced. He's been deceiving mankind for so long that unless we are walking within the circle of light, we don't even notice. (In *Thy Word Is a Lamp*, 50.)

Susa Young Gates

If we are perfectly careless and heedless of the commandments of God, Satan does not take much notice of us, he does not need to. But if we are trying our best to live our religion and to live up to every commandment, then, Satan will set a strong watch upon us, and seek to fathom our thought and then to hinder and circumvent our every plan. (In *Young Woman's Journal*, Oct. 1896, 26.)

A great many . . . people accept the comfortable theory that if a person does no particular harm in the world, and lives a good and decent life, he will be all right in this world and the next. That is one of the most pernicious doctrines which we can accept. (In *Young Woman's Journal*, Mar. 1898, 110.)

Beppie Harrison

Satan . . . might whisper in our ears that all is lost and that there's no point in trying further once we've chosen unwisely. But we didn't follow him then and there's no reason to believe him now. (*Day at a Time*, 57.)

Patricia T. Holland

Satan uses that very delicate line between self-confidence and pride to blind us. He can keep us so frenzied in our efforts to protect our self-esteem that we are blinded to the one quality that would assure it— true dependence upon the Lord. (In *BYU Speeches*, 21 Jan. 1986, 58.)

Elaine L. Jack

The adversary will stop at nothing to catch our attention and then ever so slyly lead us away from the work of the Lord. (In *Ensign*, Aug. 1994, 65.)

This is the dispensation of the fulness of times. We have been given the fulness of the gospel. To entice us from the path, Satan suggests a salad bar of sin—a little here and a little there until the plate is piled high and the price is paid. (In *Ensign*, Aug. 1994, 65.)

Satan loves dissension in any form. He encourages harsh feelings, angry words, ruthless judgments, scorn, pride, and the cruelest of actions. (In *Ensign*, Aug. 1994, 67.)

Today we see all around us the adversary at work—and he is succeeding. He has twisted truths to his purposes, and throngs have followed. Either we are holding fast to the iron rod or, perhaps, unconsciously, we are letting go by just a few fingers and are slowly slipping away. . . . None of us is exempt. Nor are we immune to sidesteps in a frantic rush to do it all, the desire to have it all, and the justification to need it all—

now. Satan is ruthless, and his efforts are never ending. (In *Ensign*, Nov. 1993, 98.)

LUCILE JOHNSON

The main thrust of adversarial forces is to whisper at every opportunity, "You are worthless. You are helpless. You are a failure. You have no value." Satan wants to feed our feelings of inferiority, to negate our faith in our real genealogy. (*Enjoy the Journey*, 22.)

SHERRIE JOHNSON

Satan and his premortal followers cannot have a mortal body. They cannot have a true counterpart and be one flesh with that person in order to make themselves complete, whole. They cannot pass onto others the great gift of mortal flesh and blood. Because they cannot do these things they will never have joy. Therefore in their selfish, malicious ways Satan and his followers try to keep us from joy and growth. (*Man, Woman, and Deity*, 107.)

ARDETH GREENE KAPP

Television and video programs portray immorality as an exciting and acceptable act of love. Exposure to these messages of deception will dull your senses until what appeared alarming to you at first becomes of little concern and even acceptable. If this happens, that falsehood is unmasked. Your dreams become nightmares, and your hopes destroyed. (In *Ensign*, Nov. 1990, 94.)

CAMILLA EYRING KIMBALL

Technology has never been so sophisticated, and the forces of evil are using that technology to bombard us all with false standards. (*Writings*, 98.)

JANET S. SCHARMAN

I believe lack of hope to be Satan's most powerful tool. (In *Arms of His Love*, 41.)

We are most often not tempted to major sins. But if, over time, we can be pushed to the point of giving up, of believing that what we have been asked to do is either not reasonable or really not very important, then all else becomes meaningless to us and Satan has won. (In *Arms of His Love*, 41.)

Satan is the one who stirs up our fear, self-doubt, and feelings of abandonment. . . . If he can confuse us, distract us, or encourage us to let go of what we know to be true, then he has won a very powerful victory not only over us but over all those we can influence. (In *Arms of His Love*, 41.)

MICHELE R. SORENSEN

At first that great deceiver uses nothing more than a "flaxen cord." Because his victim isn't struggling to get away, one little flaxen cord is plenty. But by the time the poor slave discovers his bondage, strong chains have been locked into place. (*Chainbreakers*, 124.)

M. CATHERINE THOMAS

Satan's thoughts are made very compelling even though many of them are thoughts of misery or lead to misery. But here is one of life's major tutorials of eternal significance: we have the power to *turn him off*. (*Selected Writings*, 217.)

SUZANNE TRUBA

The devil's parade is very colorful, and life on the world's terms can be engaging and gratifying, even satisfying and entertaining. . . . But this I know to be true: The adversary's parade leads down a one-way street to transitory pleasure and ultimate sorrow. (In *Arms of His Love*, 299.)

SUSAN L. WARNER

Part of Satan's evil design is to give our children mistaken ideas of who they are—lies for them to remember. (In *Ensign*, May 1996, 78.)

Satan wants us to be slow to remember what we have received and heard. He wants us to minimize and even forget the quiet witnesses of the Spirit that have told us who we really are. (In *Ensign*, May 1996, 78.)

WENDY L. WATSON

We need to be bold in exposing Lucifer and his lies. We need to rise up and with ever-increasing clarity point out his counterfeits, his deceptions, his trickery. (In *Arms of His Love*, 204.)

Scripture

Blessings from the Scriptures

JANETTE HALES BECKHAM

The words of the scriptures will strengthen you in times of temptation. The scriptures have been given to us to help us find peace and reassurance in times of crisis, to help us find solutions to our everyday challenges, to strengthen us in times of temptation. The scriptures will help us improve our behavior as we come to know our Savior, Jesus Christ. (In *Ensign*, May 1995, 91.)

ELAINE CANNON

When you look for a scripture to solve a certain problem, you find so many wonderful thoughts on a variety of other subjects that hope wipes out worry. (In *My Soul Delighteth*, 132.)

With the help of the plates of Laban and the plates of Nephi, the posterity of Father Lehi . . . had God's commandments always before their eyes. . . . Learning the truth is important for any generation, given the reality of an active adversary who has been conniving for the souls of men since the war in heaven. (In *My Soul Delighteth*, 124.)

JOANNE B. DOXEY

If we immerse ourselves daily in the scriptures, particularly the Book of Mormon, we will have increased discernment. We will have power to do good and to resist evil, and our ability to solve problems will be expanded. Messages to help us in our day were foreseen by the Lord and were divinely placed on the pages of the scriptures to assist us and our families. (In *Ensign*, Nov. 1989, 89.)

AMY HARDISON

When we give scripture study enough importance that we read daily, we will be blessed with strength, wisdom, and inspiration. We will find valuable ways to apply the scriptures in our daily lives. We will gain knowledge. And with that knowledge, we will also gain a feeling, a closeness to our Father, an awareness of spiritual things. In other words, as we study the scriptures we will gain spiritual strength. (*How to Feel Great*, 98.)

PATRICIA T. HOLLAND

Meeting God in scripture has been like a divine intravenous feeding for me—a celestial I.V. that my son once described as an "angelical" cord. (In *Best of Women's Conference*, 198.)

LAEL LITTKE

I loved the beauty of the words [of the scriptures] my mother read to me and my siblings, and I memorized many of my favorite passages. As I grew older I found those remembered verses coming to my aid as I tried to deal with life. The word of God became my center, the final authority when a question arose. (In *My Soul Delighteth*, 22.)

LAURA OWEN

Those who read and, more importantly, *know* God's words . . . can have a constant light with them. The light and the lamp that David sings about [Psalm 119:105] are a personal testimony of Heavenly Father that calls forth self-confidence-evoking courage and appreciation for . . . abilities through the knowledge that they are gifts from God. (In *Thy Word Is a Lamp*, 138.)

Because of the spirit that comes from studying the word, there is a light that lasts long after the book is closed, a light that helps . . . anyone . . . who reads the scriptures to discover qualities and abilities. (In *Thy Word Is a Lamp*, 138–39.)

CAROLYN J. RASMUS

As we study the scriptures we can learn about God, his dealings with men throughout the ages, the gift of Jesus Christ to each of us, and the testimony of others who believed in God. As we study these things, our memories will be enlarged and we will increase our understanding of things pertaining unto God. (*In the Strength of the Lord*, 57.)

TAMRA T. REEVES

It is in the scriptures that we find the words of Christ, which penetrate our hearts, inspire our minds, reflect our Savior's love, and illuminate our paths. The spiritual light and truth we receive through study of the Savior's words leave no doubt in our minds of his love for each of us. (In *Thy Word Is a Lamp*, 23.)

The light of Christ and the light of truth are synonymous. Is it any wonder, then, that our paths will be made much clearer and brighter if we will feast upon the truths contained in the scriptures? (In *Thy Word Is a Lamp*, 20.)

CHERRY B. SILVER

Loving the scriptures and reading in them regularly allows the Lord to send us daily messages. (In *Knit Together in Love*, 9.)

BARBARA B. SMITH AND SHIRLEY W. THOMAS

Many specific blessings come to us through the scriptures. They bring peace and comfort in the face of anxiety, understanding to augment learning, direction when uncertainty confuses. (*Words for Women*, 36.)

BELLE S. SPAFFORD

Individuals have not always been fortunate in having copies of the scriptures in their possession for their individual use. . . . Today, we are abundantly blessed in that everyone who will do so may possess these valuable volumes which contain the will of God for his children, the divine plan of life and salvation, the gospel of Jesus Christ, which is

the power of God unto salvation. (In *Relief Society Magazine*, Nov. 1962, 797.)

WENDY L. WATSON

Of all the how-to instruction books on relationships, the scriptures are by far the best. (In *May Christ Lift Thee Up*, 46.)

BARBARA SORENSON WILDE

How reassuring it is to follow the words of Christ, trusting in him to know the way. When we have the scriptures for a beacon in our lives, we can journey through this life putting our faith in our Savior and in his love for us. We need not fear the darkness and evil surrounding us. (In *Thy Word Is a Lamp*, 83.)

Need to Search the Scriptures

BARBARA DI CONZA

The wattage of the light received [from the scriptures] increases exponentially with the time and effort expended. The Lord's math is so mercifully, beautifully, lovingly perfect. (In *Thy Word Is a Lamp*, 7.)

JOANNE B. DOXEY

If we treat the scriptures lightly, letting them gather dust on the shelves, unopened and unread, they are unable to bless our lives as planned. We will be denied the sweet whisperings of the Spirit in guiding our lives and the lives of our families unless we pay the price of studying, pondering, and praying about the scriptures. (In *Ensign*, Nov. 1989, 89.)

LANA A. EDWARDS

If we only realized the treasure buried inside the covers of our scriptures, we would be feasting daily. (In *Thy Word Is a Lamp*, 95.)

SUSA YOUNG GATES

One may learn more of a man's attitude on any question by reading what he says, himself, than by reading what others say about him. Hence it is that the reading of the scriptures is far more profitable than reading any number of commentaries and stories about them. Let us go to the fountain head for light. (In *Improvement Era*, Dec. 1905, 182.)

BETTY BAKER GILFILLAN

As I listen to the news each day, I can almost hear the earth groan from the burden of corruption. The light of gospel truth must pierce this deep gloom of evil. We, Heavenly Father's children, must fill our lamps each day by reading our scriptures. We must pray always that the light might not flicker. (In *Thy Word Is a Lamp*, 14.)

AMY HARDISON

In every facet of our lives, the scriptures can give us insight and direction. But we cannot apply something we do not know. So our first step is to study the scriptures on a daily basis. . . . Whatever method we use is immaterial. What matters is that we do it. (*How to Feel Great*, 97.)

ARDETH GREENE KAPP

Can you imagine being away from home and receiving a letter from your parents and not bothering to open it or read it? This is what happens when we don't read these precious records. The holy scriptures are like letters from home telling us how we can draw near to our Father in Heaven. (In *Ensign*, Nov. 1985, 94.)

We live and will one day die. And when we do, we will know our Savior, for we will have searched the holy scriptures and felt His nearness as He walks with us on our journey home. (In *Ensign*, Nov. 1985, 95.)

ANN N. MADSEN

We should . . . read the words of those who have seen the Lord or who have established a secure relationship with Him. There is such power in their words. Their words have been preserved for this very purpose so that we can feel that power. They are His witnesses. (In *As Women of Faith*, 156.)

VIRGINIA H. PEARCE

The fundamental curriculum for all classes in the Church is the scriptures—they contain the unchanging doctrines of the kingdom of God. These truths are what brought us into the Church. If we fail to continue learning them, we may not stay. (In *Ensign*, Nov. 1996, 12.)

CHERRY B. SILVER

Scriptures, keys to heavenly power, may unlock spiritual doors for us. In them daily messages from deity await us. We desire to *possess*, not simply *process*, the word of Christ. (In *Knit Together in Love*, 8.)

BARBARA SORENSON WILDE

To help us see in the dark, the Lord has provided the light of the scriptures, which will lead us on the path of truth and happiness in this life and in the life to come. The scriptures are the words of Christ. They contain the road map, the compass, and the lamp to light our way. (In *Thy Word Is a Lamp*, 81.)

Searching the Scriptures

MARILYN ARNOLD

Encourage your children or grandchildren to work out the meanings of scriptural passages in their journals and share them with you or with the family. Knowing that they intend to write about what they are reading will change the way your children read and study scripture. It will also change the way you read scripture. Your reading will, I think, become more deep and attentive and less mechanical and superficial. Your appreciation will grow, and your life

will take on new purpose. (In *Clothed with Charity*, 284–85.)

ARDETH GREENE KAPP

Learning to love the scriptures is a lot like learning to walk. At first you're unsure—you sometimes stumble, and you don't get anywhere very fast. If you stopped trying to walk, just because you fell down a few times, you'd never know the joy of walking. But once you learn how to walk, soon you can run and go places you couldn't go before. (In *Ensign*, Nov. 1985, 93.)

Open your scriptures and read them every day. Why? So you can have a sure testimony of his love for you. So you can know the gospel plan and the blessings that come through obedience and right choices. . . . If you will ask Heavenly Father in your daily prayers to help you understand the messages, and if you will strive to keep the commandments, you can have the spirit of the Holy Ghost to teach you and to open your mind to the special messages that are there for you for your needs at particular times in your life. (*I Walk by Faith*, 28.)

SHERRIE JOHNSON

We need to pray to understand the things we are reading, but it does not end there. We must also pray to be able to incorporate the things we learn into our lives. Studying the scriptures without praying is like brushing our teeth without toothpaste. If we ask in prayer, we will be better able to understand the things we read. (*Spiritually Centered*, 14.)

Kristen D. Randle

Reading the scriptures has to be more of a mystical experience than an intellectual one—allowing the spirit to use the words in ways that surpass our greatest hope for the usefulness of language. (In *My Soul Delighteth*, 79.)

M. Catherine Thomas

We can prepare ourselves to hear the word of the Lord by realizing that in opening up the scriptures, we are about to have a conversation with the Lord. . . . Thus we approach such an encounter in a spiritual, prayerful, thoughtful, and solemn way. We read trying to feel, to listen, to hear, and even to make notes. (*Selected Writings*, 57.)

Anne G. Wirthlin

The Savior has given us a pattern to follow as we study the scriptures. We hear the word, we ponder upon its meaning, we ask our Heavenly Father to help us understand, and then our minds and hearts are prepared to receive the promised blessings. (In *Ensign*, May 1998, 9.)

Pondering [the scriptures] is more than reading words; it is searching for meanings that will help us as we relate to one another and as we make choices in our lives. It is allowing the word to move from our minds to our hearts. The Spirit bears witness to our hearts as we prayerfully seek to know the things of our Heavenly Father. When we have that witness and knowledge, we think and live and relate to each other in more Christlike ways. (In *Ensign*, May 1998, 9.)

Book of Mormon

Susan Easton Black

In our fast-paced . . . lives, most individuals would not be inclined to read a double-columned book of over five hundred pages if it were presented merely as something of interest to the scholar, the curious, or the well-meaning. If we were to recognize, however, that through pondering its message we could comprehend, as we could in no other way, the nature of our Father in Heaven, his Son Jesus Christ, and the Holy Ghost, we would understand why so many continue to read the Book of Mormon with intensity. (*Finding Christ*, 13.)

The Holy One was revealed to the ancient prophets of the Book of Mormon by the power of the Holy Ghost. By the power of the Holy Ghost, these prophets wrote a second witness for Jesus Christ—the Book of Mormon—and by that same power, the ancient prophets knew that their writings would bear testimony to us that Jesus is the Christ. If we do not seek it, we can almost completely miss that testimony. If we do seek it, it reverberates, dominates, and thunders on every page, in every chapter, in every verse, and in nearly every sentence! (*Finding Christ*, 15.)

Christ is the central theme on every page of the Book of Mormon. His reality has inspired thousands of faithful Latter-day Saint missionaries who since 1830 have spent millions of dollars to travel the globe, sharing the Book of Mormon. They have certainly not labored merely to share a book of high adventure, a treatise on archaeological ruins, a manuscript on the origin of some American Indians, or a comparative study of Indian legends. . . . It is not. Christ is the central purpose. (*Finding Christ*, 12.)

ARDETH GREENE KAPP

As we read and study the Book of Mormon, the spirit of the book penetrates into our hearts, and we come to really know and love our Lord and Savior Jesus Christ. We become more aware of his infinite love for us. We learn of the Atonement and of the way to salvation provided through the ordinances and covenants of the gospel of Jesus Christ. We learn how to qualify ourselves for all the blessings our Father has in store for his children who are obedient. We learn how to repent and how to forgive and how to love one another as our Savior loves us. We gain a longing, an intense desire to be with him and be like him. (*Rejoice!* 111–12.)

EMMA SMITH

My belief is that the Book of Mormon is of divine authenticity. I have not the slightest doubt of it. . . . Though I was an active participant in the scenes that transpired, and was present during the translation of the plates . . . and had cognizance of things as they transpired, it is marvelous to me, "a marvel and a wonder," as much so as to anyone else. (In *Elect Ladies*, 20.)

I am satisfied that no man could have dictated the writing of the manuscripts unless he was inspired. For when [I acted] as his scribe, [Joseph] would dictate to me hour after hour; and when returning after meals or after interruptions, he would at once begin where he had left off, without either seeing the manuscript or having any portion of it read to him. . . . It would have been improbable that a learned man could do this, and for one so . . . unlearned as he was, it was simply impossible. (*Saints Herald*, 1 Oct. 1879, 289–90.)

LUCY MACK SMITH

Joseph would occasionally . . . describe the ancient inhabitants of this continent, their dress, mode of traveling, and the animals upon which they rode; their cities, their buildings, with every particular; their mode of warfare; and also their religious worship. This he would do with as much ease, seemingly, as if he had spent his whole life among them. (*History of Joseph Smith*, 83.)

That book was brought forth by the power of God, and translated by the gift of the Holy Ghost; and, if

I could make my voice sound as loud as the trumpet of Michael, the Archangel, I would declare the truth from land to land, and from sea to sea, and the echo should reach every isle. . . . For I do testify that God has revealed himself to man again in these last days. (*History of Joseph Smith*, 204.)

M. CATHERINE THOMAS

All major journeys in the Book of Mormon are allegorical as well as actual, and reflect not only the different kinds of the Lord's deliverances but also the principles on which the deliverances depend. All these journeys typify every person's sojourn on earth and the tasks that each is given to accomplish. (In *Doctrines of the Book of Mormon*, 186.)

The Book of Mormon was provided, at least in part, to illustrate how grace and atonement actually work in the lives of those who come to Christ. (*Selected Writings*, 72–73.)

BARBARA W. WINDER

The Book of Mormon emphasizes a recurring theme: the need to choose between being spiritually minded or carnally minded. (In *BYU Speeches*, 13 Mar. 1990, 105.)

Self-Development

JANENE WOLSEY BAADSGAARD

Sometimes, I think, we're not supposed to wait for bigger wings or leaner bodies. Sometimes we have to take a chance, lace up our tap shoes, and go for it. Sometimes true freedom doesn't require wings at all. (*Families Who Laugh*, 86.)

GENEVIEVE DeHOYOS

All people, male and female, are challenged to apply all their energies to develop intellectually, socially, and above all spiritually, so that they may fulfill the purpose of their existence. (*Stewardship*, 103.)

JOANNE B. DOXEY

Only God knows our individual possibilities and limitations. He blesses us according to his plan for us, consistent with our need to grow. We must be sensitive to the whisperings of the Spirit, which often come in peaceful, unexpected ways. (In *Ensign*, Apr. 1987, 32.)

LINDA J. EYRE

You don't have to go on not liking things about yourself. You can set a goal and work on a plan to grow and progress and work out the kinks in your personality. (*Joyful Mother*, 125.)

MICHAELENE P. GRASSLI

Sometimes courage takes the form of tenacity—the ability to hold on and face the unpleasant when it is necessary, and to master personal weaknesses without giving up. Sometimes courage involves seeking greater information or knowledge in order to better one's life or to improve the circumstances of another. Sometimes courage means doing the right thing in the face of criticism, condemnation, and pain. (*What I Have Learned*, 73.)

CLAIRE HAWKINS

Change does not come from big institutions; it comes from the heart. (In *Women in the Covenant*, 105.)

CAMILLA EYRING KIMBALL

Worthwhile things have to be learned and then practiced. Habits are made by repetition. "What you are to be, you are now becoming." (*Writings*, 135.)

JO ANN LARSEN

Viewing ourselves as having a "single spark of divinity" implies the vital need to take care of ourselves—physically, emotionally, intellectually, and spiritually. It is to consider ourselves forever-growing human beings worthy of investing in our own well-being, for our own sakes. It is to remember that in our later years, we are or will be the reapers of any harvests we sow for ourselves; that however short we will eventually be on youth, we can be long on maturity; and that as long as we live,

we can continue to make of ourselves all that we can. (*Heart of Goodness*, 93.)

SHARON G. LARSEN

God can make much more out of our lives than we can—if we will let him. (In *Arise*, 304.)

NEILL MARRIOTT

We should not take counsel from our fears. To resist their counsel, we must first identify those fears and self-doubts. . . . Be honest with yourself, and you can begin to free yourself. (In *Hearts Knit Together*, 123.)

MARGARET D. NADAULD

The combination of directed effort on your part and living close to the Spirit will get you to where you really should be. (*Write Back Soon!* 70–71.)

CHIEKO N. OKAZAKI

I hope you have a beach part of your personality where there's a lot of scrambling and laughing and sunning. But I hope there's also a part of you that wants to leave the shallow, sandy self and go into the deep. And sometimes . . . powerful currents of mortality carry us into the deeps—into the deeps of sorrow and suffering and soul-searching. There in the deeps, we discover who we really are and who the Savior really is. (In *Ensign*, Nov. 1995, 95.)

SANDRA PETREE

Easy things do not build power. We must study the scriptures. We must accept challenging callings. We must strive diligently and powerfully to teach our children (and our partners) the gospel of Jesus Christ. And we must develop ourselves to our fullest and finest potential. . . . To make your own dance a thing of beauty, you must *do hard things*—and do them cheerfully and well. (In *Clothed with Charity*, 158–59.)

ESTHER RASBAND

Diligence is . . . a matter of honesty. We know if we are being all we can be. It is . . . a matter between you and the Lord. No excuses. No judgments of others. Just honesty and two-way love. (*Confronting the Myth*, 13.)

ELLIS R. SHIPP

If our attempts are *but feeble* they will make us better and nobler than if we made no effort whatever. (*While Others Slept*, 161.)

IONE J. SIMPSON

Don't be content to do the easy thing. Look for opportunities to stretch farther than you think you can. (In *Best of Women's Conference*, 491.)

ELIZA R. SNOW

By seeking to perform every duty, you will find that your capacity will increase, and you will be astonished at what you can accomplish. (In *Women of Covenant*, 126.)

EMMA LOU THAYNE

Only as my fulfilled self can I maintain a pitcher full enough to pour from for anyone or any place that calls my name. (*As for Me*, 27.)

MARTHA H. TINGEY

We all know that every time we express a good thought or a good desire, it is a stimulant to try to carry that out in our lives and to live it a little more closely than we have ever done before. (In *Young Woman's Journal*, July 1909, 328.)

WENDY C. TOP

The only way we will ever completely escape our self-defeating behaviors—or truly change any kind of negative behavior, for that matter—is by immersing ourselves in the pure doctrines of Christ through the holy scriptures, the words of the living prophets, and the teachings of the temple, coupled with fasting and prayer. (*Getting Past the Labels*, 31–32.)

EMMELINE B. WELLS

It makes, perhaps, but little difference to mankind at large, whether we are happy or unhappy but the greatest difference to ourselves whether our characters and faculties are developed to the utmost or dwarfed and stunted in their growth. (In *Woman's Exponent*, 15 Sept. 1874, 55.)

MARGARET J. WHEATLEY

The process of changing ourselves is never easy, but it becomes easier as we stop berating ourselves for our failings and instead think of the process as digging deep into ourselves to rediscover our essential goodness. (In *Women and the Power*, 172.)

DWAN J. YOUNG

It's not enough just to grow. Even the weeds and the biblical tares can do that. It is expected of us that we . . . will successfully negotiate the bumps and curves by enlarging upon our talents, by disciplining ourselves, so that our mortal experience brings us toward greater and greater mastery of those characteristics which make us worthy of association with the Divine. (In *Ensign*, May 1982, 93–94.)

Goals

ANITA R. CANFIELD

Goals without action equal nothing. (*Young Woman*, 25.)

JAROLDEEN ASPLUND EDWARDS

Impatience for the goal will not speed the steps. The very best, most celebratory way to live is to enjoy each day's journey as well as its arrivals. Choose great goals and work toward them patiently, consistently. Let time and increments of progress work together to accomplish mighty things. (*Celebration!* 47.)

We are so eager to get to the final accomplishments that we forget to enjoy the process of achieving them. If our trip is well begun, well planned, and in the direction we desire, then each turn of the wheels, each step of the hike, each push of the bicycle wheel should be a joy along the way and will add up to arrival at our destination. (*Celebration!* 47.)

MARGARET D. NADAULD

We don't want to willfully set goals for ourselves with no thought of what Heavenly Father might have for us to do. Pray for divine guidance so he can direct your efforts on a path that will bless you. (In *BYU Speeches*, 2 Nov. 1997, 51.)

Work hard at the goals you've set for yourself, and the Lord will bless you in your efforts. The combination of directed effort on your part and living close to the Spirit will get you to where you really should be. (In *BYU Speeches*, 2 Nov. 1997, 51.)

Remember that there really is a law of the harvest. It's unrealistic to suppose that lofty goals and ambitions can be met without hard work, discipline, and focused effort. So each day, each step along the way, ask for and then listen for divine guidance. (In *BYU Speeches*, 2 Nov. 1997, 51.)

BARBARA B. SMITH

We can plan our lives and, to the degree that it is possible, determine the end from the beginning by building upon God-given principles to provide the security of truth. (In *LDS Women's Treasury*, 277.)

Goals are stars to steer by, not sticks to beat yourself with. (In *LDS Speaker's Sourcebook*, 157.)

When we see in our minds the great vision, then we discipline ourselves by steady, small steps that make it happen. It is important to realize this correlation between the large and the small. (In *Ensign*, Nov. 1980, 86.)

BELLE S. SPAFFORD, MARIANNE C. SHARP, AND LOUISE W. MADSEN

Today's dreams may be tomorrow's fulfillments if we choose aright, and having chosen, exercise the self-discipline and self-mastery that lead to action in accordance with our choices. (In *Relief Society Magazine*, Jan. 1960, 1.)

Talents

NORMA B. ASHTON

Everyone has a special assignment. No one else has your talent; no one else will be in your place at your time. Our Father in heaven has given you a special touch, so you can succeed where others fail. (In *BYU Speeches*, 8 Feb. 1972, 6.)

ANYA BATEMAN

What we can find when we consecrate our gifts to the betterment of this world and the building of the

kingdom is that the gifts we thought were so small seem to have magnified. (*Talent Race*, 58.)

We often think that the word *talent* can't mean just any ability or strength, only a few that quickly come to mind. But no guidebook I know of lists abilities and strengths that count or abilities and strengths that don't count. That's because they all count. (*Talent Race*, 11.)

When we use our gifts for good, they glow and grow—and no wonder, when heavenly light is reflected from them. (*Talent Race*, 58.)

ANITA R. CANFIELD

The gifts given to us in the pre-existence are special, and unless we use them, they will be taken away. We must discover them, develop them, and then use them for the right purposes. (*Young Woman*, 40.)

CONNIE DUNCAN CANNON

Our Heavenly Father . . . knows better than anyone else the talents that lie within each of his children and how best to nurture them. (In *To Rejoice As Women*, 221.)

MARY ELLEN EDMUNDS

Part of magnifying talents is giving them away, investing in others and allowing them to be successful. It includes not being threatened by the fact that eventually someone you have taught will play the piano or do something else better than you can. (*Love Is a Verb*, 102.)

JANET G. LEE

Appreciating the abilities and resources of others should lift us, not diminish us in any way. Every time we see or hear something of merit, we should be better because of it. The Lord must have intended it to be that way, because each of us has been given different gifts, unique abilities, and varying insights. (In *BYU Speeches*, 24 Jan. 1995, 92.)

MARILYNNE TODD LINFORD

If I am kept busy responding to the pressures to be like someone else, I won't have time to develop my own talents (*Woman Fulfilled*, 60.)

BROOKIE PETERSON

As each new season of our lives unfolds we develop significant attributes, but often we don't give ourselves enough credit for this progress. We don't think of these qualities as talents. We, as well as others, often place too much emphasis on valuing ourselves because of outward accomplishments. But we should come to realize that our homespun traits that bless others are of great worth and consequence. (*Woman's Hope*, 21.)

SHIRLEY W. THOMAS

What you have is enough if you recognize it and use it. (In *Ensign*, Feb. 1982, 61.)

EMMELINE B. WELLS

If we possess gifts, talents, or abilities, are we justified in allowing them to perish for the want of use, any more than the miser in hoarding up his gold while the poor around him are starving? I think not. (In *Woman's Exponent*, 1 Mar. 1874, 146.)

God has not given us faculties to lie dormant; they wither and almost disappear if not used, while the proper exercise of what is best within us, develop strong characteristics that not only have this effect and influence upon others about us but descend and mold the generations to come. (In *Woman's Exponent*, 15 Sept. 1874, 55.)

Women and Personal Improvement

ELAINE CANNON

I plead for a stir among the sisters of The Church of Jesus Christ of Latter-day Saints for intelligent and prayerful preparation and performance that is in line with what our Heavenly Father wants for us personally and what he needs for us to do as women. (In *Ensign*, Nov. 1979, 107.)

KAREN LYNN DAVIDSON

The Savior taught that both men and women must move forward in the development of spirituality, that all must seek wisdom and knowledge. (In *Best of Women's Conference*, 121.)

SUSA YOUNG GATES

Cultivate a taste for beautiful thoughts beautifully expressed. Learn to think for yourself; think your own thoughts. . . . Cultivate an instinctive feeling for the value of words. (In *Relief Society Magazine*, June 1921, 333.)

BEPPIE HARRISON

There is an undeniable serenity about a still house in the darkness, and when the distractions are all quieted—everyone asleep and the phone finally silent—it's a marvelous freedom to move through familiar rooms so unfamiliarly empty of other people and their needs. To be able to read the scriptures and think about them, to pray wholeheartedly without being interrupted, even just to sit and read a spiritual book or magazine article with time to mull over the author's words—it becomes a way of connecting again, of filling up the empty space. (*Needles*, 71.)

ELAINE SORENSEN MARSHALL

Within each woman is the capacity to strive for improvement and the freedom to choose her own path. Our challenge is to choose a path that will offer to each of us the assurance that our chosen course of life is acceptable and according to the will of God. (In *Woman's Choices*, 32.)

A woman involved in her own total education may feel the same stirrings of satisfaction when she learns a new quilting stitch or when she teaches her child to pray as when she composes a poem or passes a college final examination. . . . It is not difficult to see why the celebration of education has endured. (In *Woman's Choices*, 27.)

LOUISE Y. ROBISON

Greater faith is built through knowledge, but belief is incomplete unless merged into action, so yours is the opportunity to stimulate women to read, to think, and to apply in their lives the truths which they believe; to establish ideals which will hold them true. (In *Relief Society Magazine*, Nov. 1935, 685.)

TESSA MEYER SANTIAGO

We are equally under covenant both to rear and to teach our children and to recognize and develop our own considerable talents for the service of God. (In *May Christ Lift Thee Up*, 208.)

BARBARA B. SMITH

It takes a lifetime of conscious effort, of striving and learning and living, to become an holy woman. (In *Ensign*, Nov. 1979, 108.)

BELLE S. SPAFFORD

Women should make every effort to build and strengthen the spiritual qualities of life through faith in God, through participation in church activities, through developing well-defined religious concepts and beliefs and teaching them to their children, and through cultivating their innate spiritual natures. (*Today's World*, 136.)

The restored gospel gives to women a position of dignity and respect. It recognizes their spiritual and mental powers and their right to use their inborn talents to the full. (In *Relief Society Magazine*, Dec. 1945, 751.)

EMMELINE B. WELLS

Women . . . should not only make an effort to be capable of judging for themselves, and carrying their own individual burdens, . . . but . . . they should be so earnest and practical as to accomplish something real for themselves. (In *Woman's Exponent*, 15 Dec. 1877, 105.)

Self-Esteem

The Spiritual Source of Self-Esteem

DIANE BILLS

True self-esteem doesn't come from being popular out in the world . . . true self-esteem comes from God. (In *Serving with Strength*, 39.)

True self-worth comes from drawing close to God. It comes from building a true relationship with Heavenly Father, and in coming to see ourselves as he sees us. (*Trust in the Lord*, 8.)

RUTH E. BRASHER

Self-esteem and self-confidence flourish in the bonds of love. (In *BYU Speeches*, 12 July 1983, 159.)

Knowing our Father loves us and that He created each of us and endowed us with the capacity to fulfill the purposes of life provides us the basis for understanding our worth. (In *BYU Speeches*, 12 July 1983, 159.)

JOANNE B. DOXEY

True personal worth comes from a secure relationship with Heavenly Father. Individual worth is intrinsic; it is internal; it is eternal. It is something that cannot be taken from us when the blossom of youth fades, when economic conditions leave us desolate, when sickness or handicaps befall us, or when prominence and visibility are obscured. (In *Ensign*, Nov. 1987, 91.)

CLAUDIA FUHRIMAN ELIASON

To those of us who are building self-esteem, gaining a testimony should be the first stepping-stone, the foundation stone that we work on. (In *Woman's Choices*, 70.)

PATRICIA T. HOLLAND

We all need a higher image of ourselves, but Satan would have us believe it comes totally from the praise of others when in fact it comes from our relationship with God. (In *BYU Speeches*, 10 Sept. 1985, 2.)

JANET G. LEE

The Lord doesn't think in terms of quotas—only qualities. He does not accept just the top ten percent. He wants all of us. He sees our worth from where we are today and what we can become tomorrow. (In *BYU Speeches*, 24 Jan. 1995, 93.)

MARILYNNE TODD LINFORD

Our Father in Heaven wants you to think highly of yourself. He wants you to be successful. You are his child, with a divine mission. He can help you build your self-esteem. . . . He can bring ideas to your mind, open doorways, provide opportunities, and change attitudes—whatever you need. Ask for his help. (*Mother's Self-Esteem*, 21.)

BARBARA DAY LOCKHART

Love for self; a deep, abiding peace; and knowing who you really are come from only one source— from God. (In *BYU Speeches*, 12 May 1992, 97.)

As each person is as precious in his sight as the other, each one has ready access to honest, lasting, real self-acceptance. (In *BYU Speeches*, 12 May 1992, 98.)

Worldly self-esteem is never satisfied; you achieve or acquire more and more but still feel empty inside. (In *BYU Speeches*, 12 May 1992, 98.)

CHIEKO N. OKAZAKI

We hear a lot about self-esteem these days. Self-esteem—the kind that really counts—comes from a relationship with Jesus Christ and Heavenly Father that is real and solid and alive. Not a secondhand relationship of listening to someone else talk about them, but a firsthand relationship of talking with them, of experiencing their love, of being their hands in serving others. (*Lighten Up!* 159.)

ESTHER RASBAND

Genuine confidence . . . is a byproduct of our accomplishment and the Savior's atonement—a combination of what we do with God's help, and what God has done for us. (*Confronting the Myth*, 2.)

HEIDI S. SWINTON

No one can take away what is in your heart. (In *Arms of His Love*, 232.)

M. CATHERINE THOMAS

Being filled with the love of God [is] of far greater worth than any sense of self-confidence. (In *BYU Speeches*, 7 Dec. 1993, 48.)

WENDY C. TOP

True self-confidence does not come in obsessing over ourselves, . . . but in losing ourselves completely in the soul-building service of God. Lasting self-security comes not in what we make of ourselves but in what God makes of us. (*Getting Past the Labels*, 9.)

We Are Beings of Eternal Value

NORMA B. ASHTON

All of us come to earth as God's creation. Each has an innate nobility. . . . All the Lord asks of us is to be the best we can be with what we have. (In *Best of Women's Conference*, 16.)

JULENE BUTLER

Our awareness of our individual eternal nature will gradually unfold to our view as we focus on our strengths, listen to the feedback of our loved ones, find ways to compensate for our weaknesses, ponder and pray over our experiences, and invite the spirit of understanding into our lives. (In BYU *Speeches*, 9 June 1998, 270.)

ANITA R. CANFIELD

If you could see how great you were before you came here, your self-mastery and self-esteem would never be in question. (*Self-Esteem*, 41.)

LUCILE JOHNSON

Our worth and our happiness is not dependent upon our performance or the possessions we acquire on this earth. God our Father loves us without condition. Worth was incorporated into the spirit in our premortal existence. It does not have

to be earned all over again here on earth. (*Enjoy the Journey*, 20.)

ARDETH GREENE KAPP

In times of loneliness or when we may feel worthless, we are not alone and we are not worthless. We did not come to this earth life to gain our worth. We brought it with us. (*Joy of the Journey*, 137.)

JO ANN LARSEN

Within every eternal soul there is a rose—the Godlike qualities planted with us at birth, growing amid the thorns of our earthly defects or lacks. (*Heart of Goodness*, 167.)

JANET G. LEE

Never will our eternal value be measured in comparison with another's performance. (In BYU *Speeches*, 24 Jan. 1995, 93.)

Each Is a Child of God

ANYA BATEMAN

The knowledge that we are the offspring and embryo of Deity indicate . . . the marvelous potential we have all been given, [and] we realize that we need never again say, "I have little in the way of talents or strengths." (*Talent Race*, 8.)

DIANE BILLS

There is not an award, an honor, a presidency, or a queenship that man can bestow upon man, that even begins to compare to the stature we already enjoy in the sight of God. (In *Serving with Strength*, 39.)

There is a key to feeling good inside. . . . I believe this key lies in seeing ourselves as God sees us and basing our worth on who we really are. This spiritual insight can give us a foundation to help us meet any challenge in life with confidence. (*Trust in the Lord*, 2.)

JUTTA BAUM BUSCHE

When we come to understand this *unknown treasure*—the knowledge of who we really are—we will know that we are entitled to the power that comes from God. It will come when we ask for it and when we trust his leadership in our lives. (In *Best of Women's Conference*, 72.)

ELAINE CANNON

You are a daughter of God and he loves you more than you can ever imagine. . . . Our Heavenly Father is . . . great, perfect, in charge, and loves you no matter what. Because he abides in the eternal laws according to justice, he has his ways of showing love. Let him! Turn to him. (*Bell Ringer*, 2.)

You have the spark of the divine in you. Whatever you do or don't do won't change this fact. Your spirit was marvelously created in the premortal world. . . . We don't know much about this, but if you ask in prayer, the Holy Ghost will witness to your spirit of your divine beginnings. (*Bell Ringer*, 2.)

MARJORIE P. HINCKLEY

Man is an individual created in the likeness of God, with divinely bestowed free agency, and . . . the development of the human individual soul is so important a thing that God himself has called it His greatest work and glory. (In *Glimpses*, 16–17.)

LUCILE JOHNSON

Worth is an innate part of each of us, programmed into us before we were born. . . . When you finally and honestly understand and believe you are a child of God and that he loves you unconditionally (you have to believe it with all your heart), your life will be happier. (*Enjoy the Journey*, 20–21.)

DEBORAH ELDREDGE MILNE

I have learned that I am both a grown up and a child, especially in my Heavenly Father's eyes. Knowing this about myself, I can allow the people I love to be both grown up and child; for at times, I can learn from young people, and at other times, comfort and teach those who are older. When I see any person, I want to look beyond his mortal trappings—a destructible body that may be tall or short, wrinkled or smooth—and see a literal and eternal child of God. (*Reflections*, 35–36.)

CHIEKO N. OKAZAKI

Someday we will all know who we are, because the Savior, who truly knows us, will look at us and we will see ourselves through his eyes—pure, eternal, and all-knowing—rather than through our own mortal, short-sighted, dim perspective. And when we see ourselves as he sees us, we will recognize our glory. (*Lighten Up!* 112–13.)

When we feel [God's] inexhaustible love springing up in our hearts, acts of service and mercy and kindness will flow from us. (*Cat's Cradle*, 126.)

LOUISE PLUMMER

I believe that we are all God's "workmanship," as Paul says, "created in Christ Jesus unto good works" (Ephesians 2:10) and that through his divine grace and through faith, families as well as individuals can be made whole. This is my strength. (*Grasshopper*, 49.)

BARBARA B. SMITH

[God] places an infinite value on his children, with no arbitrary inferior or superior comparative labels. He wants us to be about his business, . . . and his business is eternal, life-giving work. (In *BYU Speeches*, 9 Feb. 1978, 15.)

Of all the creations of God, men and women are the ones that are to become as he is. We are his children. He has given us a plan, a model, and teachings that will help us gain his attributes. (In *LDS Women's Treasury*, 277.)

The simple and magnificent message of the restored gospel is that godhood is the birthright of every child of God. (*Love*, 63.)

The light of truth discloses our eternal nature. If we work hard enough and long enough, and pray diligently enough, the excellence that is our divine potential is possible to each one of us. (In *Ensign*, May 1982, 97.)

M. CATHERINE THOMAS

If one grand objective of earth life is to gain access to the grace of Jesus Christ for our trials and divine development, then we will immediately realize that self-confidence is a puny substitute for God-confidence. (In *BYU Speeches*, 7 Dec. 1993, 48.)

MARGARET J. WHEATLEY

As we remember more of our divine goodness, we find that the people around us exhibit more of their divine goodness. (In *Women and the Power*, 172.)

The process of our lives is a moving toward an awareness of our essential, divine nature. . . . Our forgetfulness of our divinity causes us much grief and, I believe, saddens our Father as well. (In *Women and the Power*, 170–71.)

DWAN J. YOUNG

To have faith and understand that each of us is truly a child of God gives assurance to our sense of worth. (In *Ensign*, Nov. 1983, 86.)

The Worth of the Individual

NORMA B. ASHTON

A copy is never as valuable as the original. Each of us is an original made by God, and we diminish ourselves and our Maker when we question our worth. (In *Best of Women's Conference*, 18.)

DONNA LEE BOWEN BARNES

The traits that really matter, that determine who we are . . . are traits that are largely invisible to the outsider. (In *Women Steadfast*, 278.)

CLAUDIA FUHRIMAN ELIASON

I believe that nothing is so unequal as equal treatment of unequals. (In *Woman's Choices*, 75.)

JAMIE GLENN

Heavenly Father doesn't compare us to anyone else. Who we are is who he wants to come to him. Who we are is who he loves. If we doubt our worth, we are doubting his ability and his creations. (*Walk Tall*, 16.)

MICHAELENE P. GRASSLI

Differences are not faults. They are differences. (*LeaderTalk*, 49.)

AMY HARDISON

People are not merchandise and should not be valued or dismissed because they have or lack certain traits and abilities. People are complex, multifaceted individuals, each possessing different qualities and strengths. We are not the same on the inside or out—nor are we meant to be. Each person was purposely created by God with different strengths and weaknesses. . . . If everyone's talents and abilities were the same, life would lack variety, uniqueness, and excellence. It would be very boring. Moreover, some very important qualities and abilities would be lacking. (*How to Feel Great*, 5–6.)

BARBARA DAY LOCKHART

Jesus did not wait to see how we would live before he gave his life for us. (In *BYU Speeches*, 12 May 1992, 100.)

A person may lose sight of his or her worth, but that person's worth is always great in the sight of God. (In *BYU Speeches*, 12 May 1992, 100.)

It is difficult to realize our worth to God if we are not living his commandments. (In *BYU Speeches*, 12 May 1992, 100.)

The worth of each unique life is divine, infinite, and cannot be taken away. The worth of the soul means worth of the whole soul, the whole person—spirit and body. Our worth cannot be manipulated by others, it cannot be increased or decreased. . . . Worth is an absolute aspect of life, it will always exist. (In *BYU Speeches*, 12 May 1992, 100.)

A human life is always of utmost worth because that worth is eternal and cannot be erased. . . . Worthless is not an option. (In *BYU Speeches*, 12 May 1992, 100.)

CHIEKO N. OKAZAKI

Because you are an individual, unique in the universe, irreplaceable, and inexpressibly precious to our Heavenly Father, you can never be blotted out or erased by the actions that anyone else does to you. (*Sanctuary*, 95.)

ANNE OSBORN POELMAN

It is trite but nevertheless true that each of us is unique. Like a multifaceted diamond, we are polished one surface at a time. Like that precious jewel, no two of us are alike. The Lord certainly never intended us to render the same service or follow identical schedules of personal development. (In *LDS Women's Treasury*, 116.)

MARY ELLEN SMOOT

We may *each* be an instrument in the hands of God. Happily, we need not all be the same kind of instrument. . . . Neither is it necessary for us to all serve the Lord in the same way. (In *Ensign*, Nov. 2000, 90.)

EMMA LOU THAYNE

What I must learn to be is myself. . . . Only God and I can know who I am and what is the full measure of my creation. . . . My family will learn from my sense of myself and my world, and my responsibilities will be lighter for their being born of loving what I have to do. (*As for Me*, 27–28.)

Guilt and Self-doubt

ANYA BATEMAN

The poor self-image that we get from emphasizing our weaknesses can keep us from changing. . . . If we constantly dwell on our own problems, we may convince ourselves we are not good people and therefore act as if we are not. Our predictions about ourselves tend to be self-fulfilling, especially when we intensify our own self-doubts by telling others of our follies. (In *Ensign*, Aug. 1979, 69.)

JANETTE HALES BECKHAM

Faith helps us overcome our deficits whether they are sins or other feelings of inadequacy. We really become who we become because of the gift of the Atonement. (In *Keepers*, 175.)

Sometimes we make the mistake of feeling we are alone just because we are not getting recognition. Only a small part of what we do takes place in a public setting. (In *Ensign*, May 1992, 80.)

SHERI L. DEW

It's quite the irony that the gospel of the great Jehovah, which contains the power to save every human being and to strengthen every soul, is sometimes interpreted in such a way that feelings of inadequacy result. (In *Best of Women's Conference*, 128.)

The adversary promotes feelings of guilt—about anything. Pick a topic. . . .

Guilt does not originate with the Savior, who invites us to step to a higher way of living and a more ennobling way of thinking, to do a little better and perhaps a little more. Promptings that come from him are hopeful and motivating rather than defeating or discouraging. (In *Best of Women's Conference*, 135.)

BEPPIE HARRISON

Feeling guilty does not multiply my capabilities. (*Plain and Precious*, 19.)

PATRICIA T. HOLLAND

To be successful in the many skirmishes of life, you cannot afford to be your own worst enemy. And taking the battles inside—firing mortar shells into your very soul—is potentially one of the most damaging of all human activities. Believe it or not, you can recover from poor grades or a missed date or a flat tire and dead battery on the car. But if you turn such outside matters into self-recrimination and self-criticism, letting them damage your spirit and your sense of self-worth and esteem, then you have begun a battle with a

very high mortality rate indeed. (In *BYU Speeches*, 6 Sept. 1988, 24.)

ARDETH GREENE KAPP

In times of discouragement and self-doubt, we must try to remember who we are, or better, whose we are; and when we make a mistake, we must never give up on ourselves. When we hear a beautiful violin that is out of tune, we wouldn't throw the violin away. It has not lost its value. It just needs to be tuned by tightening a string. (*Joy of the Journey*, 135.)

CHIEKO N. OKAZAKI

You can never be made to feel like nothing or to become a nobody without your cooperation and consent. You can do it to yourself, but no one can do it to you. (*Sanctuary*, 95.)

Possibilities that seem more desirable to us but that are not possible sap the strength from our hands and the courage from our hearts. They become a snare to our feet so that we stumble and lose our way. All we can do is our best. (In *Best of Women's Conference*, 418.)

REBECCA GWYNN STRADLING

When we fear humiliation or pain or the criticism of others, we are forgetting who we are and what we can become. (In *Ensign*, July 1981, 29.)

Some, weighted down by a serious transgression, may give up the search for personal perfection in a frenzy of self-deprecation. This despair is very different from constructive self-criticism. . . . Despair is potentially one of the most destructive aspects of human experience. (In *Ensign*, July 1981, 29.)

Forgetting Ourselves

JANENE WOLSEY BAADSGAARD

We must never define our worth by what we do for a living, but instead by the meaning we bring to the work. (*Family Finances*, 121.)

ANITA R. CANFIELD

It is an eternal principle that when you build and raise others, you build and raise yourself. (*Young Woman*, 57.)

PATRICIA T. HOLLAND

Whatever you toss out mentally or verbally comes back to you. . . . If your mind is constantly seeing good in others, that . . . will return, and you will truly feel good about yourself. (In *Ensign*, June 1984, 53.)

ESTHER RASBAND

Torment comes about when we buy into the belief of society that we must first seek our own *self* and serve *it*. The worldly theory is that when we find *ourselves* all else will be added unto us.

But it seems to me that the gospel teaches us that when we *stop looking* for ourselves, God can add all else unto us. It is the *search* for self-

esteem that tortures us, not our lack of it. If we could stop "seeking our own," as Paul identified it in 1 Corinthians 13:5, we could get rid of the feeling that we live in a vice. (*Confronting the Myth*, 3.)

We must be willing to lay our self-esteem at the feet of the Lord and seek instead to love him and obey him. (*Confronting the Myth*, 13.)

Ultimately, a great and marvelous self-esteem will be a gift from God to those who do not seek it—who diligently lose themselves in his service. (*Confronting the Myth*, 13.)

We live in an age when we are told, in essence, that our problem is not in whether or not we are valuable, but whether or not we *believe* we are valuable. Focusing therefore on ourselves, we see little else. (*Confronting the Myth*, 15.)

Self-esteem will never work as a substitute for the Atonement. Only Jesus Christ, the Son of God, will truly give us the power and strength and peace we long for. That peace or confidence is the by-product of putting aside our self-awareness in total heartfelt obedience to our Father in Heaven. It is the process of abasing ourselves in order to be exalted. (*Confronting the Myth*, 129.)

M. CATHERINE THOMAS

What if one ceased defining self-esteem or justifying one's pursuit of it, and just ignored it? What if, instead, one just began to obey whatever divine instruction one was not obeying, to sacrifice whatever needed sacrificing, and to consecrate whatever one was holding back? What if one just set out to "seek this Jesus"? (Ether 12:41.) (*Spiritual Lightening*, 30.)

Valuing Ourselves Brings Strength

PATRICIA T. HOLLAND

Appropriately loving ourselves requires looking within ourselves deeply, honestly, and . . . serenely. It requires a loving look at the bad as well as the good. The more we understand and know, the more we love. (*On Earth*, 69.)

SHERRIE JOHNSON

A woman who is not at peace with herself, who has never learned who she is or where she is going, who has not mastered herself, and who does not like herself cannot effectively teach her children because of her own distress. (*Spiritually Centered*, 20.)

ARDETH GREENE KAPP

People who don't know who they are or whose they are tend to wander from the straight and narrow path searching to find themselves. (*Rejoice!* 95.)

BARBARA DAY LOCKHART

With reverence for self based on God's love, we will reject the temp-

tations that otherwise would draw us to the pride of the world. We would love nothing more than God. (In *BYU Speeches*, 12 May 1992, 97.)

Acceptance of self based on God's love is real. This true reverence for self is deep, filled with gratitude and peace, and is ever-present even in the face of life's most difficult trials. (In *BYU Speeches*, 12 May 1992, 98.)

BROOKIE PETERSON

We need to be tolerant, honest, and loving about our own worth. Feelings of self-approval are essential to our happiness and to healthy relationships. To increase regard for ourselves we need to begin with low-key, believable praise of our good qualities. (*Woman's Hope*, 32–33.)

The way a woman feels about herself will determine the way she presents herself. . . . Thus our self-image influences the messages we send to others. Also it serves as a filter through which messages we receive from others must pass. . . . In many ways self-concept governs communication, and communication promotes or limits a person's success. (*Woman's Hope*, 31.)

In learning to value ourselves it is important to concentrate on our positive accomplishments. We should remember to put our mistakes and failures out of our minds after we have learned the lessons they teach, and we should concentrate on giving ourselves credit for the good things we are doing. We need to reflect on every success, major or minor, frequently. (*Woman's Hope*, 23.)

CAROLYN J. RASMUS

Every time you make a right choice, your self-confidence will improve. Others will be drawn to you because they will see your light. (In *Living the Young Women Values*, 53.)

EMMELINE B. WELLS

One of the greatest blessings given to us is self-content, the feeling that God's gifts have not been wasted in our hands, the sense of an approving conscience; and we cannot possess this (unless we are inordinately vain, conceited and self-glorifying) without having done our best; and that development of character must have taken place in us whose influence is felt in immense circles, ever widening like ripples in the sea. (In *Woman's Exponent*, 15 Sept. 1874, 55.)

Self-Knowledge

MARILYN S. BATEMAN

Knowledge of our inner self lifts us above criticism, above discouragement, and above failure. (In *BYU Speeches*, 9 Sept. 1997, 4.)

There are two important pieces of knowledge that we need to understand and internalize to be happy. The first is that we are children—spiritual children—of our Heavenly Father. There is divinity within us. Every person on this earth is a child of God. Every one!

Second, our Heavenly Father loves us. He has endowed us with gifts of the Spirit that make us uniquely who we are. Our challenge is to know our real self—to live lives congruent with the Spirit inside us. (In *BYU Speeches*, 9 Sept. 1997, 10–11.)

JUTTA BAUM BUSCHE

Self-honesty is the foundation for developing other spiritual strengths. Self-honesty will determine whether obstacles and problems we face in life are stepping stones leading to blessings or stumbling stones leading to spiritual graveyards. (In *LDS Women's Treasury*, 369.)

JULENE BUTLER

It is important to examine our weaknesses, but we must keep them in perspective and let them motivate us to stretch for better things rather than allowing them to obscure the view of our eternal potential. (In *BYU Speeches*, 9 June 1998, 267.)

ANITA R. CANFIELD

Prayer is the way to know Heavenly Father loves you. It is the way to feel His love for you and see yourself through His eyes. And when that happens, you begin to have eternal perspective and the joy of knowing who you really are. (*Young Woman*, 14.)

ELAINE CANNON

There are two important days in a woman's life; the day she is born and the day she finds out why. . . . The day a woman of any age comes to understand . . . God's will for her . . . is the day she finds out why she was born. It is the day of her own giant step. (*Gatherings*, 90–91.)

SHERI L. DEW

Faith in Jesus Christ is the key to vision, to seeing ourselves as the Lord sees us. So to improve our vision, we must increase our faith in and connection to the Savior. (In *Best of Women's Conference*, 126.)

There is a direct relationship between our personal experience with the Lord and how we see ourselves. The closer we grow to him, the more clear and complete becomes our vision of who we are and what we can become. (In *Best of Women's Conference*, 128.)

ELAINE L. JACK

What does a patriarchal blessing say? Have you ever heard of one which says, "I am sorry—you're a loser. Do the best you can on earth, and we'll see you in about seventy years." Of course not! And you never will, because of the divine

qualities each of God's children has inherited. A patriarchal blessing is like a road map, a guide, directing you in your walk through life. It identifies your talents and the good things that can be yours. (In *Ensign*, Nov. 1989, 87.)

KATE L. KIRKHAM

We can *seek to increase our capacity to discern*. Our lives are complex, our circumstances varied. Failure to develop our spiritual capacity to discern could leave us overwhelmed, overdependent on others for meaning, overcommitted, or overreacting to the next thing that pops up. (In *BYU Speeches*, 19 May 1987, 147.)

DEBORAH ELDREDGE MILNE

Throughout my life, I am working to visualize the ideal me that God began creating long before I was born. When that vision of self seems lost because of challenges and pain, I can ask God to help me remember who I really am. (*Reflections*, 82.)

LESLIE BALLIF ROGERS

The word of God comes to us not only in a patriarchal blessing but through the scriptures, living prophets, the temple, prayer, fasting, and personal inspiration. . . . Our patriarchal blessings are unique from the scriptural perspective, however, in that they are directed to one particular child of God. (In *Thy Word Is a Lamp*, 162–63.)

MARGARET J. WHEATLEY

Through all his struggles and temptations, Christ never forgot who he was. I believe that he was trying to show us our own essential goodness as well, to call us to remembrance of our own divine natures. Jesus was a model of what it means to keep in mind one's eternal identity and to act from one's divine power. He never lost sight of who he was. Our forgetfulness of our divinity causes us much grief and, I believe, saddens our Father as well. (In *Women and the Power*, 170–71.)

Self-Mastery

RUTH E. BRASHER

Understanding who we are and that we are loved enhances our awareness of the opportunity to strive for perfection, to experience the process—the eternal process. In this context, growth in self-control and self-mastery can become an adventure of stimulating proportions, not just an agony of restraint. (In *BYU Speeches*, 12 July 1983, 160.)

ANITA R. CANFIELD

Resolve to make commitments and then commit to those resolutions. Lack of self-discipline grows on people; it starts with cobwebs and ends in iron chains. (*Self-Esteem*, 110.)

ELAINE CANNON

Look to your habits and attitudes. Look to your responses to situations. Don't choose to be a problem. Be a problem solver. Be a burden lifter. Value the word of God and the place of God in your life. (*Gatherings*, 286.)

It is true that environment and even heredity have some force in a person's actions and decisions. But always there is the element of choice. Here is a truth that we can lean to—we can be master of our fate. . . . We can do anything we want to if we want to badly enough. (*Gatherings*, 281.)

People are mature or immature depending on how they react to what life thrusts upon them; but because we cannot always direct events, we must learn self-control—to govern ourselves. If we fail in responding appropriately to life's challenges, we pay a high price. (*Gatherings*, 280.)

To ensure the greatest amount of happiness in this life, you must learn to bridle all your passions and appetites. Bad habits enslave us and restrict our freedom. . . . By living in harmony with gospel principles you will be filled with the Holy Ghost and be further strengthened to resist temptation. (In *Why Say No*, 125.)

LUCY GRANT CANNON

I may not be brilliant, but I can be good. (In *Keepers*, 51.)

SUSA YOUNG GATES

When we have learned to control self, we have obtained power over every unclean and evil spirit or influence which tempts us from the path of duty. (In *Young Woman's Journal*, May 1900, 232.)

The gift of the Holy Ghost will lead us into all truth, self-knowledge, self-reverence and self-control, if we but cherish it and obey its teachings. (In *Young Woman's Journal*, May 1900, 232.)

It is self-control which gives faith, trust, hope, calmness in the midst of trial, power over every force and power in the universe. The world and all eternity lies within our own soul. (In *Young Woman's Journal*, May 1900, 233.)

BEPPIE HARRISON

Self-control isn't just about temper . . . Self-control is about keeping command of yourself in general. It takes self-control to resist the seduction of passing impulse. (*On Being a Parent*, 75.)

MARJORIE P. HINCKLEY

We know when we are doing our best and when we are not. If we are not doing our best, it leaves us with a gnawing hunger and frustration. But when we do our level best, we experience a peace. (In *Glimpses*, 41.)

SHERRIE JOHNSON

[Self-discipline] builds self-esteem and allows us to be at peace with ourselves, thereby freeing us from inner turmoil. (*Spiritually Centered*, 20.)

JO ANN LARSEN

You exist separate and apart from others. There are no shared brains, no lifelines from you to others that connect your moods to theirs, no buttons others can push to create anger and frustration inside you. That means that you, not others, are in charge of your moods. (*I'm a Day Late*, 93.)

MARILYNNE TODD LINFORD

All habits are learned. All habits can be unlearned. To accomplish this, bring an unwanted habit to the level of awareness. Catch yourself in the act and intervene by quitting cold turkey, substituting a better habit, using rewards or punishments, visualizing yourself without the habit, utilizing time by humming your favorite tune or by playing one of your favorite mental videos as a temporary distraction. (*Woman Fulfilled*, 45–46.)

CAROLINE EYRING MINER

The real reward for achievement is in the joy of knowing one has been adequate to the challenge placed before him. (In *Relief Society Magazine*, May 1962, 351.)

CHIEKO N. OKAZAKI

There are no limits on the amount of good you can do in the world if you build in yourself the spiritual muscles of self-discipline. (*Disciples*, 90.)

If you've been thinking that your life needs some changes, then discipline yourself for action, for work, for good. Remember that a rut is just a grave with both ends kicked out! (*Disciples*, 91.)

BELLE S. SPAFFORD

In man self-control is the key to useful and happy living while lack of it brings untold misery. The individual without self-control is like a ship without sail or rudder and is apt to be dashed against the rocks and destroyed. (*Woman's Reach*, 147.)

Weakness

ANYA BATEMAN

Weaknesses, it seems, are often weaknesses only because we lack experience, know-how, or exposure. (*Talent Race*, 70.)

ANITA R. CANFIELD

If you want to turn your weaknesses into strengths, you must first acknowledge your weaknesses with hope. Remember what the Lord said? If men *humble* themselves, if men come unto him, he will show them their weaknesses. He does this with a spirit of love by the power of the Holy Ghost. We end up feeling *inspired*, not discouraged, motivated to be a better person. (In *Sunshine for the LDS Woman*, 179.)

Negative thoughts and discouragement are Satan's tools, not the Lord's. Yes, you must be conscious of your weaknesses and failings, and repent of them. But it is Satan who causes you to dwell on them and leaves you feeling weaker and weaker and doubting your self-worth. The Lord wants to strengthen you and give you power to overcome your weaknesses. (*Self-Esteem*, 16.)

SUSA YOUNG GATES

The strength of the chain is exactly the strength of the weakest link; and no matter what your power may be in other directions, if you are to clean out evil from your soul, you must get power over your own body and your every weakness must be conquered and made strength. (In *Young Woman's Journal*, Jan. 1895, 192.)

MICHAELENE P. GRASSLI

Our heavenly Father in his wisdom blessed us with opportunities to rid ourselves of the great sin of pride. As we do so, his grace can turn our very weaknesses into our strengths. (*What I Have Learned*, 40.)

BEPPIE HARRISON

We are not the first to feel hopeless, from time to time, about the intractability of our weaknesses and the frequency of our wrong choices.

The medieval scholars and theologians had a name for it. They called it *despair,* and listed it as one of the seven deadly sins, right up there with lust and avarice and pride. Despair, they said, was a deadly sin because it had elements of blasphemy; despair denied that the power of God was great enough to bring you back into the light. (*Day at a Time,* 70–71.)

CAROL CORNWALL MADSEN

God knows we are weak. . . . And he knows that most of us will demonstrate our weaknesses many times over before we leave this life. This is the risk of agency. But as he so wisely knew, it is through our weakness that we discover humility, and it is through humility that we find God. (In *Best of Women's Conference,* 333.)

BETTE S. MOLGARD

Satan recognizes our spiritual endowments, and sends armies to counteract them. He knows where to find the gaps in our armor. . . .

The Lord has all of the powers and gifts that are needed (his grace is sufficient) to help us to know how to strengthen that weak part of our armor. With his help, the weak place will become a strength. (*Everyday Battles,* 133–34.)

The difference between the Savior's recovery program is that the worldly recovery programs work from the outside, on your mortal body. We were created spiritually first and temporally second. To successfully overcome our weaknesses, we must improve in that same order. This is the true order for every problem we encounter in life. (*Everyday Battles,* 102–3.)

ELLIS R. SHIPP

How hard it is to always do right! Even when we think we are most strong we are suddenly made conscious of our utter weakness. Oh, for wisdom, for knowledge and great understanding that I may ever have power to discern right from wrong, truth from error. (*While Others Slept,* 72.)

Gaining a deeper understanding of my inner nature—of its frailties and weaknesses—increases the desire to bring them into subjection. I know that can be accomplished in only one way—by the aid and assistance of the Holy Spirit. (*While Others Slept,* 69.)

IONE J. SIMPSON

Heavenly Father knows us better than we know ourselves. . . . He will help us build on our strengths and overcome our weaknesses, if we ask him. (In *Hearts Knit Together,* 118.)

BELLE S. SPAFFORD

We must not be so sensitive to our shortcomings that we fail to recognize and magnify our strengths. As we magnify our strengths our weaknesses will become submerged. (*Today's World,* 67.)

EMMELINE B. WELLS

We are all mortals and liable to make mistakes, but even the very mistakes we may make, may teach us useful lessons of a severe but practical experience. (In *Woman's Exponent*, 15 Dec. 1875, 110.)

Service

Service Leads to Happiness

LILLIAN S. ALLDREDGE

When you lose yourselves in service, you find the very thing that will make you supremely happy in this life. (In *Wisdom's Paths*, 193.)

GEORGIA LAUPER GATES

To use one's God-given gifts to serve him can be the highest order of joy. I expect that he would like nothing less from his children. (In *Wisdom's Paths*, 207.)

CHIEKO N. OKAZAKI

Sometimes we get discouraged because the needs in the world around us seem so great and our resources seem so few. . . . When we think like that, we focus on what is left undone, and we lose the joy that comes with service. . . . Lighten up. Concentrate on the joy, not the job. (*Aloha!* 21.)

MARY ELLEN SMOOT

The paradox of life is that service *to others* is the well-spring of joy and happiness *for us*. (*Sweet Is the Work*, 108.)

JERI J. WINGER

In helping others, we help ourselves, because when we give, we gain and we grow. And the pay is good. We are paid in smiles and in happiness, which is the currency of love. . . . We have God's promise that what we give will be given back many times over. (In *Woman's Choices*, 160.)

Building Others through Service

CAROL K. ANDERSON

Peace comes from unobtrusive acts of decency and consideration for those in need, who can take courage because of some small act of caring. (In *Balm of Gilead*, 73.)

ELAINE CANNON

God often works his wonders through the life and goodness of a person sensitive to inspiration. (*Count Your Blessings*, 103.)

One cries out to God for help and sometimes he sends it through an earth angel. . . . One prays, God listens, and the helper must be in tune with the silent throbbing of instruction from heaven to meet a need. (*Count Your Blessings*, 103.)

DEANNA EDWARDS

Nothing brings more joy in this life than helping to ease the pain of someone who is suffering. It takes a desire to risk walking closely with someone who is wounded so we can involve ourselves in a process of giving and receiving. We all have gifts to give and lessons about life to teach one another. (*Grieving*, 131.)

ARDETH GREENE KAPP

Love expressed through service can bring light where there is darkness, hope where there is despair, and repentance where there is transgression. (In *Living the Young Women Values*, 68.)

Our acts of service may be small or large, lengthy or brief, public or private, but when we serve in a spirit of love and sincere concern for the welfare and happiness of another, the Spirit of the Lord is felt and the Lord can work through us to bless others. (In *Living the Young Women Values*, 68.)

MARILYNNE TODD LINFORD

One way we can give service is to share with others our happy and spiritual thoughts, our achievements, the answers we receive to prayer, the precious moments we experience. (*Standing Ovation*, 46.)

As I share uplifting experiences or happy thoughts, others respond to me on the same level. We share. We learn. We hug. (*Standing Ovation*, 46.)

JILL C. MAJOR, LAUREN C. LEIFSON, AND HOLLIE C. BEVAN

When we choose to give our wholehearted support to others we will be aware of their temporal needs, take their hands and walk a few steps with them when they are emotionally downtrodden, and offer spiritual support through prayers and sharing the gospel, reminding them that, above all, they are children of God. (*Encircled by Love*, 30.)

CHIEKO N. OKAZAKI

We are literally answers to prayers when we are willing to serve. (*Aloha!* 21.)

We never know how far the effects of our service will reach. We can never afford to be cruel or indifferent or ungenerous, because we are all connected. (In *Ensign*, May 1993, 85.)

MARY ANN RASMUSSEN

It is said that if you are not in the habit of saving, you can establish that habit simply by saving a dollar a week. . . . This principle also applies to helping other people; if we stretch a little bit more than we think we can, somehow we will find the money and the time to help more people more often. (In *Women Steadfast*, 164.)

LOUISE Y. ROBISON

I wonder if there is any one . . . who does not need the human touch, who does not . . . have the opportunity of watching the one hour with those who are bearing heavy burdens! Look after those who have heavy burdens. You have been given that privilege, you can comfort and bless souls. (In *Relief Society Magazine*, Nov. 1939, 781.)

BARBARA B. SMITH

We must seek out those among us with need and, using our God-given talents for charity and our means for relieving others, coordinate the two. (In *Ensign*, Mar. 1997, 37.)

We should tune our souls to the point that we may find those in need and offer friendship, help as needed, and courage to meet each day's challenges. (In *Ensign*, Mar. 1997, 37.)

One person can make a difference. In fact, the only differences that are ever made are made by individuals who take action. (In *Ensign*, June 1984, 61.)

One person responding to human needs will in a lifetime give much assistance and great comfort. There is no end to the good we can do when every act we perform is a great work of love. (In *Ensign*, June 1984, 61.)

SUSAN L. WARNER

If it is our desire to bless the lives of others, [the Savior] will help us give up that which hath no life and open the way for us, in turn, to help those who need that which giveth life. (In *Women Steadfast*, 182.)

Often when we feel unhappy or unfulfilled, we try to fill our own need in the world's way by buying, acquiring, spending time and energy in indulgent activities. But . . . our spiritual need is satisfied when we lift the burdens of others. . . . It is our spiritual need not only to know but to choose to help. (In *Women Steadfast*, 182.)

EMMELINE B. WELLS

If we extend to another the comfort of loving words in the hours of sorrow, of doubt, or temptation, we are even in this sweet ministration doing deeds worthy to be engraven in the heraldry of good works. (In *Woman's Exponent*, 15 Apr. 1877, 171.)

In humility, laying all upon the altar of our faith, trusting in God for guidance and support, let us exert every faculty we possess, in the great work of advancement and redemption. Let us stretch forth a hand to the weak and erring, lift up the fallen, raise the bowed down, help the tempted to resist temptation, and stimulate those who are dilatory to prompt and decided action. (In *Woman's Exponent*, 1 Mar. 1874, 146.)

Blessings of Service

ANYA BATEMAN

There is a replenishing and strengthening process in giving our best and sharing and helping. (*Talent Race*, 58.)

EARLENE BLASER

I see the gospel in action as life shaping, not just as performing good deeds. Self-esteem and confidence burst forward in huge bounds when children find themselves doing good. (In *Emotional First Aid*, 92.)

ELAINE CANNON

In the end we love best those things for which we have sacrificed and those dear ones whom we have served. (*Love You*, 41.)

CAMILLE FRONK

When we vicariously feel the heartache of another, we often gain the strength and wisdom from a particular trial without having to experience that trial ourselves. (In *Arms of His Love*, 66.)

RUTH HARDY FUNK

One of the reasons God gives us the handicapped is to help to refine the souls of those of us who care for and teach and nurture children. We have handicaps and must be our brother's keeper. (In *Keepers*, 105.)

MICHAELENE P. GRASSLI

As you pray for, teach, care for, and work for the members you have been called to serve, your love for them will increase. This seems to be an eternal natural law, because it always works, if we will let it. (*LeaderTalk*, 10.)

In serving others we are serving our Heavenly Father, the source of love. The Apostle John taught that when we love one another, we come to know God (see 1 John 4:7). When we know God, our capacity for love increases. As your love for your brothers and sisters increases, your effectiveness with and for them will increase. What a satisfying cycle! (*LeaderTalk*, 10.)

CLAIRE HAWKINS

I am a firm believer in the power of service—the converting power, the retaining power of charity. Charity is the pure love of Christ. He is the converting power. He changes lives as we communicate his love through service in his name. (In *Women in the Covenant*, 105.)

ARDETH GREENE KAPP

I have found that communion with the infinite most often occurs when we are in the act of serving someone else. (*My Neighbor*, 61.)

In Monterrey, Mexico, a sister and I walked along a dirt path shaded by olive trees. We were on the Lord's errand. . . . I contemplated the possibility of our having the Lord with us, a companion. And while we did not see Him, I did witness a burning within, an excitement, an assurance, a witness of the Spirit that

He walked with us on our way, which was His way. (*My Neighbor*, 61.)

LOUISE Y. ROBISON

There is always a value in striving; always compensation for effort. When these efforts have an aim to relieve and bless, the result is a gain in priceless experience, and a growth in spiritual power. (In *Relief Society Magazine*, Mar. 1931, 144.)

In our desire to serve those of our Father's children who are in distress, we strengthen our own faith. (In *Relief Society Magazine*, May 1939, 348.)

BARBARA B. SMITH

Growth in understanding and living of the gospel is neverending. . . . All that one learns shapes each day's new experience. (*Grand-mothering*, 124.)

SHIRLEY W. THOMAS

Caring for others, like the "quality of mercy," is "twice blest: Bless[ing] him that gives and him that [receives]" (William Shakespeare, *Merchant of Venice*, act 4, sc. 1, lines 184, 186–87). In giving we grow in patience, humility, faith—all the elements of that pure love called charity. (In *Ensign*, May 1980, 87.)

SUSAN L. WARNER

Our spiritual need is satisfied when we lift the burdens of others. (In *Women Steadfast*, 182.)

BARBARA W. WINDER

Peace can come to both the giver and the receiver as we follow the promptings of the Spirit to serve one another. (In *Ensign*, Nov. 1985, 96.)

How Shall We Serve?

ELAINE CANNON

Nothing can touch the sweetness of the work of silent servants. (*Count Your Blessings*, 24.)

KAREN LYNN DAVIDSON

When we see a wrong, let's be capable of more than just indignation. Let's be skilled enough to express our indignation in a way that will convince other people and then be able to suggest and carry out some solutions. (In *Best of Women's Conference*, 121.)

MARY ELLEN EDMUNDS

Sometimes we may be waiting for a chance to serve and help in a huge, visible way, or in a faraway place. But there are many right around us who hunger and thirst for friendship, attention, and someone to care. (*Happiness*, 131.)

CAMILLE FRONK

We all want to succeed, progress, and improve, and we serve best when we support and encourage others in their development without robbing them of the pain, exertion, and ultimate exhilaration that are a part of doing it themselves. Selecting service projects by this rule of thumb ensures greater probability of fulfillment and more meaningful use of time and energy. (In *Redeemer*, 165.)

BEPPIE HARRISON

There is no way we can assume ownership of anybody else's problems. We can help, we can support, we can encourage, but we cannot do anybody else's job of living for them. (*Day at a Time*, 32.)

ARDETH GREENE KAPP

Many lives will be healed and blessed when we reach out in a spirit of love and concern. I think of a little girl who visited a neighbor's house where her little friend had died. "Why did you go?" questioned her father. "To comfort her mother," she said. "What could you do to comfort her?" "I climbed into her lap and cried with her," she said. (In *Best of Women's Conference*, 254–55.)

The value and far-reaching effect of our service, however small, has nothing to do with our age or material wealth. It has to do with our willingness to give of our time and be led by the Spirit. (In *Women and the Power*, 35.)

When we learn to listen to the Spirit in answer to our prayers, our service becomes customized by the Spirit, and we will do things that we might not otherwise have known to do. (*Joy of the Journey*, 98.)

CAMILLA EYRING KIMBALL

Never suppress a generous impulse to word or deed. (*Writings*, 129.)

CHIEKO N. OKAZAKI

The needs of the world are enormous. We can't do everything. We can't even do all of the good things there are to do. But please, set your priorities. Keep time for yourselves so that you can draw close to the Savior. Keep time for your families. Keep time for your sisters. And then find . . . a silence into which your voice can bring the note of sympathy and love. Find the loneliness that your smile can dispel. Find the need that your hand can fulfill. And find the human soul that yours can meet as a sister—not as faceless, anonymous charity. (*Cat's Cradle*, 174.)

[Service is] not complicated at all. You see a need—you meet that need, just as quickly as you can, doing the very best you can right at that moment with the resources that you have. That's the rhythm: see and act. Perceive and do. (*Cat's Cradle*, 36.)

Don't feel that you are not old enough, not educated enough, or not rich enough to serve. Don't worry too much about product or the outcome. Feel the rhythm of seeing needs, of meeting needs. We can trust that rhythm. (*Cat's Cradle*, 37.)

MARY ELLEN SMOOT

Some of the most important services we ever perform are sharing the gospel of Jesus Christ and otherwise relieving spiritual suffering. The "casseroles" of faith and hope that we give to a friend, the "cookies" of kindness that we extend to our own families, the "coats" of charity that we gently place on others' shoulders when their hearts need spiritual warming—these are some of the most vital services. (In *Arise*, 6.)

Attitude toward Service

LINDA R. ARCHIBALD

There is joy in every kind of service, and big service projects are no more valid than daily acts of kindness. It is also true that service done abroad in the world is no more important than that offered sincerely within the walls of our own homes. (*Sunshine in My Soul*, 76.)

Whether acts of service are large or small, one of the certainties is that calls to serve rarely come when we are waiting for them. . . . Unexpected cries for help should not be resented. Since we can never predict when someone else's needs will cross our path, we must cultivate perpetual spontaneity. (*Sunshine in My Soul*, 77.)

MARY ELLEN EDMUNDS

We must not ever ignore an impulse to serve when there's something we could do. When it's within our power to give love, we should never withhold it. If we feel compassion or empathy without doing

something, we may diminish our power to act, to respond. (*Love Is a Verb*, 3.)

For me I feel close to the Savior when I can do in a small way for someone else, what He would do if He were there. In a way, that's what being an instrument is all about . . . to make it possible for His love to reach more of His children. (In *Ensign*, Nov. 1985, 96.)

MARIE K. HAFEN

If we sit and wait for others to come and wipe our tears, we may miss the opportunity to wipe the tears of a neighbor or a friend. (In *Clothed with Charity*, 44.)

We can sit at home behind seemingly safe walls, or we can push beyond our comfort zones and break through our walls of judgment and criticism to someone else who needs us. (In *Clothed with Charity*, 44.)

BETTY JO JEPSEN

We can serve others. Serving others in any way is an indication of our desire to respond to the Savior's invitation to come unto Him. (In *Ensign*, Nov. 1992, 77.)

JOAN B. MACDONALD

Imagine doing all your work or good deeds as if to or for the Savior. Where is there room for feelings of competition or proving? When your work or service are done and they are good, they are just that. Good. And you don't feel pride, for you've only been a vehicle, a conduit for the Lord. You feel privileged, you feel humble, and you feel grateful. (*Holiness of Everyday Life*, 93.)

Chieko N. Okazaki

When our hearts are centered on the Savior, we don't have to drag ourselves to do good works. They spring up generously and abundantly. They don't fatigue us or frighten us or drain our energy. They give us energy. They make us want to do more. And simultaneously, we become less attached to what we do because we see that it is truly the Savior working through us. (*Aloha!* 77.)

It is the desire in individual hearts that powers not only small, individual acts of service, but also the great acts that become mass movements and even revolutions. You have that power, too. (In *Ensign*, May 1992, 95.)

If your service is starting to feel like a job, then you need to change things to get the joy back. (*Cat's Cradle*, 42.)

Virginia H. Pearce

It seems that every task I do . . . becomes ennobled if I do it in the spirit of an offering to God. (In *Best of Women's Conference*, 430.)

Belle S. Spafford

A conception of excellence . . . should imbue the volunteer in her free-will service, . . . just as it should in any other activity in which she

may engage. (In *Relief Society Magazine*, Nov. 1960, 713–14.)

Just as there should be excellence and full intent of heart in the performance of free-will service, so it is equally important that it be discriminately rendered and wisely directed; otherwise it could be unfair both to the giver and the recipient, also to the cause one is trying to serve. (In *Relief Society Magazine*, Nov. 1960, 714.)

Service performed in the spirit of conversion to and love for the Master's cause and in obedience to eternal and righteous principles brings to one a fullness of joy. . . . Such joy is not the reward of superficial, spare-time, begrudgingly given performance; such joy is reserved for those who enter into the work with full purpose of heart. (In *Relief Society Magazine*, Nov. 1955, 721.)

Giving of Self

Afton J. Day

Remove your bushel, lengthen your fuse, or otherwise get fired up, because whether you are at work, at home, or at church, the positive effect you have on others will be limited to the warmth and light you generate yourself. (*Coming Up*, 120.)

Mary Ellen Edmunds

Love without service, like faith without works, is DEAD! (In *LDS Speaker's Sourcebook*, 434.)

JOY F. EVANS

Almost everyone can do or be something for someone else in need. (In *Ensign*, May 1989, 75.)

CAMILLA EYRING KIMBALL

Anything we can do for Christ's cause in bringing the people of the earth to recognize him as their Savior is insignificant compared with what he has done for us, but it is our challenge. We must serve well. (*Writings*, 82.)

KATE L. KIRKHAM

When we accept more fully the attention of our Savior to our life and to our every need, when we acknowledge that he knows the desires of our hearts, when we remember to seek first the kingdom of God, we will have ample substance to impart. (In *BYU Speeches*, 12 Apr. 1994, 146.)

MAREN M. MOURITSEN

Somehow, some way, it is significant and important that we get outside of ourselves; that we not be so overwhelmingly consumed by our own self-interests. When that happens, you will be willing to deny yourselves of all ungodliness and love God with all your might, mind, and strength. (In *BYU Speeches*, 2 Apr. 1996, 201.)

KATHLEEN "CASEY" NULL

When our hearts are full our vision is clear. We can see the needs of others and feed sheep. If we are empty we cannot see the needs of others, we cannot see beyond our own needs. (*Where Are We Going?* 128.)

LOUISE Y. ROBISON

It is required that each person do his best, and all of his best, for only the very best is enough in the service of God. (In *Relief Society Magazine*, Dec. 1925, 651.)

ELIZA R. SNOW

How much better—how much nobler the principle of habituating yourselves to derive pleasure by contributing to the happiness of those around you than to seek it in the indulgence of that little selfishness of feeling which extends no farther and has no other object than mere personal gratification. (*Personal Writings*, 68–69.)

BELLE S. SPAFFORD

The gospel of Jesus Christ encompasses all that is good. Charity toward one's fellows is part and parcel of the gospel of Christ. The sister filled with the spirit of testimony is impelled toward seeking after objects of charity and administering to their wants. (In *Relief Society Magazine*, Nov. 1953, 717.)

M. CATHERINE THOMAS

Cease searching for that elusive self-fulfillment and consciously, deliberately, give to others what we, ourselves, hunger for most. (In *Women and the Power*, 189.)

PAULA THOMAS

When we discover what we could do to lighten someone else's load we should not walk but run to accomplish our mission. (In *Finding the Light*, 73.)

EMMELINE B. WELLS

How necessary are good works to the complete life of a Saint of God; the performance of good works is something to be desired: if our part in life be ever so lowly, our means of doing good for others ever so limited, with what we have in our charge we may devote ourselves to accomplishing some good work. (In *Woman's Exponent*, 15 Apr. 1877, 171.)

HELEN MAR WHITNEY

Every one of us have a mission upon this earth, and it is only the willing hands and hearts, and those who will sacrifice *self* to the good of others that will gain an everlasting triumph, and be crowned to reign throughout the glorious eternities to come. (*Woman's View*, 478.)

Serving in Church Callings

AFTON J. DAY

I challenge you to look at your next assignment in terms of an opportunity to get closer to one or more of your Father in Heaven's children and, as a result, to get closer to your Father in Heaven. (*Coming Up*, 120.)

When we magnify our callings the callings cease to be a source of irritation and become instead a source of inspiration. (*Coming Up*, 120.)

SUSA YOUNG GATES

No matter what your station or calling in life may be, yours or mine, if we are not as happy in performing the smallest necessary task as we would be to accept the honors of the world, we have not chosen the better part. (In *Young Woman's Journal*, Jan. 1895, 275.)

The field is always white for the harvest, and the laborers are always few. And there is a place for every man just as big and as great as is the man who is to fill that place. (In *Improvement Era*, Oct. 1905, 912.)

MICHAELENE P. GRASSLI

The Lord knows us better than we do. We may not feel qualified for a calling in ways we think we should be, but he knows that either there is something we need to learn or we have something that's needed at the time. Probably both! We grow into our callings. When we accept opportunities to serve as they are offered to us, we are accepting opportunities to grow. (*LeaderTalk*, 4.)

Fear is a common response to a new calling. Fear even causes some people to decline serving. But as Paul wrote to Timothy, fear is not of God. Instead, his gifts of power, love, and sound minds are strengths on which we can draw for courage to go forward. (*LeaderTalk*, 1.)

PATRICIA T. HOLLAND

The Lord uses us *because* of our unique personalities and differences rather than in spite of them. (In *BYU Speeches*, 17 Jan. 1989, 73.)

ELAINE L. JACK

I find many parallels with building a temple and fulfilling a calling. We begin with bare ground, and we start to work. We survey the situation, pray for inspiration, thoughtfully formulate plans, send them for review, adjust, and plan again. We firm up a foundation and then add walls, a roof, and even gardens. Each administration builds on the solid bedrock of the past. (In *Ensign*, May 1997, 74.)

CHIEKO N. OKAZAKI

Our real calling to be a compassionate Christian came when we stepped out of the waters of baptism. . . . We don't need a bishop's assignment to be kind. We don't need to sign up to be thoughtful. We don't need to be sustained by our wards to be sensitive. Rejoice in the power you have within you from Christ to be a nucleus of love, forgiveness, and compassion. (In *Ensign*, Nov. 1991, 89.)

VIRGINIA H. PEARCE

Callings and assignments are easy ways to become involved in the lives of others. Paradoxically, as we concentrate on the needs of others,

our own needs become less controlling. (In *Ensign*, Nov. 1993, 80.)

BELLE S. SPAFFORD

The Lord's . . . work must go on. Its progress depends upon the strength we lend it. . . . Each of us is called to a particular work because of some strength we possess. It is our responsibility to accept his calls, to grow in his service to such stature that our weaknesses and our limitations will not impede the progress of his work. (*Today's World*, 67.)

PEGGY ST. CYR

There are times when we are reluctant to accept a calling because we feel we do not have the training, the background, or the expertise to do well in a particular area. We need to realize that the Lord will provide ways for us to learn and grow so that we might fulfill those callings. (*Conversion to Commitment*, 51.)

Every calling is a blessing, an opportunity. Certainly we enjoy some more than others, but each one allows us the chance to grow and change in one way or another, and the Lord is far more cognizant of our needs than we are. He knows of the weaknesses we need to overcome, the talents we need to develop, the understanding that needs to expand. (*Conversion to Commitment*, 54.)

LEAH D. WIDTSOE

It is useless for anybody to try to do very much in this Church without the assistance of the Lord. (In *Improvement Era*, Aug. 1923, 921.)

Sin and Temptation

MARILYN ARNOLD

To give up sins may be a greater sacrifice than to give up kingdoms. (*Sweet Is the Word*, 150.)

We want salvation, and we long for purity, but too often we do not truly wish to change, to "give away" our sins—even to know God. (*Sweet Is the Word*, 150.)

ELAINE CANNON

Sin is forbidden by God because it is hurtful. It is not hurtful because it is forbidden. The best counsel you can get is not to sin. (*Bell Ringer*, 48.)

SHERI L. DEW

It is easy to let the blinding glare of the adversary's enticements distract us from the light of Christ. (In *Ensign*, Nov. 1999, 97.)

MARY ELLEN EDMUNDS

We could love more if we sinned less, because sin drains our batteries. (*Love Is a Verb*, 7.)

MARIE K. HAFEN

Once sin's swift current carries us downstream, we can't always just turn around at will and swim back, against the current, to our point of beginning. (In *BYU Speeches*, 9 May 1995, 171.)

CAMILLA EYRING KIMBALL

There is no place so high that it is beyond difficulty or temptation. (*Writings*, 27.)

ANN N. MADSEN

We may be enticed in opposite directions in a tug-of-war between light and darkness, but we are always the tie-breakers. (In *Every Good Thing*, 310.)

Even when we can't see the light clearly, we can always move away from the darkness. (In *Every Good Thing*, 310.)

BETTE S. MOLGARD

The power of the Lamb of God gives us a full suit of armor to fight the forces of evil during our personal battles. (*Everyday Battles*, 124.)

We all fight the same battles against discouragement, fear, priority choices, addictions, gossip, and perfectionism. What many of us are not aware of, however, is that these familiar battles all originate as subtle snares of the adversary. Like a group relishing the aroma while walking past a bakery, we don't even realize that we have been deliberately distracted. (*Everyday Battles*, 3.)

CHIEKO N. OKAZAKI

We can give our lives piece by piece into captivity until we no longer have the power to wrench it away again. (In *Ensign*, Nov. 1996, 89.)

When we're trying to do our best and we make a mistake, it is not the same thing as being guilty of a sin. The difference between a mistake and a sin lies in two characteristics: first, you must know that one choice is right and another is wrong; and second, you must have the ability to choose between them. (*Cat's Cradle*, 108.)

BARBARA B. SMITH

Each of us has or will have our times of trial. . . . The tests, whenever they come or whatever they are, force upon us this choice: Can we walk in faith and by strict obedience, or will we put aside the things of the Lord in favor of the earthly options offered by the great Tempter? (*Grandmothering*, 111–12.)

We rarely succumb to temptation in one overpowering moment. The strength of living by a principle is built line upon line, time upon time, of facing a moment of challenge and responding appropriately. Every important choice is the inevitable result of a hundred earlier choices. (In *BYU Speeches*, 16 Feb. 1982, 92.)

ELIZA R. SNOW

How strangely is the human countenance changed when the powers of darkness reign over the empire of the heart! (*Personal Writings*, 80.)

PEGGY ST. CYR

If we pray, study the scriptures, heed the words of the prophet and of the other General Authorities, attend meetings, obey the Lord's commandments—in other words, if we stay close to the Lord, we keep Satan at bay. If our lives are built upon the foundation of the gospel, Satan has little power over us. (*Conversion to Commitment*, 16.)

We must strengthen ourselves continually so that the devil's efforts will be weak and futile against our will to resist. He can tempt us only as far as we allow him to, and if we stay spiritually strong, the Lord helps us to resist. (*Conversion to Commitment*, 16.)

The power of prayer is our greatest weapon against the power of Satan. (*Conversion to Commitment*, 16.)

CAROL B. THOMAS

Every time you pray or bear testimony or stand for the right, you shut down the powers of evil in your life. (In *Ensign*, May 1999, 93.)

HELEN MAR WHITNEY

The sorrows and privations and all the persecutions endured by the Saints of God are light, when compared with the punishment of a guilty conscience. (*Woman's View*, 223.)

Single Adults

JOYCE BACA

The single life is so much more than waiting to be married. It is a time to get to know, love, and appreciate ourselves and our Father in Heaven. (*Divorce*, 97.)

MARION JANE CAHOON

As a single person, I've never been particularly depressed that my garden hasn't yielded a bridal bouquet yet. Instead of focusing on the flowers that aren't there, I've chosen to truly savor the flowers that have bloomed. . . . I have a life like my mother's English country garden—full of drifts and banks and spots of variety, full of spiritual harvest, and some stubborn weeds that keep me on my knees. (In *Singular Life*, 74.)

JOAN OKELBERRY CLISSOLD

One of the most difficult adjustments for me as a single person was to find meaning in the role I play rather than wishing for a different role. . . . Now, it is much clearer to me that exaltation is an individual process, achievable through a variety of roles. (In *Singular Life*, 175.)

KAREN LYNN DAVIDSON

A true adult, whether she is married or single, establishes as happy a life as her opportunities allow, cultivates a close relationship with her Father in Heaven, and does not wait for another person to make her happy. (*Thriving*, 44.)

GENEVIEVE DEHOYOS

Our Lord is so loving and kind that the promise is given that if we qualify, even though we have no [worthy] spouse at our side, we will be given to a worthy one and allowed to pass through the gate to reside with God forever. (*Stewardship*, 103.)

MARY ELLEN EDMUNDS

What seems critical to me . . . is not whether I am married or single, but that I am striving towards being perfect: whole, complete, and pure, prepared for what God has in mind for me. (In *Singular Life*, 151.)

FLORENCE S. JACOBSEN

You girls who feel you should have married by this time and are not married: there is much you can do. . . . Give yourself to other people. Give yourself to the Church. Give yourself to your own relatives and family. Make yourself as attractive as possible. Read books. Become educated. Learn everything there is to learn. Forget about your greatest desire of being married, but live worthy for that temple marriage, and you will be prepared for whatever blessing the Lord has for you. (In *Ensign*, Mar. 1972, 39.)

CHIEKO N. OKAZAKI

Let us consecrate our singleness, naming it specifically, to God. . . . What could the Lord do with our singleness if we offered it to him instead of complaining about it, suffering over it, or apologizing for it? (*Disciples*, 90.)

Singleness is not a sickness, a sin, or a problem. Single people are not broken, and they do not need to be fixed. (*Disciples*, 90.)

SHEILA OLSEN

The advice I would give to any woman . . . is to assume responsibility for your own emotional welfare. . . . In the final analysis, we alone are responsible for our own well-being, together with a loving Heavenly Father, and we alone must take charge of our own feelings of self-worth. Along with that, we also have a responsibility to reach out in love and service to others. (In *Women of Wisdom*, 47.)

CAROLYN J. RASMUS

Too often, singles in the Church . . . say they have no family. But we all have and are a part of a family. . . . They include our "genealogy families"—our parents and siblings . . . ; our "gospel families"—members of the Church . . . ; and our "neighborhood families," who . . . can be the first to whom we turn when we need help, friendship, or just a kind word. (In *Ensign*, Mar. 1988, 48.)

BARBARA B. SMITH

Even if a woman is without a family to share her home, she can build a haven established on gospel principles. (In *Ensign*, Mar. 1979, 22.)

Spirituality

The Need for Spirituality

SUSA YOUNG GATES

Let your heart learn to expand and to seek first to build up the spiritual and its interests and afterwards work for the temporal. That's the way the law reads. First are given the spiritual commandments, then follow all the promises of temporal blessings and prosperity. (In *Young Woman's Journal*, Sept. 1895, 569.)

MICHAELENE P. GRASSLI

The human spirit thrives on love, knowledge of its origin, and teachings of a spiritual nature. It is important that we provide a favorable environment for spiritual growth and the peace that will accompany it. This peace I speak of will result in quiet assurances even in the midst of worldly pressures and turmoil. (In *Ensign*, Nov. 1988, 78.)

AMY HARDISON

With spirituality, we have greater wisdom in disciplining our children. We have a greater love within our marriage and have a greater ability for unselfishness and service for our husbands. We find greater joy and fulfillment in all we do. And spirituality creates inner strength. (*How to Feel Great*, 90.)

Developing spirituality needs to be high on our list. Spirituality will help us resist the temptations of Satan. It will put us in touch with the Holy Ghost for personal revelation. And it will increase our level of faith. (*How to Feel Great*, 90.)

ELAINE L. JACK

When the Lord says "walk with me" (Moses 6:34), He is asking us to become more spiritual by being obedient to His word. Developing spirituality is critical to our eternal progress. (In *Ensign*, May 1994, 15.)

SHERRIE JOHNSON

Too often society has tagged spirituality with dull, overpious, unsmiling, no-enjoyment associations. But if we look at the lives of righteous people, analyze the beautiful, exciting world the Lord has created for us, we soon realize these tags are part of Satan's work. Everything—*everything*—in life becomes more enjoyable, more exciting, more meaningful when we

concentrate on the spiritual and gain the companionship of the Holy Ghost. (*Spiritually Centered*, 6.)

ARDETH GREENE KAPP

Just as the Lord sent the sea gulls to destroy the crickets, He has provided safety and protection for you and me. Spirituality allows us to have the Spirit of the Lord with us, and when we do, we will never be deceived. (In *Ensign*, Nov. 1990, 94.)

When our time is spent in the accumulation of experiences that nourish the spirit, we see with different glasses things that others do not see and cannot understand. (*Joy of the Journey*, 9.)

AMY BROWN LYMAN

It is religion, spirituality, and faith which help people to understand the sacredness of human personality and the doctrine of the Fatherhood of God and the brotherhood of man, and which help them to face the vicissitudes of life. (In *Relief Society Magazine*, Nov. 1941, 767.)

It is evident that there is need to work not only for economic recovery and for health, but also for moral and spiritual recovery—for moral and spiritual rearmament. (In *Relief Society Magazine*, Nov. 1939, 777–78.)

JOAN B. MACDONALD

We are pitchers, not fountains; we simply have nothing to offer without frequent trips to the well. (*Holiness of Everyday Life*, 44.)

CHIEKO N. OKAZAKI

Rather than think of spiritual life as a separate room, let's think of it as paint on the walls of all the rooms, or maybe a scent in the air that drifts through the whole house— . . . becoming part of the air we breathe. Our spiritual lives should *be* our lives, not just a separate part of our lives. (*Lighten Up!* 173.)

LOUISE Y. ROBISON

Spirituality is the only power that keeps human beings steady and unshaken when overwhelming sorrow comes. Outside of spiritual interpretation there is no solution for the problems of life. (In *Relief Society Magazine*, Nov. 1938, 768.)

BARBARA B. SMITH

We must fortify ourselves so that when hard or lonely moments come, we can call upon God for his strength, wisdom, and vision, that we might act according to righteous principles. (In *Ensign*, Nov. 1979, 108.)

BELLE S. SPAFFORD

Spiritual strength, faith in God, and a reliance on his providences are essential to well being. (*Today's World*, 136.)

M. CATHERINE THOMAS

Many Saints in the Church hunger and thirst after greater righteousness and spiritual experience, just as our father Abraham did (see Abraham 1:2). The hunger is our birthright. (In *Temples*, 490.)

WENDY L. WATSON

Distinguishing good from evil, light from darkness, is critical in these latter days. . . . Our spiritual wattage will often be increased or diminished, depending on the distinctions we make and hold to. (In *Every Good Thing*, 39.)

LEAH D. WIDTSOE

The spiritual activities of life are always those which give the deepest, most lasting joy and satisfaction. (In *Improvement Era*, May 1938, 269.)

BARBARA W. WINDER

Qualities of spirituality do not come without effort. Like any other talent with which we are blessed, they must be constantly practiced. (In *Ensign*, Nov. 1988, 88.)

Growing in Spirituality

JANETTE HALES BECKHAM

Growing up spiritually requires us to see beyond our own desires and to enlarge our way of seeing things. We not only have to let go of our selfishness but sometimes let go of things we want very badly to come to understand our Heavenly Father's point of view. (In *Ensign*, May 1994, 96.)

JANET E. BUCK

I have discovered that you don't "find time" for anything. You make time. This is especially true when speaking of spiritual nourishment. Often we do not recognize our spiritual hunger pangs for what they really are. We give them other labels: discouragement, depression, anger, resentment, loneliness, self-pity. Yet these are all indications of spiritual starvation. (In *Ensign*, Apr. 1991, 42.)

CAROLE OSBORNE COLE

There are any number of ways to feed ourselves spiritually. Basic, of course, is attendance at Sunday meetings. Partaking of the sacrament is necessary to spirituality. Individual scripture study, fasting and prayer, education days or weeks, reading books by General Authorities, and keeping a journal are all ways to keep our spirituality viable and the motivating force it should be in our lives. [We] feast spiritually from a visit to the temple. (In *Building a Love*, 27.)

AFTON J. DAY

Success builds upon success, and common sense tells me that as we increase our spirituality life becomes more stimulating, if not easier, and our capacity for love becomes greater. (*Perfect Wife*, 6.)

When you learn unconditional love from a spiritual interaction with your Father in Heaven, who is the source of love, a change takes place that is more than a mere assimilation of ideas. Your emotions are educated, not only your intellect. While it will still take practice and a conscious effort to put your knowledge into practice, you are less resistant to change because you are moving away from your "natural man" and toward your spiritual self. (*Coming Up*, 74.)

Each level of progression up the ladder of spirituality brings increased rewards—the kind of rewards you can feel and use in your everyday life, not just an added wing to your heavenly mansion. (*Perfect Wife*, 6.)

SHERI L. DEW

There are many ways to draw near, seek, ask, and knock. If, for example, your prayers offered to Heavenly Father in the name of Christ have become a little casual, would you recommit yourself to meaningful prayer, offered in unrushed solitude and with a repentant heart? . . . Tonight would be a wonderful time to begin. (In *Ensign*, Nov. 1997, 92.)

The best way I know to strengthen our personal testimonies and protect ourselves from evil is to seek to have as many experiences with the Lord as possible. (In *Arms of His Love*, 393.)

We are told that if we ask, we will receive; if we inquire, the mysteries of God will be unfolded to us; and if we build our lives upon the rock of Jesus Christ, neither earth nor hell will prevail against us. (In *Arms of His Love*, 393.)

MARJORIE P. HINCKLEY

There is something about spirituality that is central to the life of a woman.

I do not mean the kind of spirituality that only takes you to church on Sunday. Sitting in church will not necessarily make you into a Christian anymore than sitting in a garage will make you into a car. I am talking about the kind of spirituality that makes you behave like a child of God.

I am talking about the kind of spirituality that breathes reverence into every act and deed.

I am talking about the spirituality that makes you loving and grateful, and forgiving, and patient, and gentle, and long-suffering. . . .

I am talking about the kind of spirituality that compels you to get in touch with your Heavenly Father every single day of your life. (In *Glimpses*, 23–24.)

ELAINE L. JACK

Our spiritual growth comes from seeing the Lord's hand in our lives. There is little comparison between a worldly check register and our account in the Lamb's Book of Life. (In *Ensign*, Aug. 1994, 66.)

The physical characteristics that we inherit from our parents are obvious. The spiritual characteristics we inherit from our heavenly parents have to be developed. You have been born with all the godlike gifts that Christ has. They are within you, but you have to choose to cultivate and develop them. Spiritual growth doesn't just happen without our best efforts. (In *Ensign*, Nov. 1989, 87–88.)

Without question, those progressing eternally are those on the straight and narrow; they are spiritual and charitable. (In *Ensign*, May 1994, 16.)

Spirituality is all about feeling the Spirit of God, wanting it with us, sharing the Spirit with others, and heeding its prompting. (In *Ensign*, May 1994, 16.)

SHERRIE JOHNSON

We need to recognize self-discipline as a basic part of spirituality. In order to grow close to our Father in Heaven, we must overcome the things of this world. We must have spirits that are stronger than our bodies, stronger than mortal appetites and passions. (*Spiritually Centered*, 19.)

CAMILLA EYRING KIMBALL

Of all we learn in life, the single most important knowledge we can attain is a firm testimony of the Lord Jesus Christ as our Savior and an understanding of the path he would have us follow. (*Writings*, 86.)

AMY BROWN LYMAN

We are sometimes inclined to think that if we go to Church and testify vigorously of the blessings that we receive, that that is all that is necessary, but there are a great many things that are fundamental to a spiritual life and we cannot reach the highest development unless we live up to the standards of the gospel set for us by the Savior. (In *Relief Society Magazine*, June 1922, 322.)

The women who have accomplished things in the Relief Society must be women who have their minds always set on a very high goal. Those who work for the highest in life cannot afford to entertain any thoughts but those that are the most elevating. (In *Relief Society Magazine*, June 1922, 324.)

If we would get in the habit of committing to memory some of the splendid scriptural sayings that we read all too lightly; . . . it would set our minds to thinking along the lines that would develop us and help us to be splendid leaders in Zion. (In *Relief Society Magazine*, June 1922, 324.)

The greatest asset to any home is spirituality. It is the most dynamic force for good that we know anything about. Real spirituality, however, does not just happen, it is not a thing separate and apart from our every day lives, to be had and enjoyed at will. It comes as a natural result of faithful, consistent, righteous daily living and obedience to God's laws. (In *Relief Society Magazine*, Mar. 1936, 143.)

BETTE S. MOLGARD

Taking time to ponder allows important whisperings to settle in our mind long enough to capture them. Taking the time to write down our impressions, then praying to make sure we understood correctly and asking if there is anything else will increase our knowledge a hundredfold. (*Everyday Battles*, 129.)

At the conclusion of a blessing of any kind, write what you can remember and then ponder, pray, and write some more. Sacred experiences written down following the same pattern can blossom into powerful spiritual experiences. (*Everyday Battles*, 129.)

Banish the darkness from your mind and let your Savior fill it with light. Pray *before* you read your scriptures and feel the Lord fill your mind with the light of understanding. Listen to the whisperings of the Spirit, then act on those promptings. Pray *before* you go to the temple, then bask in the flood of light that will fill your mind and spirit. The strength of even a small piece of that light is able to lock out discouragement. Darkness cannot tolerate light. (*Everyday Battles*, 26.)

MARGARET D. NADAULD

All of us need to have more reverence in our lives, more holiness, more times of quiet and peace and calm. We need a place where our souls can be nourished and tutored and blessed. Temples are such places.

Home can be such a place. (*Write Back Soon!* 97.)

CHIEKO N. OKAZAKI

We don't have to be in a sacred place for spiritual things to happen. The Sacred Grove was just a stand of trees before Joseph Smith walked into it. It became sacred because of what happened there. (*Lighten Up!* 73.)

Heavenly Father doesn't save up all his spiritual experiences just for sacrament meeting or the temple. (*Lighten Up!* 73.)

CAROLYN J. RASMUS

Spirituality . . . requires daily effort. It also requires time and practice. It means acting when we feel impressed to—not in big, grand, glorious ways, but responding to small impressions that come. (In *Woman's Choices*, 40.)

Learning to live by the Spirit . . . suggests that we need to expect that we can receive inspiration. (In *Woman's Choices*, 40.)

MARY ELLEN SMOOT

The stronger our spiritual footings, the greater our capacity to build the kingdom—and the greater our joy. As you write your family histories, as you tend to lost sheep, as you nurture the seedlings of faith in others, you will find yourself saying, "Is it already the end of the day?" rather than "Will this day ever end?" (In *Ensign*, Nov. 1997, 13.)

BELLE S. SPAFFORD

There is no excuse for robbing the Lord's day of its sanctity. Work should be so planned and affairs so managed that on the Sabbath we may lay aside our week-day tasks, pay our devotions to our Heavenly Father, and obtain needed physical and spiritual refreshment. (In *Relief Society Magazine*, Oct. 1943, 613.)

A proper observance of the duties and devotions of the Sabbath Day will give us the best rest that we can obtain, as well as a great renewal of spiritual strength. (In *Relief Society Magazine*, Oct. 1943, 613.)

To attend sacrament meeting on the Sabbath should be regarded by Latter-day Saints not as a burdensome requirement, but as a glorious privilege. The sacrament meeting provides opportunity for us to partake of the sacrament, thereby renewing our covenants with our Heavenly Father and testifying that we are willing to serve Him and keep His commandments; it is a period wherein we may worship the Father in humility and prayer; it is an hour of repentance, and a time for meditation upon God's great plan of life and salvation. (In *Relief Society Magazine*, Oct. 1943, 613.)

M. CATHERINE THOMAS

Many Saints in the Church hunger and thirst after greater righteousness and spiritual experience. . . . It is common to discourage such people out of fear that they will go off the track somehow in their pursuit, and of course that danger continually presents itself. . . . But the opposite risk is that members will struggle in the foothills of spiritual experience. (*Selected Writings*, 155.)

Susan L. Warner

Each of us has memories of spiritual feelings. . . . Remembering our spiritual feelings draws us to our Heavenly Father and to His Son, Jesus Christ. It gives us a sense of our true identity. . . . Recalling spiritual feelings reminds us of who we really are. (In *Ensign*, May 1996, 78.)

Success

Amy Hardison

Success, more than anything else, is the consistent advancement toward predetermined goals. It is a journey and not a destination. (*How to Feel Great*, 21.)

Sharlene Wells Hawkes

Success is simple. It begins—and ends—on the inside. (*Living*, 240.)

There are a great many things in life that we cannot control, but we can determine how successful we *feel* by choosing what kind of success we are after. Achieving inner peace and being at peace with the world *is success*. (*Living*, 240.)

Marilynne Todd Linford

Failing doesn't make a person a failure. Failing means that we have discovered one way something won't work. If we think of ourselves as failures, we are—in our own minds. Failing can be a firm stepping stone.

If nine out of ten things fail, then we must have the courage to try ten times as many things. Discovering one way something won't work makes the path to success a little closer. (*Woman Fulfilled*, 11.)

Amy Brown Lyman

Wisely has it been said that effort can be fully evaluated, not by what the hours, but what the years and the centuries say. (In *Relief Society Magazine*, Mar. 1944, 139.)

Virginia H. Pearce

Success is an affliction to the soul unless it is recognized for what it is—God's working in our lives. (In *Best of Women's Conference*, 433.)

With success, as well as adversity, we pray that our performance will be consecrated for the welfare of our souls. . . . Then desperate days refine us rather than destroy us. And [good] days become days of worship and gratitude rather than days of pride and boasting. (In *Best of Women's Conference*, 433.)

LOUISE Y. ROBISON

We accomplish in any line of endeavor only in proportion to the study and thought given to that subject. (In *Relief Society Magazine*, May 1932, 319.)

Thought and study must be given to our simplest task if we are to succeed. Each adult person should acknowledge the opportunities in life, and give time to each in proportion to its value. (In *Relief Society Magazine*, May 1932, 319.)

BARBARA B. SMITH

Many times the solutions to our problems await only our discovery that we already have the key to the answer. The need is for us to learn to use it effectively. (In *Ensign*, Nov. 1982, 83.)

Teaching

ANNETTE PAXMAN BOWEN

Any teacher knows that the most valuable teaching is done one-to-one. Those are the moments when a teacher can have the greatest influence. (*Doughnuts, Letters*, 85.)

ARDETH GREENE KAPP

It was the Master Teacher who opened the gate, allowing each of us to learn the lessons, even the difficult ones, that would ensure our continued growth, allowing us the opportunity to reach our divine destiny. He marked the way and invited us to follow. (*More Miracles*, 59–60.)

I believe that if a teacher is ever to be allowed into the private, sacred realm of a child's heart, where lasting changes take place and lasting imprints are made, a sensitivity to the inner spirit of each child and a reverence for teaching moments is required. This sensitivity is difficult to teach, but is unquestionably the most important quality to be learned. (*Gentle Touch*, ix.)

A teacher can't always remove the problem and may not even help lift the load, but a teacher who really cares can avoid adding additional burdens to young shoulders often weighted down unmercifully by outside pressures. (*Gentle Touch*, 46–47.)

It is in teaching diligently that we are instructed more perfectly. (*My Neighbor*, 52.)

Bodies are born only once, but many rebirths take place as teachers gently and reverently lead their students to discover their own gifts and endowments, talents and abilities so generously bestowed by a divine Father. (*My Neighbor*, 144.)

Into the sacred realms of another's heart, the teacher must proceed reverently, with deep respect, and teach clearly and forcefully truths to which the Spirit can bear witness. (*My Neighbor*, 146.)

It is not in knowing perfectly the twenty-third Psalm and then teaching with great skill the meaning of each word that a teacher experiences the ultimate joy. It is, rather, in coming to know the Shepherd and then reverently guiding another person to that same knowledge. Only then is a teacher privileged to take part in His work, which is also our work. (*My Neighbor*, 146.)

JENNIE B. KNIGHT

The words from the lips of those who have faith in God and his son Jesus Christ, coupled with the testimony of the divine mission of Joseph Smith, when spoken will do much to substitute confidence and faith for skepticism and doubt. (In *Relief Society Magazine*, May 1935, 283.)

Words of truth directed by well prepared teachers will banish ignorance and give knowledge. (In *Relief Society Magazine*, May 1935, 283.)

Love must be the keynote in all our teachings of obedience. (In *Relief Society Magazine*, Feb. 1939, 128.)

AMY BROWN LYMAN

Teachers are considered to be greatly blessed in their field and the opportunity it gives them. . . . With this opportunity there comes . . . the responsibility of influencing human behavior and molding human lives. (In *Relief Society Magazine*, Nov. 1941, 737.)

MARGARET D. NADAULD

Christ must be at the forefront of all of our teaching, as well as the pattern for our daily life. (In *BYU Speeches*, 2 Nov. 1997, 12.)

VIRGINIA H. PEARCE

Because the daily life of people varies so much in the 160 different countries where [the Church has] organized classes, the stories and examples in the manuals may sometimes confuse the learners. Teachers can prayerfully make adaptations, always taking care that the learning activities chosen truly reflect the doctrine. (In *Ensign*, Nov. 1996, 12.)

LOUISE Y. ROBISON

It is a glorious privilege to be called to teach—not merely to tell things which one knows, but to influence people to have higher, more stimulating thoughts. Ideas have power. In the end, right ideas will rule the world and you have the privilege of helping to bring this change about. (In *Relief Society Magazine*, Nov. 1936, 688.)

In teaching the three R's, the most important are Reason, Reverence and Responsibility. (In *Relief Society Magazine*, Jan. 1939, 3.)

ELLIS R. SHIPP

We cannot give what we do not possess, nor teach what we do not know. (*While Others Slept*, 283.)

SUSAN L. WARNER

Our efforts to help our children establish a heritage of rich spiritual memories are never wasted. Sometimes, the seeds we plant may not bear fruit for years, but we may take comfort in the hope that someday the children we teach will remember how they have "received and heard" the things of the Spirit. They will remember what they know and what they have felt. They will remember their identity as children of Heavenly Father, who sent them here with a divine purpose. (In *Ensign*, May 1996, 78.)

Temples and Temple Ordinances

COLLEEN W. ASAY

It is worth every price we must pay to be able to enter and involve ourselves in the blessings of the House of the Lord. (In *Wisdom's Paths*, 132.)

JANETTE HALES BECKHAM

As we make sacred covenants with our Heavenly Father in the temple, He promises us that we will be able to live with Him again. (In *Ensign*, May 1997, 91.)

Just as the early pioneers sacrificed to make their way to the Rocky Mountains, modern pioneers like . . . all of you are also on the trail to a mountain—"the mountain of the Lord's house" (Isa. 2:2). That's the way the prophet Isaiah referred to latter-day temples. (In *Ensign*, May 1997, 91.)

ELAINE CANNON

The keys to eternity and the gladness of being part of a bit of heaven on earth are available to any person who becomes prepared for entry inside the sacred walls of a temple in that person's part of the world. (*Sunshine*, 40.)

SUSA YOUNG GATES

Perhaps there is no other principle which so antagonizes the powers of evil as that of temple building and temple work. (In *Young Woman's Journal*, Jan. 1909, 25.)

PATRICIA T. HOLLAND

On those days when I feel off center, out of focus, or off balance, when I feel that I don't have enough time, insight, or strength to solve my problems, I know that comfort is as close as the temple. (In *LDS Women's Treasury*, 104.)

The temple provides protection and it provides patterns and promises that can settle and strengthen and stabilize us, however anxious our times. (In *LDS Women's Treasury*, 94.)

ELAINE L. JACK

In the temple, we sisters receive all the blessings of the priesthood, not by ordination but by being as fully endowed with the power of the priesthood as are the men. Both men and women wear the garments of the holy priesthood and make the same sacred covenants with God. They both perform priesthood ordinances, having authority to do so. (*Eye to Eye*, 138.)

The endowment itself is an endless opportunity for schooling. . . . Sacred and important information as to the nature and functioning of godhood is revealed to us in the endowment ceremony, and we are imbued with spiritual power. (*Eye to Eye*, 137–38.)

Making covenants is essential to receiving an endowment of spiritual power and knowledge from God. The temple is a house of learning where the Spirit teaches, when we seek that Spirit. (*Eye to Eye*, 137.)

ARDETH GREENE KAPP

In the temple we participate in ordinances and covenants that span the distance between heaven and earth. They prepare us to one day return to God's presence and enjoy the blessings of eternal families and eternal life. (In *Ensign*, May 1992, 79.)

ANN N. MADSEN

The temple is the Lord's university. . . . To qualify [for entrance] the Lord asks only that you bring a broken heart and a contrite spirit to his altar. You must be willing to consecrate yourself, with the integrity to keep sacred things in your heart and with a tremendous desire to serve the Lord Jesus Christ. (In *Best of Women's Conference*, 349.)

The temple is the bridge of love between this world and the next. (In *Best of Women's Conference*, 362.)

BETTE S. MOLGARD

Nowhere on earth does eternity link hands with mortality more than in our holy temples. (*Everyday Battles*, 116.)

The peaceful setting of the temple provides us with a clear view of what the world would look like if everyone set aside Satan's yardstick and clung tightly to the Savior's. (*Everyday Battles*, 116.)

VIRGINIA H. PEARCE

Eternal perspective is what the temple offers us. . . . The more clear our understanding of the big picture, the more energy we will have to live the details. (In *Arise*, 270.)

MARY ELLEN SMOOT

The temple is the house of God, and as a Relief Society we are committed to helping each other back home. The temple helps us become women of covenant rather than women of the world. (*Sweet Is the Work*, 173.)

CAROL B. THOMAS

The spiritual atmosphere of the temple curbs our appetite for worldly things. (In *Ensign*, May 1999, 13.)

M. CATHERINE THOMAS

The Savior's at-one-ment is another word for the sealing power. By the power of the at-one-ment, the Lord draws and seals his children to himself in the holy temples. (In *Temples*, 388.)

This . . . is the temple endowment: having been cast out, to search diligently according to the revealed path, and at last to be clasped in the arms of Jesus (see Mormon 5:11). (In *Temples*, 389.)

EMMELINE B. WELLS

There is, in the Temple, a heavenly influence so exalting and inspiring that one seems to be near the other shore. We ought to be willing to sacrifice our worldly interests once in a while to do some of this great work. (In *Woman's Exponent*, 15 Sept. 1874, 55.)

LEAH D. WIDTSOE

The obligations which you assume in the ordinances of the Temple are all uplifting and for your own enrichment, and are not difficult to carry out. You may not comprehend the full meaning of all the ceremonies at first, but repeated visits will make them clearer and more enjoyable. Each time you go in the right spirit, you will have "light added unto light" and your soul will be truly fed and uplifted. (In *Improvement Era*, Apr. 1938, 220.)

ZINA D. H. YOUNG

Think of the affinity between the dead and us. They are looking to us for deliverance. Shall we not help them? (In *Woman's Exponent*, 1 and 15 Jan. 1895, 226.)

Testimony

The Blessing of Testimony

JUTTA BAUM BUSCHE

As I walk down our street and pass all the beautifully tended homes of my neighbors, I am inclined to think that all is well with them, that they do not struggle as I do. It is through the honest testimonies they bear that I learn to see their hearts, and we become united in feelings of love. (In *Best of Women's Conference*, 72.)

SUSANNE JOHNSON DAVIS

Our testimony of the gospel is one of our most precious possessions. It will bring us closer to our Savior and guide our thoughts and actions. A testimony is of the utmost importance. (In *BYU Speeches*, 5 Aug. 1997, 350.)

CLAUDIA FUHRIMAN ELIASON

A testimony can bring peace, joy, and assurance. It should also bring self-respect, for at the very heart and core of each of our testimonies should be that sure knowledge that we are literally sons and daughters of our Heavenly Father, each of us a child of God. . . . Among all the peoples of the world, we know who we are, whence we have come, and why we are here. (In *Woman's Choices*, 69–70.)

ELAINE L. JACK

Personal faith is a reality you need in your life. It is a source of strength and comfort and resolution under the happiest and most trying moments of your life. If you want to get a life, get a testimony. (In *Ensign*, July 1995, 49.)

CAMILLA EYRING KIMBALL

Your greatest asset will be a positive conviction and testimony of the gospel of Jesus Christ. If you have a firm commitment to follow this star with unwavering trust, numerous decisions will be ready made for you. (*Writings*, 87.)

JENNIE B. KNIGHT

It has always seemed as natural to me to believe the gospel of Jesus Christ as it has for me to eat or to breathe. (In *Relief Society Magazine*, June 1928, 340–41.)

AMY BROWN LYMAN

A testimony is . . . a combination of knowledge, conviction, faith and inspiration. It is dynamic and forceful in character. . . . It is the greatest armor one can have as a protection against temptation, weakness and sin, and the greatest sustaining force in trials and tribulations. (In *Relief Society Magazine*, May 1941, 346.)

My testimony has been my anchor and my stay, my satisfaction in times of joy and gladness, my comfort in times of sorrow and discouragement. (In *Elect Ladies*, 142.)

JOAN B. MACDONALD

When we bear testimony to one another, we need to do more than tell each other what we know to be true. We need to tell each other why and how we know it. . . . Describing to each other, in testimony, the ways Heavenly Father has been involved with our lives results in a litany of God's good works—the kind of praise and worship found in the scriptures. (*Holiness of Everyday Life*, 132.)

BERTHA S. REEDER

I . . . find the fire of testimony lighting my path into a lifetime of happiness here and everlasting life hereafter. (In *Relief Society Magazine*, Sept. 1956, 577.)

LOUISE Y. ROBISON

The most vital influence in life is a calm, positive testimony that God lives and that He is really our Father. To know positively that our Father and His Son Jesus Christ did visit the earth and restore the Gospel through the Prophet Joseph Smith . . . —this knowledge is more precious than life. (In *Relief Society Magazine*, Nov. 1938, 768.)

ELIZA R. SNOW

The "testimony of Jesus" will light up a lamp that will guide my vision through the portals of immortality, and communicate to my understanding the glories of the Celestial kingdom. (In *Elect Ladies*, 40.)

BELLE S. SPAFFORD

A testimony of the truth of the gospel of Jesus Christ is a priceless possession. He who has one is indeed blessed. His life has direction and purpose. He is fortified to meet the tempests, and his soul knows peace. He has an appreciation of the true and abiding values of life, while the glittering, shallow, superficial things which challenge the efforts and waste the energies of many men, do not trouble him. He goes forth to meet each day with a love of God and man in his heart and with the calm assurance that God whom he loves also loves him and will direct his course and bless his pursuits. (*Today's World*, 19.)

The surest and strongest protective armor a child can possess is a testimony of the gospel of Jesus Christ. (In *Relief Society Magazine*, Nov. 1953, 719.)

ZINA D. H. YOUNG

We are not working under a mere belief, but we have the blessing of assurance. (In *Woman's Exponent*, 15 Nov. and 1 Dec. 1899, 74.)

Gaining a Testimony

SUSA YOUNG GATES

The thing of the utmost and deepest importance, is the obtaining of a testimony that God lives, that Jesus is His Son, and that this gospel is from God, and that Joseph Smith was the prophet of this dispensation. After this by carefully nourishing this beautiful testimony, knowledge will be added to knowledge, and light to light. (In *Young Woman's Journal*, Jan. 1896, 189.)

JAMIE GLENN

Often the beginning of knowing that the Plan is true is *desiring* to know if it is true. We can let this desire work in us *and* experiment upon the Lord's words. As we continue to make efforts, nourish our understanding, and live as if the Plan is true, our faith will be increased. (*Walk Tall*, 7.)

MARJORIE P. HINCKLEY

We must get [a testimony] through the Holy Ghost. . . . It cannot be bought with money. It can be had only when we have made ourselves worthy and have sought the Lord in humility and diligence. Then it will surely be ours. (In *Glimpses*, 7.)

There are very few big and spectacular miracles in most of our lives. But it is a quiet multitude of little miracles that makes life sweet and adds to our testimonies. (In *Glimpses*, 205.)

SARAH S. LEAVITT

The whole of Joseph's vision and what the Angel Moroni had said came to my mind in a moment. . . . This was the message . . . for me and not for me only, but for the whole world, and I considered it of more importance than anything I had ever heard before. (In *Women's Voices*, 3.)

CHERRY B. SILVER

To testify that moral living brings positive results, to say with certainty that commitment and sacrifice and paying tithing yield blessings, to witness that prayers are answered—all these testimonies come when we exercise our faith to live these principles and find that they come of God. (In *Knit Together in Love*, 4.)

BATHSHEBA W. SMITH

Teach your children to love the gospel—your sons and your daughters—so that they can have a testimony for themselves; every soul that is honest in heart may receive a testimony that they cannot deny. (In *Woman's Exponent*, vol. 34, no. 1, 7.)

ELIZA R. SNOW

To hear men testify that they had seen a holy angel—that they had listened to his voice, bearing testimony of the work that was ushering in a new dispensation; that the fullness of the gospel was to be restored and that they were commanded to go forth and declare it, thrilled my inmost soul. (In *Women of Mormondom*, 63–64.)

BELLE S. SPAFFORD

Testimony is not reserved for God's prophets alone; it is not alone for those who bear the Priesthood. It is for all God's children, his daughters as well as his sons. (In *Relief Society Magazine*, Nov. 1953, 718.)

To have a testimony contemplates that one accepts, without reservation, that Christ is the Son of God; that he came to earth to redeem God's children; that he suffered and died to atone for the sins of man; that he arose from the dead, bringing to pass the resurrection; that he will come again in his glory. . . . Testimony contemplates a full acceptance of all of the doctrines taught by Christ, and given again in this day by the Lord through the Prophet Joseph Smith. (In *Relief Society Magazine*, Nov. 1953, 717.)

EMMELINE B. WELLS

When I came up the river on the boat and standing on the top of the boat to see the prophet on the landing . . . , I knew instantly then that the gospel was true by the feeling that pervaded me from the crown of my head to the end of my fingers and toes, and every part of my body. (In *Relief Society Magazine*, Oct. 1920, 561.)

ZINA D. H. YOUNG

Seek for a testimony, as you would . . . for a diamond concealed. . . . If you will dig in the depths of your own hearts you will find, with the aid of the Spirit of the Lord, the pearl of great price, the testimony of the truth of this work. (In *Elect Ladies*, 58.)

Being Valiant in Testimony

RUTH MAY FOX

The gospel has meant everything to me. It has been my very breath, my mantle of protection against temptation, my consolation in sorrow, my joy and glory throughout all my days, and my hope of eternal life. "The Kingdom of God or nothing" has been my motto. (In *Keepers*, 49.)

SUSA YOUNG GATES

One apostatizes only from truth, not error. (In *Improvement Era*, Apr. 1905, 464.)

Men do not go to the death for a lie. If they are ready to put their lives in the breach of their statements, they have some measure of truth, you may depend upon it. (In *Improvement Era*, Mar. 1907, 349.)

MARJORIE P. HINCKLEY

My testimony of this wonderful work grows every day. . . . If I can just be one more voice to say that God lives and that this is His work, I will be satisfied. (In *Glimpses*, 1.)

CAMILLA EYRING KIMBALL

A testimony can be starved until it dies. The unhappiness of those who lose this witness strengthens my resolve to be steadfast. (*Writings*, 88.)

The first essential credential of a true Christian is a personal testimony of the divinity of Christ. Our eternal life depends on our individual testimony. (*Writings*, 86.)

LOUISE Y. ROBISON

It is not enough for us to have a testimony of the Gospel, we must do more than just know it, we must live it. (In *Relief Society Magazine*, May 1934, 293.)

How thankful we should be for the great blessing of faith and the knowledge which our Father has given us. How careful we should be to keep this precious gift. Only our own actions can deprive us of it. (In *Relief Society Magazine*, Nov. 1938, 768.)

Naomi M. Shumway

[A] little girl, . . . when asked by an evangelist which church she belonged to, answered proudly, "I'm a Mormon." "Well," he said, "and if you did not choose to be a Mormon, what would you be?" Shyly but with conviction she replied, "I'd be ashamed!" (In *Ensign*, Nov. 1979, 104.)

Emma Smith

I know Mormonism to be the truth, and [believe] the church to have been established by divine direction. I have complete faith in it. (In *Early Mormon Documents*, 1:538–39.)

Lucy Mack Smith

I often wonder to hear brethren and sisters murmur at the trifling inconveniences which they have to encounter . . . , and I think to myself, salvation is worth as much now as it was in the beginning of the work. But I find that "all like the purchase, few the price will pay." (*History of Joseph Smith*, xvii–xviii.)

Mary Fielding Smith

I would not give up the prospect of the latter-day glory for all that glitters in this world. (*Mary Fielding Smith*, 100.)

Helen Mar Whitney

I truly rejoice that I have had the privilege of being numbered with those who have come up through much tribulation and gained a knowledge for myself that this is the work of God which neither wealth nor worldly honors could tempt me to part with. (*Woman's View*, x.)

Thoughts

Janene Wolsey Baadsgaard

I admit it isn't always easy to reverse a bad mood. When I'm having a bad day or dark thoughts, I can usually change the way I feel by changing the way I think. (In *Best of Women's Conference*, 27.)

Anita R. Canfield

No one really knows how far the mind can actually go in influencing our lives. . . . It can produce great spirituality within us, and it can delineate our personal qualities to any height or depth. It can carry a soul to the point of desperation or insanity, or to the heights of accomplishment and achievement. All these are possible, depending on what and how we think. (*Self-Esteem*, 16–17.)

Karla C. Erickson

One of the traits of being in charge of one's life is being in charge of one's thoughts. Those who are in charge of their lives and thoughts are usually happy people. (*Make Time Count*, 23.)

JAMIE GLENN

If we do not decide what we will think, then the influences of the world and the subtleties of Satan will decide for us. It takes more than just not allowing negative or obscene thoughts. We must also consciously direct and control our thoughts in uplifting and positive ways. (*Walk Tall*, 71.)

SUZANNE L. HANSEN

You are the result of a lifetime of thinking. . . . Since you are in control of what you think about, you can change your life *immediately*, just by changing your thoughts. (In *Living the Legacy*, 82.)

If you want things to be different, you must be different. First, change your attitude. If you want a brighter, happier life, be a brighter, happier person. It all starts with how you think. (In *Feeling Great*, 111.)

AMY HARDISON

In addition to free agency of action, we also have the free agency of thought. We can choose what we will think and no one can take away that right unless we voluntarily relinquish it. (*How to Feel Great*, 74.)

ARDETH GREENE KAPP

The process of cleansing the vessel by eradicating inappropriate thoughts . . . requires continuous,

arduous, daily effort to control our thoughts. Satan fights with psychological warfare. . . . Our minds become the battleground. Pure thoughts are the weapons that conquer the enemy. It is not a task to be trivialized. (*Rejoice!* 103.)

CAMILLA EYRING KIMBALL

It isn't what we think we are; it is, What we think, we are. Our actions are the end result of our thoughts. "As a man thinketh in his heart, so is he." (*Writings*, 99.)

MARILYNNE TODD LINFORD

Thoughts are private routes leading anywhere we choose, from the debasing to the ennobling. Thoughts precede attitudes, which precede actions. What we think, we become. (*Woman Fulfilled*, 9.)

BETTE S. MOLGARD

When discouraging thoughts come into your mind, don't let them linger for a moment. You can say as Moses did, "Get thee hence, Satan; deceive me not." (*Everyday Battles*, 23.)

HEIDI S. SWINTON

The thoughts we fill our heads with—what we read, what we watch on television, what we talk about with our friends, what we peruse on the Internet—either enhances our communication with the Lord or interrupts it. What we think about determines much of who we are. (In *Arms of His Love*, 235.)

M. CATHERINE THOMAS

When we learn to keep the mind occupied with God's things, gradually the Spirit comes and takes up residence, bringing comfort and direction and fulfilling ancient promises. (*Selected Writings*, 217.)

You and I have absolute stewardship over our mind. We can change the contents of our mind. We can put into it what we want and what we put in has creative power over our soul. (*Selected Writings*, 268.)

The real work of living the gospel begins in the microdots of the mind, in planting mental virtue deeply, in keeping my mind firm. . . . What we sow in our minds and actions, we reap in our emotions. (In *Women and the Power*, 189.)

Time

MARY ELLEN EDMUNDS

Time is a gift . . . from God. We can't demand more, and we can't insist on less. We can't buy more, and we can't sell any. . . . Everyone in the world receives the same amount of time every day. . . . Time is our life—it's our day to prepare to be with God forever and ever. Time is given to us for that preparation, for repenting and forgiving and trying to be good and do good. (In *Every Good Thing*, 251.)

Eventually, the night will come and the day will be finished when we could have done our work. We will either have used our time well and done the things that mattered most, or we will not have done. (In *Best of Women's Conference*, 150.)

We must . . . remember that we who love the Lord have covenanted to give him time. (In *Best of Women's Conference*, 150.)

Somehow, when we do what God asks us to do, the best we can, keeping first things first, our time seems to come back to us, added upon and multiplied. It's a miracle. (In *Best of Women's Conference*, 150.)

We who love the Lord have covenanted to give him time. (In *Best of Women's Conference*, 150.)

Skills and relationships and testimony and character traits—there are a lot of things that take time. For the most part, the things in our life that matter the most will have to be attended to. We will have to budget some time—make and take some time—for them. It's a process, sometimes a lifelong process. (In *Every Good Thing*, 252.)

I don't want to mistake busyness for being effective or using time well. (In *Best of Women's Conference*, 147.)

JULIA P. M. FARNSWORTH

Punctuality is the doing of the right thing at the right time. (In *Relief Society Magazine*, June 1921, 336.)

CAMILLA EYRING KIMBALL

Time is what life is made of, and how we use our time determines what sort of life we have. The present time is the raw material out of which we make whatever we will. Do not brood over the past or dream idly over the future, but seize the instant and get your lesson from the hour. (*Writings*, 136.)

Great men have always been misers of moments. (*Writings*, 136.)

JILL C. MAJOR, LAUREN C. LEIFSON, AND HOLLIE C. BEVAN

Time is precious. . . . Time is essential to forming loving relationships. . . . People learn that they are valuable when others take time to listen to them, talk to them, and be with them. (*Encircled by Love*, 31.)

EMMA LOU THAYNE

I cannot afford to forget the value of fifteen minutes. . . . What is eternal progression but the relishing of its particulars? (*As for Me*, 26.)

Procrastination

MARY BRENTNALL

Procrastination is not only a delaying, wasteful habit in itself, but it also puts you bang up against all the difficult emergencies of life. (In *Improvement Era*, May 1949, 281.)

JANENE WOLSEY BAADSGAARD

Procrastination is the age-old answer to all life's little problems. It removes a little misery now so you can save it up and feel a whole bunch of misery later. (*Families Who Laugh*, 126.)

MARY ELLEN EDMUNDS

Procrastination is deadly. It can destroy time, energy, and other resources. And it can become a very strong habit—hard to break. (In *Every Good Thing*, 261.)

BEPPIE HARRISON

The problem with procrastination is that you are always rushing to complete things at the last moment, not having begun to do them until the next-to-the-last moment. (*Plain and Precious*, 261.)

ELAINE L. JACK

Putting off to tomorrow is to fall behind, to step backward, and open the door to the subtle influences of Satan. (In *Ensign*, May 1994, 15.)

ANN N. MADSEN

Procrastination leaves a person . . . powerless. Planning but never acting results in lamps without oil—no matter how many gallons are planned—and people are left without satisfaction, left with only a shadow, never a light. (In *Redeemer*, 53.)

Woman

Woman's True Worth and Potential

Aileen H. Clyde

God, who knows his children's needs, compares maternal love with his power to give comfort. Perhaps that's our best evidence of woman's divine nature and potential. Such love has as its goal a homecoming, a returning to the source of our spiritual creation, a sitting down together in heaven. (In *Hearts Knit Together*, 177.)

Sheri L. Dew

No woman is a more vibrant instrument in the hands of the Lord than a woman of God who is thrilled to be who she is. (In *Ensign*, Nov. 2000, 96.)

Jaroldeen Asplund Edwards

Womanhood is the great mystery, adventure—and endless possibility. (*Things I Wish I'd Known*, 101.)

Women are like wildflowers. To our Heavenly Father we are each rare and precious. When we are born our nature is sown with dormant seeds. Talents, wisdoms, questions, characteristics, dreams, capabilities—all broadcast within us as silent, fragrant possibilities. Each condition and season of our lives causes different seeds to sprout within us. And many still continue to lie dormant, just waiting for the right conditions to bloom with unexpected beauty. (*Things I Wish I'd Known*, 54.)

Patricia T. Holland

God has a view of women, who they are, what they do incomparably, and what eternally they will be. Women must seize that vision and embrace it, or they—and the human family with it—will perish. (In *To Rejoice As Women*, 107.)

Virginia U. Jensen

When we fully understand that we are daughters of God with rights and privileges that extend throughout eternity—that we are entitled to blessings from Him, dependent upon our faithfulness—then we will look at the world, and our place in it and our responsibility to it, in a different way. (In *Ensign*, Nov. 1998, 92.)

Camilla Eyring Kimball

Each woman in the Church who lives her life according to the commandments will know eternal exaltation in its fullest meaning, which is marriage with increase. Living to claim this promise is every woman's business. (*Writings*, 113.)

JULIA MAVIMBELA

I give thanks to God that He has made me a woman. I give thanks to my creator that He has made me black; that he has fashioned me as I am, with hands, heart, head to serve my people. It can, it should be a glorious thing to be a woman. (In *Women of Wisdom*, 63.)

CAROLE MIKITA

Look at yourself . . . as one who very much belongs in the forefront, a woman with a mission to be true to her heart and mind and to her Lord. (In *Arise*, 287–88.)

MARGARET D. NADAULD

May mothers and fathers understand the great potential for good their daughters inherited from their heavenly home. We must nourish their gentleness, their nurturing nature, their innate spirituality and sensitivity, and their bright minds. (In *Ensign*, Nov. 2000, 15.)

You were born to womanhood, and that is a special privilege. You can't even imagine how much Heavenly Father loves you and wants to see you succeed in your life. (*Write Back Soon!* 48.)

Thank Heavenly Father for the privilege of being born to womanhood, for it is a divine and priceless blessing. (*Write Back Soon!* 7.)

BARBARA B. SMITH

Each woman faces the challenge of being true to the principles of the gospel if she would improve the quality of her mortal life and make herself worthy of the opportunity of eternal progression. She should begin by understanding who she is and that she has a magnificent potential as a daughter of God. (In *Ensign*, Nov. 1979, 107.)

Though scriptural references to [Eve] are few, I search them, believing that in finding her I find something of myself and the beginning of what is womanly. I look for the promise and potential of woman that Heavenly Father intended from the beginning. For women, Eve is mother, model, and mentor. (In *Wisdom's Paths*, 236.)

BELLE S. SPAFFORD

The Church has always accorded to women a position of dignity and respect. Its teachings on the position of woman in the eternal plan reach to the divine. The sacredness of the individual is a fundamental doctrine of the Church. The gospel teaches that the Lord loves his daughters just as he loves his sons. Salvation and exaltation in the Father's kingdom are for all the honest in heart in all the world, men and women alike, through individual obedience to the laws and ordinances instituted by the Lord upon which these blessings are predicated. (In *Improvement Era*, May 1958, 335.)

ELMINA S. TAYLOR,
MARIA Y. DOUGALL, AND
MARTHA H. TINGEY

Woman's mission is so comprehensive, her influence so potent, her power so great, that it requires a thorough understanding of her position, with a well-balanced mind, . . . and the full development of her spiritual nature, to enable her to use her natural forces for her own best interest, and the greatest benefit to the human family. (In *Young Woman's Journal*, Oct. 1890, 28.)

M. CATHERINE THOMAS

When a woman is in full alignment with that which was bestowed on her before this world, her life is filled with power, with clarity, and with a passion to live and fulfill her own unique purposes. This knowledge and power are available to every woman who seeks to know the Lord Jesus Christ and his divine plan for her. (*Selected Writings*, 163.)

With the Restoration came a greatly enhanced view of marriage, of the exalted position and destiny of women, and of their calling to the work of atonement. (In *Women and Christ*, 91.)

Woman's Influence

MICHAELENE P. GRASSLI

Satan wants you. Having you on his side is the best victory of all for him because not only will he have cheated you out of your eternal blessings, but he will also cheat others whom you could have influenced through your good example. (In *Ensign*, Apr. 1994, 62.)

VIRGINIA U. JENSEN

Sometimes this world is a frightening place to be. I believe, however, that women have unique opportunities and special gifts and talents to protect, nurture, and influence others. We can create places of security where marriages, children, and families can thrive and avoid the evil of the world. (In *Ensign*, Nov. 1997, 89.)

As women, we have natural tendencies to love and nourish. Women teach children, bolster friends, encourage husbands, and cheer on the disheartened. Women are givers of life and nurturers of the living. Every one of us has something to give, something to share, and someone to serve. (In *Ensign*, Nov. 1998, 92.)

The actions of righteous women ripple on and on through time and space and even generations. (In *Ensign*, Nov. 2000, 93.)

AMY BROWN LYMAN

I believe it is apparent that there is a place for women among the world's thinkers and doers. (In *Relief Society Magazine*, May 1934, 289.)

BETTE S. MOLGARD

Always keep in mind that you, as a daughter of your Heavenly Father, can be a mighty force for good as you access spiritual gifts, line upon line, precept upon precept. (*Everyday Battles*, 129.)

TESSA MEYER SANTIAGO

A woman's circle of influence does not stop at the curb bordering her home. We must not underestimate the power and responsibility of our womanhood. (In *May Christ Lift Thee Up*, 208.)

BARBARA B. SMITH

A woman's attitude and response [to welfare projects] will set the tone for the entire family and for others. Her enthusiasm can be contagious, and filling such assignments provides her with a golden opportunity to teach gospel principles of love and service, of work and self-reliance, of stewardship and consecration. (In *Ensign*, Nov. 1976, 122.)

ELIZA R. SNOW

There is no sister so isolated, and her sphere so narrow but what she can do a great deal towards establishing the kingdom of God upon the earth. (*Women's Exponent*, 15 Sept. 1873, 62.)

BELLE S. SPAFFORD

Love of woman for her sister, love of woman for humanity, love of woman for that which is pure, ideal, and sacred is God-implanted in her heart. This love is the most potential service power known to society. (*Today's World*, 112–13.)

MERCY FIELDING THOMPSON

At one time after seeking earnestly to know from the Lord if there was anything that I could do for the building up of the Kingdom of God, a most pleasant sensation came over me with the following words. Try to get the Sisters to subscribe one cent per week for the purpose of buying glass and nails for the Temple. I went immediately to Brother Joseph and told him what seemed to be the whispering of the still small voice in me. He told me to go ahead and the Lord would bless me. (*Mary Fielding Smith*, 155.)

JANICE MADSEN WEINHEIMER

If Satan can undermine the high standards of womanhood, he will lower the standards of the entire human race. (*Families Are Forever*, 120.)

EMMELINE B. WELLS

To live for others; to bless them; to sustain them; to be an example of the perfection of womanhood, are possibilities which ought to fertilize the most barren soul. (In *Woman's Exponent*, 15 Sept. 1874, 55.)

LEAH D. WIDTSOE

The strength and virility of any cause, people, or nation, may be judged by the strength and virility of its women. When the mothers of men are strong and loyal, they breed strength and loyalty in their sons. (In *Improvement Era*, May 1935, 289.)

Responsibilities of Women

COLLEEN W. ASAY

The influence of women upon their husbands and children would be enhanced significantly if while under the influence of the divine tutelage of the temple they would seek an understanding of their ministry in the home. (In *Wisdom's Paths*, 130.)

ELAINE CANNON

We need more women who know Jesus Christ and who will teach and testify of him. We need women who are studying the scriptures, who know the word of God and experiment upon the word; women who will move by knowledge and also by faith. (In *Woman to Woman*, 73.)

We each have a mighty errand to do. It may or may not include marriage and motherhood at this time, but ours is the errand of influence. (In *Ensign*, Nov. 1979, 10.)

God has revealed the divinely appointed opportunities for women. No matter how the world carries on—demeaning women, exploiting their beauty and promise, keeping them chattels and slaves, expecting them to single-handedly carry the burdens of parenting in any situation . . . — no matter, God gave to woman to be his arm of love. (*Gatherings*, 84.)

WINNIFRED SAVILLE CANNON

How glorious to be born a woman, although it is not an easy task to fill all the requirements of wife and mother! A woman must learn to take the bitter with the sweet and keep on smiling. (In *Relief Society Magazine*, July 1943, 367.)

JOANNE B. DOXEY

The Lord loves you for being His partner in His plan. Be of good cheer as you perform your divinely ordained task of guiding the destiny of this generation, that they may then pass the baton of righteousness on to generations yet unborn. (In *Ensign*, Nov. 1989, 91.)

JAROLDEEN ASPLUND EDWARDS

The rewards of society, the things on which any satisfying society rests—humanity, family, education, love, order, and nests—are contained within our errand from the Lord. (*Things I Wish I'd Known*, 101.)

I believe it is essential for every woman to recognize that one of her most important roles in life is the creation of homes. This is a cherished gift we can give, both to ourselves and to others. (*Things I Wish I'd Known*, 38.)

LINDA J. EYRE

In these days when we hear so much of women's rights, it is time we turned our thoughts to women's responsibilities. (*Joyful Mother*, 4.)

MARJORIE P. HINCKLEY

Some of us are married. Some of us are not (yet). Some of us have children and grandchildren. Some have none. Some are widowed, some divorced. But we can all do what is our responsibility to do. We can all bless lives. (In *Glimpses*, 240.)

VIRGINIA U. JENSEN

Virtue and power are found in everyday, ordinary work, in all the daily tasks of caring for our families, and in our regular service to others. (In *Ensign*, Nov. 2000, 93.)

There is evidence all around us that the world desperately needs women who stand for something good and noble and righteous—even if that stand may not be popular. The world needs women who in their daily acts and deeds exemplify a higher standard. (In *Arise*, 13.)

JENNIE B. KNIGHT

Every woman should have words of warning, tempered with tolerance for the wayward, and words of righteous indignation to be used against all forms of injustice and oppression. (In *Relief Society Magazine*, May 1935, 283.)

SYDNEY SMITH REYNOLDS

We feel that by being in the home full time we make the most important contribution a woman can make in this life. We are not home because we are not clever enough to be somewhere else. We are home because we chose to be there. (In *Ensign*, Oct. 1979, 67.)

LOUISE Y. ROBISON

It will depend upon the mothers in the home to hold aloft the standards for our husbands and young people, to help them to see that money is not the big thing; money is not the rich thing. As Henry Ford says, money is dead, but character and the things that the human heart produces are the things that will live on. (In *Relief Society Magazine*, Nov. 1932, 673.)

The standards of any home are largely the standards of the women of that home. (In *Relief Society Magazine*, June 1927, 295.)

Latter-day Saint women should have homes where the spirit of God resides, and from which we may give to the world boys and girls who are clean, pure, and honest. (In *Relief Society Magazine*, June 1929, 312.)

From the very beginning our women have willingly and lovingly sent forth husbands and sons, and in the later years, their daughters, to proclaim the Gospel, and it seems to me that it is one of the greatest contributions that women have ever made. (In *Relief Society Magazine*, June 1931, 333.)

We owe an incalculable debt of gratitude to those heroic women who patiently endured pain and persecution for the sake of the liberty which the women of today enjoy. But we must remember that the spirit of any event must be kept alive by adherents of that event in order that it may not die. (In *Relief Society Magazine*, Mar. 1932, 154.)

BARBARA B. SMITH

Let us as women in the Church today make happy, provident living a life-style in our homes, approaching this goal in a spirit of challenge and innovation and thanksgiving. (In *Ensign*, Nov. 1980, 86.)

Let us see what creativity can do to heighten the standard of our living, not reduce it—to be provident without becoming penny-pinching, miserly, or ungenerous. (In *Ensign*, Nov. 1980, 86.)

The homemaker is healer, comforter, and counselor; architect, builder, and maintenance engineer of a learning and research center equal to any university; artist, sculptor, creator of the greatest masterpiece: a human being. (In *Ensign*, Mar. 1979, 22.)

MARY ELLEN SMOOT

Sisters, we are needed here—by the Lord, by our priesthood leaders, by our families, and by each other. The Lord needs us to embrace our eternal callings and fill the measure of our creation. (In *Ensign*, Nov. 2000, 90.)

ELIZA R. SNOW

There are many . . . whose labors are not known beyond their own dwellings and perhaps not appreciated there, but what difference does that make? If your labors are acceptable to God, however simple the duties, if faithfully performed, you should never be discouraged. (In *Elect Ladies*, 37.)

BELLE S. SPAFFORD

There is no other calling as high, no other function so glorious, no greater responsibility for woman than to protect and guide the spirit children of our Heavenly Father entrusted to her so that, embodied, they may return to his presence having triumphed over the temptations and evils of earth life. (In *Improvement Era*, May 1958, 354.)

Just as woman shares with man the privileges and blessings of the Church, so, she bears with him responsibility in building the kingdom of God on earth. The Lord has endowed her with special talents and abilities which he expects her to develop and use in the furtherance of his work. (In *Improvement Era*, May 1958, 354.)

SHIRLEY W. THOMAS

For a . . . woman, the wholeness that is so closely related to holiness is achieved, in part, through her acceptance of the responsibility to establish a home whatever her circumstances—and then to bring to that home, learning and the light of the gospel. (In *Ensign*, Nov. 1980, 107.)

WENDY C. TOP

[A] tendency to overdo things is often an occupational hazard of womanhood. Our sensitivity to detail can, when held in balance, beautify and soften the world, but when it gets out of balance it can have just the opposite effect. We can actually make ourselves and everyone around us crazy! We lose what we sought to gain and "spend . . . [our] labor for that which cannot satisfy" (2 Nephi 9:51). (*Getting Past the Labels*, 29–30.)

EMMELINE B. WELLS

That motherhood brings into a woman's life a richness, zest and tone that nothing else ever can I gladly grant you, but that her usefulness ends there, or that she has no other individual interests to serve I cannot so readily concede. (In *Elect Ladies*, 85.)

Blessings Available to Women

MAUREEN URSENBACH BEECHER

Women of the Restoration were spiritually gifted, as were their brothers. . . . In matters of the Spirit, women received with men from the Lord's store of gifts. (In *Women Steadfast*, 55.)

JILL MULVAY DERR AND MAUREEN URSENBACH BEECHER

Ours is a heritage of abundance. . . . It is the inheritance of charity.

. . . By praying for, receiving, and exercising charity, we become like unto the Son, in purpose one with the Son. . . . We are the fruits of his harvest, his jewels, his own. Faithful stewards are no more servants but the sons and daughters of God, heirs and joint heirs with Christ. (In *Women and Christ*, 102.)

SHERI L. DEW

A woman led by the Lord knows where to turn for answers and for peace. She can make difficult decisions and face problems with confidence because she takes her counsel from the Spirit, and from her leaders who are also guided by the Spirit. (In *Ensign*, Nov. 1998, 95–96.)

JAROLDEEN ASPLUND EDWARDS

I testify that the Lord loves women. He watches over us and loves our womanhood—the duties and the responsibilities of our gender—and he can speak to us directly with spiritual messages that are necessary for our personal welfare and for the callings in which we are engaged. (*Things I Wish I'd Known*, 100.)

LOUIE B. FELT

God is at the helm, and He . . . loves you for the sacrifices you make; He loves every sister . . . whose heart is in her work; He loves you with a love that you cannot understand, and He will bless you and will comfort you, as He has done me. (In *Children's Friend*, July 1908, 276.)

FLORENCE S. JACOBSEN

That which people, especially women, seek as they cry for liberation is already in their midst; it is so close they do not see it, so simple that they cannot understand it: the gospel of Jesus Christ. (In *Ensign*, Mar. 1972, 36.)

SHERRIE JOHNSON

The beauty of the gospel plan is that both God's sons and daughters can deal directly with him. Even though the man presides as to government, a woman's access to her Father in Heaven is in no way limited; nor is it different from a man's. God places no restrictions on a woman's prayers. (*Man, Woman, and Deity*, 27.)

ARDETH GREENE KAPP

It is my fervent and humble testimony that the heavens are very much open to women today. . . . We can pull down the blessings of heaven through obedience to law. These divine and sacred blessings are not reserved for others alone. Visions and revelations come by the power of the Holy Ghost. The Lord has said, "On my servants and on my hand-maidens I will pour out in those days of my Spirit; and they shall prophesy." (Acts 2:18.) (In *Woman to Woman*, 63.)

TESSA MEYER SANTIAGO

We are entitled through our noble birthright as daughters of God to personal revelation and inspiration concerning our circles of influence. And we are duty-bound to work to obtain that inspiration. (In *May Christ Lift Thee Up*, 216.)

IDA SMITH

If we as Latter-day Saints really understand the gospel of Jesus Christ and all that it portends for women, we will realize that no blessing can be withheld from us if we are prepared and worthy to receive it. (In *Woman to Woman*, 48.)

Jesus Christ and Women

PATRICIA T. HOLLAND

We will always see God's infinite care in the process of making us who we are and what we are becoming. We see the gentle way he kneels to brush back our hair or even to wipe away a tear. He adjusts the angle of the light and works his wonders with lines and scars and shadows. Ever so softly he whispers for us to endure difficulty or discouragement for what it may hold of illumination and eternal beauty. Under his hand our inner person becomes the outer person, and the artist shapes his perfect image. (In *LDS Women's Treasury*, 91.)

SHERRIE JOHNSON

Jesus Christ is not only the way and the model for the men of the Church but for the women also. There is only one way, and Jesus is that way. (*Man, Woman, and Deity*, 43.)

CAROLE MIKITA

The Lord knows where he needs each of us and he will place us there with whatever help we need to get the job done. (In *Arise*, 287.)

KATHRYN H. SHIRTS

There are important differences between the Savior and ourselves to be overcome during our mortal existence, but gender is not one of them. Being female is not something we have to repent of. (In *Women Steadfast*, 98.)

Relying on the Savior as a model and as a mentor . . . we can immerse ourselves in the scriptures and, at the same time, by being open to the influence of his Spirit, relate them to our own lives and circumstances. In the intercessory prayer recorded in 3 Nephi, the resurrected Lord prays that those who believe in him might be purified, "that I may be in them as thou, Father, art in me." (19:29.) The intimacy of that relationship . . . brings women as well as men into the very center of the story. (In *Women Steadfast*, 101.)

Qualities of Righteous Women

ELAINE CANNON

When we covenant with the Lord to take upon us his name, we also take upon us the burden of helping mankind in our special, womanly way. (*Count Your Blessings*, 69.)

A thinking woman knows who she is and who she is coming to be. She doesn't spend her time shadow-boxing with gospel fundamentals or sulking over something she doesn't have full information about. . . . A thinking woman takes her responsibilities seriously, but not her achievements. . . . She forgives herself quickly for not being perfect—yet! Her confidence is in the Lord, and she doesn't flinch—much. (*Gatherings*, 74.)

SHERI L. DEW

The Lord . . . needs us to speak up for what is right, even when doing so is unpopular. He needs us to develop the spiritual maturity to hear the voice of the Lord and detect the deceptions of the adversary. He delights in women who keep their covenants with precision, women who reverence the power of the priesthood, women who are willing to "lay aside the things of this world, and seek for the things of a better" (D&C 25:10). (In *Ensign*, Nov. 1997, 93.)

ELAINE L. JACK

No greater heroine lives in today's world than the woman who is quietly doing her part. (In *Ensign*, Nov. 1990, 89.)

VIRGINIA U. JENSEN

A woman who keeps the commandments is using our Heavenly Father's blueprint to build a place of security for herself and her family. Those around her know they can trust her. They can feel safety and peace within her influence. Adherence to the Lord's commandments is the foundation of her fortress. (In *Ensign*, Nov. 1997, 90.)

ARDETH GREENE KAPP

Let us all be filled—filled with the light, the strength, the faith that comes from prayer, scripture study, and obedience to God's commandments each day of our lives. Let us stand united together, shoulder to shoulder, heart to heart, and hand in hand, bonded together by that light that never grows dim. (In *Ensign*, Nov. 1988, 95.)

JENNIE B. KNIGHT

Women should specialize in kind, gentle, beautiful words, they are to our language what fragrance is to the flowers, essentially joy giving. (In *Relief Society Magazine*, May 1935, 283.)

AMY BROWN LYMAN

[Women] have sympathy, imagination, patience, a spontaneous eagerness to help, and a warm good will, all of which are real assets and help them to find their way easily into the hearts of those who suffer. (In *Relief Society Magazine*, Mar. 1944, 137.)

Women are especially well fitted by nature for welfare work. They seem naturally to be able to alleviate distress, to eliminate bitterness, and to lessen despair. In turn, such work is very satisfying to them. (In *Relief Society Magazine*, Mar. 1944, 137.)

MARGARET D. NADAULD

Women of God can never be like women of the world. The world has enough women who are tough; we need women who are tender. There are enough women who are coarse; we need women who are kind. There are enough women who are rude; we need women who are refined. We have enough women of fame and fortune; we need more women of faith. We have enough greed; we need more goodness. We have enough vanity; we need more virtue. We have enough popularity; we need more purity. (In *Ensign*, Nov. 2000, 15.)

DONNA TOLAND SMART

The need to nourish, to be nourished and the need for beauty, the need to learn and to make use of learning, and the need to share with loved ones—woman's common umbilical cord, spans through the centuries backward as far as Eve. (In *Mormon Women Speak*, 117.)

BARBARA B. SMITH

[The] giving of self to others is as old as Eve, and the happiness that accompanies it she knew too. Teachers know this, nurses know it, neighbors too. Because of woman's assignment by the Lord to nurture and care for all living, she will, by nature, find fulfillment in nurturing those who need a caring heart of sincere concern. (In *Wisdom's Paths*, 246.)

BARBARA B. SMITH AND SHIRLEY W. THOMAS

Loyalty is probably a learned characteristic, but for the willing and determined it is not hard to learn. And it is impossible to think of a Christlike person who doesn't possess that quality. (*Words for Women*, 98.)

BATHSHEBA W. SMITH

Cultivate a happy and kind disposition, and never sacrifice the natural pride and reserve that a pure and lovely woman always carries. (In *Young Woman's Journal*, Jan. 1892, 186.)

ELIZA R. SNOW

Woman's faith can accomplish wonders. (In *Women of Mormondom*, 392.)

BELLE S. SPAFFORD

Kind, helpful service to those in need is a realm wherein God and nature destined woman to serve and bless mankind. (*Today's World*, 112.)

CLARISSA S. WILLIAMS

I think nothing greater could be said of any woman than that she is a peace maker. (In *Relief Society Magazine*, Dec. 1921, 696.)

Latter-day Saint Women

JANETTE HALES BECKHAM

As we become righteous, problem-solving women of faith, we will learn to represent [Jesus] and do His work. (In *New Era*, Nov. 1994, 41.)

ELAINE CANNON

A woman whose attitude is mellowed by a closeness to God, whose life is sweetened by gospel experiences, . . . enlightened by religious training, strengthened by saving ordinances, and directed by inspired leadership, is bound to have a unique view of why she was born. No matter how broad-minded or emancipated, liberated or sophisticated she may claim to be, deep down she knows she is a cherished child of God. She is the recipient, with others of his children both male and female, of all the blessings of a plan of eternal life. (*Gatherings*, 90–91.)

We must pursue a course of a covenant people. We must secure those traditions which are sacred to good people everywhere. . . . Your course should become clear, your priorities ought to be known to you as a daughter of God. (In *Ensign*, Nov. 1978, 107.)

KAREN LYNN DAVIDSON

I am continually impressed by the ways in which the women of our Church are able to rise above their past. Once a woman comes to understand the Atonement, she knows she does not have to live with past mistakes. Disadvantage and injustice need not drag us down. Our sisters find a way to go on, with faith and strength. (In *Women and the Power*, 15.)

Sheri L. Dew

We are distinct from the women of the world not only because of what we know but because of the spiritual privileges that accompany those gifted with the Holy Ghost and endowed with power in the house of the Lord. (In *Arms of His Love*, 393.)

That we are here now is no accident. For aeons of time our Father watched us and knew He could trust us when so much would be at stake. We have been held in reserve for this very hour. We need to understand not just who we are but who we have always been. For we are women of God, and the work of women of God has always been to help build the kingdom of God. (In *Ensign*, Nov. 2000, 95.)

As women of God we must stand tall so that we will stand out from the rest of the world. Only in doing so may we hope to find joy. For finding joy and standing tall, not in feet or inches but as ambassadors for the Lord, are directly connected. (In *Ensign*, Nov. 2000, 94.)

What we must all do is work to sink our spiritual roots deep—deep enough that when the winds of life blow (as they most certainly will) we'll be prepared to face them and to give them the kind of nurturing strength [women are] known for. (In *Ensign*, Sept. 1989, 26.)

From the adversary's point of view, we are dangerous. Righteous women dedicated to the Lord and united in the cause of goodness threaten his work. Of course he would target and attempt to deceive us, women who have a clear understanding of who we are. . . . We are not ordinary women. (In *Arms of His Love*, 389.)

Michaelene P. Grassli

My dear sisters, . . . you are the ones who can touch hearts, change lives, and lead others to our Heavenly Father. We women of the Church have significant and critical work to do for the Lord. (In *Ensign*, Apr. 1994, 62.)

Elaine L. Jack

As women of covenant we seek exaltation and the peace that attends eternal life in the kingdom of heaven. With that resolve comes the quiet assurance that speaks softly to our souls and reaffirms to us that peace and love, hope and gentility, reverence, joy, and obedience bring about change and good works. (In *Ensign*, Nov. 1993, 98.)

To be a woman of covenant is a sacred and holy responsibility. It is uniquely ours. It is not by chance that we are on the Lord's errand at this time. It is by choice that we came to this earth to follow the path of the Savior. (In *Ensign*, Nov. 1993, 98.)

Virginia U. Jensen

We cannot be ordinary women. We cannot be women who seem too much like women of the world. We must speak up for righteousness without apology. We . . . are unique. (In *Ensign*, Nov. 2000, 93.)

CAMILLA EYRING KIMBALL

A woman of faith . . . is one whose heart and soul, mind and strength are committed to the pursuit of true values. First, in her heart and soul, a faithful woman acknowledges God's role in all things. Then, with her mind she seeks to understand the divine plan for this world. And finally, with the strength of her hands, she undertakes to . . . keep God's commandments and give unselfish service to His children. (In *Heritage of Faith*, 4.)

Women of faith will know that the Lord lives and will follow that knowledge, whatever the cost. (In *Heritage of Faith*, 10.)

BETTE S. MOLGARD

We, as Latter-day Saint women, . . . pose a disturbing threat to Satan and his armies. We have been placed on this earth to fulfill a specific role in the plan of salvation. No matter what our station in life, we have been placed in this time of all times, in our particular circumstances to fill the measure of our creation. (*Everyday Battles*, 4.)

LOUISE Y. ROBISON

As mothers in Israel we should be just as valiant in the cause of truth as were our former sisters. We may not have to face mobs, and be driven from our homes, but we should stand just as firmly for the principles of the Gospel as did those blessed sisters. (In *Conference Report*, Apr. 1930, 144.)

BARBARA B. SMITH

The women of the Church have an important work to do. That work requires great strength of character, faith in the Lord Jesus Christ, and a pure heart that will be a light unto the world and a bulwark of righteousness against the darkness that covers the earth with contention and evil. (In *Ensign*, May 1984, 30.)

MARY ELLEN SMOOT

Sisters who know right from wrong stand firm on the Lord's side, making choices that set them apart from the rest of the world. (In *Ensign*, Nov. 1999, 92.)

It is a new day, the dawning of a new era. It is our time, and it is our destiny to rejoice as we fill the earth with greater kindness and gentleness, greater love and compassion, greater sympathy and empathy than has ever been known before. It is time to give ourselves to the Master and allow Him to lead us into fruitful fields where we can enrich a world filled with darkness and misery. (In *Ensign*, Nov. 1999, 92.)

Each of us, no matter who we are, no matter where we serve, must arise and make the most of each opportunity that comes. We must follow the counsel given by the Lord and His servants and make our homes houses of prayer and havens of security and safety. We can and must deepen our faith by increasing our obedience and sacrifice. In this individual process a miracle will take place. (In *Ensign*, Nov. 1999, 92.)

Each of us has a vital role, even a sacred mission to perform as a daughter in Zion. (In *Ensign*, Nov. 1999, 92.)

We each have a purpose and reason for being. *Every sister has a thread to weave in the tapestry of time.* Discover your thread and begin to weave. (*Sweet Is the Work*, 20.)

Eliza R. Snow

[We are] women of God—women filling high and responsible positions—performing sacred duties—women who stand, not as dictators, but as counselors to [our] husbands, and who, in the purest, noblest sense of refined womanhood, [are] truly their helpmates. (*Deseret News Weekly*, 19 Jan. 1870, 555.)

[Latter-day Saint women] occupy a more important position than is occupied by any other women on the earth. Associated as they are, with apostles and prophets inspired by the living God—with them sharing in the gifts and powers of the Holy Priesthood . . . participating in those sacred ordinances, without which, we could never be prepared to dwell in the presence of the Holy Ones. (In *Woman's Exponent*, 15 July 1874, 28.)

Do you know of any place on the face of the earth, where woman has more liberty, and where she enjoys such high and glorious privileges as she does here, as a Latter-day Saint? No! (In *Women of Mormondom*, 391.)

It is the duty of each one of us to be a holy woman. We shall have elevated aims, if we are holy women. We shall feel that we are called to perform important duties. No one is exempt from them. There is no sister so isolated and her sphere so narrow but what she can do a great deal towards establishing the kingdom of God upon the earth. (In *Woman's Exponent*, 15 Sept. 1873, 62.)

Belle S. Spafford

The women of the Church must prove themselves a steadying and unwavering influence in their homes and in their children. . . . They [must] build faith and enlarge their own understanding, and that of their families, of God's great plan and purposes, so that when the bitter experiences of life come the doctrines and teachings of the Church will be a living reality with unbounded sustaining influence and power. (In *Relief Society Magazine*, Nov. 1950, 727.)

Latter-day Saint women are not immune to present-day trends, attitudes, opinions, influences, and practices. . . . However, there are no women in all the world so well positioned to make wise decisions. . . . They have the doctrine and teachings of the Church to guide them. They know the essential elements of good home and family life. They know the factors that are important in the well-being of children. (In *Relief Society Magazine*, Nov. 1958, 719.)

Our primary concern, . . . is that we shall firmly position ourselves in preserving the enduring, spiritual values which time and the prophets have taught us are unchangeable, and which are the guarantee of the stability of our homes, and the eternal well-being of our children. (In *Relief Society Magazine*, Nov. 1961, 720–21.)

Latter-day Saint women have at their command the firm and infallible guidelines that lead toward the full development and total usefulness of womankind. (In *BYU Speeches*, 11 Feb. 1975, 49–50.)

Truly women *should* rejoice in the brighter day which dawned for womankind with the restoration. As the rays of the gospel shed their light upon the earth, the lofty position accorded woman in the gospel plan and the importance of her divinely ordained earthly mission were made clearly visible, and new vistas for development and purposeful living, under the guidance of the priesthood, were opened to her view. (In *Relief Society Magazine*, Nov. 1966, 804.)

In my experience in working with . . . women of good conscience but living by man-defined rather than God-revealed truths, I have countless times had to call upon all the courage I possessed in order to stand firm for what I knew to be right. In doing so, I have never once lost a friend—temporarily perhaps, but never permanently. (Address, Weber State College Institute, 2 Feb. 1973, 15.)

Possessing revealed truth and the words of the prophets as they relate to the responsibility of the Latter-day Saint woman and her role in life, we have an unwavering duty to uphold these teachings in our speech and actions, and to direct our lives in harmony with them. (In *BYU Speeches*, 11 Feb. 1975, 45.)

The Latter-day Saint woman knows that motherhood is a divine calling. . . . [She] knows that no other work to which she might set her hand could be so broad and inspiring, so filled with interest, so demanding of intelligence and capability, so rewarding. (*Woman's Reach*, 117.)

WENDY C. TOP

We can show our sisters around the world that the family system ordained by God really works and is the greatest hope for society. . . . We can influence the world to respect and honor women without having to reinvent them. (*Getting Past the Labels*, 138.)

Latter-day Saint women have a long history and a strong precedent of being progressive, capable, educated, contributing members of society, serving both in and outside of their homes. Women of the Church today have the obligation to carry on this tradition to the best of their ability and according to the guidance of the Lord. (*Getting Past the Labels*, 138.)

We have got to get past the labels *married, single, mother, childless, professional, homemaker,* and any other pigeon-holing definition and see ourselves first and foremost as daughters of God, each with her own equally important mission and unique powers and abilities. (*Getting Past the Labels*, 5.)

Although we will not convert every person to the gospel and bring all directly into the brilliant light of Christ, perhaps if we hold that light up high enough, a few of its warming rays will scatter over the world and make the way a little less cold and dark for others. (*Getting Past the Labels*, 139.)

WENDY L. WATSON

Far too many of us are far too content to live far beneath our privileges as women of covenant. (In *Arise*, 166.)

EMMELINE B. WELLS

There are many heroines in the "Mormon" Church whose names will ring down the ages. Their faith in God is as strong as the everlasting hills, that cannot be moved. They are self-sacrificing and reverent women. (In *Woman's Exponent*, Jan. 1908, 48.)

[Mormon women] should be the best informed of any women on the face of the earth, not only upon our own principles and doctrines but on all general subjects. (In *Elect Ladies*, 88.)

ELIZABETH ANN WHITNEY

My heart goes out to all those who are seeking to walk the narrow way and keep fast hold of the iron rod. The Father has great blessings in store for His daughters; fear not, my sisters, but trust in God, live your religion and teach it to your children. (In *Their Own Words*, 201.)

BARBARA W. WINDER

Sisters, it is so important that each of us be willing to do whatever is required of us wherever we are called. We do not pick and choose what we will accept, just as we do not choose which commandments to obey. (In *Ensign*, Nov. 1987, 96.)

Sisterhood among Women

JULENE BUTLER

If we are to thrive spiritually, or simply survive spiritually, we need each other. (In *Best of Women's Conference*, 75.)

ELAINE CANNON

It is time . . . for the women of the Church to behave with a sense of belonging instead of a sense of separateness. We are not women of the world, after all. We are sisters.

We are daughters of God. We are children of the covenant who are marching to the same drummer, though we may be singing a separate song. (In *Woman to Woman*, 66.)

KAREN LYNN DAVIDSON

"Sister" as a form of address carries within it a significant, symbolic message: we are equals, working side by side, doing our best in our individual ways to build the kingdom. As sisters we can strengthen ourselves and each other. As sisters we can find unity in our diversity. As sisters we can thrive on our differences. (*Thriving*, 112.)

SUZANNE BARNES ENGEMANN

We need to allow each other to be who we are by seeing each other as daughters of God instead of judging who looks most like any particular culture's vision of ideal. (In *Hearts Knit Together*, 202.)

MARJORIE P. HINCKLEY

We are all in this together. We need each other. . . . It is a sociological fact that women need women. We need deep and satisfying and loyal friendships with each other. These friendships are a necessary source of sustenance. We need to renew our faith every day. We need to lock arms and help build the kingdom so that it will roll forth and fill the whole earth. . . . Let us "watch over one another . . . that we may all sit down in heaven together." (In *As Women of Faith*, 11–12.)

PATRICIA T. HOLLAND

It is often only when other women find us pleasant and worthy that we find ourselves pleasant and worthy. If we have this effect on each other, why aren't we more generous and loving with one another? (In *Ensign*, June 1984, 50.)

Isolation can be one of the most frightening and stressful circumstances of the human heart. We all need other people and strong, sweet relationships if it is possible to have them. . . . Relief Society offers us a sisterhood that we can cherish and association with others who believe what we believe, hope what we hope, and who love the things of God. (In *Clothed with Charity*, 2–3.)

MARILYNNE TODD LINFORD

Competition is really an illusion. Reality is who we are and why. (*Woman Fulfilled*, 60.)

I can show I feel good about me and about others by just being myself and by replacing one-upmanship, name-dropping, and hints of superiority with sincere compliments. (*Woman Fulfilled*, 60.)

Competitive relationships stifle growth. (*Woman Fulfilled*, 60.)

Women can be their own support network. One woman can dry another's tears and be another's temporary crutch. I can sustain you. You can sustain me. Your smile, your kind word, your help when I need you, your pat on my back, my commitment never to gossip about you and yours to never gossip about me, will bless me as nothing else can. (*Mother's Self-Esteem*, 108.)

JILL C. MAJOR, LAUREN C. LEIFSON, AND HOLLIE C. BEVAN

Women should be allies: showing love, building up, and lifting each other. . . . We need to recognize what a great force our nurturing nature can be in helping build the self-worth of those around us. . . . It takes a strong foundation of confidence and self-esteem for all women to go forward and accomplish their missions here on earth. (*Encircled by Love*, 40.)

JULIA MAVIMBELA

It is important for women to be aware of their common lot. It is important for women to stand together and rise together to meet our common enemies—illiteracy, poverty, crime, disease, and stupid unjust laws that have made women feel so helpless as to be hopeless. (In *Women of Wisdom*, 63.)

CHERYL B. PRESTON

Our code as Christian soldiers, our handbook of instructions, is the scriptures. They reverberate with pleas for solidarity and refraining from judgment. They urge us to seek the unity that underlies a Zion society. . . . They remind, "Every [sisterhood] divided against itself is brought to desolation; and a house divided against a house falleth." (Luke 11:17.) . . . As sisters in the gospel, we have promised to bear

one another's burdens, not increase them. (In *Women in the Covenant*, 183.)

Women's Relationship with Men

ANITA R. CANFIELD

Men and women are equal before God. The same laws, rules, and covenants apply to both equally. However, they are equal, but not the same. . . . In a song there is both melody and harmony—same song but different parts. The respective calling of each sex simply reflects the unique qualifications and temperaments of each. (*Self-Esteem*, 112.)

The highest degree of Godhood is gained through the perfect blending of the qualities of man and woman. (*Self-Esteem*, 112.)

ELAINE CANNON

When we come to understand and obey the gospel of Jesus Christ and the whole exquisite plan of life, we will know that God established the difference in the roles of men and women so that it is not possible for one to be exalted without the other. (*Gatherings*, 84–85.)

LUCILE JOHNSON

Men and women are equal, but they are not the same. It isn't that either sex or either role is inferior, they are just different. . . . These unique differences . . . were ordained before the world was. Men and women are not to be competitors. They are to be companions—to enhance one another. (*Sunny Side Up,* 43–45.)

Men and women—husband and wives together—should be on the Lord's side—not on women's side or men's side. (*Enjoy the Journey,* 209.)

SHERRIE JOHNSON

Often as husbands and wives we would be greatly helped if we would forget about the overemphasized differences between men and women and remember that they are more alike than they are different. Men and women both need to be loved. Both need to feel capable and worthwhile and wanted. Both have egos. Both need to be understood. Both have dreams and goals to work toward and a divine mission to fulfill. Both have the same spiritual needs, and both need to have faith in Jesus Christ. (*Man, Woman, and Deity,* 93.)

KATE L. KIRKHAM

In my mind and heart, nothing about our male-female differences equates with subordination or with diminished value of either gender. Instead, our gender differences and our authority differences offer the greatest opportunity to learn what Christ is trying to teach us through his gospel: that charity and oneness are available to us; that the pursuit of our individual salvation is inextricably linked to others'; that this life is a time of opportunities to teach and learn from one another. (In *Women Steadfast,* 263–64.)

IDA SMITH

It is important for a woman to learn in this life her eternal role so that when she is sealed she will be prepared and ready—with all her heart—to function . . . as a full partner in a celestial team—without having to look *up* because of any feeling of inferiority, or look *down* because of any feeling of superiority, but look *across* into the eyes of an equally prepared, equally magnificent eternal mate. (In *Women and the Power,* 60–61.)

The Prophet Joseph Smith did more than just preach that men and women were of equal value and importance in the sight of God. He preached that in order for a man to achieve his highest potential (the celestial kingdom and godhood), he must have a woman—equally exalted—by his side and sealed to him forever. (In *Woman to Woman,* 44.)

ELIZA R. SNOW

In the Kingdom of God, woman has no interests separate from those of man—all are mutual. (*Deseret News Weekly,* 19 Jan. 1870, 555.)

[Some women] are so radical in their extreme theories that they would set [for themselves an] antagonism to man . . . [and] make [their sisters] adopt the more reprehensible phases of character which men present, and which should be shunned or improved by them instead of being copied by women. (In *Woman's Exponent*, 15 July 1872, 29.)

A. D. SORENSEN

In carrying out their stewardships in obedience to the law of consecration, all persons in the kingdom, women as well as men, labor together within the system of equality required by divine love. (In *As Women of Faith*, 67.)

In divine love woman and man are equal—absolutely equal. . . . Their total, and therefore equal, caring for each other helps make possible fulness of life together. (In *As Women of Faith*, 65.)

BELLE S. SPAFFORD

The gospel teaches that women have an appointed place in the plan of salvation and that the Lord loves his daughters as he loves his sons and that the promised blessings are the same for both. (In *Relief Society Magazine*, Dec. 1945, 751.)

BARBARA W. WINDER

The prophets have taught that in his wisdom and mercy our Father made men and women dependent upon each other for the full flowering of their potential. Because their natures are somewhat different, they can complement each other. Because they are in many ways alike, they can understand each other. Let neither envy the other for their

differences; let both discern what is superficial and what is basic in those differences and act accordingly. (In *BYU Speeches*, 8 Jan. 1989, 65.)

Challenges of Modern Women

JANENE WOLSEY BAADSGAARD

It would be such a relief to admit that we're human and that all life's choices are difficult at times. It would be like taking off a new girdle: Suddenly everyone would see that we're not perfect—but we'd be a lot more comfortable. (*Potted Plant*, 91.)

SHERI L. DEW

This is a day when the adversary has launched an all-out attack against womanhood, because he knows . . . that the influence of a righteous woman is enormous and that it spans generations. . . . At all costs, he wants to keep us at arm's length from Jesus Christ. For if we don't come unto Christ . . . we will go through our probation here on our own rather than experiencing what the Savior promised when He said, "Come unto me, all ye that labour and are heavy laden, and I will give you rest" (Matt. 11:28). (In *Ensign*, Nov. 1997, 92–93.)

Sisters, we can't afford *not* to seek the things of the Spirit! There is too much at stake. Too many people are depending on us as mothers, as sisters, leaders, and friends. (In *Ensign*, Nov. 1998, 95.)

PATRICIA T. HOLLAND

If . . . [one] wanted to destroy a society, I think [he] would stage a full blown blitz on its women. [He] would keep them so distraught and distracted that they would never find the calming strength and serenity for which their sex has always been known. Satan has effectively done that. (In *BYU Today*, June 1987, 48.)

CAMILLA EYRING KIMBALL

The opportunities for women to excel are greater today than ever before. We should all be resourceful and ambitious, expanding our interests. Forget self-pity and look for mountains to climb. (In *Woman to Woman*, 9.)

MARILYNNE TODD LINFORD

Be the best you can be. . . . Use your individual talents, aspirations, faults, and trials to mold a woman, a mother, who paces her running with her strength, her desires with reality, and who travels life's journey with high self-esteem. (*Mother's Self-Esteem*, 110.)

We've all heard statements like . . . "Get out of the home. . . . Do something meaningful." . . . These seeds breed discontentment and, if nourished, blossom into dissatisfaction and diminish self-esteem. A mother with poor self-esteem begets both friction in her marriage and children with low self-esteem. These

seedlings then grow more and more complicated. (*Mother's Self-Esteem*, 3.)

LENORE ROMNEY

Our generation will be judged not so much by the numbers of women in the halls of science or the legislatures as by how the next generation turns out. (In *Ensign*, June 1974, 25.)

MARY ELLEN SMOOT

Despite the great challenges we individually and collectively face today, I'm sure you will agree, this is a wonderful time to be alive. In the context of world history, there has never been a more exciting time to sojourn on earth. Do you suppose that you were chosen to be born for such a time as this? (In *Ensign*, Nov. 1997, 86–87.)

BELLE S. SPAFFORD

The richness, the hope, the promise of life today, are exciting beyond belief. Nonetheless, we need stout hearts and strong characters; we need knowledge and training; we need organized effort to meet the future—a future pregnant with unborn events, big with possibilities, stupendous in its demands, and challenging in its problems. (*Woman's Reach*, 27.)

A woman's world is as broad as the universe. There's scarcely an area of human endeavor that a woman cannot enter if she has the will and preparation to do so. (In *Elect Ladies*, 160.)

When the spiritual natures deeply embedded in women become dormant or choked out, we have real cause to fear. (*Today's World*, 136.)

WENDY C. TOP

Satan's merciless promotion of comparison and self-contempt . . . causes us to be inordinately preoccupied with ourselves. . . . We are so absorbed in . . . how we look and what we need and whether or not other people like us . . . that we have little time and energy to think about and serve others or to seek God's will instead of our own. (*Getting Past the Labels*, 9.)

Satan has cleverly switched one form of oppression—the undervaluing of women by men—for another and perhaps more devastating form—the undervaluing of women by themselves. (*Getting Past the Labels*, 6.)

Work

JANENE WOLSEY BAADSGAARD

A career is not a life. A career is something we do to sustain life. Problems occur in paid employment when we fail to understand the equally important work of our hearts. We forget our eternal purpose in life when we throw ourselves off balance by spending too much time earning a living and not enough time living. (*Family Finances*, 120.)

The truest reward from work is not what we get, but what we become. We do our best not always because the work is worth it, but because we are. If we work only for the wage, we have chosen work that pays us little. (*Family Finances*, 121.)

The work we do fulfills a divine purpose if it is done with love. To avoid labor is to lose step with the infinite plan. Work is not a curse. When we work, we begin to fulfill the measure, the hope, of our creation. When we choose to work with love, we choose to embrace life. If we fashion the work of our hands into the work of our hearts, all work is honorable. (*Family Finances*, 103.)

JAROLDEEN ASPLUND EDWARDS

We need to create grace notes of celebration in the pattern of our work. (*Celebration!* 27.)

A happily examined life can help us look at the things we do—regardless of our current life situation—and realize that we have power within us to do things better. (*Celebration!* 27.)

With our labors under control, we are relieved of feelings of guilt or unworthiness when we make time for play and celebration. (*Celebration!* 21.)

Work accomplished gives us feeings of personal worth and self-esteem. When we finish tasks, we feel capable and valued—empowered. We feel renewed confidence when we are able to achieve orderliness in our environment and responsibilities. (*Celebration!* 21.)

SUSA YOUNG GATES

If we begin with our burden or work, when it is small, and go steadily and regularly forward, it is amazing the amount we can do or carry, in the end. (In *Improvement Era*, Sept. 1905, 843–44.)

BEPPIE HARRISON

Joseph, [Jesus'] father in the eyes of the world, was a carpenter and Jesus learned to be a carpenter as well. I don't suppose that makes carpentry a more holy occupation than any other; what that means to me is that ordinary work is meant to be part of our life here on earth. (*Plain and Precious*, 118.)

We were not sent here to waste our time on trivial pleasures: We came to learn to use our hands, our minds, and above all our free agency, and one of the best uses of free agency is to choose to be good at whatever you do. (*Plain and Precious*, 118.)

BARBARA BARRINGTON JONES

I'm afraid there are no magic pills and no easy ways. If you really want to . . . obtain any worthy goal, you must be willing to work. (In *Feeling Great*, 81.)

JOAN B. MACDONALD

We must not compromise our values in order to succeed at work. We must not sacrifice our family relationships in order to succeed at work. And, finally, we must remain conscious of our values and priorities while we are at work. (*Holiness of Everyday Life*, 12.)

Work and career can become so important to us that even personal values can be pushed aside as we rush after the goal of success. (*Holiness of Everyday Life*, 12.)

CAROLINE EYRING MINER

The world of work is an adventure, if our minds are set to make it so. (In *Relief Society Magazine*, Oct. 1962, 721.)

We do well the things we like to do. (In *Relief Society Magazine*, Oct. 1962, 721.)

CHIEKO N. OKAZAKI

We should seek work in which we can be attended by the Spirit of the Lord. (In *Ensign*, Nov. 1994, 93.)

LOUISE Y. ROBISON

It is just to the degree of excellence with which we do our work whether or not we will have joy in it. (In *Relief Society Magazine*, Nov. 1933, 649.)

BELLE S. SPAFFORD

Work becomes drudgery only so long as what is done is done only because of the letter of the law and without the spirit. (In *Relief Society Magazine*, Nov. 1955, 721.)

EMMELINE B. WELLS

Work is not done by looking on. (In *Elect Ladies*, 91.)

LEAH D. WIDTSOE

How I honor those who give of their brain and their muscle that earth may yield her treasure for man's sustenance. (In *Improvement Era*, Aug. 1936, 470.)

Youth

MARIE K. HAFEN

Sometimes . . . a young person can be tempted to "live it up," so long as he or she "just repents" before the deadline. Paul describes these foolish ones as wanting "to enjoy the pleasures of sin *for a season*" (Hebrews 11:25; emphasis added). But when the season ends, as seasons inevitably do, the stain of sin is still there when the pleasures have turned to ashes. Some even feel it is their "right" to romp in the mud of transgression right up to the moment they take their spiritual shower of repentance. This kind of thinking is like acting in a dress rehearsal, unrealistically relaxing in the knowledge that the real performance is not now but in the future. (In *BYU Speeches*, 9 May 1995, 170.)

LUCILE JOHNSON

We need to take the time and make the effort with our young people, to embrace them, to let them know how much they're loved and how special they are. The more difficult and unlovable a person is, the more evidence you have of how greatly that person needs your love! (*Sunny Side Up*, 106.)

ARDETH GREENE KAPP

Parents and leaders, I am convinced that most youth will respond when they see no faltering, wavering, or weakening on our part. (In *Ensign*, Nov. 1990, 94.)

AMY BROWN LYMAN

If our boys will adhere strictly to the standards of the Church and the teachings of the Gospel, and keep themselves intelligently informed, they stand a very good chance of being safe from all evil. (In *Relief Society Magazine*, May 1941, 299–300.)

BERTHA S. REEDER

Each youth in the Church has within himself, waiting to be lighted, the fire of testimony. . . . Once it is lighted, no one except himself can take its powers or blessings away from its possessor. (In *Relief Society Magazine*, Sept. 1956, 574.)

Nature in her various moods and forms has something for everyone in his teens. (In *Improvement Era*, June 1954, 470.)

JOANN SHIELDS

Adults must teach youngsters the truth about the Father and the Savior and help them erase human foibles . . . from their understandings of deity (Moses 6:55–62; Ezekiel 18). Because God himself gave us scriptures specifically to help us learn about him, it is spiritual abuse not to pass these truths on to our youth. (In *To Rejoice As Women*, 188.)

Young people need to know God's will would be their will if they were omniscient too! Only then can youngsters form their own relationship with the Father independent of their family relationships and all other life elements. That independent relationship could greatly ease the individuation process that naturally occurs during adolescent years as teens seek to identify themselves apart from their families. (In *To Rejoice As Women*, 189.)

Once young people feel the Lord's pleasure, they will not be desperate to please others. The difference is palpable. It is easier to please God than to please people. (In *To Rejoice As Women*, 189.)

Adults can help young people make mature decisions by suggesting they ask the Father themselves and by telling stories and more stories about the miracles he has performed. Even when adults do pray for young people, they often repeatedly ask the Father to do something *for* youth, when he wants to do something *in* them. (In *To Rejoice As Women*, 193.)

SUSAN WINDER TANNER

In our competitive society, young people will not find happiness unless they first have a sense of their eternal natures and find value in who they are intrinsically. (In *To Rejoice As Women*, 288.)

MARTHA H. TINGEY

There is no power that can enable the youth of Zion to withstand the temptations and the trials and the opposition with which they have to contend today except this testimony of the Spirit of God, the companionship of the Holy Spirit. (In *Young Woman's Journal*, July 1909, 329.)

JANICE MADSEN WEINHEIMER

Parents have to spoon-feed teenagers spiritually a dose at a time. When they have received a sufficient portion, they will take over and start feeding themselves. Until they reach that point, we must guard cautiously against the worldly termites that would come in and invade and tear down from within the structure we are so patiently trying to build. (*Families are Forever*, 128.)

One of the most important things we can do to help our teenagers is to pray for them. (*Families Are Forever*, 125.)

LEAH D. WIDTSOE

It takes the mettle of which heroes are made for a youth to meet daily and resist the wiles and tempting ease of a custom which is hourly enslaving the appetites and wills of the majority of the young people of this and other nations. (In *Improvement Era*, May 1935, 291.)

God bless our girls, and help their mothers and fathers to set them the right example! Our destiny as a people is in their hands; but they will not fail, for they love righteousness, and are willing to prove it. (In *Improvement Era*, May 1935, 291.)

Wise leaders recognize that young people must have an outlet for their youthful energies and if it can be made legitimate and up-building then their whole being is benefited. (In *Improvement Era*, June 1935, 382.)

Loving kindness as an integral character bulwark is essential for all who would lead youth. (In *Improvement Era*, June 1935, 356.)

Advice to Youth

MARILYN S. BATEMAN

All of us are on earth for a sacred and glorious purpose. It is not by chance that you have been reserved for this time—the dispensation of the fullness of times. Your birth was foreordained in the eternities. (In *BYU Speeches*, 8 Sept. 1998, 1.)

JANETTE HALES BECKHAM

I believe that there are some things that help in these growing-up times so we don't feel so alone. Spend more time talking to Heavenly Father and reading the scriptures. Listen to the still, small voice. . . . When we start to think of others, we feel less alone. (In *Ensign*, May 1992, 79–80.)

ARDETH GREENE KAPP

Young women, you are needed. Never before in the history of the Church has there been such a need for young women who are willing to sacrifice popularity if necessary, suffer loneliness if required, even be rejected if needed, to defend the gospel of Jesus Christ. . . . Your good example helps others to find their way in a darkening world. (In *Ensign*, Nov. 1988, 94.)

MARGARET D. NADAULD

The time is here for you to stand up for what you know is right. You must judge right from wrong. You can't afford to be complacent, or go with the flow, or wonder what to do. You must decide now which path you will follow, which answer you will give. Decide well in advance, before the pressure is on, what you stand for. (*Write Back Soon!* 30.)

[Heavenly Father] wants you to fill your life with so much goodness and truth that others will be attracted to it and want to embrace it. (*Write Back Soon!* 48.)

In preparation for your future, may I invite you to do something. . . . Would you please go to your journal and write in it all about the kind of woman you would like to become? And then will you work toward making that dream of your future become a reality in your life?

In this way you will be turning your heart to the family you will one day have. (In *Ensign*, May 1998, 90.)

Always remember to *tell* Heavenly Father you love Him when you talk to Him in prayer. Never miss an opportunity to *show* Him you love Him by the love you give to others. (*Write Back Soon!* 142.)

BERTHA S. REEDER

If I were a young girl or boy at the very threshold of life, I would resolve to have a plan or goal to follow in building that life. . . . I would not want to leave to chance the kind of life I wanted to build for myself. (In *Relief Society Magazine*, Sept. 1956, 577.)

Sources

Periodicals

BYU Today. 1981–1992.

The Children's Friend. 1902–1970.

Conference Report. 1897–.

Deseret News Weekly. 1850–. (Later changed to The Deseret News.)

The Ensign. 1971–.

The Improvement Era. 1897–1970.

Journal of Collegium Aesculapium. 1983–.

Juvenile Instructor. 1866–1929.

The New Era. 1971–.

Relief Society Magazine. 1914–1970.

The Woman's Exponent. 1872–1914.

Young Woman's Journal. 1889–1929.

Books

Anderson, Susan Noyes. At the End of Your Rope, There's Hope. Salt Lake City: Deseret Book, 1997.

Archibald, Linda R. Sunshine in My Soul: Discovering the Magic in Everyday Life. Salt Lake City: Deseret Book, 1999.

Arise and Shine Forth: Talks from the 2000 Women's Conference. Salt Lake City: Deseret Book, 2001.

The Arms of His Love: Talks Selected from the 1999 Women's Conference. Salt Lake City: Deseret Book, 2000.

Arnold, Marilyn. Sweet Is the Word: Reflections on the Book of Mormon—Its Narrative, Teachings, and People. Salt Lake City: Covenant Communications, 1996.

As a Woman Thinketh (full title: Elaine Cannon's As a Woman Thinketh). Edited by Elaine Cannon. Salt Lake City: Bookcraft, 1990.

As Women of Faith: Talks Selected from the BYU Women's Conferences. Edited by Mary E. Stovall and Carol Cornwall Madsen. Salt Lake City: Deseret Book, 1989.

Austin, Mildred Chandler. *Woman's Divine Destiny.* Salt Lake City: Deseret Book, 1978.

Baadsgaard, Janene Wolsey. *Families Who Laugh . . . Last.* Salt Lake City: Deseret Book, 1992.

———. *Family Finances for the Flabbergasted.* Salt Lake City: Deseret Book, 1995.

———. *Is There Life after Birth?* Salt Lake City: Deseret Book, 1983.

———. *Why Does My Mother's Day Potted Plant Always Die?* Salt Lake City: Deseret Book, 1988.

Baca, Joyce. *Divorce: Making It a Growth Experience.* Salt Lake City: Deseret Book, 1985.

The Balm of Gilead: Women's Stories of Finding Peace. Salt Lake City: Deseret Book, 1997.

Banfield, Jill Todd. *Draw Near unto Me.* Salt Lake City: Bookcraft, 1983.

Bateman, Anya. *I Didn't Place in the Talent Race But . . .* Salt Lake City: Deseret Book, 1990.

Behold Your Little Ones. Edited by Barbara B. Smith and Shirley Thomas. Salt Lake City: Bookcraft, 1999.

The Best of Women's Conference. Salt Lake City: Deseret Book, 2000.

Bills, Diane. *Trust in the Lord: Letting the Spirit Be Your Guide.* Salt Lake City: Covenant Communications, 1996.

Black, Susan Easton. *Finding Christ through the Book of Mormon.* Salt Lake City: Deseret Book, 1995.

Bowen, Annette Paxman. *Doughnuts, Letters, Midnight Phone Calls.* Salt Lake City: Deseret Book, 1991.

Building a Love That Lasts: Outstanding Articles on Marriage. Salt Lake City: Deseret Book, 1985.

Buntin, Kathleen Rawlings. *All Alone: Surviving the Loss of Your Spouse.* Salt Lake City: Deseret Book, 1995.

Canfield, Anita R. *A Perfect Brightness of Hope.* Salt Lake City: Deseret Book, 1993.

———. *Self-Esteem for the Latter-day Saint Woman.* Salt Lake City: Bookcraft, 1988.

————. *The Young Woman and Her Self-Esteem.* Salt Lake City: Deseret Book, 1990.

Cannon, Elaine. *Be a Bell Ringer.* Salt Lake City: Bookcraft, 1989.

————. *Count Your Many Blessings.* Salt Lake City: Bookcraft, 1995.

————. *Gatherings: Favorite Writings by Elaine Cannon.* Salt Lake City: Deseret Book, 2000.

————. *Love You!* Salt Lake City: Bookcraft, 1991.

————. *Mothering.* Salt Lake City: Bookcraft, 1993.

————. *Not Just Ordinary Young Men and Young Women.* Salt Lake City: Bookcraft, 1991.

————. *Sunshine.* Salt Lake City: Bookcraft, 1994.

The Children's Friends: Primary Presidents and Their Lives of Service. Coauthored by Janet Peterson and LaRene Gaunt. Salt Lake City: Deseret Book, 1996.

Clothed with Charity: Talks Selected from the 1996 Women's Conference. Edited by Dawn Hall Anderson, Susette Fletcher Green, and Dlora Hall Dalton. Salt Lake City: Deseret Book, 1997.

Davidson, Karen Lynn. *Thriving on Our Differences.* Salt Lake City: Deseret Book, 1990.

Day, Afton J. *Coming Up from Down in the Dumps.* Salt Lake City: Bookcraft, 1986.

————. *How to Be a Perfect Wife and Other Myths.* Salt Lake City: Bookcraft, 1977.

DeHoyos, Genevieve. *Stewardship—the Divine Order.* Bountiful, Utah: Horizon Publishers, 1982.

Doctrines of the Book of Mormon: 1991 Sperry Symposium on the Book of Mormon. Edited by Bruce A. Van Orden and Brent L. Top. Salt Lake City: Deseret Book, 1992.

Early Mormon Documents. Compiled and edited by Dan Vogel. 3 vols. Salt Lake City: Signature Books, 1996–2000.

Edmunds, Mary Ellen. *Happiness: Finders, Keepers.* Salt Lake City: Deseret Book, 1999.

————. *Love Is a Verb.* Salt Lake City: Deseret Book, 1995.

Edwards, Deanna. *Grieving: The Pain and the Promise.* Salt Lake City: Covenant Communications, 1997.

Edwards, Jaroldeen Asplund. *Celebration! Ten Principles of Joyous Living*. Salt Lake City: Deseret Book, 1995.

————. *Things I Wish I'd Known Sooner . . . : Personal Discoveries of a Mother of Twelve*. Salt Lake City: Deseret Book, 1991.

Eldridge, Erin. *Born That Way? A True Story of Overcoming Same-Sex Attraction with Insights for Friends, Families, and Leaders*. Salt Lake City: Deseret Book, 1994.

Elect Ladies: Presidents of the Relief Society. Coauthored by Janet Peterson and LaRene Gaunt. Salt Lake City: Deseret Book, 1990.

An Emotional First-Aid Kit for Mothers. Edited by Linda J. Eyre. Salt Lake City: Bookcraft, 1997.

Erickson, Karla C. *Take Time to Make Time Count*. Salt Lake City: Bookcraft, 1984.

————. *Take Time to Smell the Dandelions*. Salt Lake City: Bookcraft, 1979.

Every Good Thing: Talks Selected from the 1997 Women's Conference. Edited by Dawn Hall Anderson, Dlora Hall Dalton, and Susette Fletcher Green. Salt Lake City: Deseret Book, 1998.

Eyer, Mary Sturlaugson. *He Restoreth My Soul*. Salt Lake City: Deseret Book, 1982.

Eyre, Linda J. *I Didn't Plan to Be a Witch*. New York: Simon & Schuster, 1996.

————. *A Joyful Mother of Children*. Salt Lake City: Bookcraft, 1983.

Feeling Great, Doing Right, Hanging Tough: Favorite Talks from Especially for Youth. Salt Lake City: Bookcraft, 1991.

Finding the Light in Deep Waters and Dark Times: Favorite Talks from Especially for Youth. Salt Lake City: Bookcraft, 1992.

Flynn, Johanna, and Anita Canfield. *Visiting Teaching: A Call to Serve*. Salt Lake City: Deseret Book, 1989.

Glenn, Jamie. *Walk Tall, You're a Daughter of God*. Salt Lake City: Deseret Book, 1994.

Glimpses into the Life and Heart of Marjorie Pay Hinckley. Edited by Virginia H. Pearce. Salt Lake City: Deseret Book, 1999.

Grassli, Michaelene P. *LeaderTalk*. Salt Lake City: Bookcraft, 1996.

————. *What I Have Learned from Children*. Salt Lake City: Deseret Book, 1993.

Hardison, Amy. *How to Feel Great about Being a Mother*. Salt Lake City: Deseret Book, 1987.

Harrison, Beppie. *A Day at a Time: A Woman's Look at Perfection*. Salt Lake City: Bookcraft, 1994.

———. *Needles in the Basket: Looking at Patterns of a Woman's Life*. Salt Lake City: Deseret Book, 1991.

———. *On Being a Parent: The Crash Course in Character Development*. Salt Lake City: Bookcraft, 1995.

———. *Plain and Precious: An LDS Daybook of Renewal and Joy*. Salt Lake City: Deseret Book, 1997.

Hawkes, Sharlene Wells. *Living In but Not of the World*. Salt Lake City: Deseret Book, 1997.

Hearts Knit Together: Talks Selected from the 1995 Women's Conference. Edited by Dawn Hall Anderson, Dlora Hall Dalton, and Susette Fletcher Green. Salt Lake City: Deseret Book, 1996.

A Heritage of Faith: Talks Selected from the BYU Women's Conferences. Edited by Mary E. Stovall and Carol Cornwall Madsen. Salt Lake City: Deseret Book, 1988.

Heroic Mormon Women. Edited by Ivan J. Barrett. American Fork, Utah: Covenant Communications, 1991.

Heuston, Kimberley Burton. *Single Parenting: Help for Latter-day Saint Families*. Salt Lake City: Deseret Book, 1998.

High Fives & High Hopes: Favorite Talks from Especially for Youth. Salt Lake City: Deseret Book, 1990.

Holland, Patricia T. *On Earth As It Is in Heaven*. Coauthored with Jeffrey R. Holland. Salt Lake City: Deseret Book, 1994.

Jack, Elaine L. *Eye to Eye, Heart to Heart*. Salt Lake City: Deseret Book, 1992.

Johnson, Lucile. *Enjoy the Journey*. Compiled and edited by Arlene Bascom. Salt Lake City: Covenant Communications, 1996.

———. *Sunny Side Up: Breakthrough Ideas for Women from One of the Most Loved Speakers in the Church*. Compiled and edited by Arlene Bascom. Salt Lake City: Covenant Communications, 1993.

Johnson, Sherrie. *Man, Woman, and Deity*. Salt Lake City: Bookcraft, 1991.

———. *Spiritually Centered Motherhood*. Salt Lake City: Bookcraft, 1995.

Joy. Salt Lake City: Deseret Book, 1989.

Joy in the Journey: Favorite Talks from Especially for Youth. Salt Lake City: Deseret Book, 1998.

Kapp, Ardeth Greene. *The Gentle Touch*. Salt Lake City: Deseret Book, 1978.

————. *I Walk by Faith*. Salt Lake City: Deseret Book, 1993.

————. *The Joy of the Journey*. Salt Lake City: Deseret Book, 1992.

————. *Lead, Guide, and Walk Beside*. Salt Lake City: Deseret Book, 1998.

————. *Miracles in Pinafores and Bluejeans*. Salt Lake City: Deseret Book, 1979.

————. *More Miracles in Pinafores and Bluejeans*. Salt Lake City: Deseret Book, 1981.

————. *My Neighbor, My Sister, My Friend*. Salt Lake City: Deseret Book, 1990.

————. *Rejoice! His Promises Are Sure*. Salt Lake City: Deseret Book, 1997.

————. *What Latter-day Stripling Warriors Learn from Their Mothers*. Salt Lake City: Deseret Book, 1996.

Keepers of the Flame: Presidents of the Young Women. Coauthored by Janet Peterson and LaRene Gaunt. Salt Lake City: Deseret Book, 1993.

Kimball, Camilla Eyring. *The Writings of Camilla Eyring Kimball*. Edited by Edward L. Kimball. Salt Lake City: Deseret Book, 1990.

Knit Together in Love: A Focus for LDS Women in the 1990s. Coauthored by Carol L. Clark, Mary Ellen Edmunds, Anne C. Pingree, and Cherry B. Silver. Salt Lake City: Deseret Book, 1991.

Larsen, Jo Ann. *The Heart of Goodness*. Salt Lake City: Shadow Mountain/ Deseret Book, 1999.

————. *I'm a Day Late and a Dollar Short . . . and It's Okay!* Salt Lake City: Deseret Book, 1991.

The LDS Speaker's Sourcebook. Compiled by Aspen Books. Salt Lake City: Aspen Books, 1991.

LDS Women's Treasury: Insights and Inspiration for Today's Woman. Salt Lake City: Deseret Book, 1997.

Linford, Marilynne Todd. *Give Mom a Standing Ovation*. Salt Lake City: Bookcraft, 1996.

————. *Is Anyone Out There Building Mother's Self-Esteem?* Salt Lake City: Deseret Book, 1986.

————. *A Woman Fulfilled*. Salt Lake City: Bookcraft, 1992.

Living the Legacy: Favorite Talks from Especially for Youth. Salt Lake City: Deseret Book, 1996.

Living the Young Women Values. Salt Lake City: Bookcraft, 1999.

Lyman, Amy Brown. *In Retrospect*. Salt Lake City: General Board of the Relief Society, 1945.

MacDonald, Joan B. *The Holiness of Everyday Life*. Salt Lake City: Deseret Book, 1995.

Major, Jill C., Lauren C. Leifson, and Hollie C. Bevan. *Encircled by Love*. Salt Lake City: Deseret Book, 1989.

May Christ Lift Thee Up: Talks from the 1998 Women's Conference. Salt Lake City: Deseret Book, 1999.

Milne, Deborah Eldredge. *Reflections from a Broken Mirror: Spiritual Values I Learned As an LDS Child of Divorce*. Salt Lake City: Deseret Book, 1998.

Molgard, Bette S. *Everyday Battles: Rising Above the Adversary's Subtle Snares*. Salt Lake City: Bookcraft, 1999.

Mormon Women Speak: A Collection of Essays. Edited by Mary Lythgoe Bradford. Salt Lake City: Olympus Publishing Co., 1982.

Morris, Carroll Hofeling. *"If the Gospel Is True, Why Do I Hurt So Much?": Help for Dysfunctional Latter-day Saint Families*. Salt Lake City: Deseret Book, 1991.

Motherhood: A Partnership with God. Compiled by Harold Lundstrom. Salt Lake City: Bookcraft, 1956.

Mothers of the Prophets. Coauthored by Leonard J. Arrington, Susan Arrington Madsen, and Emily Madsen Jones. Rev. ed. Salt Lake City: Deseret Book, 2001.

My Soul Delighteth in the Scriptures: Personal and Family Applications. Edited by H. Wallace Goddard and Richard H. Cracroft. Salt Lake City: Bookcraft, 1999.

Nadauld, Margaret D. *Write Back Soon! Letters of Love and Encouragement to Young Women*. Salt Lake City: Deseret Book, 2001.

Null, Kathleen "Casey." *I Used to Think People My Age Were Old*. Salt Lake City: Bookcraft, 1995.

————. *Where Are We Going Besides Crazy?* Salt Lake City: Bookcraft, 1989.

Okazaki, Chieko N. *Aloha!* Salt Lake City: Deseret Book, 1995.

————. *Cat's Cradle*. Salt Lake City: Bookcraft, 1993.

————. *Disciples*. Salt Lake City: Deseret Book, 1998.

————. *Lighten Up!* Salt Lake City: Deseret Book, 1993.

————. *Sanctuary*. Salt Lake City: Deseret Book, 1997.

The Personal Writings of Eliza Roxey Snow. Edited by Maureen Ursenbach Beecher. Salt Lake City: University of Utah Press, 1995.

Personal Writings of Joseph Smith. Edited by Dean C. Jessee. Salt Lake City: Deseret Book, 1984.

Peterson, Brookie. *A Woman's Hope*. Salt Lake City: Bookcraft, 1991.

Plummer, Louise. *Thoughts of a Grasshopper: Essays and Oddities*. Salt Lake City: Deseret Book, 1996.

Poelman, Anne Osborn. *The Amulek Alternative: Exercising Agency in a World of Choice*. Salt Lake City: Deseret Book, 1997.

————. *The Simeon Solution: One Woman's Spiritual Odyssey*. Salt Lake City: Deseret Book, 1995.

Rasband, Ester. *Confronting the Myth of Self-Esteem: Twelve Keys to Finding Peace*. Salt Lake City: Deseret Book, 1998.

Rasmus, Carolyn J. *In the Strength of the Lord I Can Do All Things*. Salt Lake City: Deseret Book, 1990.

The Redeemer: Reflections on the Life and Teachings of Jesus Christ. Salt Lake City: Deseret Book, 2000.

Serving with Strength throughout the World: Favorite Talks from Especially for Youth. Salt Lake City: Deseret Book, 1994.

Sharing the Light in the Wilderness: Favorite Talks from Especially for Youth. Salt Lake City: Deseret Book, 1993.

Shipp, Ellis R. *While Others Slept: Autobiography and Journal of Ellis Reynolds Shipp*. Salt Lake City: Bookcraft, 1985.

A Singular Life: Perspectives on Being Single by Sixteen Latter-day Saint Women. Edited by Carol L. Clark and Blythe Darlyn Thatcher. Salt Lake City: Deseret Book, 1987.

Smith, Barbara B. *Growth in Grandmothering*. Salt Lake City: Bookcraft, 1986.

————. *The Love That Never Faileth*. Salt Lake City: Bookcraft, 1984.

Smith, Barbara B., and Shirley W. Thomas. *Women of Devotion*. Salt Lake City: Bookcraft, 1990.

————. *Words for Women: Promises of Prophets*. Salt Lake City: Bookcraft, 1994.

Smith, Lucy Mack. *History of Joseph Smith*. Salt Lake City: Bookcraft, 1979.

Smoot, Mary Ellen W. *Sweet Is the Work: How Relief Society Helps Brings Women to Christ*. Salt Lake City: Deseret Book, 2000.

Sorensen, Michele R. *Chainbreakers*. Salt Lake City: Deseret Book, 1993.

Spafford, Belle S. *Address*. Weber State College Institute. 2 February 1973.

————. *A Woman's Reach*. Salt Lake City: Deseret Book, 1974.

————. *Women in Today's World.* Salt Lake City: Deseret Book, 1971.

St. Cyr, Peggy. *From Conversion to Commitment.* Salt Lake City: Bookcraft, 1996.

Sunshine for the Latter-day Saint Woman's Soul. Salt Lake City: Bookcraft, 1999.

Temples of the Ancient World. Edited by Donald W. Parry. Salt Lake City: Deseret Book, 1994.

Thayne, Emma Lou. *As for Me and My House.* Salt Lake City: Bookcraft, 1989.

Their Own Words (full title: *In Their Own Words: Women and the Story of Nauvoo*). Edited by Carol Cornwall Madsen. Salt Lake City: Deseret Book, 1994.

They Knew the Prophet. Edited by Hyrum L. Andrus and Helen Mae Andrus. Salt Lake City: Deseret Book, 1974.

Thomas, M. Catherine. *Selected Writings of M. Catherine Thomas.* Salt Lake City: Deseret Book, 2000.

————. *Spiritual Lightening.* Salt Lake City: Bookcraft, 1998.

Thy People Shall Be My People and Thy God My God: 1993 Sperry Symposium on the Old Testament. Edited by Paul Y. Hoskisson. Salt Lake City: Deseret Book, 1994.

Thy Word Is a Lamp: Women's Stories of Finding Light. Salt Lake City: Deseret Book, 1999.

To Rejoice As Women: Talks Selected from the 1994 Women's Conference. Edited by Susette Fletcher Green and Dawn Hall Anderson. Salt Lake City: Deseret Book, 1995.

Top, Wendy C. *Getting Past the Labels: How the Truth Makes Women Free.* Salt Lake City: Deseret Book, 2000.

Voices of Old Testament Prophets: 1997 Sidney B. Sperry Symposium on the Old Testament. Salt Lake City: Deseret Book, 1997.

Weinheimer, Janice Madsen. *Families Are Forever . . . If I Can Just Get Through Today!* Salt Lake City: Deseret Book, 1979.

Why Say No When the World Says Yes: Resisting Temptation in an Immoral World. Compiled by Randal A. Wright. Salt Lake City: Deseret Book, 1993.

Wisdom's Paths (full title: *In Wisdom's Paths: Insights and Inspiration for LDS Women over Fifty*). Edited by Barbara B. Smith and Shirley W. Thomas. Salt Lake City: Deseret Book, 2000.

Wise, Gayla. *The Sign of the Son of Man.* Salt Lake City: Covenant Communications, 1991.

Woman to Woman: Selected Talks from the BYU Women's Conferences. Salt Lake City: Deseret Book, 1986.

A Woman's Choices: The Relief Society Legacy Lectures. Salt Lake City: Deseret Book, 1984.

A Woman's View: Helen Mar Whitney's Reminiscences of Early Church History. Edited by Jeni Broberg Holzapfel and Richard Neitzel Holzapfel. Provo, Utah: Religious Studies Center, Brigham Young University, 1997.

Women and Christ—Living the Abundant Life: Talks Selected from the 1992 Women's Conference. Edited by Dawn Hall Anderson, Susette Fletcher Green, and Marie Cornwall. Salt Lake City: Deseret Book, 1993.

Women and the Power Within: To See Life Steadily and See It Whole. Edited by Dawn Hall Anderson and Marie Cornwall. Salt Lake City: Deseret Book, 1991.

Women in the Covenant of Grace: Talks Selected from the 1993 Women's Conference. Edited by Dawn Hall Anderson and Susette Fletcher Green. Salt Lake City: Deseret Book, 1994.

Women of Covenant: The Story of Relief Society. Edited by Jill Mulvay Derr, Janath Russell Cannon, and Maureen Ursenbach Beecher. Salt Lake City: Deseret Book, 1992.

The Women of Mormondom. Edited by Edward W. Tullidge. New York: Tullidge & Crandall, 1877.

Women of Nauvoo. Coauthored by Richard Neitzel Holzapfel and Jeni Broberg Holzapfel. Salt Lake City: Bookcraft, 1992.

Women of Wisdom and Knowledge: Talks Selected from the BYU Women's Conference. Edited by Marie Cornwall and Susan Howe. Salt Lake City: Deseret Book, 1990.

Women Steadfast in Christ: Talks Selected from the 1991 Women's Conference. Edited by Dawn Hall Anderson and Marie Cornwall. Salt Lake City: Deseret Book, 1992.

Women's Voices: An Untold History of the Latter-day Saints, 1830–1900. Edited by Kenneth W. Godfrey, Audrey M. Godfrey, and Jill Mulvay Derr. Salt Lake City: Deseret Book, 1982.

Authors

Those who desire more information about a given author can usually find it by going to the source of the quotation used.

Alldredge, Lillian S.
Allen, Deanne Ernst
Allen, Lucy Diantha Morley
Anderson, Carol K.
Anderson, Geraldine P.
Anderson, Susan Noyes
Archibald, Linda R.
Archibald, Margaret Hafen
Arnold, Marilyn
Asay, Colleen W.
Ashton, Karen J.
Ashton, Norma B.
Atkinson, Pamela J.
Austin, Mildred Chandler

Baadsgaard, Janene Wolsey
Baca, Joyce
Baird, Nancy
Baker, Dixie Drawhorn
Baker, Karen
Ballard, Suzanne
Ballif-Spanvill, Bonnie
Banfield, Jill Todd
Barlow, Sally H.
Barnes, Donna Lee Bowen
   (Some of Sister Barnes's writings were originally published under the name Donna Lee Bowen.)
Barnes, Kathleen H.
Barthel, Mildred
Bartholomew, Sherlene Hall
Bateman, Anya
Bateman, Marilyn S.

Beckham, Janette Hales
   (Some of Sister Beckham's writings were originally published under the name Janette C. Hales.)
Beecher, Maureen Ursenbach
Bell, Elouise
Bennion, Francine R.
Benson, Flora Amussen
Berg, Lori
Bevan, Hollie C.
Bills, Diane
Black, Susan Easton
Black, Traci Cutler
Blakemore, Connie L.
Blaser, Earlene
Boswell, Lisa Johnson
Bowen, Annette Paxman
Bowen, Barbara Timothy
Bouley, Sandra
Boyer, Marian R.
Brasher, Ruth E.
Brentnall, Mary
Breyton, Hannah
Brigham, Janet
Brinton, Sally Peterson
Brown, Cheryl
Buck, Janet E.
Buntin, Kathleen Rawlings
Busche, Jutta Baum
Butler, Julene

Cahoon, Marion Jane
Canfield, Anita R.
Cannon, Connie Duncan
Cannon, Elaine

Cannon, Janath R.
Cannon, Lucy Grant
Cannon, Winnifred Saville
Carlson, Paula
Carver, Janiel Reeve
Child, Hortense H.
Choules, Marilyn Jeppson
Christensen, Catherine
Christensen, Janet Nelson
Christianson, Stace Hucks
Clark, Carol L.
Clifford, Dixie R.
Cline, Vivian R.
Clissold, Joan Okelberry
Clyde, Aileen H.
Cole, Carole Osborne
Cook, Nadine Q.
Cornwall, Marie
Covey, Sandra Merrill

Dalton, Elaine S.
Dastrup, Suzanne Little
Davidson, Karen Lynn
Davies, Courtney Carr
Davis, Susanne Johnson
Day, Afton J.
DeHoyos, Genevieve
Derr, Jill Mulvay
Dew, Sheri L.
Di Conza, Barbara
Dick, Lauren A.
Dougall, Maria Y.
Doxey, Joanne B.
Durham, Christine
Durham, Louise

Edmunds, Mary Ellen
Edwards, Deanna
Edwards, Jaroldeen Asplund
Edwards, Lana A.
Eldridge, Erin
Eliason, Claudia Fuhriman
Embry, Jessie L.

Engemann, Suzanne Barnes
England, Kathy
Erickson, Karla C.
Evans, Joy F.
Eyer, Mary Sturlaugson
Eyre, Linda J.

Farnsworth, Julia P. M.
Farnworth, Xanthe K.
Felt, Louie B.
Flynn, Johanna
Forste, Renata Tonks
Foulger, Mary F.
Fox, Ruth May
Freeze, Lillie Tucket
Fronk, Camille
Funk, Ruth Hardy

Garff, Gertrude R.
Gates, Georgia Lauper
Gates, Susa Young
Gibb, Sara Lee
Gilfillan, Betty Baker
Glenn, Jamie
Goodliffe, Bonnie L.
Gough, Janet D.
Grace, Cindy Bishop
Grassli, Michaelene P.
Gunnell, Kim Novas

Hafen, Marie K.
Hales, Mary
Hall, Elizabeth Huntington
Hanks, Darla
Hansen, Elizabeth
Hansen, Suzanne L.
Hardison, Amy
Hardy, Nedra
Harmer, Adrienne Aikele
Harris, Kathryn Kay
Harrison, Beppie
Hatch, Elaine Hansen
Hawkes, Sharlene Wells
Hawkins, Claire

Ottesen, Carol C.
Ottley, JoAnn
Owen, Laura

Pahnke, Vickey
Parkin, Bonnie D.
Pearce, Virginia H.
Perry, Janice Kapp
Peterson, Brookie
Petree, Sandra
Pinborough, Jan Underwood
Pinegar, Patricia P.
Plummer, Louise
Plunk, Helen M.
Poelman, Anne Osborn
    (Some of Sister Poelman's writings
    were originally published under the
    name Anne G. Osborn.)
Pratt, Mary Ann
Preston, Cheryl B.
Price, Lynn F.
Pullins, Kathy D.
Putnam, Jeanne Kane

Randle, Kristen D.
Rasband, Esther
Rasmus, Carolyn J.
Rasmussen, Mary Ann
Raynes, Marybeth
Reeder, Bertha S.
Reeves, Tamra T.
Reese, Ann S.
Reid, Rose Marie
Reynolds, Emily Madsen
Reynolds, Sydney Smith
Richards, Barbara N.
Richards, Hepzibah
Richards, Jane Snyder
Richardson, Marilyn
Ritchie, Dolores
Robison, Louise Y.
Rogers, Leslie Ballif
Rogers, Sandra

Romney, Lenore
Ruppel, Wendy Evans

Santiago, Tessa Meyer
Scharman, Janet S.
Sharp, Marianne C.
Shields, Joann
Shipp, Ellis R.
Shirts, Kathryn H.
Shumway, Kristen
Shumway, Naomi M.
Silver, Cherry B.
Simpson, Ione J.
Smart, Donna Toland
Smith, Barbara B.
Smith, Bathsheba W.
Smith, Emma
Smith, Ida
Smith, Kathryn S.
Smith, Lucy Mack
Smith, Mary Fielding
Smoot, Mary Ellen
Snow, Eliza R.
Sommerfeldt, Susan Champion
Sorensen, A. D.
Sorensen, Marian P.
Sorensen, Michele R.
Sorensen, Mollie H.
Spafford, Belle S.
Squires, Gwen
St. Cyr, Peggy
Stoddard, Marian Jeppson
Stone, Karen Sedgwick
Stout, Mary Kay
Stovall, Mary
Stradling, Rebecca Gwynn
Swinton, Heidi S.

Tanner, Sandra
Tanner, Susan Winder
Taylor, Elmina S.
Taylor, Sally
Taylor, Teri H.

Thayer, Donlu DeWitt
Thayne, Emma Lou
Thomas, Carol B.
Thomas, M. Catherine
Thomas, Margaret W.
Thomas, Paula
Thomas, Shirley W.
Thompson, Mercy Fielding
Tingey, Martha H.
Todd, Sally M.
Tollestrup, Myra
Top, Wendy C.
Trotter, Elouise
Truba, Suzanne
Tueller, Anna
Turner, Lisa Ray

Umoren, Mary Wilson

Voorhees, Kathleen E.

Warner, Susan L.
Watson, Wendy L.

Watts, Emily Bennett
Weinheimer, Janice Madsen
Wells, Emmeline B.
Wheatley, Margaret J.
Wheeler, Leann P.
Whitaker, Eileen N.
Whitney, Elizabeth Ann
Whitney, Helen Mar
Widtsoe, Leah D.
Wiederhold, Mercedes
Wilde, Barbara Sorenson
Williams, Clarissa S.
Winder, Barbara W.
Winger, Jeri J.
Wirthlin, Anne G.
Wise, Gayla
Woods, Debra
Wright, Ruth B.

Young, Dwan J.
Young, Emily D. Partridge
Young, Zina D. H.

Index

An index of topics and subtopics, with suggested cross-references.